D0372247

Rio de Janeiro

"All you've got to do is decide to go
and the hardest part is over.

So go!"

TONY WHEELER, COFOUNDER – LONELY PLANET

THIS EDITION WRITTEN AND RESEARCHED BY
Regis St Louis

Contents

Plan Your Trip   4

Welcome to
Rio de Janeiro 4

Rio de Janeiro's
Top 10 6

What's New 13

Need to Know 14

Top Itineraries 16

If You Like...................... 18

Month by Month 20

With Kids 24

Carnaval 26

Eating 33

Drinking & Nightlife... 37

Entertainment 40

Samba............................ 43

Shopping...................... 47

Sports
& Activities...................49

Explore Rio de Janeiro   52

Ipanema & Leblon 56

Gávea, Jardim
Botânico & Lagoa..........76

Copacabana
& Leme 85

Botafogo, Humaitá
& Urca.............................99

Flamengo & Around 110

Centro &
Praça Mauá..................120

Santa Teresa & Lapa...136

Zona Norte 148

Barra da Tijuca
& Western Rio.............. 155

Sleeping 163

Understand Rio de Janeiro   177

Rio de Janeiro Today...178

History.......................... 180

The Sounds of Rio 191

Football........................ 196

Architecture................200

Survival Guide   203

Transportation 204

Directory A–Z 209

Language 215

Index 223

Rio de Janeiro Maps   234

(left) **Copacabana Beach p87** A stunning 4km stretch of sand

(above) **Pão de Açúcar p101** Aerial views

(right) **Cristo Redentor p112** Rio's open-armed savior

Zona Norte
p148

Centro & Praça Mauá
p120

Santa Teresa & Lapa
p136

Flamengo & Around
p110

Botafogo, Humaitá & Urca
p99

See Barra da Tijuca & Western Rio Inset

Gávea, Jardim Botânico & Lagoa
p76

Copacabana & Leme
p85

Ipanema & Leblon
p56

Inset

Barra da Tijuca & Western Rio
p155

Welcome to Rio de Janeiro

Golden beaches and lush mountains, samba-fueled nightlife and spectacular football matches: welcome to the Cidade Maravilhosa.

Tropical Landscapes

Looking out from the 710m peak of Corcovado, you will see why Rio is called the Cidade Maravilhosa (Marvelous City). Lushly forested mountains fringe the city, shimmering beaches trace the shoreline and a string of tiny islands lie scattered along the seafront. Far from being mere cinematic backdrop, this seaside beauty hosts outstanding outdoor adventures: hiking in the Tijuca rainforest, cycling alongside the lake and beaches, sailing across Baía de Guanabara, and surfing, rock climbing and hang gliding amid one of the world's most stunning urban landscapes.

Captivating Beaches

Rio's beaches have long seduced visitors. Copacabana Beach became a symbol of Rio during the 1940s, when international starlets would jet in for the weekend. Hogging the spotlight these days is Ipanema Beach, its fame and beauty unabated since bossa nova stars Tom Jobim and Vinícius de Moraes introduced the world to its allure in the 1960s. For *cariocas* (residents of Rio), the beach is their backyard – a playground that's free and open to all, offering endless enjoyment in the form of football, volleyball, surfing, snacking, drinking or simply relaxing amid the passing parade of people.

The Rhythms of Rio

Music is the lifeblood of Rio, with a soundtrack of rock, old-school bossa nova, hip-hop, funk and Brazil's many regional styles. Above all there's samba, a rapid-fire style of music with African influences and an infectious beat that is synonymous with Rio. You can hear it all over town, but the soul of samba resides in Lapa, an edgy red-light district that is home to dozens of live-music halls and an enormous weekend street party that draws revelers from all walks of life. Samba is also the integral sound during Carnaval, and the danceable backing music to street parties and all-night parades.

Joie de Vivre

Speaking of Carnaval, Rio knows how to party. Whether you call it joie de vivre, *Lebensfreude* or lust for life, *cariocas* have it in spades. Carnaval, and the buildup to it, is the most obvious manifestation of this celebratory spirit. But Rio has many other occasions for revelry: celebrations after a big Flamengo (or Vasco, Fluminense or Botafogo) football match, weekend samba parties around town, *baile* funk parties in the favelas (slums, informal communities), and boat parties on the bay – not to mention major fests such as Réveillon (New Year's Eve) and the Festas Juninas.

Why I Love Rio de Janeiro

By Regis St Louis, Writer

There's no other place like Rio. It's a combination of many things that I find so captivating: walking through parks inside the city and seeing monkeys and toucans, spending the evening catching music jams around Lapa, joining a few friends amid the roaring crowds at Maracanã, or greeting the sunrise (after an early morning or late night) from Copacabana Beach. In moments like these you realize you're hooked. I also love the *carioca* spirit: spontaneous and good-natured, with the urge to live life to the fullest.

For more about our writer, see p264.

Top: Cristo Redentor (p112) looking out towards Pão de Açúcar (p101)

Rio de Janeiro's
Top 10

Carnaval (p26)

1 Get plenty of sleep before you board the plane, because once you land, it's nonstop revelry until Ash Wednesday brings it all to a close (sort of). With around 500 street parties happening in every corner of town, you will not lack options. For the full experience, join a samba school and parade amid pounding drum corps and mechanized smoke-breathing dragons before thousands of roaring fans in the Sambódromo. Or assemble a costume and hit one of the Carnaval balls around town. The buildup starts weeks in advance.

🎊 *Carnaval*

Ipanema Beach (p58)

2 This enchanting beachfront attracts a wide mix of *cariocas* (residents of Rio). Different crowds – surfers, volleyballers, bohemians, muscle boys – congregate at each section, or *posto*, including famous *posto* 9 where Ipanema's young and beautiful frolic. The principal activities of the day are people-watching, surf-side walks and sunset-watching – best from Arpoador, at Ipanema's east end. You can also eat and drink on the sand. Roaming vendors will come to you, and *barracas* (stalls) set you up with chairs, umbrellas and caipirinhas. All you need to do is show up.

👁 *Ipanema & Leblon*

CATARINA BELOVA / SHUTTERSTOCK ©

LAZYLLAMA / SHUTTERSTOCK ©

Copacabana Beach (p87)

3 The Copacabana experience is about many things: rising early and going for a run along the sand, playing in the waves on a sun-drenched afternoon, or whiling away the evening over cocktails and appetizers at a beach-front kiosk. Regardless, you'll probably notice the incredibly seductive view: 4km of wide, curving sand framed by Rio's ubiquitous green peaks. Head uphill for even better views; rooftop bars and forts at either end of the beach make great settings for taking it all in.

◉ *Copacabana & Leme*

Pão de Açúcar (p101)

4 Some will tell you to arrive around sunset for the best views from this absurd confection of a mountain. But in truth, no matter what time you come, you're unlikely to look at Rio (or your own possibly comparatively lackluster city) in the same way. From up here on Sugarloaf Mountain the landscape is one of pure undulating green hills and golden beaches lapped by blue sea, with rows of skyscrapers sprouting along the shore. The ride up is good fun, too: all-glass aerial trams whisk you up to the top. The adventurous can rock-climb their way to the summit.

◉ *Botafogo, Humaitá & Urca*

Nightlife in Lapa (p142)

5 The Arcos da Lapa form the gateway to Rio's most animated nightlife. Pass through the arches of the 64m-high aqueduct and stroll the packed, bar-lined streets while samba spills out from 19th-century facades. While you'll encounter drinks (from curbside beer and caipirinha vendors) and music (from impromptu jam sessions) all around, venture inside an old-school dance hall to see the city at its most dynamic. From the band on stage come the rhythms of samba, some of the world's most infectious beats. Grab a partner and join the mayhem on the dance floor.

☆ *Santa Teresa & Lapa*

Cristo Redentor *(p112)*

6 The open-armed savior has stood atop his lofty perch (710m-high Corcovado), gazing peacefully over Rio, since 1931. The statue of Christ the Redeemer is a remarkable work of artistry, but most people don't come up here to admire the art deco design. They come for the mesmerizing panorama – a combination of tropical rainforest, beaches, islands, ocean, bay and verdant peaks – that surrounds this unlikely metropolis. There are various ways to reach the top, including a memorable (and steep!) ascent on a cog train.

◉ *Flamengo & Around*

Santa Teresa *(p55)*

7 Overlooking downtown Rio, the hilltop neighborhood of Santa Teresa – where people live in houses rather than high-rises – has a village-like vibe. Its aging 19th-century mansions and bohemian spirit offer a dramatic counterpoint to Rio's better-known seaside persona. Here you'll find old-school bars, art-loving B&Bs and lush backyards where marmosets often roam, with sweeping views over downtown and the bay. The downside: it's still rough around the edges. But the locals and expats who live here couldn't imagine living anywhere else.

◉ *Santa Teresa & Lapa*

LATITUDESTOCK - BILL BACHMANN / GETTY IMAGES ©

Maracanã Football Stadium *(p150)*

8 Fresh from a sparkling makeover for the 2014 World Cup, Maracanã is hallowed ground among Brazilians. It has been the site of both triumph (Pelé's 1000th goal) and catastrophe (losing to Uruguay in the final match of the 1950 World Cup). Games here are simply spectacular, with tens of thousands of cheering fans sending up an earth-shaking roar when the home team (and Rio has four of them) scores. Whether or not you're a football fan, don't pass up the chance to see a game inside this historic arena.

☆ *Zona Norte*

Floresta da Tijuca (p161)

9 New York has Central Park; Rio has the Floresta da Tijuca, a vast swath of rainforest with hiking trails, sparkling waterfalls and abundant greenery that makes other parks look like playgrounds. There are a number of fine walks you can take, as well as some climbs up rocky 900m peaks, where rewarding views await. If you prefer flying to walking, take a hang-gliding flight from Pedra Bonita inside the Tijuca boundaries for a magnificent (if somewhat terrifying) view over Rio's wondrously green backyard.

🏃 *Barra da Tijuca & Western Rio*

INGO ROSLER / GETTY IMAGES ©

JANE SWEENEY / GETTY IMAGES ©

Lagoa Rodrigo de Freitas (p78)

10 'Saltwater lagoon' may not be the first thing you think of when you hear the words 'Rio de Janeiro,' but this picturesque body of water plays a key role in the city's psyche. By day *cariocas* cycle, jog and stroll the 7km path that loops around it. By nightfall a different crowd arrives to eat and drink in the open-air kiosks scattered along the shore. In December Lagoa is home to a massive floating Christmas tree; its glittering lights and nightly displays are pure magic for kids and adults alike.

◉ *Gávea, Jardim Botânico & Lagoa*

What's New

Praça Mauá

Rio's once derelict port has had a dramatic makeover. The Praça Mauá is now home to several stunning new museums, including the beautiful Museu do Amanhã, designed by Santiago Calatrava. (p128)

Botafogo & Humaitá

All eyes are on these twin neighborhoods north of Copacabana. Some of the city's best new restaurants have opened here, along with atmospheric gastropubs, creative art spaces and buzzing nightspots such as Cabaret Lounge. (p105)

Metro Expansion

In preparation for the 2016 Summer Olympics, six new metro stations are opening at long last. The new *linha* 4 connects Ipanema with Jardim Oceânico in Barra via Leblon, Gávea and São Conrado.

Light Rail

A new light rail, called the VLT, now provides efficient, speedy transport around downtown. This is a great way to reach Praça Mauá and to travel east–west between Praça Tiradentes and Praça XV (Quinze) de Novembro. (p126)

Favela Chic

There's a lot happening in Rio's favelas. You can find great hostels, lively bars and first-rate restaurants in the informal communities near the Zona Sul – all of which make fine use of those fantastic hilltop views. (p89)

Microbrews

The craft-beer scene has exploded in Rio, and there's now a wide range of brewpubs across the city, such as As Melhores Cervejas do Mundo. You can sample locally made beers as well as unique brews from across Brazil, including from brewers who use fruits and spices from the Amazon. (p96)

Copacabana on the Rise

A renaissance is under way in this seaside neighborhood, with the arrival of creative new restaurants, microbrew-loving bars and a fantastic music and film museum. (p88)

The Bonde Returns

The quaint yellow streetcar has returned to the rails, meaning you can once again make the scenic journey from Centro to Santa Teresa across the Arcos da Lapa. (p139)

Bikes

New bike lanes have been added to the city, with another 33km on the way. Rio also has a bike-share program – Bike Rio – though you'll need a local phone number to use it. (p205)

Foodie City

An infusion of globally minded new restaurants are helping to reshape the dining scene. New arrivals include authentic Mexican, Peruvian and Spanish eateries, along with places that showcase Brazilian recipes in inventive new ways.

For more recommendations and reviews, see **lonelyplanet. com/brazil/rio-de-janeiro**

Need to Know

For more information, see Survival Guide (p203)

Currency
Real (R$)

Language
Portuguese

Visas
Many nationalities require them, including citizens of the US, Canada and Australia.

Money
ATMs widely available. Credit cards accepted in most mid-range and top-end hotels and restaurants.

Cell Phones
Local SIM cards can be used in unlocked European and Australian phones, and in US phones on the GSM network.

Time
Rio is three hours behind GMT. Daylight savings pushes the clocks one hour forward between mid-October and mid-February.

Tourist Information
Riotur (www.rioguiaoficial.com.br) has offices and kiosks for getting maps, transport info and tips on attractions and events.

Daily Costs

Budget: under R$200
➡ Hostel bed: R$40–70
➡ Sandwich and drink in a juice bar: R$15
➡ Coconut water on the beach: R$5

Midrange: R$200–600
➡ Standard double room in Copacabana: R$350
➡ Dinner for two: R$100–150
➡ Guided bicycle tour: R$100–125
➡ Admission to a samba club: R$20–50

Top end: over R$600
➡ Boutique hotel room: from R$600
➡ Dinner for two at a top restaurant with drinks: R$350
➡ Rock climbing up Pão de Açúcar: R$375

Advance Planning

Nine months before Book a room if visiting during Carnaval or on New Year's Eve.

Three months before Organize your visa (if you need one) and book accommodations.

Two weeks before Book guided tours and activities such as rock climbing, rainforest tours and tandem gliding.

One week before Book a table at top restaurants. Check concerts and events on www.rioguiaoficial.com.br.

Useful Websites

Insider's Guide to Rio (www.ipanema.com) Tips and planning info, with special sections on Carnaval and gay Rio.

Lonely Planet (www.lonelyplanet.com) Destination information, travel forum and bookings.

Riotur (www.rioguiaoficial.com.br) Rio's official tourism authority.

Rio Times (www.riotimesonline.com) English-language resource on current events.

WHEN TO GO

High season runs from December to March, when Rio is festive, pricey and hot. To beat the crowds and higher prices, visit from May to September.

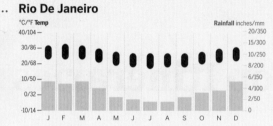

Rio De Janeiro

Arriving in Rio de Janeiro

Aeroporto Internacional Antônio Carlos Jobim Most international flights arrive at this airport (also called Galeão), located 15km north of the city center. From there, Premium Auto Ônibus (www.premiumautoonibus.com.br; tickets R$15) operates buses approximately every 30 to 40 minutes to Flamengo, Copacabana, Ipanema, Leblon and other neighborhoods. It takes 75 minutes to two hours depending on traffic. Radio taxis charge a set fare of R$130 to Copacabana and Ipanema (45 to 90 minutes). Less-expensive metered yellow-and-blue *comum* (common) taxis cost between R$60 and R$90.

For much more on **arrival,** see p204

Getting Around

➡ **Metro** The most convenient way to get around. Trains run from 5am to midnight Monday through Saturday, and from 7am to 11pm on Sundays and holidays. Single rides cost R$3.70.

➡ **Bus** Buses are frequent and cheap; destinations are listed above the windscreen. Fares on buses cost around R$3.

➡ **Taxi** Useful at night. Fares start at R$5.20 plus R$2.05 per kilometer. Rates are higher at night and on Sundays.

➡ **Bike** Shared-bike scheme Bike Rio (p205) has numerous stations around town. You'll need a local cell phone (mobile) number to release the bikes at each station.

For much more on **getting around**, see p205

Sleeping

Rio's most popular accommodations include high-rise hotels on the beachfront, small art-minded guesthouses (particularly in Santa Teresa) and stylish hostels. With a growing number of accommodation options, rates are fairly competitive (with prices slightly less than in the US). Keep in mind you'll pay a premium (double or triple the normal price) during Carnaval and on New Year's Eve, with minimum stays (four to seven nights) usually required. You can save money by renting an apartment.

Book at least two or three months in advance during high season.

Useful Websites

➡ **Airbnb** (www.airbnb.com) Hundreds of rooms and apartments listed across Rio.

➡ **Cama e Cafe** (www.camaecafe.com.br) Rent a room from local residents in Santa Teresa.

➡ **Blame It on Rio 4 Travel** (www.blameitonrio4travel.com) Excellent agency that rents apartments in Copacabana and Ipanema.

For much more on **sleeping,** see p163

DANGERS & ANNOYANCES

Crime in Rio is a concern. It's wise to be cautious.

➡ Take nothing of value to the beach.

➡ Avoid deserted parts of Centro on weekends.

➡ Don't wear expensive-looking accessories.

➡ Carry a copy of your passport, one credit card and enough cash for the day; leave the passport, extra cash and cards in your hotel safe.

Top Itineraries

Day One

Ipanema & Leblon (p56)

 Spend the first day soaking up the rays on **Ipanema Beach**. Be sure to hydrate with *maté* (cold, sweetened tea) and *agua de côco* (coconut water), sample a few beach snacks (or a sandwich at **Uruguai**) and take a scenic stroll down to Leblon.

> ✖ **Lunch** CT Boucherie (p65) serves excellent grilled dishes and creative sides.

Ipanema & Leblon (p56)

In the afternoon, wander through the streets of Ipanema, doing some window-shopping on Rua Garcia d'Ávila, stopping for ice cream at **Vero**, and getting a coffee fix at **Cafeína**. Later, stroll over to **Ponta do Arpoador**, and watch the sunset behind Dois Irmãos.

> ✖ **Dinner** Creative dishes with Eastern influences at Zazá Bistrô Tropical (p64).

Ipanema & Leblon (p56)

 Catch a concert at **Vinícius Show Bar**, an intimate space for bossa nova and live jazz. Afterwards, head up the street to **Barzin**, a festive bar and live-music venue that always draws a crowd. End the night at **Usina**, a stylish lounge in Leblon.

Day Two

Flamengo & Around (p110)

 Start off in Cosme Velho, and take the cog train up Corcovado to admire the view beneath the open-armed **Cristo Redentor**. Nearby, visit the **Museu Internacional de Arte Naïf do Brasil**, which is full of colorful folk art from Brazil and beyond.

> ✖ **Lunch** Have a leisurely lunch at Bar do Mineiro (p141), a Santa Teresa classic.

Santa Teresa & Lapa (p136)

Wander through Santa Teresa, Rio's most atmospheric neighborhood. Browse for handicrafts at **La Vereda**, admire the views from the **Parque das Ruínas** and check out the eclectic art collection and lush gardens of **Museu Chácara do Céu**. Stop for a pick-me-up bite at **Cafecito**.

> ✖ **Dinner** Feast on beautiful Amazonian dishes at Espírito Santa (p141).

Santa Teresa & Lapa (p136)

 Take a taxi downhill to Lapa for a late night of samba and caipirinhas. Start the evening by taking in the street party around the **Arcos da Lapa**, before making your way to **Rio Scenarium**, a beautiful antique-filled club where you can join samba-loving crowds on the dance floor or simply watch the evening unfold from an upper balcony.

Day Three

Barra da Tijuca & Western Rio (p155)

 In the morning, go for a hike in **Floresta da Tijuca**, which has rainforest-lined hiking trails, refreshing waterfalls and spectacular views from craggy summits.

> **Lunch** Try Rio's signature pork and black bean at Casa da Feijoada (p64).

Copacabana & Leme (p85)

In the afternoon, take in the sun and surf on **Copacabana Beach**. If you're feeling active, try your hand at stand-up paddleboarding. After a few hours in the sun, stroll to the southern end of the neighborhood, where you can visit the **Forte de Copacabana**. Here you'll find a small museum and several relaxing open-air cafes with memorable views across the sweep of Copacabana Beach.

> **Dinner** Enjoy tapas and sangria at El Born (p90) in buzzing Baixo Copa.

Gávea, Jardim Botânico & Lagoa (p76)

 After dinner, go for creative cocktails and serene views at the open-air lakeside bar of **Palaphita Kitch**. If you're still going strong, end the night at **00 (Zero Zero)**, which has a small, fired-up dance floor and top-notch DJs.

Day Four

Centro & Praça Mauá (p120)

Start the morning in the newly redesigned streets around Praça Mauá. Admire the view from the **Museu de Arte do Rio** and check out the futuristic exhibits inside the **Museu do Amanhã**. Peek in the lavish **Mosteiro de São Bento** en route to Praça XV (Quinze) de Novembro and check out other impressive colonial sights, including **Paço Imperial** and the **Igreja de Nossa Senhora do Carmo da Antiga Sé**.

> **Lunch** Enjoy rich seafood dishes and bay views at AlbaMar (p130).

Botafogo, Humaitá & Urca (p99)

 Spend the afternoon down in Urca. Take the cable car to the top of **Pão de Açúcar**, from where Rio spreads before you in a stunning panorama. Afterwards, have drink and a snack at waterfront **Bar Urca**.

> **Dinner** Dine at much-celebrated Lasai (p105).

Botafogo, Humaitá & Urca (p99)

 Stick around Botafogo for libations in some of the neighborhood's creative new drinking dens. Sip microbrews in the rock-and-roll refuge of **Caverna**; hang out with the artsy set at **Comuna**; and join the dance party at the bordello-esque **Cabaret Lounge**.

If You Like...

Beaches

Ipanema There's never a dull moment on Rio's most famous beach, with volleyball games, food and drink vendors, and those inviting waves. (p58)

Copacabana Planted with high-rises and framed by mountains, curving Copacabana Beach is truly magnificent. (p87)

Praia Vermelha Hidden near the cable-car station to Pão de Açúcar, this tiny, well-concealed beach boasts a magnificent panorama. (p103)

Barra da Tijuca A picturesque, seemingly endless stretch of sand located west of Leblon. (p157)

Prainha You'll find good surf and a striking setting of rainforest-backed beachfront with little development in sight. (p160)

Outdoor Adventures

Parque Nacional da Tijuca Lush rainforest, waterfalls, scenic views atop rocky cliffs – Tijuca National Park is a must for outdoor lovers. (p161)

Hang gliding Take the plunge off Pedra Bonita for an unforgettable airborne adventure. (p50)

Pão de Açúcar Forget the cable car; for an adrenaline rush sign up for a rock-climbing excursion to the top of Sugarloaf Mountain. (p101)

Lagoa Rodrigo de Freitas By day you can jog or cycle around the picturesque lake; by night enjoy cocktails at waterfront kiosks. (p78)

Pista Cláudio Coutinho This trail is steep and slippery, but you can take it up Morro da Urca (stage

ROGER DE LA HARPE / GETTY IMAGES ©

Tropical greenery in Jardim Botânico (p79)

one of Pão de Açúcar) for cinematic views above Rio. (p102)

Parks & Gardens

Jardim Botânico This beautifully set botanical garden makes a refreshing escape from the city. (p79)

Parque Lage Home to a historic mansion and rainforest-lined walking trails, including one challenging trail that ascends Corcovado. (p80)

Parque do Flamengo A long, narrow park with magnificent bay views that makes a great setting for a bike ride. (p114)

Parque da Catacumba Trails lead up to a peak with spectacular views over the lake and the peaks beyond. (p80)

Sítio Burle Marx It's a long journey to get here, but this beautifully landscaped estate is a verdant wonderland. (p157)

Historical Sights

Museu da República The former presidential palace has historical artifacts, including an eerily preserved room where one president took his own life. (p114)

Igreja de Nossa Senhora do Carmo da Antiga Sé Magnificently restored church where several Portuguese kings were crowned. (p125)

Forte Duque de Caxias Stand atop an old colonial fort and enjoy sweeping views over Copacabana and Pão de Açúcar. (p88)

Igreja São Francisco da Penitência This gilded masterpiece stands atop one of Centro's last remaining hills. (p124)

Museu Histórico Nacional The former royal arsenal provides a fascinating glimpse into Rio's royal days. (p122)

Mosteiro de São Bento A gold-laden work of art, and one of Brazil's finest colonial churches. (p128)

Art & Architecture

Museu de Arte do Rio The city's best new art museum is a showcase for great photography, painting and sculpture. (p127)

Museu do Amanhã The spectacular new – and thought-provoking – museum designed by Santiago Calatrava. (p128)

Museu do Imagem e Som An artfully configured museum that celebrates Brazilian music and film. (p88)

Museu Nacional de Belas Artes An impressive collection of 19th- and early-20th-century paintings in the heart of downtown. (p123)

Museu de Arte Moderna A massive postmodern building that houses works by some of Brazil's best-known 20th-century artists. (p123)

Theatro Municipal One of Rio's most striking buildings, this theater was recently restored to its former splendor. (p123)

Museu do Índio A beautifully curated collection of indigenous objects, photos and sound recordings. (p102)

Museu Chácara do Céu You'll pass through lush gardens en route to this small museum, which has an outstanding collection of modern art. (p139)

For more top Rio de Janeiro spots, see the following:

➡ Eating (p33)

➡ Drinking & Nightlife (p37)

➡ Entertainment (p40)

➡ Samba (p43)

➡ Shopping (p47)

➡ Sports & Activities (p49)

Free Attractions

Centro Cultural Banco do Brasil Massive arts center that is home to some of the city's top exhibits. (p126)

Centro de Arte Hélio Oiticica A little-visited gem that has cutting-edge contemporary exhibitions. (p124)

Real Gabinete Português de Leitura The elegant Portuguese reading room is one of Rio's few buildings of the Manueline style. (p124)

Parque das Ruínas High up in Santa Teresa, the ruins of this former mansion have magnificent views over Rio. (p139)

Museu de Folclore Edison Carneiro A small but worthwhile collection of Brazilian folk art next door to the former presidential palace. (p115)

Instituto Moreira Salles Fascinating gallery of temporary exhibits in a restored villa surrounded by Burle Marx–designed gardens. (p79)

Centro Cultural Justiça Federal The handsome building that once housed Brazil's Supreme Court today hosts diverse exhibitions. (p123)

PLAN YOUR TRIP IF YOU LIKE...

Month by Month

TOP EVENTS

Carnaval, February

Festas Juninas, June

Portas Abertas, July

Gay Pride Rio, October or November

Réveillon, December

January

Rio starts the year in high gear, with steamy beach days, open-air concerts and the buzz of pre-Carnaval revelry.

✷ Dia de São Sebastião

The patron saint of Rio is commemorated on January 20 with a procession that carries the image of São Sebastião from Igreja de São Sebastião dos Capuchinos (Rua Haddock Lobo 266) in Tijuca to the Catedral Metropolitana in Lapa.

February

High season is in full swing, with people-packed beaches, sold-out hotel rooms and the revelry of Carnaval. Thunderstorms bring some relief from the sweltering humidity.

✷ Rio Music Conference

Despite the bland name, this event (www.riomusicconference.com.br) features a stellar lineup of electronic-music gurus. Past guests at the five-night fest have featured Fatboy Slim, Bob Sinclair and Alesso. Headliners appear in the Marina da Glória.

✷ Carnaval

Brazil's biggest fest is celebrated with abandon in Rio, with hundreds of street parties as well as costume balls and elaborate samba-fueled parades that attract revelers from all corners of the globe.

March

After Carnaval the visiting crowds disperse, though the weather stays hot and the tropical rain showers continue. Ongoing summer concerts and events make it a festive time to visit.

✷ Dia da Fundação da Cidade

The city commemorates its founding in 1565 with a March 1 Mass in the church of its patron saint, Igreja de São Sebastião dos Capuchinos. A procession, concerts, a children's parade and one massive birthday cake are part of the festivities.

✷ Sexta-Feira da Paixão

In March or April (depending on when Easter falls), Good Friday is celebrated throughout the city. The most important ceremony re-enacts the Stations of the Cross under the Arcos da Lapa (p140), with more than 100 actors.

☆ Festival Internacional de Documentários

Latin America's most important documentary film festival (www.itsalltrue.com.br) takes place over 10 days in March or April; more than 100 films from Brazil and abroad are screened at theaters in Rio and São Paulo.

April

After the sweltering heat of summer, April remains warm but pleasant with slightly cooler temperatures and fewer rainstorms. Following

the festive January to March period, *cariocas* (residents of Rio) return to work, and the kids are back in school.

🎎 Dia do Índio

April 19 pays homage to Brazil's indigenous cultures, with a week of special events held at the Museu do Índio (p102). Exhibitions, dance and film presentations are staged daily.

🎎 Dia de São Jorge

On April 23 the city pays its respects to St George, an important figure in the Afro-Brazilian community. There's a Mass at Igreja de São Jorge (Rua da Alfândega 382, Centro) followed by a procession. Food vendors abound.

June

June brings milder weather, with temperatures in the low 20s (Celsius) and little rainfall. Although it's low season, there's much merriment in the air during the fun-loving Festas Juninas.

🎎 Festas Juninas

Spanning the month of June, the feast days of various saints mark some of the most important folkloric festivals in Brazil. Celebrations are held in various public squares, with food stands, music, fireworks and bonfires. The big days are June 13, 24 and 29.

🏃 Rio Marathon

Set along the coast, with the ocean always at your side, this marathon course ranks among the world's loveliest. The annual 42km run (www.maratonadorio.com.br) typically happens in June or July (but sometimes as early as late May), when the weather is mild. There are also 6km and 21km runs.

🎎 Festa da São Pedro do Mar

The fishing fraternity pays homage to its patron saint in late June. A maritime procession of decorated boats leaves from the fishing community of Caju and sails to the statue of São Pedro in Urca.

July

The cooler days of winter arrive, with little rainfall, clear blue skies and mild temperatures. There aren't many visitors in town, and accommodation prices are near their lowest.

🎎 Portas Abertas

Artists in Santa Teresa open their studios for a week in July during this lively annual festival (www.artedeportasabertas.com.br). Expect music, a diverse crowd and inventive installations that make good use of the atmospheric bohemian 'hood.

🎎 Festa Literária Internacional de Parati

This important literary festival (www.flip.org.br) brings authors from around the world to Paraty (four hours west of Rio) for five days in July or August. Well-known writers Jhumpa Lahiri, Colm Tóibín and Richard Flanagan have been among the guests in past years.

August

With continuing cool weather but sunny skies, it's an excellent time to take advantage of outdoor activities such as cycling, rock climbing, and hiking in the Tijuca forest.

🎎 Festa de NS da Glória do Outeiro

On August 15 the historic church (p115) overlooking Glória and the bay holds a procession, stages a concert and hosts colorful stalls. Festivities start in the morning and continue all day.

🎎 Rio das Ostras Jazz e Blues Festival

Located 170km east of Rio, en route to Búzios, pretty Rio das Ostras hosts one of Brazil's best jazz and blues fests (www.riodasostras jazzeblues.com), with four days of concerts on outdoor stages by international performers.

🍴 Rio Gastronomia

During the month of August, Rio hosts Brazil's biggest culinary event (www.riogastronomia.com.br). Some 400 restaurants around the city offer a special signature dish (or multicourse meal) at reduced prices. Other events happen at the Joquei Clube (p84), such as tastings, workshops and cooking lessons.

September

The temperatures are heating up, and although Carnaval is still months away, samba-school rehearsals get underway, making it a great opportunity to get a taste of the excitement out of season.

☆ Rock in Rio

One of the biggest rock festivals on earth has recently returned to Rio (after rotating between Lisbon and Madrid). Expect a stellar lineup of bands and huge, celebratory crowds for this event, happening in Rio in 2017 and 2019. Check out www. rockinrio.com.br.

☆ Samba-School Rehearsals

Samba schools begin hosting open gatherings once a week (usually on Friday or Saturday nights). In spite of the name, these are less a dress rehearsal than just an excuse to dance (to samba, of course) and to celebrate. All are welcome.

☆ Dia de Independência do Brasil

Independence Day is celebrated on September 7 with a large military parade down Av Presidente Vargas in Centro. It starts at 8am at Igreja de Nossa Senhora de Candelária (p126) and goes down just past Praça XI.

☆ Festival do Rio

Rio's international film festival (www.festivaldorio. com.br) is one of the biggest in Latin America. Some 400 films from more than 60 countries are shown at 30 theaters. It runs over two weeks, and kicks off either in September or October.

(Top) Gay Pride Rio parade
(Bottom) Rio Marathon (p21)

SU JUSTEN / SHUTTERSTOCK ©

A. RICARDO / SHUTTERSTOCK ©

October

October brings an increasing number of beach days and a touch more daylight – Rio pushes the clock ahead one hour from mid-October to mid-February. The comfortable temperatures make it an excellent time to be in the tropics.

⭐ Festa da Penha

Held on Sundays in October, this religious fest draws thousands of pilgrims who ascend the 365 steps to the dramatically set Igreja da Penha (p153) in the northern suburb of Penha. In the plaza below, food and drink stalls and live music create a festive environment.

November

Summer has nearly arrived and the city begins to gear up for festive days and nights ahead, with a big Gay Pride parade, a dance festival and more activities on the city's sands.

⭐ Gay Pride Rio

Although not as large as São Paulo's massive parade, the Rio Gay Pride event (www.gaypridebrazil.org) gets bigger each year, with more than a million people turning out in recent years. It usually takes place in October or November.

☆ Festival Panorama de Dança

Spanning two weeks in November, the Festival Panorama (www.panorama festival.com) showcases the work of dozens of contemporary dance groups from across the globe, bringing together a mix of experimental troupes as well as traditional performers.

✕ Mondial de la Bière

This four-day event (www. mondialdelabiererio.com) in November draws brew lovers from far and wide to an extravaganza of food and beer tasting. It's currently held on Praça Mauá.

December

While the northern hemisphere shivers, *cariocas* strip down to the bare essentials for hot days on the beach and steamy nights at samba parties around town.

⭐ Lighting of the Lagoa Christmas Tree

Throughout December, the world's largest floating Christmas tree (85m) glows brightly on Lagoa Rodrigo de Freitas (p78). To celebrate its lighting, the city throws a concert in Parque Brigadeiro Faria Lima, on the west side of the lake, usually on the first Saturday in December.

⭐ Festa de Iemanjá

This December 31 Candomblé festival celebrates the feast day of Iemanjá, the goddess of the sea. Celebrants dress in white and place their petitions on small boats, sending them out to sea. If their petitions return, their prayers will not be answered.

⭐ Réveillon

Rio's biggest holiday after Carnaval takes place on Copacabana Beach, when some two million people pack the sands to welcome the new year. Fireworks light up the sky as top bands perform on stages built on the sands.

With Kids

Rio may not be the obvious choice for a family holiday, but there are plenty of activities to keep kids amused: sandy fun on the beach; bike rides around Lagoa; aerial cable-car rides; boat trips and rainforest walks; and plenty of great treats – juices, ice creams and pastries – along the way.

Ilha Fiscal (p127)

DANIELA FERRAZ / EYEEM / GETTY IMAGES ©

Top Snacks

Sorvete
Treat the kids to ice cream, especially from Vero (p60) or Felice Caffè (p62).

Agua de Côco
Drink coconut water straight from the nut at beachside kiosks.

Pão de Queijo
This small, round, cheese-filled bread is available at any juice bar.

Pastel de Nata
Sample these tasty custard tarts at beautiful art deco Confeitaria Colombo (p129).

Sucos
Try creamy *açaí* and many other juice flavors.

Green Spaces

Jardim Botânico
These verdant gardens (p79) offer a fine break from the sun on a hot day. Explore a lily-filled pond, a playground, a cafe and shaded walking trails.

Parque Lage
About 1km northeast of the Jardim Botânico, Parque Lage (p80) has extensive walking trails, plus a playground, a small fish pond and a good outdoor cafe; it's also a great spot to see monkeys.

Floresta da Tijuca
At this vast wilderness (p161) northwest of the Zona Sul you can take short or long hikes, enjoy picturesque views and take a dip beneath a waterfall.

Panoramic Views

Cristo Redentor
Most kids will get a huge kick out of the steep cog train that takes visitors through dense forest to the massive Christ the Redeemer statue (p112).

Pão de Açúcar

The journey by aerial gondola to the summit of Sugarloaf Mountain (p101) is probably the best part of the experience for kids; afterwards, you can walk to the small, pretty beach of Praia Vermelha.

The Beach

If traveling with younger kids, check out **Baixo Bebê Leblon**. The family-friendly beach area between *postas* 11 and 12 in Leblon has a netted-off play area with slides and such.

Older kids will find lots to see and do on the beach: football and volleyball games, boogie boarding and stand-up paddling, and sampling snacks from roaming food vendors.

The Lake

At **Parque dos Patins**, on the west side of Lagoa Rodrigo de Freitas, you can hire bikes, scooters, tricycles, toys and huge family-sized pedal bikes for a spin along the lakeside path.

On the east side of the lake, at **Parque do Cantagalo**, you can hire pedal boats for a glide around the lake (in a swan-shaped boat, no less).

If you're around in December, pay a visit to the lake at night, when a giant floating Christmas tree lights up the lakeside.

Climbing Adventures

Near the east side of Lagoa Rodrigo de Freitas you'll find Parque da Catacumba (p80), which is a great spot for older kids. The outfit known as Lagoa Aventuras (p84) has a zipline, a rock-climbing wall, treetop walks and rappelling (abseiling). There are also short but steep hiking trails that take you to a lookout with pretty views over the lake.

Boat Trips

Older kids might enjoy a boat ride out on the bay. For a full-day outing you can take the ferry to Ilha de Paquetá (p125). Once

you're on the car-free island, you can get around by bicycle or horse-drawn carriage. There are also shorter cruises most days, as well as the ferry to Niterói, which offers great, inexpensive views of the bay.

Top Attractions for Kids
AquaRio

New in 2016, this is South America's biggest aquarium (p128), with hands-on areas for kids.

Ilha Fiscal

A Cinderella-esque castle (p127), reached by a short boat ride.

Museu do Índio

Native music, headdresses, weaponry, recreated huts and activities for kids (p102).

Quinta da Boa Vista

The former home and gardens (p152) of the Portuguese royals now contains a natural-history museum and a zoo (p152).

The Bonde

Ride the little yellow streetcar (p139) up to Santa Teresa, and enjoy the views along the way.

Markets

You'll find fruit markets all across town; they're the perfect spot to assemble a picnic, while sampling delicacies you won't find back home.

Planetário

Astronomic fun and stargazing (p79).

Carnaval

If you haven't heard by now, Rio throws one of the world's best parties, with music and dancing filling the streets for days on end. Officially, Carnaval is just five days of revelry – from the Friday to the Tuesday before Ash Wednesday – but the city begins partying months in advance.

Carnaval float, Sambódromo (p153)

Experiencing Carnaval

The culmination of the big fest is the brilliantly colorful parade through the Oscar Niemeyer–designed Sambódromo (p153) arena, with giant mechanized floats, pounding drummers and whirling dancers. But there's lots of action in Rio's many neighborhoods for those seeking more than just the stadium experience.

Out-of-towners add to the mayhem, joining *cariocas* (residents of Rio) in the street parties and costumed balls that erupt throughout the city. There are free concerts to be found (in Largo do Machado, Arcos da Lapa and Praça General Osório, among other places), while those seeking a bit of decadence can head to the various balls.

Whatever you do, prepare yourself for sleepless nights, an ample dose of caipirinhas (cocktails consisting of lime, sugar and sugarcane rum) and samba, and plenty of mingling with the joyful crowds spilling out of the city.

Joining the *bandas* and *blocos* (street parties) is one of the best ways to have a *carioca* experience. These marching parades consist of a procession of brass bands (in the case of *bandas*) or drummers and vocalists (in the case of *blocos*), and are followed by anyone who wants to dance through the streets. Some *bandas* suggest costumes (such as drag or Amazonian attire), while others expect people simply to show up and add to the good cheer.

History

Although the exact origins of Carnaval are shrouded in mystery, some believe the festival originated as a pagan celebration of spring's arrival sometime during the Middle Ages. The Portuguese brought the celebration to Brazil in the 1500s, but it took on a decidedly local flavor by adopting indigenous costumes and African rhythms. The origin of the word itself probably derives from the Latin *'carne vale'* – 'farewell, meat' – whereby the Catholic population would give up meat and other fleshly temptations during the 40 days of Lent.

The first festivals in Rio de Janeiro were called *entrudo,* during which locals danced through the streets in colorful costumes, throwing mud, flour and various suspect liquids at one another. In the 19th century Carnaval meant attending a lavish masked ball, or participating in the orderly and rather vapid European-style parade. Rio's poor citizens, bored by the finery but eager to participate in a celebration, began holding their own parades, dancing through the streets to African-based rhythms. Then, in the 1920s, the new sound of samba emerged in Rio. It was music full of African flavors, brought to the city by former slaves and their poor descendants – a sound that would forever more be associated with Carnaval.

Since those days, Carnaval has grown in leaps and bounds, and its elaborate parades have spread from Rio de Janeiro to other parts of Brazil. It has also become a huge commercial enterprise; visitors to the city spend in excess of R$1 billion each year.

Carnaval on the Streets

Rio's street parties – the *bandas* and *blocos* – have exploded in recent years. Ten years ago, there were only a handful of these events happening around town. These days there are around 500 street parties, filling every neighborhood in town with the sound of pounding drums and old-fashioned Carnaval songs – not to mention thousands of merrymakers. For many *cariocas,* this is the highlight of Carnaval. You can don a costume (or not), learn a few songs and join in; all you have to do is show up. For Zona Sul fests, don't forget to bring your swimsuit for a dip in the ocean afterwards.

For complete listings, pick up a free *Carnaval de Rua* guide from **Riotur** (www.rioguiaoficial.com.br) or check www.ipanema.com/carnival for times, dates and meeting spots of Rio's best *bandas.* The following are some of the better-known street parties, and each attracts anywhere from 1000 to hundreds of thousands. Although the dates are usually reliable, the times sometimes change, so it's wise to confirm before heading out.

AfroReggae (Av Atlântica, near Rainha Elizabeth; ☯10am Carnaval Sun) A massive and hugely popular *bloco*, with a heavy rhythm section, that celebrates along the beachfront in Copacabana.

NEED TO KNOW

➡ **Carnaval 2017** February 24–28

➡ **Carnaval 2018** February 9–13

➡ **Carnaval 2019** March 1–5

➡ **Riotur** (⏹2271-7000; www.rioguia oficial.com.br; 9th fl, Praça Pio X; ☯9am-6pm Mon-Fri) The tourist organization in charge of Carnaval.

➡ **LIESA** (Map p254; ⏹3213-5151; http://liesa.globo.com; Av Rio Branco 4, Centro; ☯10am-4pm Mon-Fri Sep-Carnaval) For information on buying tickets to the big parades in the Sambódromo.

➡ **Ipanema.com** (www.ipanema.com/carnival) For street-parade times.

Banda de Ipanema (Praça General Osório, Ipanema; ☯4pm 2nd Sat before Carnaval, Carnaval Sat & Carnaval Tue) This long-standing *banda* attracts a wild crowd, complete with drag queens and others in costume. Don't miss it.

Banda de Sá Ferreira (cnr Av Atlântica & Rua Sá Ferreira, Copacabana; ☯5:30pm Carnaval Sat) This popular Copacabana *banda* marches along the ocean from *posto* 1 to *posto* 6.

Banda Simpatia é Quase Amor (Praça General Osório, Ipanema; ☯4pm Sat before Carnaval & Carnaval Sun) Another Ipanema favorite, with a 50-piece percussion band.

Barbas (cnr Rua Assis Bueno & Rua Arnoldo Quintela, Botafogo; ☯4pm Carnaval Sat) One of the oldest *bandas* of the Zona Sul parades through the streets with a 60-piece percussion band. A water truck decked out in red and white follows along to spray the crowd.

Carmelitas (cnr Rua Dias de Barros & Ladeira de Santa Teresa, Santa Teresa; ☯1pm Carnaval Fri & 10am Carnaval Tue) A crazy mixed crowd (some dressed as Carmelite nuns) parades through Santa Teresa's streets.

Céu na Terra (Curvelo, Santa Teresa; ☯8am Carnaval Sat) Follows the tram tracks on a memorable celebration through Santa Teresa en route to Largo das Neves.

Cordão do Bola Preta (Primeiro de Março, near Rua Rosário, Centro; ☯9am Carnaval Sat) The oldest and biggest *banda* still in action. Costumes are always welcome, especially those with black-and-white spots. More than two million join the festivities.

Samba-school parade

Dois Pra Lá, Dois Pra Cá (Rua da Passagem 145, Botafogo; ☺10am Carnaval Sat) This fairly long march begins at Casa de Dança Carlinhos de Jesus and ends at the Copacabana Palace.

Monobloco (Av Rio Branco, near Pres Vargas, Centro; ☺7am 1st Sun after Carnaval) Rise and shine! This huge *bloco* attracts upwards of 400,000 revelers. Nursing hangovers (or perhaps still inebriated), they gather in Centro for a final farewell to the Carnaval mayhem.

Que Merda É Essa? (Garcia d'Ávila, near Nascimento Silva, Ipanema; ☺2:30pm Carnaval Sun) This playful gathering (which means 'What the shit is this?') is yet another big draw in Ipanema – and eventually makes its way along the beach.

Suvaco de Cristo (Rua Jardim Botânico, near Rua Faro, Jardim Botânico; ☺10am Sun before Carnaval) Very popular *bloco*, the name of which means 'Christ's armpit' in reference to the open-armed Redeemer looming overhead. It also meets on Carnaval Saturday, but doesn't announce the time (to avoid overcrowding), so ask around.

Carnaval Balls & Parties

Carnaval balls are giant, sometimes costumed, parties with live music and dancing, and an ambience that runs the gamut from staid and formal to wild and a bit tawdry. The most famous and for-

mal ball (you'll need a tux) is held at the Copacabana Palace (p171), where you'll have the opportunity to celebrate with Rio's glitterati as well as international stars. Tickets cost upwards of R$1600.

Popular but less pricey balls and parties (under R$120) are held at Rio Scenarium (p144), the Joquei Clube (p84) and at Circo Voador (p144), among other places. The most extravagant gay balls are found at Le Boy (p96). These are good places to don a costume to help get in the mood.

Tickets go on sale about two weeks before, and balls are held nightly during Carnaval. The *Veja Rio* insert in *Veja* magazine has details.

Samba-School Parades

The highlight of any Carnaval experience is attending (or participating in) a parade at the Sambódromo (p153). Here, before a crowd of some 90,000 (with millions more watching on TV), each of 12 samba schools has its 80 minutes to dance and sing through the open Oscar Niemeyer-designed stadium. The pageantry is not simply eye candy for the masses. Schools are competing for top honors in the parade, with winners announced (and a winner's parade held) on the Saturday following Carnaval.

The Big Event

Here's what to expect: each school enters the Sambódromo with amped energy levels, and dancers take things up a notch as they move through the stadium. Announcers introduce the school, the group's theme colors and the number of *alas* (literally, wings – subgroups within a school, each playing a different role). Far away the lone voice of the *puxador* (interpreter) starts the samba. Thousands more voices join him (each school has 3000 to 5000 members), and then the drummers kick in: 200 to 400 per school. The pounding drums drive the parade. Next come the main wings of the school, the big allegorical floats, the children's wing, the celebrities and the bell-shaped *baianas* (women dressed as Bahian 'aunts') twirling in elegant hoop skirts. The *baianas* honor the history of

Above: African-themed float by Salgueiro samba school

Right: Samba parade in the Sambódromo (p153)

the parade itself, which was brought to Rio from Salvador da Bahia in 1877. Costumes are fabulously lavish, with 1.5m feathered headdresses; long, flowing capes that sparkle with sequins; and rhinestone-studded G-strings.

Parade Nights

The Sambódromo parades start with the *mirins* (young samba-school members) on the evening of Carnaval Friday, and continue on through Saturday night, when the Group A samba schools strut their stuff. Sunday and Monday are the big nights, when the 12 best samba schools in Rio (the Grupo Especial) parade: six of them on Sunday night and into the morning, and six more on Monday night. The following Saturday, the six top schools strut their stuff again in the Parade of Champions, which generally has more affordable tickets than on the big nights. Each event starts at 9pm and runs until 4am.

Winner Takes All

The whole procession is an elaborate competition. A handpicked set of judges chooses the best school on the basis of many components, including percussion; the *samba do enredo* (theme song); harmony between percussion, song and dance; choreography, costumes, story line, floats and decorations. The dance championship is hotly contested, with the winner becoming the pride not just of Rio but of all Brazil.

Tickets

Getting tickets for the parades at legitimate prices can be tough, even for locals. LIESA (p27), the official samba-school league, begins selling tickets in December or January, most of which are immediately snatched up by travel agencies and then later resold at higher prices. Check with Riotur (p27) about where you can get tickets, as the official outlet can vary from year to year.

➡ **Prices** At face value, tickets run from R$140 to R$500, though you'll probably have to pay

about twice that (or more) if you buy just before Carnaval.

➡ **Where to sit** The best seating areas, in order of preference, are sectors 9, 7, 11, 5 and 3. The first two (9 and 7) have great views and are in the center, which is the liveliest place to be.

➡ **Last-minute options** By Carnaval weekend, most tickets will have sold out, but there are lots of scalpers. If you buy a ticket from a scalper (no need to worry about looking for them – they'll find you!), make sure you get both the plastic ticket with the magnetic strip and the ticket showing the seat number. The tickets for different days are color-coded, so double-check the date as well. If you haven't purchased a ticket but still want to go, you can show up at the Sambódromo during Carnaval at around midnight, three or four hours into the show, when you can get grandstand tickets for about R$50 from scalpers outside the gate. Make sure you check which sector your ticket is for. Most ticket sellers will try to sell their worst seats. And if you can't make it during Carnaval proper, there's always the cheaper Parade of Champions the following Saturday.

Getting Involved

Most visitors stay for three or four schools, and come to see their favorite in action (every self-respecting *carioca* has a school they support, just as they have a favorite football team). If you're really gung-ho, wear your school's colors and learn the theme song (the words are found on the website of each school), so you can sing along when it marches through the Sambódromo. Mangueira (pink and green) and Salgueiro (red and white) are two of the most popular schools.

Getting to the Sambódromo

The best way to get to the Sambódromo is by metro; several stations are within walking distance of the arena. The metro runs around the clock during Carnaval, from Saturday morning until Tuesday evening. This is also a great opportunity to check out the paraders commuting in costume.

If you take the metro, the stop at which you get off depends on the location of your seats. For sectors 2, 4 and 6, exit at Praça Onze. Once outside the station, turn to the right, take another right and then walk straight ahead on Rua Júlio Carmo to sector 2. For sectors 4 and 6, turn right at Rua Carmo Neto and proceed to Av Salvador de Sá. You'll soon see the Sambódromo and hear the roar of the crowd. Look for signs showing the entrance to the sectors. If you are going to sectors on the other side (1, 3, 5, 7, 9, 11 and 13), exit at metro stop Central. You'll then walk about 700m along Av Presidente Vargas until you see the Sambódromo.

If you go by taxi, make sure you tell your taxi driver which side of the stadium your seats are on.

Joining a Samba School

Those who have done it say no other part of Carnaval quite compares to donning a costume and dancing through the Sambódromo before roaring crowds. Anyone with the desire and a little extra money to spare can march in the parade. Most samba schools are happy to have foreigners join one of the wings.

To get the ball rolling, you'll need to contact your chosen school in advance; it will tell you the rehearsal times and when you need to be in the city (usually it's a week or so before Carnaval). Ideally you should memorize the theme song as well, but it's not essential (you can always lip sync).

The biggest investment, aside from the airfare to Rio, is buying a *fantasia* (costume), which will cost upwards of R$600. If you speak some Portuguese, you can contact a school directly; many Rio travel agencies can also arrange this.

Those seeking an insider's perspective on samba schools should read Alma Guillermoprieto's excellent book, *Samba*.

Rio Folia

Lapa becomes one of the major focal points during Carnaval. Rio Folia consists of open-air concerts held in front of the Arcos da Lapa on the Praça Cardeal Câmara. About half-a-dozen different bands play each night (samba, of course). The music starts at 10pm and runs until past 2am,

Woman in Carnaval costume

though revelers pack Lapa until well past sunrise.

Samba Land & Samba City

Another festive space for concerts is the Terreirão do Samba (Samba Land), an open-air courtyard next to the Sambódromo's sector 1, where a variety of bands play to large crowds throughout Carnaval (beginning the weekend before). There are also dozens of food and drink vendors. The action starts around 8pm and continues until 5:30am. Admission is R$15.

For a behind-the-scenes look at Carnaval, plan a visit to Cidade do Samba (p153). Located north of Centro near the port, the 'samba city' is actually made up of 14 large buildings in which the top schools assemble the Carnaval floats.

Visitors can take a tour through the area or attend a live show, which features costumed dancers, live music and audience participation, and comes with free drinks and appetizers. It's touristy and pricey, but some visitors enjoy the Carnaval-style show nonetheless. Confirm times and prices with Cidade do Samba, or check with Riotur.

Samba Glossary for Parade-Goers

Alas Literally the 'wings.' These are groups of samba-school members responsible for a specific part of the central *samba do enredo* (theme song). Special *alas* include the *baianas* (women dressed as Bahian 'aunts' in full skirts and turbans). The *abre ala* of each school is the opening wing or float.

Bateria The drum section is the driving beat behind the school's samba and is the 'soul' of the school.

Carnavalesco The artistic director of each school, responsible for the overall layout and design of the school's theme.

Carros alegóricos The dazzling floats, usually decorated with near-naked women. The floats are pushed along by the school's maintenance crew.

Desfile The parade. The most important samba schools *desfilar* (parade) on the Sunday and Monday night of Carnaval. Each school's *desfile* is judged on its samba, drum section, master of ceremonies and flag bearer, floats, leading commission, costumes, dance coordination and overall harmony.

Destaques The richest and most elaborate costumes. The heaviest ones usually get a spot on one of the floats.

Diretores de harmonia The school organizers, who usually wear white or the school colors; they run around yelling and 'pumping up' the wings, making sure there aren't any gaps in the parade.

Enredo The central theme of each school. The *samba do enredo* is the samba that goes with it. Radio stations and dance halls prime *cariocas* with classic *enredos* in the weeks leading up to Carnaval.

Passistas The best samba dancers of a school. They roam the parade in groups or alone, stopping to show off some fancy footwork along the way. The women are usually dressed in short, revealing skirts, and the men usually hold tambourines.

Puxador The interpreter of the theme song. He (a *puxador* is invariably male) works as a guiding voice, leading the school's singers at rehearsals and in the parade.

Rio's traditional seafood stew, *moqueca*

Eating

Despite top-notch chefs, ethnically diverse cuisine and a rich bounty from farm, forest and sea, Rio hasn't earned much of a culinary reputation abroad. Within Brazil, however, it's a different story, with cariocas (residents of Rio) convinced that there's no place quite like home for sitting down to a first-rate meal.

The Dining Scene

Restaurants come in many forms in Rio, which is unsurprising given the large immigrant population. Lebanese, Japanese, Spanish, German, French and Italian cuisines are among the standouts, though there's an equally broad selection of regional Brazilian restaurants.

Diners can sample rich, shrimp-filled *moqueca* (seafood stew cooked in coconut milk) from Bahia or tender *carne seca* (jerked meat) covered in *farofa* (manioc flour), a staple in Minas Gerais. Daring palates can venture north into Amazonia, enjoying savory *tacacá* (a soup of manioc paste, lip-numbing jambu leaves and dried shrimp) or *tambaqui* (a large Amazonian fish) and other meaty fishes from the mighty Amazon. Cowboys and the *gaúcho* from the south bring the city its *churrascarias,* Brazil's famous all-you-can-eat barbecue restaurants, where crisply dressed waiters bring piping-hot spits of freshly roasted meats to your table.

Wherever you end up, try to pace yourself. Brazilian dishes are normally quite large – and some dishes are meant for two. When in doubt, ask the server to clarify.

NEED TO KNOW

Price Ranges

The price symbols in reviews indicate the cost of a main course.

$	less than R$30
$$	R$30–75
$$$	more than R$75

Opening Hours

Most restaurants open from noon to 3pm and 6pm to 11pm. On Sundays many restaurants open only for lunch, if at all. Juice bars open around 7am or 8am and close at midnight or later.

Tipping

A 10% tip is usually included in restaurant bills. When it isn't included, it's customary to leave 10%.

Reservations

Most restaurants accept reservations for both lunch and dinner, so call ahead to avoid a wait. Reservations are essential at high-end restaurants, and the answering host will usually speak English.

Lunch Specials

Some restaurants serve multicourse lunch specials, which often provide decent value for money. Prices hover around R$30, but can go upwards of R$50 for more elaborate offerings.

Dress Code

Cariocas (residents of Rio) are quite casual when it comes to dress, and dining out is no exception. Even at the nicest places, a pair of smart jeans and a collared shirt or blouse will do just fine.

Etiquette

Brazilians can be fastidious when it comes to eating. Use a knife and fork when eating pizza. In fact, never touch your food with bare hands: always use a napkin when eating sandwiches, bar snacks etc.

Juice Bars

Most *cariocas* start off their morning with a stop at the local juice bar, where they can enjoy two or three dozen varieties of vitamin-filled elixirs, including the very popular *açaí* (healthful juice made from an Amazonian berry and whipped up to a thick consistency – it's eaten with a spoon).

Other unique flavors to try: *cupuaçu* (Amazonian fruit), *caju* (fruit from the cashew-nut tree), *acerola* (tropical cherry), *carimbola* (star fruit), *graviola* (custard apple), *fruta do conde* (sugar apple) and *cacau* (made from the creamy pulp of the cocoa pod; nothing like cocoa). More traditional fruits include *maracujá* (passion fruit), *manga* (mango), *goiaba* (guava) and *tomate de árbol* (tamarillo).

Juices are made from frozen pulp, with added sugar. To order it without sugar, request *'sem açúcar'.*

Juice bars also serve snacks (on display in the counters), hot sandwiches such as *misto quente* (toasted ham and cheese sandwich) and other bites served up in a hurry.

Per-Kilo Restaurants

At lunchtime, locals favor pay-by-weight restaurants, which range from simple, working-class affairs to sumptuous buffets lined with fresh salads, grilled meats, pastas, seafood dishes and copious desserts. These are found all across the city, and are a great way to sample a wide variety of Brazilian dishes.

Most places charge around R$50 to R$70 per kilogram, with a sizable plate of food costing about R$35 to R$50.

Snacks

Snack stands, juice bars and *botecos* (small open-air bars) serve up a variety of delicious, if unhealthy, *salgados* (snacks). After a day at the beach, they go quite nicely with a few rounds of *chope* (draft beer).

A few top picks:

Bolinho de bacalhau Deep-fried codfish balls.

Coxinha Pear-shaped cornmeal balls filled with shredded chicken.

Esfiha Triangular pastry filled with meat and spices, spinach or other fillings.

Pão de queijo Bite-sized cheese-filled rolls.

Kibe Deep-fried Middle Eastern snack with a thin whole-wheat crust and a filling of ground beef and spices.

Pastel de carne/camarão/queijo Squares of deep-fried dough filled with meat, shrimp or cheese.

Tapioca Crepes made from manioc flour, filled with chicken, cheese, fruit preserves and more. Found primarily at food markets.

Food Markets

The *feiras* (produce markets) that pop up in different locations throughout the week are the best places to shop for juicy mangoes, papayas, pineapples and other fruits. For an authentic slice of homegrown *carioca* commerce, nothing beats wandering through a market and taking in the action. The best time to go is in the morning (from 9am to noon). The *feiras* end by 2pm or 3pm.

In addition to the markets we list, stop in at Ipanema's Hippie Fair (p70) on Sundays for delectable Bahian fare.

Cobal do Humaitá (Map p252; ☎2266-1343; Voluntários da Pátria 446, Botafogo; ☺7am-4pm Mon-Sat), the city's largest farmers market, sells plenty of veggies and fruit; it also has cafes and restaurants, and a huge open-air pavilion for alfresco dining.

Cobal do Leblon (p69) has fruit stalls, indoor-outdoor restaurants and bars.

Other neighborhood markets worth visiting include the following:

Copacabana Markets are held Wednesdays on Praça Edmundo Bittencourt; Thursdays on Rua Ministro Viveiros de Castro and Rua Ronald de Carvalho; Saturdays on Rua General Azevedo Pimentel; and Sundays on Praça Serzedelo Correia.

Gávea Friday market on Praça Santos Dumont.

Glória Sunday market on Av Augusto Severo.

Ipanema Markets are held Mondays on Rua Henrique Dumont, Tuesdays on Praça General Osório and Fridays on Praça NS da Paz.

Jardim Botânico Saturday market on Rua Frei Leandro.

Leblon Thursdays on Rua General Urquiza.

Leme Monday market on Gustavo Sampaio.

Santa Teresa Fridays on Rua Felicio dos Santos.

Urca Sundays on Praça Tenente Gil Guilherme.

Feijoada

As distinctively *carioca* as Pão de Açúcar (Sugarloaf Mountain) or Cristo Redentor (Christ the Redeemer), the *feijoada completa* is a dish that constitutes an entire meal, and often begins with a caipirinha aperitif.

A properly prepared *feijoada* consists of black beans slowly cooked with a great variety of meat – including dried tongue and pork offcuts – seasoned with salt, garlic, onion and oil. The stew is accompanied by white rice and finely shredded kale, then tossed with croutons, fried *farofa* and pieces of orange.

Feijoada has its origins in Portuguese cooking, which uses a large variety of meats and vegetables; fried *farofa* (inherited from the indigenous inhabitants) and kale are also Portuguese favorites. The African influence comes with the spice and the tradition of using pork offcuts, which were the only part of the pig given to slaves.

Traditionally, *cariocas* eat *feijoada* for lunch on Saturdays, though a few restaurants serve it on other days. Among the top places to sample the signature dish is Casa da Feijoada (p64), which is one of the few places in Rio that serves *feijoada* daily. Vegetarians can sample tasty meat-free versions of *feijoada* at Vegetariano Social Club (p65).

Eating by Neighborhood

➡ **Ipanema & Leblon** Best assortment of dining, from inexpensive juice bars and per-kilo places to award-winning restaurants. (p59)

➡ **Gávea, Jardim Botânico & Lagoa** Charming upscale neighborhood options, plus dining with views at open-air lakeside kiosks. (p80)

➡ **Copacabana & Leme** Humble rotisseries, ethnic fare and beachfront kiosks, plus hidden gems on the side streets. (p88)

➡ **Botafogo, Humaitá & Urca** High-end eateries along Rua Conde de Irajá; casual open-air options along Rua Nelson Mandela. (p103)

➡ **Flamengo & Around** Small selection of midrange and downmarket options and a few well-concealed surprises (Lebanese, Japanese and Rio's best pizzas). (p115)

➡ **Centro & Praça Mauá** Atmospheric lunch options on cobblestone streets near Praça XV, but few dinner options. (p128)

➡ **Santa Teresa & Lapa** An enticing collection of eateries, with the densest concentration around Largo do Guimarães. (p140)

Lonely Planet's Top Choices

Espírito Santa (p141) Superb Amazonian dishes and creative cocktails in Santa Teresa.

CT Boucherie (p65) Juicy grilled dishes and limitless servings of interesting sides.

Zazá Bistrô Tropical (p64) Handsomely converted mansion with contemporary Asian-inspired fare.

Aprazível (p141) Beautiful setting with views over the city.

Lasai (p105) One of Rio's best and most creative restaurants.

Ferro e Farinha (p116) Wonderful pizza in an atmospheric but hard-to-find space.

Best by Budget

$

Talho Capixaba (p65) Delectable sandwiches and antipasti.

Cafecito (p140) Charming open-air cafe in Santa Teresa.

Boulangerie Guerin (p88) The best bakery (and pastries) in Rio.

Galeto Sat's (p89) Lively and fun grilled-chicken joint.

$$

TT Burger (p90) Outstanding burgers, a short stroll from the beach.

Mironga (p130) Stylish and good-value lunch spot in Centro.

Volta (p81) Creative Brazilian comfort fare in a pretty villa.

Frontera (p62) Excellent per-kilo joint in Rio, with a huge variety of dishes.

$$$

Churrascaria Palace (p92) Rio's best all-you-can-eat joint, with sizzling cuts of meat in an elegant setting.

Olympe (p82) An imaginative fusion of Brazilian and French cooking.

Tèréze (p141) French decadence at the plush Hotel Santa Teresa.

Zuka (p66) Brilliantly executed dishes on Leblon's main eat street.

Best for Seafood

La Carioca Cevicheria (p82) Mouthwatering ceviche and other Peruvian fare.

Laguna Restaurante (p157) Seafood in a lush island setting reached by boat.

AlbaMar (p130) High-end seafood in a historic building overlooking the bay.

Sushi Leblon (p66) Famous for its inventive dishes and mouthwatering sashimi.

Best for Snacks

Sírio Libaneza (p116) Rio's best Middle Eastern snacks.

Tacacá do Norte (p115) Simple tiled lunch counter with mind-blowing *tacacá* (an Amazonian soup).

Bibi Sucos (p68) Sandwiches and snacks that go nicely with the huge variety of Brazilian juices.

Vero (p60) Creamy rich gelato in Ipanema.

Nega Teresa (p140) Scrumptious Bahian street food served with a smile.

Best for Views

Bar Urca (p105) Sit on the seawall, nibble on great snacks and admire the view.

Cafe Colombo (p91) Unbeatable views across Copacabana Beach, plus tasty brunch fare.

Best for Atmosphere

Rústico (p140) Creative cooking in an open-air setting in Santa Teresa.

Bar do Mineiro (p141) An old-fashioned favorite for traditional Brazilian cooking and lively ambience.

Brasserie Rosário (p129) An old-world bistro on a peaceful cobblestone lane.

Cais do Oriente (p130) Delectable fare and a classy 19th-century setting.

Best for Sharing Plates

Venga! (p62) Buzzing atmosphere and satisfying tapas.

El Born (p90) Great tapas and beer that pay homage to Barcelona.

Casa Momus (p142) Delicious Mediterranean fare in a picturesque setting in Lapa.

Meza Bar (p103) A trendy spot in Rio's most food-centric neighborhood.

Bar do David (p89) Tasty bar snacks and first-rate seafood in the Babilônia favela.

Stuzzi (p65) Italian *stuzzichini* (sharing plates), great wine and a festive atmosphere.

Best for Vegetarians

Prana Vegetariano (p116) The best vegetarian cooking (and juices) in town.

Govinda (p128) Beautifully prepared vegetarian dishes served by Hare Krishnas.

Vegetariano Social Club (p65) A small, elegant favorite in Leblon.

Drinking & Nightlife

Any night of the week you'll find plenty of ways to experience Rio's electrifying nightlife: alfresco bars by the lake; festive outdoor drinking spots on the colonial streets of Centro; beachfront kiosks; stylish lounges and nightclubs; and warm and welcoming botecos (small, open-air bars) that are scattered across the city.

The Scene

As in most places in the world, there are a few different subcultures (models and modelizers, surfers, hipsters and hippies) within the nightlife circuit, though there's plenty of crossover between groups. The well-heeled crowd from the Zona Sul tends to favor high-end nightclubs in Gávea and Barra, while an alternative crowd heads to the clubs in Botafogo. Lapa's mix of bars and dance halls attracts a greater diversity of people from all backgrounds, who have little in common aside from a love of samba.

Venues come and go – and the best parties are often one-off events in unique spots – so it helps if you can get the latest from a local source. If you can read a bit of Portuguese, pick up the *Veja Rio* insert in *Veja* magazine, which comes out each Sunday. *Rio Show,* the entertainment insert that comes in the Friday edition of *O Globo,* also has extensive listings

Botecos & Brewhouses

For an insight into Rio's drinking culture, familiarize yourself with one of the great sociocultural icons of the city: the *boteco*. These casual, open-sided bars are scattered all over town, and draw in a broad cross-section of society. You'll find young and old, upper class and working class, men and women, black and white mixing over ice-cold *chope* (draft beer) or caipirinhas (cocktails made from lime, sugar and sugarcane alcohol), flirting and swapping the latest gossip as bow-tied waiters move deftly among the crowd.

Just as most *cariocas* (residents of Rio) have a favorite football team, nearly every local also has a favorite *boteco* to call their own. These range from hole-in-the-wall joints where canned beer is handed out to drinkers slouched over plastic tables to classic, wood-paneled bar rooms with murals on the walls, expertly mixed drinks and a history dating back several generations. Wherever you go in the city, you'll find food is an important part of the experience, as *cariocas* rate bars not just on the drinks and the vibe but on the menu as well.

Lately the beer scene has improved immensely thanks to the rise of the craft-brewing industry across Brazil. New bars featuring top microbrews from within the state and beyond have opened all across Rio, and *cariocas* are discovering their inner beer nerd.

Nightclubs

Rio has some great places to shake your *bunda* (booty). DJs pull from the latest house, drum 'n' bass and hip-hop favorites, as well as uniquely Brazilian combinations such as electro-samba and bossa-jazz. In addition to local DJs, Rio attracts a handful of vinyl gurus from São Paulo, New York and London to spin at bigger affairs. Flyers advertising dance parties can be found in boutiques in Ipanema and Leblon, and in the surf shops in Galeria River (p97) by Praia Arpoador. You'll save money by getting on the guest list – this usually means adding your name on the club's event-listing page on Facebook.

NEED TO KNOW

Opening Hours

Bars From 6pm to 2am Monday to Friday, from noon on Saturday and Sunday. Most places stay open later (typically till 4am) on Friday and Saturday nights.

Nightclubs From 11pm to 5am Thursday to Saturday.

Prices

Drink prices A draft beer will set you back roughly from R$6 to R$10, with cocktails from R$14 to R$22 and up to R$30 at pricier lounges. Most bars tack on a 10% service charge.

Club admission Prices vary; women typically pay less than men. Fridays and Saturdays are the most expensive nights. On average, club admission on a weekend night is around R$50 for men and R$30 for women.

Getting In

➡ The dress code at clubs isn't strict in Rio. Neat shorts and sneakers are fine, though flip-flops and swimsuits are a no-no.

➡ Groups of single men will have a harder time getting in. Try to join up with a few females.

➡ Go before midnight to beat the crowds.

Consumption Card

At many clubs in Rio you'll receive a consumption card when you enter. Rather than paying for individual drinks, your card will be marked each time you order. At the end of the night, you'll head to the cashier and pay for your food and drinks, plus the admission charge. Don't lose the card, as you'll be hit with a hefty fee (upwards of R$200).

Gay Rio

Rio has been a major destination for gay travelers since the 1950s. Back then the action was near the Copacabana Palace, which is still popular with a slightly older crowd (look for the rainbow-hued flag). Today, however, the party has mostly moved on, with the focal point of the LGBT scene, especially for visitors, in Ipanema. The gay beach at the end of Rua Farme de Amoedo (again, look for the rainbow flag) is the stomping ground of some of Rio's buffest men, sometimes known as 'barbies' in *carioca* slang. The bars and cafes of nearby streets – Rua Teixeira de Melo and Rua Farme – attract a mixed crowd and are a good spot to explore if you're not quite ready to jump into the beach scene.

Rio also hosts an enormously popular Gay Pride Rio festival. For more info on the gay scene in Rio, including recommendations on nightclubs, bars, cafes and guesthouses, visit **Rio Gay Guide** (www.riogayguide.com).

Drinking & Nightlife by Neighborhood

➡ **Ipanema & Leblon** Lots of *botecos,* and a handful of lounges and nightclubs. (p66)

➡ **Gávea, Jardim Botânico & Lagoa** Romantic lakeside drinking spots popular with couples. (p82)

➡ **Copacabana & Leme** Beach kiosks, *botecos,* nightclubs and bars with views in the favela above Leme. (p93)

➡ **Botafogo, Humaitá & Urca** Several popular spots in Urca; great *botecos,* and creative bars and drinking dens in Botafogo. (p105)

➡ **Centro & Praça Mauá** Atmospheric after-work drinking spots on pedestrianised streets. (p130)

➡ **Santa Teresa & Lapa** Old-fashioned bars and bohemian haunts in Santa; riotous street parties and samba clubs in Lapa. (p142)

Lonely Planet's Top Choices

Palaphita Kitch (p83) Amazonian-tinged cocktails and serene lakeside views.

Canastra (p66) A friendly French-run neighborhood bar with great food and drink.

Bar dos Descasados (p142) Romantic outdoor lounge with hilltop views.

Comuna (p105) Creative gathering space for art, music and microbrews.

Complex Esquina 111 (p66) Great cocktails and a stylish crowd flock to this outdoor Ipanema spot.

Estrelas da Babilônia (p89) Mesmerizing views from a terrace high up in Babilônia favela.

Best Lounges

Usina (p70) Upscale cocktail den in Leblon, with live music upstairs.

Baretto-Londra (p68) Very swanky party space inside Ipanema's Hotel Fasano.

Best Neighborhood Bars

Bar do Gomes (p143) Old-fashioned neighborhood bar in Santa Teresa.

Antônio's (p143) A fine spot for taking in the Lapa street scene.

Jobi (p69) Tiny, much-loved watering hole open late in Leblon.

Anexo Bar (p143) Friendly, bohemian meeting spot in Lapa.

Champanharia Ovelha Negra (p106) A festive meeting spot for the champagne lovers.

Ponto da Bossa Nova (p93) A mainstay of the outdoor drinking scene of Baixo Copa.

Best Views

Bar do Alto (p89) Intriguing cocktails, tasty snacks and great views over Copacabana.

Alto Vidigal (p70) Mesmerizing views and great parties in Vidigal.

Bar Urca (p106) Drinking in the open air with views over the bay.

Best for Dancing

00 (Zero Zero) (p82) Nightclub of choice for a fashion-conscious, electronic-music-loving crowd.

Bar Bukowski (p106) A party house in Botafogo with a dance floor, upstairs stage and a games room.

Leviano Bar (p143) Outdoor tables on Lapa's wildest street and dancing upstairs.

Cabaret Lounge (p105) Whimsically decorated bar space for cocktails and dancing.

Mais Que Nada (p96) Small Copacabana club with nights of salsa, samba and rock.

Best for Atmosphere

Crazy Cats (p105) Antique-filled drinkery with a rock-and-roll soundtrack.

Samba Caffe (p132) Raise a glass over the cobblestones of Rio's oldest neighborhood.

Bar do Zé (p117) Atmospheric and well-hidden bar tucked away in Glória.

Bar Astor (p67) Luscious cocktails and a great location across from Ipanema Beach.

Jazz In Champanheria (p132) Fun space to sip champagne in the reborn Praça Mauá district.

Mud Bug (p96) A big draw in Copacabana for both rock lovers and football fans.

Best Outdoor Spaces

Hipódromo (p82) Outdoor drinking fest that happens most nights in Gávea.

Palaphita Gávea (p82) A fun, wildly decorated outdoor club behind the track.

Sindicato do Chopp (p93) A tranquil beachfront bar in Leme.

Cobal do Humaitá (p106) Open-air eating and drinking – and a great spot to watch a game.

Best for Craft Beer

Brewteco (p69) A masculine beer-lovers gathering spot in Leblon.

Delirium Cafe (p68) Great global selections in Ipanema.

As Melhores Cervejas do Mundo (p96) A friendly place for beer nerds of all stripes.

Escondido (p93) A casual place to start the night, with good microbrews on tap.

Best Gay Clubs & Bars

Week (p132) One of the best Saturday-night party spots in Rio.

Buraco da Lacraia (p143) A trashy good time for adventure seekers in Lapa.

Tô Nem Aí (p69) Buzzing bar on Ipanema's most gay-friendly street.

Le Boy (p96) Legendary, long-running nightspot in Copacabana.

TV Bar (p96) A good-time crowd against a backdrop of TV screens and DJs.

Galeria Café (p69) A staple of the Ipanema scene.

Entertainment

Rio has a celebrated music scene, with enchanting settings to catch live performances, from cutting-edge concert halls to small and intimate neighborhood venues. Dance, theater, classical concerts and opera also have their small but loyal local following, while cinema is an even bigger deal – Rio is one of the leading film centers in Latin America.

Live Music

In addition to samba (p43), Rio is a show-case for jazz, bossa nova, Música Popular Brasileira (MPB), rock, hip-hop and fusions of these styles. Brazil's many regional styles – *forró* (traditional Brazilian music from the Northeast), *chorinho* (romantic, intimate samba) and *pagode* (relaxed and rhythmic samba) – are also a part of the music scene.

Venues range from modern concert halls seating thousands to intimate samba clubs in edgy neighborhoods. Antiquated colonial mansions, outdoor parks overlooking the city, old-school bars, crumbling buildings on the edge of town and hypermodern lounges facing the ocean are all part of the mix. Rio has a few large concert halls that attract Brazilian stars such as Gilberto Gil and Milton Nascimento, along with well-known international bands visiting Rio on world tours.

Major music festivals include the Rio Music Conference (www.riomusicconference .com.br), held in the Marina da Glória. In addition to established venues, during the summer months concerts sometimes take place on the beaches of Copacabana, Botafogo, Ipanema and Barra da Tijuca.

Dance

Rio has produced a number of successful dance troupes, including the contemporary Companhia de Dança Deborah Colker, which spends much of its time touring abroad. One homegrown talent you might catch in town is the Cia de Dança Dani Lima, an avant-garde troupe that weaves provocative pieces together through dance and aerial gymnastics. Also keep an eye out for the Lapa-based Intrépida Trupe, whose talented acrobat-dancers bring surreal works to the stage.

There is no space dedicated solely to dance; performances can take place at many venues around the city.

Rio's biggest dance festival, Festival Panorama de Dança (www.panoramafestival.com), is held in November. For classical dance, try to see a production by the Ballet do Theatro Municipal, which puts on highly professional performances at Rio's most venerable theater.

Theater

Brazil has a long history of theater. Literary greats from the 19th century, including the highly imaginative *carioca* (resident of Rio) Joaquim Machado de Assis, gave vision to the stage. Talents from the 20th century, such as the great Nelson Rodrigues and more recently Gerald Thomas, have kept the flame alive, and you may be able to catch some of their work on Rio's stages. There are more than two dozen theaters in town. Unfortunately, if you don't speak Portuguese, you won't get a lot out of an evening at the theater.

Classical Music

In the classical-music scene, Rio has several symphony orchestras, and irregular appearances are made by chamber groups and soloists. The best new venue is Barra da Tijuca's excellent Cidade das Artes (p160), where the Brazilian Symphony Orchestra plays. Other first-rate places to catch a performance include the Sala Cecília Meireles (p146), which has excellent acoustics, and the magnificent Theatro Municipal (p133). You might also attend a performance at the Centro Cultural Banco do Brasil (p126) or the Fundação Eva Klabin (p80), both of which host orchestral works periodically.

The biggest classical-music festival is Música no Museu, held in museums, churches and cultural centers around town.

Music in the Museum

Classical-music lovers should try to attend a concert held during **Música No Museu** (www.musicanomuseu.com.br; ☉Jan-Sep). Held annually over a number of months, this event features dozens of concerts (all free) each month, held at museums and cultural spaces around the city, including inside the Museu de Arte Moderna (p123), Museu da República (p114), Centro Cultural Banco do Brasil (p126) and Parque das Ruínas (p139). Most concerts are held during the daytime (typically starting sometime between noon and 3pm), making it an alternative to the beach if you need a break. Visit the website or pick up a brochure from any tourist office for the current schedule.

Cinema

There's plenty of variety at Rio's many cinemas. The market here is remarkably open to foreign and independent films, documentaries and avant-garde cinema. This isn't to say that mainstream Hollywood films are in short supply. The latest US blockbusters get ample airtime at movie megaplexes, while cultural centers, museums and old one-screen theaters offer a more diverse repertoire. Films are shown in the original language with Portuguese subtitles. On weekends, popular shows often sell out, so buy your ticket early. Prices range from R$20 to R$34 per ticket, with cheaper matinee prices from Monday to Thursday and the highest prices (and longest lines) from Friday to Sunday.

The Rio film fest is one of the biggest in Latin America; more than 400 films from 60 countries show at theaters across Rio, and there are occasional screenings at the Marina da Glória and other open-air spots around town. In past years the two-week festival has attracted more than 300,000 attendees. It runs from around the last week of September or first week of October.

NEED TO KNOW

Tickets & Reservations

Tickets for Fun (www.ticketsforfun.com.br) Sells tickets to shows at Citibank Hall and Arena HSBC, both in Barra da Tijuca. Also sells through various stores, including Lojas Saraiva, in Shopping Rio Sul (p107).

Ingresso.com Sells tickets to venues including Theatro Municipal, Sala Cecília and Espaço Tom Jobim. Purchasing online or by phone requires Portuguese, or you can buy from a distributor such as Lojas Americanas (Visconde de Pirajá 142, Ipanema).

Listings

Rio Guia Oficial (www.rioguiaoficial.com.br) The city's tourism authority maintains up-to-date listings of major events.

Time Out (www.timeout.com.br/rio-de-janeiro) Maintains a weekly calendar of key concerts and events in Portuguese.

Rio Show (http://rioshow.oglobo.globo.com) Published inside the Friday edition of *O Globo* newspaper; has extensive listings in Portuguese.

Veja (http://veja.abril.com.br) The *Veja* insert included with this magazine, which comes out on Sundays, is a good (but Portuguese-only) source of info.

Although there's a wide variety of international fare screened here, the festival often sets the stage for the success of Brazilian films aimed at wide release. For more info, visit www.festivaldorio.com.br.

Entertainment by Neighborhood

➡ **Ipanema & Leblon** A handful of theaters, cinemas and live-music venues. (p70)

➡ **Gávea, Jardim Botânico & Lagoa** Live-music spots at lakeside kiosks. (p83)

➡ **Botafogo, Humaitá & Urca** Several cinemas and creative venues. (p106)

➡ **Flamengo & Around** Small concert halls in arts spaces. (p118)

➡ **Centro & Praça Mauá** Large selection of concert halls and theaters. (p132)

➡ **Santa Teresa & Lapa** Many live-music venues in Lapa. (p144)

➡ **Barra da Tijuca & Western Rio** Home to megasized concert halls. (p160)

Lonely Planet's Top Choices

Theatro Municipal (p123) Grand dame of a theater that showcases some of Rio's best performing arts.

Cidade das Artes (p160) Massive R$500-million home to the Brazilian Symphony Orchestra.

Odeon Petrobras (p132) Classic old-fashioned cinema on Praça Floriano in Centro.

Circo Voador (p144) Creative open-air space for top concerts in the heart of Lapa.

Espaço Tom Jobim (p79) Concerts and plays in a historic setting in Jardim Botânico.

Best Cinemas

Estação Net Botafogo (p107) Brazilian and foreign films.

Estação Net Rio (p106) Good location near the metro.

Estação Net Ipanema (p70) Perfect rainy-day escape in Ipanema.

Espaço Museu da República (p118) Contemporary and classic films.

Cinema Leblon (p70) Screens the latest releases on Leblon's main drag.

Best Jazz & Bossa Nova

Maze Inn (p118) Fabulous setting for a jazz party high up in Tavares Bastos favela.

TribOz (p144) Some of Rio's best jazz shows in a beautifully decorated house in Lapa.

Vinícius Show Bar (p70) Long-running Ipanema gem with good bossa nova.

Beco das Garrafas (p97) An intimate club in the legendary birthplace of bossa nova.

Best Música Popular Brasileira & Rock

Miranda (p83) Upscale venue with good food and drink overlooking Lagoa.

Usina (p70) Posh Leblon club with an upstairs area where bands sometimes play.

Barzin (p67) In addition to DJs, this Ipanema spot hosts an eclectic lineup of live music.

Teatro Odisséia (p145) A Lapa mainstay with rock and MPB bands.

Fundição Progresso (p146) A showcase for top names and up-and-coming groups in Lapa.

Teatro Rival Petrobras (p133) Downtown venue where you can eat, drink and catch MPB.

Best Theaters

Espaço Tom Jobim (p79) Dramas, puppet shows and live music in Jardim Botânico.

Teatro do Leblon (p70) Stages thought-provoking fare.

Casa da Cultura Laura Alvim (p70) Diverse works showcased in a restored mansion facing Ipanema Beach.

Centro Cultural Banco do Brasil (p126) A downtown cultural icon for its performances (and exhibitions).

Best Dance Venues

Ginga Tropical (p132) See an amazing range of folkloric dances from across Brazil.

Espaço SESC (p97) Wide-ranging cultural fare, with global dance groups and plenty of experimentation.

LONELY PLANET / GETTY IMAGES ©

Samba band, Lapa

 # Samba

Samba is the great soundtrack of Rio. It plays all across town, but if you're looking for its heart, you'll probably find it in the bohemian neighborhood of Lapa. In this neighborhood, addictive rhythms spill out of old-fashioned dance halls, drawing music lovers from far and wide. Samba also takes center stage during Carnaval, where percussive beats and singsong lyrics are essential to the big fest.

Samba Clubs

Gafieiras (dance halls) have risen from the ashes of a once-bombed-out neighborhood and reinvigorated it with an air of youth and song. The neighborhood in question is Lapa, and after years of neglect it has reclaimed its place as Rio's nightlife center. In the 1920s and '30s Lapa was a major destination for the bohemian crowd, who were attracted to its decadent cabaret joints, brothels and *gafieiras*. Today its vintage buildings hide beautifully restored interiors set with wide dance floors.

Inside you'll find some of Rio's top samba groups, playing to crowds that often pack the dance floor. The nostalgic settings inside the clubs add to the appeal, and even if you don't feel like dancing, the music and festive crowd set the scene for a great night out.

Samba da Mesa

by Carmen Michael

On Friday nights Rio's samba community congregates in front of the faded colonial facades of Rua do Mercado under a canopy of tropical foliage to play *samba da mesa* (literally, 'samba of the table'). On the worn

NEED TO KNOW

Opening Hours

There's always something going on in Lapa, though many clubs are closed on Sundays and Mondays. Typical opening times are from about 8pm to 1am during the week, and till 3am or 4am on weekends.

When to Go

On weekends, Lapa packs huge crowds and many people come for the festive ambience on the streets. If you plan to visit a samba club on a Friday or Saturday, go early to beat the lines, and have a few backup options just in case.

Cover Charges

Cover charges typically range from R$20 to R$50, and women generally pay less than men. Often a portion of the charge covers drinks. As with other clubs, you'll be given a consumption card to keep track of your drinks, which you'll pay for at the end of the night.

Security

Lapa is still scruffy around the edges, so keep your wits about you. Stick to well trafficked areas, be mindful of pickpockets in crowded areas, and leave the valuables at home.

Resources

Rio Guia Oficial (www.rioguiaoficial.com. br) Free monthly publication that lists samba venues and upcoming concerts. Available free at tourist-info kiosks.

Rio Carnival (www.rio-carnival.net) A decent website for checking times and reading up on other Carnaval-related activities.

cobblestones a long table stands, altar-like. Around it the musicians sit and the crowd gyrates, paying homage to their favorite religion. *Samba da mesa* in Rio today is a grassroots movement of musicians and appreciators passionately committed to keeping their music on the street and in an improvised form.

It typically involves a table, at least one *cavaquinho* (small, ukulele-like instrument) player, an assortment of *tambores* (drums) and any number of makeshift instruments such as Coke cans, knives and forks that will make a rattle. The standard of the music can be outstanding, and it is not uncommon to catch sight of a samba *bamba* (big-name samba performer) keeping the beat for the group or belting out one of its tunes. Depending on which bohemians have blown through for the night, you might even catch a duel, in which two singers will pit their wits against each other in a battle of rhymes. It is a challenge of the intellect, and the topics include everything from love to poverty to the opponent's mother. Even if you speak some Portuguese, you probably won't understand the slang and local references, but the delight of the crowd is infectious.

Street samba has taken a battering from the commercialization of music and space, the rising popularity of funk in the favelas (slums, informal communities) and the police clampdown on 'noise pollution' in public spaces. However, for those still interested in a little piece of bohemian Rio, there are several established places that support free, improvised street music. On Friday nights Rua do Mercado and Travessa do Comércio near Praça XV (Quinze) de Novembro in Centro attract a younger, radical chic set. On Sunday and Thursday nights Bip Bip (p96), a tiny bar in Copacabana, caters for hard-core *sambistas* (samba singers). If you're around on December 2, Dia de Samba (Samba Day), you can join the samba train bound for Oswaldo Cruz with the rest of Rio's samba community. The musicians disembark in the dusty backstreets of this working-class suburb, which is transformed every year into a labyrinth of makeshift bars and stages that host a 24-hour marathon of *samba da mesa*.

Impromptu street gatherings in Rio are more elusive at other times and finding them can sometimes be challenging. But it's an unforgettable experience when you find one. There are few fixed places for these parties, and they move from one week to the next. Lapa, in particular Rua Joaquim Silva, generally has something going on, but if not, keep your ears open for the unmistakable sound of the *samba bateria* (percussive-style samba) – follow that sound and you will find a party. Pay heed to the local etiquette: ensure you do not talk over the music; don't use cameras with a flash; and don't sit down unless you are a contributing musician.

Samba Schools

In preparation for Carnaval, most big samba schools open their weekly rehearsals to the public, starting around September. An *escola de samba* (samba school) is a professional troupe that performs in the grand samba parade during Carnaval. Schools typically charge between R$10 and R$30 at the door (admission can go upwards of R$50 as Carnaval nears), and you'll be able to buy drinks. These are large dance parties, not specific lessons in samba (although you may learn to samba at some of them), that are fun to watch and visitors are always welcome to join in.

Keep in mind that many samba schools are in the favelas, so use common sense and consider going with a *carioca* (resident of Rio) for peace of mind. It's best to take a taxi. Mangueira and Salgueiro are among the easiest schools to get to.

Samba schools get incredibly packed as Carnaval approaches. The schools that are most popular with visitors are generally Salgueiro and Mangueira. It's always best to confirm if there is going to be a rehearsal.

Beija-Flor (☑2233-5889; www.beija-flor.com. br; Praçinha Wallace Paes Leme 1025, Nilópolis; ⊘9pm Thu)

Grande Rio (☑2671-3585; www.academicos dogranderio.com.br; Wallace Soares 5-6, Duque de Caixas; ⊘8pm Tue & 10pm Sat)

Imperatriz Leopoldinense (☑2560-8037; www.imperatrizleopoldinense.com.br; Professor Lacê 235, Ramos; ⊘8pm Sun)

Mangueira Map p261 (☑2567-3419; www. mangueira.com.br; Visconde de Niterói 1072, Mangueira; ⊘10pm Sat)

Mocidade Independente de Padre Miguel (☑3332-5823; www.mocidadeindependente.com. br; Av Brasil 31146, Padre Miguel; ⊘10pm Sat)

DANCE CLASSES

Given samba's resurgence throughout the city, it's not surprising that there are several places where you can learn the moves. You can also find places to study *forró* (dance accompanied by the traditional, fast-paced music from the Northeast) and other styles. A dance class is a good setting to meet other people while getting those two left feet to step in time.

A few good places to learn:

➡ Casa de Dança Carlinhos de Jesus (p107)

➡ Centro Cultural Carioca (p132)

➡ Fundição Progresso (p140)

➡ Rio Samba Dancer (p98)

Portela (☑2489-6440; Clara Nunes 81, Oswaldo Cruz; ⊘10pm Fri)

Porto da Pedra (☑3707-1518; www.unidosdo portodapedra.com.br; Av Lúcio Tomé Feteiro 290, Vila Lage, São Gonçalo; ⊘8pm Wed)

Rocinha (☑3205-3318; Bertha Lutz 80, São Conrado; ⊘10pm Sat)

Salgueiro (☑2238-9226; www.salgueiro.com. br; Silva Teles 104, Andaraí; ⊘10pm Sat)

São Clemente Map p261 (☑2671-3585; www. saoclemente.com.br; Av Presidente Vargas 3102, Cidade Nova; ⊘10pm Fri)

Unidos da Tijuca Map p261 (☑2516-2749; www.unidosdatijuca.com.br; Francisco Bicalho 47, Santo Cristo; ⊘10pm Sat)

Vila Isabel (☑2578-0077; Av Blvd 28 de Setembro 382, Vila Isabel; ⊘10pm Sat)

Lonely Planet's Top Choices

Salgueiro (p45) Wonderfully festive, well-located samba school.

Rio Scenarium (p144) Touristy, but still a fantastic setting for live samba.

Democráticus (p144) Long-running club with first-class musicians.

Beco do Rato (p145) Low-key and welcoming spot; there's never a cover charge.

Bip Bip (p96) Copacabana gem famed for its *roda de samba* (informal samba played around a table).

Pedra do Sal (p132) Twice-weekly outdoor samba in a historic locale north of Centro.

Best Lapa Samba Clubs

Carioca da Gema (p144) Long-running favorite, especially on Monday nights.

Semente (p144) First-rate talent at this cozy club around the corner from the Arcos da Lapa.

Fundição Progresso (p146) Top *sambistas* and much more in a massive industrial space that was once a foundry.

Lapa 40 Graus (p144) Dance to samba and play pool, all in one multistory complex.

Vaca Atolada (p143) Small, brightly lit bar with a lively *roda de samba* most nights.

Sarau (p143) Great people-watching on the outdoor plaza with live samba and *forró* groups in the background.

Best Live Samba Outside Lapa

Trapiche Gamboa (p132) Atmospheric music club with addictive samba beats in Gamboa.

Renascença Clube (p154) Open-air celebration that draws samba fans from across Rio.

Teatro Rival Petrobras (p133) Hosts one of Rio's best samba and *feijoada* (bean-and-meat stew served with rice) parties on the last Saturday of the month.

Cariocando (p116) Head here for Saturday feasting on *feijoada* and live bands.

Mais Que Nada (p96) Youthful club in Copacabana that hosts samba one night a week.

Shopping

Unsurprisingly, beach and casual wear are a big part of the shopping scene in Rio. Less well known is the great variety of stores selling antiques, custom-made handicrafts, wine and spirits, handmade jewelry, records and CDs, coffee-table books and one-of-a-kind goods found only in Rio.

Rio's Markets

Rio's many markets are ideal places for exploring the subcultures beneath the city's surface, whether that means you're brushing elbows with antique lovers, recent migrants from the Northeast or youthful flocks of fashionistas from the Zona Sul. Several markets, such as the Feira Nordestina and the monthly Feira do Rio Antigo, are as much about food and music as they are about shopping.

A few top markets:

Av Atlântica Fair (Av Atlântica, Copacabana; ⊘6pm-midnight Mon-Sat)

Feira do Rio Antigo (p146)

Feira Nordestina (p152)

Hippie Fair (p70)

Photography and Image Fair (Parque do Catete; ⊘9am-5pm last Sun of month)

Praça do Lido Market (Praça do Lido; ⊘8am-6pm Sat & Sun)

Praça Santos Dumont Antique Fair (Praça Santos Dumont, Gávea; ⊘9am-5pm Sun)

Rio Souvenirs

Music Expand your CD collection with local favorites, such as Maria Rita, Diogo Nogueira or Mart'nália.

Cachaça Buy quality *cachaça* (high-proof sugarcane alcohol) from Minas for R$35 and up.

Swimwear Flaunt your new tan in a tiny *sunga* (Speedo) or *fio dental* (string bikini). Ipanema, along Rua Visconde de Pirajá, is the place to look.

Maracatu drums If the massive Northeastern instrument won't fit on your coffee table, consider the smaller ukelele-like *cavaquinho*.

Havaianas Find a pair for every mood at the spacious shop in Copacabana (p98).

Paintings Artists showcase their works at the Sunday Hippie Fair (p70).

Soccer jerseys Score a jersey for one of Rio's teams. Loja Fla (p97) is the go-to place for Flamengo fans.

Folk art Tap into Brazil's handicraft traditions at stores scattered about town.

Shopping by Neighborhood

➡ **Ipanema & Leblon** Loads of boutiques; high prices. (p70)

➡ **Gávea, Jardim Botânico & Lagoa** Several small but atmospheric shopping streets. (p83)

➡ **Copacabana & Leme** Loads of stores, a few markets and tourist fare. (p97)

➡ **Centro & Praça Mauá** Wine shops, bookstores and downmarket clothing shops; medina-like browsing in the pedestrian streets of Saara. (p133)

➡ **Santa Teresa & Lapa** A few handicrafts shops and galleries near Largo do Guimarães. (p146)

Lonely Planet's Top Choices

Pé de Boi (p118) Eye-catching handicrafts made by artists from around Brazil.

Hippie Fair (p70) Have fun browsing – and eating street food – in Ipanema.

Maria Oiticica (p72) Elegant jewelry made from Amazonian seeds and fibers.

Osklen (p71) Attractive men's and women's fashion from Brazil's best-known designer.

Granado (p133) High-end skin-care products in an old-fashioned pharmacy.

Gilson Martins (p97) Wallets, bags and other accessories with iconic Rio imagery.

Best Handicrafts

Índio e Arte (p107) A small range of handmade crafts at Botafogo's Museu do Índio.

La Vereda Handicrafts (p146) Unique gift ideas with a local focus in Santa Teresa.

O Sol (p83) Folk art that benefits a social-welfare organization.

Tucum (p146) Small store with Amazonian jewelry, pottery, baskets and wall hangings with pre-Columbian motifs.

Best Jewelry

Antonio Bernardo (p72) Artful, high-end creations in Ipanema.

H Stern (p59) One of the world's top jewelers, with an

on-site museum where you can see the technicians in action.

Amsterdam Sauer (p72) An iconic name with an extensive showroom.

Sobral (p133) Colorful, eye-catching pieces in resin that won't break the bank.

Best Fashion Boutiques

Dona Coisa (p83) Fun, high-end browsing in Jardim Botânico.

Forum (p71) Captivating women's and menswear.

Isabela Capeto (p84) Lovely one-of-a-kind garments sold from the studio in Jardim Botânico.

Redley (p71) Eye-catching clothing for the summer.

Zimpy (p98) Affordable skirts and summer dresses in Copacabana.

Best Bookshops

Livraria da Travessa (p133) Locations all around town, including a much-loved Centro branch.

Argumento (p72) Browse books and music, and nibble on crepes.

Best Music Stores

Berinjela (p133) Used records and CDs hidden in the bowels of a Centro shopping gallery.

Toca do Vinícius (p71) A must for bossa nova fans.

Arlequim (p133) Wide-ranging music selection, plus an appealing in-store cafe.

Bossa Nova & Companhia (p97) Copacabana's best place for delving into Rio's musical legacy.

Baratos de Ribeiro (p107) Great used-vinyl selection of unusual titles in Botafogo.

Best for Musical Instruments

Maracatu Brasil (p118) Many percussion instruments, and you can take classes upstairs.

Casa Oliveira (p133) Known for its guitars and stringed instruments.

Best Shopping Malls

Shopping Siqueira Campos (p98) Quirky place with used books and records, plus galleries and antique stores.

Shopping Leblon (p72) A great place to while away a rainy day.

Village (p161) Rio's most lavish mall, located in Barra da Tijuca.

Botafogo Praia Shopping (p107) A fine place to browse, and a food court with incredible views.

Best Unusual Stores

Gabinete (p83) A curiosity cabinet full of elegant objects for the home.

Brecho de Salto Alto (p97) Festive store with vintage-inspired designs.

Sports & Activities

Tropical rainforest, towering peaks and sparkling beaches set the stage for a wide range of adventures in this outdoors-loving city. Hiking, rock climbing, hang gliding, surfing and cycling are just a few ways to spend a sun-drenched afternoon. Rio is also a great place to watch sport; nothing quite compares to seeing the mad spectacle of a football match at hallowed Maracanã.

Walking, Jogging & Cycling

Splendid views and the sounds of the ever-present ocean are just two features of the many good walking and jogging paths of the Zona Sul. Parque do Flamengo (p114) has plenty of paths stretching between city and bay. Further south Lagoa Rodrigo de Freitas (p78) has a 7.2km track for cyclists, joggers and inline skaters. At the lakeside Parque dos Patins you can rent bicycles (R$15 per hour), tricycles or quadricycles (around R$30 per hour). A popular option is to take the seaside path from Leme to Barra da Tijuca. You can also cycle along paths from Copacabana up to Parque do Flamengo. Sunday is the best day to go, as the road is closed to traffic but open to the city's many outdoor enthusiasts.

The short Pista Cláudio Coutinho (p102), between the mountains and the sea at Praia Vermelha in Urca, is closed to bikes but open to walkers and joggers. It's open from 6am to 6pm daily.

Rio by Bike (p205) offers excellent tours that combine scenery and cultural insight, with guides pointing out key landmarks and describing events that have shaped Rio. Tours last three to four hours and travel mostly along bike lanes.

Hiking

Rio has some outstanding hikes along the trails coursing through Floresta da Tijuca. You can also go for hikes through wilderness areas around Corcovado, Morro da Urca and Pão de Açúcar (p101).

Jungle Me (☑ 4105-7533; www.jungleme.com.br; tours from R$150) This top-notch outfit offers excellent hiking tours through Parque Nacional da Tijuca, led by knowledgeable guides. The Peaks & Waterfalls tour offers challenging walks up several escarpments that boast stunning views of Rio, followed by a refreshing dip in a waterfall. The Wild Beaches of Rio tour takes you on a hike between scenic beaches in Rio's little-visited western suburbs.

Rio Natural (☑ 99992-1666; www.rionatural.com.br; hikes from R$190) Rio Natural is a reputable outfit that seemingly offers every type of outdoor adventure you can think of in Rio. You can go hiking (up Pico Tijuca, Pão de Açúcar, Corcovado, Pedra Bonita and Dois Irmãos), abseiling, paragliding, kayaking or rafting (on rivers outside of Rio).

Rio Hiking (☑ 99721-0594; www.riohiking.com.br; hikes from R$210) Founded by a mother-and-son team back in 1999, this popular outfit offers hiking trips that range from easy to strenuous and cover a variety of terrains around Rio. Popular tours include hikes up Pão de Açúcar, Corcovado and Pedra da Gávea. Other options: kayaking around Pão de Açúcar, surf lessons and all-day adventures outside of Rio (such as diving or hiking).

Rock Climbing

Rio is the center of rock climbing in Brazil, with 350 documented climbs within 40 minutes of the city center. In addition to organized outings, you can also try your hand at the rock-climbing wall in Parque da Catacumba (p80).

PLAN YOUR TRIP SPORTS & ACTIVITIES

NEED TO KNOW

Football at Maracanã

Getting to Maracanã You can take the metro to Maracanã station, and buy tickets at the gate; or go with a group organized by Brazil Expedition (p207), Be a Local (p208) or **Sergio Manhães** (http://futebolnomaracana.blogspot.com).

Game days Games take place year-round on Saturdays or Sundays, and less frequently on Wednesdays or Thursdays.

Information For results, schedules and league tables, visit www.sambafoot.com/en.

Surf Rio

Surf bus To get to the great surf spots outside Rio, catch a ride on the **Surfbus** (www.surfbus.com.br), which takes passengers and their boards down to Prainha, with stops along the way. It departs at 7am and 10am from Largo do Machado and picks up passengers in the Zona Sul en route. It returns from Prainha at 12:30pm and 4pm. Call ahead to confirm pickup location and estimated arrival time.

Surf conditions Find detailed information on all the breaks around Rio at www.wannasurf.com. If you can read Portuguese, check out www.riosurfpage.com.br.

Boards For boards and other gear, visit Galeria River (p97). Spirit Surfboards (p98) rents boards, and you can also rent boards on the beach and from some hostels.

Classes Beginners who want to learn to surf can take classes through informal *escolinhas* (schools) off Ipanema Beach and off Barra. Rio Surf 'N Stay (p176) offers lessons (in English) and overnight accommodations.

Crux Ecoadventure (☑99392-9203, 3474-1726; www.cruxecoaventura.com.br) This reputable outfit offers a range of climbing excursions and other outdoor adventures. The most popular is the rock climb up Pão de Açúcar (R$375). Other possibilities include rappelling (abseiling) down waterfalls, full-day hikes through Floresta da Tijuca, and cycling and kayaking trips.

Climb in Rio (☑2245-1108; www.climbinrio.com; half-day climbs R$230) This respected agency offers half- and full-day climbing trips led by experienced guides. Navigating more than 400 routes around Rio and the state, this is a good pick for climbing junkies.

Hang Gliding

If you weigh less than 100kg (about 220lb) and have a spare R$500 to spend, you can do the fantastic hang glide off 510m Pedra Bonita – one of the giant granite slabs that tower above Rio – onto Pepino Beach in São Conrado. Flights last about seven to 10 minutes, and no experience is necessary. Guest riders are secured in a kind of pouch that is attached to the hang glider. The winds are quite safe here and accidents are rare.

The price of the flight includes pickup and drop-off from your hotel.

Delta Flight in Rio (☑3322-5750, 99693-8800; www.riobyjeep.com/deltaflight) With more than 20 years' experience, Ricardo Hamond has earned a solid reputation as a safety-conscious and extremely professional pilot; he has flown more than 12,000 tandem flights.

Just Fly (☑2268-0565; http://justflyinrio.blogspot.com) Paulo Celani is a highly experienced tandem flyer with more than 6000 flights to his credit.

Tandem Fly (☑2422-6371, 2422-0941; www.riotandemfly.com.br) Two brothers – both very experienced pilots – run this outfit, and they also give lessons for those wanting to learn how to fly solo.

Capoeira

The only surviving martial art native to the New World, capoeira was invented by Afro-Brazilian slaves about 400 years ago. In its original form, the grappling martial art developed as a means of self-defense against slave owners. Once the fighting art was discovered, it was quickly banned and capoeira went underground. The slaves, however, continued to hone their fighting skills; they did it out of sight, practicing secretly in the forest. Later the sport was disguised as a kind of dance, allowing them to practice in the open. This is the form that exists today.

Capoeira, which is referred to as a *jogo* (game), is accompanied by hand clapping and the plucking of the *berimbau* (a long, single-stringed instrument). Initially the music was used to warn fighters of the boss' approach; today it guides the rhythm of the game. Fast tempos dictate the players' exchange of fast, powerful kicks and blows, while slower tempos bring the pace down to a quasi-dance. The *berimbau* is accompanied by the *atabaque* (floor drum) and a *pandeiro* (Brazilian tambourine).

You can see musicians and spectators arranged in the *roda de capoeira* (capoeira circle) at the weekly Feira Nordestina (p152) in São Cristóvão. If you're in town for a while, you can also sign up for classes. Fundição Progresso (p147) in Lapa offers classes three nights a week.

Surfing, Stand-Up Paddleboarding & Kayaking

Rio has some fine options when it comes to surfing, with some great breaks just outside the city. If you're not ready to leave the Zona Sul, there are a few options, including fairly consistent breaks in front of *posto* 10 in Ipanema and *posto* 11 in Leblon. Copacabana gets an OK break between *postos* 4 and 5. You'll find better waves near the spit of land dividing Copacabana from Ipanema. On the east side, off Praia do Diabo, you get right and left breaks, which can reach up to 2m high, but it's not a good spot for beginners. On the other side of the rocks is Arpoador, which is generally more consistent, with fast, hollow breaks to the left ranging from 0.5m to 3m. The big drawback here is that the place gets crowded, making maneuvering extremely difficult. To beat the crowds, go early on weekday mornings.

If you're serious about surfing, you'll want to head down to the beaches west of Rio. Just past Barra da Tijuca and Recreio is **Macumba Beach**; its left and right breaks draw both long-boarders and beginners. After Macumba is lovely **Prainha**, which is widely considered the best surf spot in the area, with waves reaching 3m on good days. If it's too packed, you can continue on to **Grumari**, where the swell isn't as good but the crowds are thinner.

Surfing aside, you can also get out on the water on a stand-up paddleboard. You can hire these out by the half-hour, or take

lessons from rental outfits located at the southern end of Copacabana Beach. You can also rent a kayak off the beach in Praia Vermelha in Urca.

LONELY PLANET'S TOP CHOICES

➡ **Best football experience** Seeing a game at Maracanã (p150).

➡ **Best bike outing** Riding the beach-side path from Leblon to Leme.

➡ **Best climb** The ascent up Pão de Açúcar (p101).

➡ **Best hiking** Scrambling through rainforest and up craggy overlooks in Floresta da Tijuca (p161).

➡ **Best surfing** The waves off Prainha.

➡ **Best airborne experience** Taking the hang-gliding plunge off Pedra Bonita.

Sports & Activities by Neighborhood

➡ **Ipanema & Leblon** Cycling or jogging the beach path. (p72)

➡ **Gávea, Jardim Botânico & Lagoa** Cycling or jogging the lakeshore path. Hikes in Parque Lage. (p84)

➡ **Copacabana & Leme** Cycling or jogging the beach path; stand-up paddleboarding off the beach. (p98)

➡ **Botafogo, Humaitá & Urca** Rock climbing up Pão de Açúcar. Walking the short Pista Cláudio Coutinho. (p107)

➡ **Flamengo & Around** Cycling or jogging through Parque do Flamengo. (p118)

➡ **Zona Norte** Watching a football game at Maracanã. (p150)

➡ **Barra da Tijuca & Western Rio** Hikes and climbs in Floresta da Tijuca. (p162)

PLAN YOUR TRIP SPORTS & ACTIVITIES

Explore
Rio de Janeiro

Ipanema & Leblon **56**

Top Sights 58
Sights 59
Eating 59
Drinking & Nightlife 66
Entertainment 70
Shopping 70
Sports & Activities 72

**Gávea, Jardim
Botânico & Lagoa** **76**

Top Sights 78
Sights 79
Eating 80
Drinking & Nightlife 82
Entertainment 83
Shopping 83
Sports & Activities 84

Copacabana & Leme . .**85**

Top Sights 87
Sights 88
Eating 88
Drinking & Nightlife 93
Entertainment 96
Shopping 97
Sports & Activities 98

**Botafogo, Humaitá
& Urca** **99**

Top Sights 101
Sights 102
Eating 103
Drinking & Nightlife 105
Entertainment 106
Shopping 107
Sports & Activities 107

**Flamengo
& Around** **110**

Top Sights 112
Sights 114
Eating 115
Drinking & Nightlife 117
Entertainment 118
Shopping 118
Sports & Activities 118

**Centro &
Praça Mauá** **120**

Top Sights 122
Sights 123
Eating 128
Drinking & Nightlife 130
Entertainment 132
Shopping 133

**Santa Teresa
& Lapa** **136**

Top Sights 138
Sights 139
Eating 140
Drinking & Nightlife 142
Entertainment 144
Shopping 146
Sports & Activities 146

Zona Norte **148**

Top Sights 150
Sights 152
Eating 153
Entertainment 154

**Barra da Tijuca
& Western Rio** **155**

Sights 157
Eating 157
Drinking & Nightlife 160
Entertainment 160
Shopping 161
Sports & Activities 162

Sleeping **163**

RIO DE JANEIRO'S
TOP SIGHTS

Ipanema Beach 58

Lagoa Rodrigo
de Freitas 78

Copacabana Beach 87

Pão de Açúcar 101

Cristo Redentor 112

Museu Histórico
Nacional 122

Escadaria Selarón 138

Maracanã Football
Stadium 150

Neighborhoods at a Glance

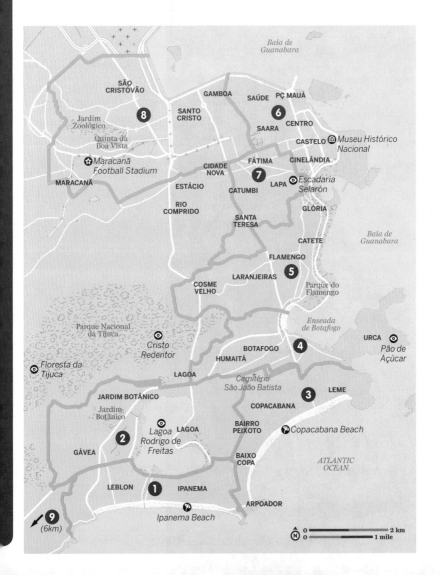

① Ipanema & Leblon p56

Ipanema and Leblon share the same stretch of south-facing shoreline. Rio's beautiful people flock to these beaches, while the tree-lined streets inland hide some of the best eating, drinking and shopping in the city.

② Gávea, Jardim Botânico & Lagoa p76

The northern border of Ipanema and Leblon is the Lagoa Rodrigo de Freitas, a saltwater lagoon fronted by the high-rent districts of Gávea, Jardim Botânico and Lagoa. Here you'll find open-air dining and drinking at lakeside restaurants, and verdant botanical gardens to the west.

③ Copacabana & Leme p85

The scalloped beach of Copacabana begins northeast of Ipanema. Once a destination for international jet-setters, Copacabana is the city's somewhat ragged tourist magnet, with dozens of oceanfront hotels and sidewalk restaurants. The population density is high here and mixes old-timers, favela kids and tourists, and high and low culture.

④ Botafogo, Humaitá & Urca p99

Just north of Copacabana, Botafogo and Humaitá are desirable neighborhoods with vibrant nightlife, cutting-edge restaurants and a few intriguing museums and galleries in the area's old mansions. East of Botafogo, Urca retains a peaceful vibe, and is famed for Pão de Açúcar (Sugarloaf Mountain), which shadows its quiet streets.

⑤ Flamengo & Around p110

To the north of Botafogo, residential neighborhoods include low-key Flamengo, leafy Laranjeiras and, further west, Cosme Velho, above which looms Cristo Redentor (Christ the Redeemer) atop Corcovado. Following the curve of the bay north is Parque do Flamengo, home to cycling trails, sports fields, and several monuments and museums. Inland from here, Catete and Glória hide history in their battered streets, including the former presidential home.

⑥ Centro & Praça Mauá p120

Centro is Rio's business hub and also one of Rio's oldest areas; it houses baroque churches, historic sites, scenic plazas and lavish theaters. Its wide boulevards are crisscrossed with narrow pedestrian streets sprinkled with colonial buildings. History aside, Centro has atmospheric open-air cafes and bars that draw the happy-hour crowd. North of Centro, Praça Mauá is the center of Rio's revitalized port district and has some outstanding new museums.

⑦ Santa Teresa & Lapa p136

On the southwestern edge of Centro, Lapa is a ramshackle neighborhood that's also the epicenter of Rio's nightlife, with dozens of samba-filled bars and clubs, and late-night street parties. Uphill from Lapa, Santa Teresa is a picturesque neighborhood of winding streets and old mansions that have been restored by the many artists and bohemian characters who have settled here.

⑧ Zona Norte p148

The big draws in Rio's northern zone are Maracanã Football Stadium, the Feira Nordestina (Northeastern Fair) and the Quinta da Boa Vista, former residence of the imperial family.

⑨ Barra da Tijuca & Western Rio p155

West of Leblon you'll find great hiking amid the rainforest of Floresta da Tijuca. Nearby, hang gliders make their soaring descent. Further out, Barra da Tijuca is a sprawling suburb with a long, pretty beach, but you'll need a car to get around. Other beaches dot the coast, and get wilder and less populated the further west you go.

Ipanema & Leblon

IPANEMA | LEBLON | VIDIGAL

Neighborhood Top Five

1 Frolicking in the waves, sipping refreshing *maté* and watching people parade on lovely **Ipanema Beach** (p58).

2 Joining fishers and couples on rocky **Ponta do Arpoador** (p59) for the nightly spectacle of sunset.

3 Feasting on Bahian snacks and browsing artwork and handicrafts at the weekly **Hippie Fair** (p70).

4 Gazing out over the length of Leblon and Ipanema at the **Mirante do Leblon** (p59).

5 Catching a concert at **Vinícius Show Bar** (p70), and following with drinks along Rua Vinícius de Moraes.

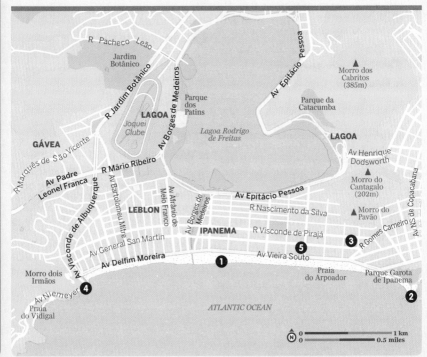

For more detail of this area, see Maps p236 and p240 →

Explore Ipanema & Leblon

The favored address for young, beautiful and wealthy *cariocas* (residents of Rio), these twin neighborhoods boast magnificent beaches and tree-lined streets full of enticing open-air cafes, restaurants and bars. They're also the epicenter of the city's high-end shopping, with dozens of colorful boutiques and multistory *galerias* (shopping centers) selling pretty things that can quickly deplete a budget. While there are few traditional sights here, you can bask on the beach and explore the leafy streets. Ipanema is also Rio's gay district, which revolves around the cafe and bar scene on and near Rua Farme de Amoedo.

Ipanema acquired international fame in the early '60s as the birthplace of the bossa nova hit song 'Girl from Ipanema.' The neighborhood became the hangout of artists, intellectuals and wealthy liberals, who frequented the sidewalk cafes and bars. These days the artists and intellectuals have moved on, and the area is better known for its high-priced apartments and luxury lifestyle. This is, after all, Rio's most affluent district. While few *cariocas* can afford to live here, the streets and beach attract a wide cross-section of society, from surf kids from the outskirts to long-time residents and fashion-conscious twenty- and thirtysomethings who pack the open-sided bars by night. Ipanema and Leblon are also among the city's top destinations for dining and drinking.

Local Life

→ **Markets** Hit a fruit market (p35) for fresh mangoes, passion fruit and snacks (such as the crepe-like tapioca).

→ **Restaurant strips** Rua Dias Ferreira in Leblon is packed with high-end restaurants that serve sushi, Italian tapas, Brazilian fusion and more.

→ **Hangouts** Ipanema and Leblon have many lively neighborhod bars. Good starting points: Belmonte (p69) in Leblon and Barzin (p67) in Ipanema.

→ **Rainy-day escapes** Shopping Leblon (p72) has plenty of rainy-day amusement, including top-end shops, a movie theater and decent restaurants – some with views.

Getting There & Away

→ **Bus** Botafogo (574); Corcovado train station (570); Urca (512); Copacabana (570); São Conrado (177); Centro (132); and Novo Rio bus station (474).

→ **Metro** General Osório and NS da Paz in Ipanema; Jardim de Alah and Antero de Quental in Leblon.

Lonely Planet's Top Tip

On Sundays the east-bound lane of the beach road closes to traffic and fills with cyclists, joggers and in-line skaters. The car-free stretch goes all the way up through Copacabana to Leme.

 Best Places to Eat

→ Zazá Bistrô Tropical (p64)
→ Zuka (p66)
→ CT Boucherie (p65)
→ Via Sete (p61)
→ La Carioca Cevicheria (p62)
→ Stuzzi (p65)

For reviews, see p59 →

Best Places to Drink

→ Canastra (p66)
→ Complex Esquina 111 (p66)
→ Alto Vidigal (p70)
→ Bar Astor (p67)
→ Academia da Cachaça (p69)
→ Brewteco (p69)

For reviews, see p66 →

Best Places to Shop

→ Gilson Martins (p70)
→ Toca do Vinícius (p71)
→ Osklen (p71)
→ Maria Oiticica (p72)
→ 10Aquim (p71)
→ Forum (p71)

For reviews, see p70 →

TOP SIGHT
IPANEMA BEACH

You've probably seen the photos and heard the jazzy theme song ('Girl from Ipanema'), but nothing quite compares to the experience of kicking off your Havaianas and strolling along the golden sands of Rio's most famous beach. The beach is the city's great backyard, free and open to all, with amusements of all kinds: from surfing and jogging along the shore to sitting back, *agua de côco* (coconut water) in hand, and watching Rio at play.

One long stretch of sun-drenched sand, Ipanema Beach is demarcated by *postos* (posts), which mark off subcultures as diverse as the city itself. *Posto 9*, right off Rua Vinícius de Moraes, is Garota de Ipanema, which is where Rio's most lithe and tanned bodies tend to migrate. The area is also known as the Cemetério dos Elefantes because of the handful of old leftists, hippies and artists who sometimes hang out here. In front of Rua Farme de Amoedo the beach is known as Praia Farme, and is the stomping ground for gay society. *Posto 8* further east is mostly the domain of favela (slum, informal community) kids. Arpoador, between Ipanema and Copacabana, is Rio's most popular surf spot.

Whatever spot you choose, you'll enjoy cleaner sands and sea than those in Copacabana. Keep in mind that if you go on a Saturday or Sunday, the sands get crowded. Go early to stake out a spot.

Once on the beach, head to your favorite *barraca* (beach stall), where you can hire chairs and a sun umbrella. There are also food and drink stalls, though roving vendors will come to you, proffering cold drinks (try the sweet tea-like *maté*) and snacks (such as crunchy *globos* – a crispy biscuit made from manioc flour).

Bring just enough cash for the day, and keep a close watch on your belongings. Petty theft is rife on the beach.

DON'T MISS...

➡ Sandwiches with fresh grilled meat from Uruguai (p60)

➡ *Globos* and *maté*

➡ Rehydrating *agua de côco*

➡ Watching *cariocas* show off their skills at volleyball and *futevôlei* (volleyball played without using your hands)

PRACTICALITIES

➡ Map p236, A5

➡ Av Vieira Souto

◉ SIGHTS

◉ Ipanema

IPANEMA BEACH   BEACH
See p58.

PONTA DO ARPOADOR   VIEWPOINT
Map p236 (Av Vieira Souto) At the far eastern end of Av Vieira Souto, this rocky point juts out into the water and serves as one of Rio's best places for watching the sunset. Throughout the day, you'll spot fishers casting off the rock, couples stealing a few kisses and photographers snapping that iconic length of Ipanema Beach that stretches off toward the towering peaks of Dois Irmãos.

You'll also see large flocks of surfers jockeying for position offshore. Around the western edge of the rock is the tiny, secluded Praia do Diabo (Devil's Beach); it's a fine place to take in the views, but swim with caution. A very rustic gym is built into the rocks (think Fred Flintstone–style barbells with concrete weights and chin-up bars).

H STERN   MUSEUM
Map p236 (☎2106-0000; www.hstern.net; Garcia d'Ávila 113; ⊙9am-6pm Mon-Fri, to noon Sat) **FREE** The famous jeweler H Stern allows visitors to get a glimpse behind the scenes at these gemological headquarters. A 12-minute audio tour shows the process of turning the rough stones into flawlessly cut jewels, and you can peer behind the laboratory windows to see craftspeople, cutters, goldsmiths and setters at work. There's a free shuttle service to and from major hotels in Rio.

While there you can also ask to visit the small museum with its display of rare mineral specimens and a large collection of tourmalines. Following the tour, you'll meet with a sales rep, which some people find uncomfortable. A polite 'No, thank you,' will usually see you to the next level (the showroom) and then on to the exit.

MUSEU AMSTERDAM SAUER   MUSEUM
Map p236 (☎2512-1132; www.amsterdamsauer.com; Garcia d'Ávila 105; ⊙9am-7pm Mon-Fri, to 4pm Sat) **FREE** On the most upscale street in Ipanema, the Amsterdam Sauer Museum houses an impressive collection of precious stones: more than 3000 items in all. Visitors can also take a peek at the two replicas of mines.

PARQUE GAROTA DE IPANEMA   PARK
Map p236 (off Francisco Otaviano, near Bulhões Carvalho; ⊙7am-7pm) This small park next to Ponta do Arpoador features a tiny playground, a concrete area popular with skaters, and a lookout with a view of Ipanema Beach. On weekends in summer there are occasional concerts held here.

**ELEVADOR DO MORRO
DO CANTAGALO**   VIEWPOINT
Map p236 (Barão da Torre & Teixeira de Melo) **FREE** Connected to the metro station of Praça General Osório, this elevator whisks passengers up to Cantagalo, a favela that's wedged between Ipanema and Copacabana. The sparkling sea views from the elevator are quite fine, though local residents are happy simply to have a convenient way to get home that doesn't mean ascending hundreds of steps. From the top, keep heading uphill for even better views over Ipanema and Lagoa Rodrigo de Freitas.

As far as security goes, Cantagalo has been safe to visit since the police pacification units arrived in 2009. Recent high-profile visitors include Lady Gaga, Carla Bruni and Brazil's president, Dilma Rousseff.

◉ Leblon

MIRANTE DO LEBLON   LOOKOUT
Map p240 (Av Niemeyer) A few fishers casting out to sea mingle with couples admiring the view at this overlook uphill from the western end of Leblon Beach. The luxury Sheraton Hotel looms to the west, with the photogenic favela of Vidigal nearby.

PRAIA DE LEBLON   BEACH
Map p240 Separated from Ipanema by the gardens and canal of Jardim de Alah, Leblon Beach attracts families and has a slightly more sedate vibe than its eastern counterpart. Parents with little ones may want to check out Baixo Bebê, between *postos* 11 and 12, where you'll find a small playground on the sand as well as other young families.

✗ EATING

Rio's best restaurants lie in the neighborhoods of Ipanema & Leblon. Along the tree-lined side streets abutting the major thoroughfares, you'll find a mix of trendy eateries, outdoor cafes and juice bars. **Price and quality generally run high here, though the stylish new flavor of the month doesn't always live up to the hype.**

✗ Ipanema

URUGUAI   SNACKS $
Map p236 (Posto 9, Ipanema Beach; sandwiches R$12-18; ◎noon-5pm) Of the many *barracas* on the beach, Uruguai is a long-term favorite and serves scrumptious grilled chicken, beef or sausage sandwiches. Look for the blue-and-white-striped Uruguayan flag flying high over the beach.

VERO   ICE CREAM $
Map p236 (☑3497-8754; Visconde de Pirajá 260; ice creams R$11-16; ◎11am-midnight) This artisanal Italian-run *gelateria* whips up Rio's best ice cream. You'll find more than two dozen rich and creamy temptations, including *gianduia* (chocolate with hazelnut), *caramelo com flor de sal* (caramel with sea salt), *figo com amêndoas* (fig with almond) and classic flavors such as *morango* (strawberry). The selection changes daily.

CAFEÍNA   CAFE $
Map p236 (☑2521-2194; www.cafeina.com.br; Farme de Amoedo 43; quiches R$10, sandwiches R$20-40; ◎8am-11:30pm; 🛜) In the heart of Ipanema, this inviting cafe with sidewalk tables is a fine spot for an espresso while watching the city stroll by. You'll also find freshly made sandwiches, salads, quiches and some very rich desserts.

DELÍRIO TROPICAL   BRAZILIAN $
Map p236 (☑3624-8164; www.delirio.com.br; Garcia d'Ávila 48; salads R$15-22; ◎11am-9pm Mon-Sat; 🖊) Delírio Tropical serves a tempting array of salads, which you can enhance by adding grilled trout, salmon carpaccio, filet mignon and other items. The open layout has a pleasant, casual ambience, but you'll need to go early to beat the lunchtime crowds.

GALITOS GRILL   BRAZILIAN $
Map p236 (☑2287-7864; Farme de Amoedo 62; mains R$18-44; ◎noon-10pm) This open-sided purveyor of roast chicken is a handy eating spot. Grab a seat at the counter and enjoy inexpensive, nicely seasoned lunch specials whipped up in a hurry.

KONI STORE   JAPANESE $
Map p236 (☑2521-9348; Maria Quitéria 77; hand rolls R$12-17; ◎11am-2am Sun-Thu, to 6am Fri & Sat) Numbering almost two dozen branches in Rio, the Koni craze shows no sign of abating. The recipe is simple: *temaki* (seaweed hand roll) stuffed with salmon, tuna, shrimp, roast beef or a combination of ingredients, which can then be devoured at one of the tiny bistro tables.

It's healthy, tasty and cheap, which are a few reasons why you'll have to wait in line among nightclub kids for a roll at 4am on a Friday.

LAFFA   KEBAB $
Map p236 (☑2522-5888; Visconde de Pirajá 175; sandwiches R$17-26; ◎11:30am-midnight) A hit on the street-food scene, Laffa is a lively little eatery that whips up piping-hot grilled lamb or turkey shawarmas, falafel sandwiches or dessert concoctions such as apple strudel or sliced strawberries with Nutella. It's all served on *laffa* (pita bread) wraps, made fresh to order.

MIL FRUTAS   ICE CREAM $
Map p236 (☑2521-1384; www.milfrutas.com.br; Garcia d'Ávila 134; ice creams R$12; ◎11am-midnight) On chic Garcia d'Ávila, Mil Frutas serves ice cream that showcases fruits from the Amazon and abroad. *Jaca* (jackfruit), *goiaba* (guava), *maracujá* (passion fruit) and *açaí* are among the several dozen varieties.

LA VERONESE   PIZZERIA $
Map p236 (☑2247-3152; Visconde de Pirajá 29; mini pizzas R$5; ◎7am-7pm Tue-Sat, 9am-2:30pm Sun) If Rio is destroying your budget, head to this friendly stand-up snack counter for one of the best deals in the Zona Sul: the R$5 mini pizza with crispy crust is excellent value, and you can top it off with a few strangely addictive *palmeiras* (palm-shaped cookies).

VEZPA   PIZZERIA $
Map p236 (Farme de Amoedo 75; pizza slices R$10; ◎noon-2am) Great for a quick slice when your energy levels are low, Vezpa serves up satisfying New York–style pizza slices and lasagna from a tiny storefront. There are a few outdoor tables for you to sit at while you munch.

HOPE IN RIO'S FAVELAS

Residents of Rio de Janeiro's favelas (slums, informal communities) face enormous obstacles. Many families live in communities lacking basic essentials such as sewers, medical clinics and roads. Children attend some of the city's worst schools; many, indeed, drop out. The long bus commute for those heading to work can often take hours on traffic-snarled roads for a salary that may not even meet their basic living expenses. There's also a social stigma attached to living in the slums, some of which – particularly those far removed from visitors' eyes – are still run by local drug lords.

Yet it isn't all gloom for Rio's estimated one million favela residents. In the last two decades locally managed organizations have begun appearing in favelas across the city. While small in scale, these nonprofits offer residents the chance to learn new skills and gain a sense of pride. They also give something often in short supply: hope.

For many poor favela children, the Grupo Cultural Afro Reggae (GCAR; www.afro reggae.org) is a lifeline. Since 1997 the GCAR has run a cultural center in the Vigário Geral favela, offering workshops in music, theater, dance, hip-hop and capoeira (Brazilian martial art). The center provides kids with a chance to get off the street, tap into their Afro-Brazilian heritage and gain self-esteem in the setting and fulfillment of goals. Owing to the center's wide popularity, these ideas have spread. GCAR and its favela affiliates now offer more than 60 different programs for poor residents around Rio.

Rocinha, Brazil's largest favela, creates similar opportunities for local residents at its Casa da Cultura. Founded in 2003 by Gilberto Gil, Minister of Culture, singer and neighbor, the center draws on the favela's rich artistic tradition, and offers classes in music, theater and painting. The favela next door, Vidigal, perched on a hillside overlooking Ipanema beach, is the base of the group Nós do Morro (Us from the Favela; www.nosdomorro.com.br). This theater group won fame after some of its young actors appeared in the award-winning film *Cidade de Deus* (City of God) and 10 of its members performed in *The Two Gentlemen of Verona* for the Royal Shakespeare Company in 2006. The organization celebrates its 30th-year anniversary in 2016 and its work has expanded to offer Vidigal kids and adults the opportunity to take courses in theater and filmmaking. Nós do Morro also hosts exhibitions, stages shows and screens open-air films in the favela.

As many have discovered, the favelas have a deep well of talent, but few opportunities. Opportunity is exactly what sociologist Maria Teresa Leal had in mind when she founded a sewing collective in Rocinha in the 1980s. The idea began during Leal's repeated trips to the favela, where she encountered many talented seamsters who had no chance to earn money for their skills. So began Coopa Roca (www.coopa-roca.org.br), comprising a small group of women, each working from home to produce quilts, pillows and craft items made of recycled fabrics and other materials. As of 2015 the co-op employs some 100 women, and makes pieces for Brazilian and international designers; its work has been displayed at museums in cities such as Rio, New York and Paris.

Favelas have made numerous contributions to the city. Rio's biggest party, Carnaval, was born in the favelas, which continue to be pivotal to the festival. That favelas throw the best parties has long been known to many *cariocas* (residents of Rio). Today, Baile Funks are a well-known aspect of the party scene, luring both rich and poor to the gritty neighborhoods on the hillsides. It's there that DJs spin a blend of Rio's bass-heavy tunes (with almost no relation to American-style funk) to packed dance floors.

For a closer look at life inside a favela, you can consider staying overnight at one of the dozens of hostels scattered around the favelas; Vidigal is the most popular destination for foreign guests.

VIA SETE INTERNATIONAL **$$**
Map p236 (☑2512-8100; Garcia d'Ávila 125; mains R$42-75; ☺noon-midnight; ☏) This restaurant on upscale Garcia d'Ávila serves a good selection of salads, burgers and unique appetizers such as calamari in manioc crust, as well as excellent grilled dishes such as tuna steak, rump steak, Black Angus and a fish of the day. You choose the side dishes and sauce to accompany your meal.

Via Sete uses 100% organic ingredients, beef included. The pleasant front-side patio is a prime spot for sipping tropical cocktails while practicing the discreet art of people-watching.

LA CARIOCA CEVICHERIA
PERUVIAN $$

Map p236 (☑2522-8184; Garcia d'Ávila 173; sharing plates R$30-37; ⊘6:30pm-1am Mon-Fri, from 1pm Sat & Sun) True to name, this Peruvian place specializes in ceviche and serves up more than a dozen varieties of the tangy, tender seafood dish. Other great plates for sharing include the *pulpo andino* (crispy octopus with potato salad and baked red pepper), *tiraditos* (fresh, thinly sliced fish) and *lomo saltado* (stir-fried steak and spices).

Take a seat on the inviting front terrace and don't forget to order a pisco sour; they're the best you'll find this side of Machu Picchu.

ALESSANDRO E FEDERICO
PIZZERIA $$

Map p236 (☑2522-5414; Garcia d'Ávila 151; mains R$43-91; ⊘noon-1am; ☎) Dominated by the wood-burning oven at center stage, this stylish two-story restaurant serves some of Ipanema's best thin-crust pizzas. A more casual Alessandro e Federico further south on the same street has a menu of freshly made panini, salads and pastas (but no pizza), with sidewalk seating.

AZTEKA
MEXICAN $$

Map p236 (Visconde de Pirajá 156; mains R$29-48; ⊘noon-11:30pm) A few steps from Praça General Osório, this small open-sided eatery fills a much lacking niche in Rio's food world: Mexican cuisine. Nibble on tortilla chips and guacamole before feasting on quesadillas and burritos. Try the Morelia (pulled pork in *tomatillo* sauce).

The chef-owner hails from Mexico and worked in the US before bringing his cooking to Rio.

VENGA!
SPANISH $$

Map p236 (☑2247-0234; Garcia d'Ávila 147; tapas R$18-40; ⊘noon-midnight) A festive spot to eat and drink, Venga! was Rio's first authentic tapas bar when it opened back in 2009. Classic wood details and a good soundtrack set the scene for noshing on *patatas bravas* (spicy potatoes), *pulpo a la Gallega* (grilled octopus), *gambas al ajillo* (garlic prawns) and other Iberian hits. Match those small plates with a glass of Spanish rioja. Also in Leblon.

FELICE CAFFÈ
FUSION $$

Map p236 (☑2522-7749; Gomes Carneiro 30; mains R$48-65, sandwiches R$35-45; ⊘noon-1am Mon-Fri, 10am-1am Sat & Sun; ✳☎) Half a block from the beach, Felice has a small shaded front terrace for taking in the passing parade of people. Head inside for air-conditioned splendor, where locals and travelers enjoy juicy grilled dishes such as sesame-crusted tuna fillet, plus risottos, steak burgers, bountiful salads and, most importantly, rich Italian-style ice cream (R$12 for two scoops).

FORNERIA SÃO SEBASTIÃO
ITALIAN $$

Map p236 (☑2239-5575; Aníbal de Mendonça 112; mains R$55-73; ⊘noon-1am) This open-sided spot on Ipanema's trendiest street serves first-rate Italian fare in a quasi-industrial interior (concrete walls, exposed bulbs), with old film posters somewhat softening the look. Start off with a brie and prosciutto salad or tuna carpaccio, before moving on to tasty thin-crust pizzas or veal with shiitake and fettuccine. Arrive early to snag an outdoor table in front.

TERZETTO CAFE
CAFE $$

Map p236 (☑2247-3243; Jangadeiros 28; mains R$43-65; ⊘8am-11:30pm Mon-Sat, to 10pm Sun) Fronting Praça General Osório, Terzetto is a lively, enticing cafe with an assortment of prepared salads and antipasti as well as focaccia, ravioli, bruschetta, grilled dishes, pizzas (after 4pm) and desserts. It's a great anytime spot with breakfast plates (such as egg dishes, fruit salad, granola and yogurt), lunch specials and decent coffees.

FRONTERA
BUFFET $$

Map p236 (☑3289-2350; Visconde de Pirajá 128; per kg R$60; ⊘11:30am-11pm) Run by a Dutch chef, Frontera offers more than 60 plates at its delectable lunch buffet, which features a mouthwatering assortment of grilled meats, baked casseroles and seafood pastas, plus salads, fresh fruits, grilled vegetables and desserts. Sushi and the dessert counter cost extra. Dark woods and vintage travel posters give it a cozier feel than most per-kilo places.

AMAZÔNIA SOUL
AMAZONIAN $$

Map p236 (☑2247-1028; Teixeira de Melo 37; mains R$27-68; ⊘11am-9pm Mon-Sat, 10am-8pm Sun) This tiny cafe doles out rich dishes of *maniçoba* (Amazon-style *feijoada* stew made with manioc leaves instead of beans), *vatapá* (a puree of manioc, dried shrimp, coconut and *dendê* oil) and *tacacá,* a complicated soup made of shrimp, lip-numbing jambu leaves and manioc paste. For something a little less daring, try the *caranguejo society* (sautéed crab meat with toasted manioc flour).

The small shop inside sells handicrafts and edible items from the Amazon.

NEW NATURAL   BRAZILIAN $$

Map p236 (☏2287-0301; Barão da Torre 167; per kg R$55; ◷8am-10:30pm; ☏) Featuring an excellent lunch buffet of organic and vegetarian fare, New Natural was the first health-food restaurant to set up in the neighborhood. Fill up on fresh pots of soup, rice, veggies and beans at the healthy buffet.

CAPRICCIOSA   PIZZERIA $$

Map p236 (☏2523-3394; Vinícius de Moraes 134; small/large pizzas R$50/80; ◷6pm-1am) This trendy high-end pizzeria serves up tasty thin-crust pizzas made with fresh ingredients. The price is higher than other pizza joints, but the chefs – working in an open kitchen next to the brick oven – are at least generous with the toppings. Among many flavorful combinations is the signature *capricciosa* (ham, bacon, egg, artichoke hearts and mushrooms).

GULA GULA   BRAZILIAN $$

Map p236 (☏2294-3023; www.gula.com.br; Henrique Dumont 87A; mains R$36-63; ◷noon-midnight) In a cozy villa on the western edge of Ipanema, Gula Gula remains a culinary favorite – which means a lot in a neighborhood ever in search of the new. Grilled meats are tops at this casual spot, but those in search of something lighter can opt for quiches and salads. Gula Gula also has branches in Centro and **Leblon** (Map p240; ☏2284-8792; Rita Ludolf 87A) among a dozen other locations.

GAROTA DE IPANEMA   BRAZILIAN $$

Map p236 (☏2522-0340; Vinícius de Moraes 49; mains R$36-96; ◷noon-2am) A mix of visitors and neighborhood regulars pack the tables at the former bar where 'The Girl from Ipanema' composers Tom Jobim and Vinícius de Moraes once held court. Although the food is fairly standard Brazilian fare, one dish stands out: the *picanha Brasileira* (R$96 for two), a scrumptious skillet of sliced sirloin brought sizzling to your table.

Wash it down with a few glasses of ice-cold *chope* (draft beer) and you'll realize why Garotas have been springing up all over the city.

BRASILEIRINHO   BRAZILIAN $$

Map p236 (☏2523-5184; Jangadeiros 10; mains R$38-59; ◷noon-11pm) Facing Praça General Osório, this rustically decorated restaurant serves good, traditional Mineiro cuisine. Favorites include *tutu a mineira* (mashed black beans with manioc), *carne seca* (dried beef) and *picanha* (rump steak). The *feijoada* (black bean and pork stew served with rice) here is tops – unsurprising given that Brasileirinho is run by the same owner as Ipanema's top-notch *feijoada* eatery Casa da Feijoada.

In the evening you can dine out on the plaza.

TEMPORADA   SEAFOOD $$

Map p236 (☏2523-0066; Av Francisco Bhering, Praia do Arpoador; mains R$48-68; ◷noon-midnight) Temporada serves an assortment of tasty grilled dishes, and the outdoor tables facing the ocean have the best beach-side setting you'll find in the Zona Sul: there's no traffic between you and the sea, only palm trees and sand. It's set behind the Aproador Inn.

Try the grilled octopus appetizer or the tuna tartar with wasabi yogurt, followed by the fish of the day with risotto of *cupuaçu* (acidic, slightly pear-like Amazonian fruit).

PAPA GUI   PIZZERIA $$

Map p236 (☏2513-3951; Teixeira de Melo 53; pizzas R$20-58; ◷noon-midnight) On the west side of Praça General Osório, Papa Gui cooks up excellent thin-crust pizza that's good value – particularly from Monday to Wednesday when there's a two-for-one deal on several varieties. It's a tight space, with a handful of outdoor tables along the sidewalk.

GRINGO CAFE   CAFE $$

Map p236 (www.gringocafe.com; Barão da Torre 240; breakfast R$22-34; ◷8am-10pm; ☏) Tired of eating *feijoada*? This open-sided American-run diner dishes up remedies in spades for the homesick: waffles, pancakes, hash browns, mac and cheese, chili (both meat and vegetarian), barbecue ribs, milkshakes etc. It even smells like a US diner.

★**ZAZÁ BISTRÔ TROPICAL** FUSION **$$$**
Map p236 (☑2247-9101; www.zazabistro.com.br;
Joana Angélica 40; mains R$60-86; ⊘7:30pm-
midnight Mon & Tue, noon-midnight Wed-Fri,
from 1pm Sat & Sun) Inside an art-filled and
whimsically decorated converted house,
Zazá serves beautifully prepared dishes
with Asian accents, and uses organic in-
gredients when possible. Favorites include
chicken curry with jasmine rice, flambéed
prawns with risotto, and grilled fish served
with caramelized plantain. Don't miss the
cocktails.

Upstairs, diners lounge on throw pillows
amid flickering candles. You can also sit at
one of the tables out the front.

BAZZAR INTERNATIONAL **$$$**
Map p236 (☑3202-2884; Barão da Torre 538;
mains R$42-90; ⊘noon-1am Mon-Sat, to 5pm
Sun) Set on a peaceful tree-lined street, this
nicely designed restaurant with a relaxing
front terrace serves creative, beautifully
executed dishes. Current favorites include
suckling pig with macadamia cream,
grilled rock lobster and a vegetarian heart-
of-palm *moqueca* (Bahian stew cooked in a
clay pot with *dendê* oil, coconut milk and
spicy peppers).

ESPAÇO 7ZERO6 BRAZILIAN **$$$**
Map p236 (☑2141-4992; http://espaco7zero6.
com.br; Vieira Souto 706; set brunch/dinner
R$72/175; ⊘noon-6pm Mon-Thu, 8am-2pm Fri-
Sun & 7pm-midnight daily) From its location
on the top floor of the Hotel Praia Ipanema,
this place has a jaw-dropping view of
Ipanema Beach. There's dinner most nights
and lunch on weekdays, but the best time
to come is for the weekend brunch, when
the restaurant spreads a banquet of tropi-
cal fruits, yogurt, freshly baked breads and
pastries, egg dishes and even waffles.

CASA DA FEIJOADA BRAZILIAN **$$$**
Map p236 (☑2247-2776; Prudente de Morais 10B;
feijoada R$78; ⊘noon-midnight) Admirers of
Brazil's iconic *feijoada* needn't wait until
Saturday, the day it's traditionally eaten,
to experience this meaty meal. The casual
Casa da Feijoada serves the rich black-bean
and salted-pork dish every day of the week.

It comes with the requisite orange slices,
farofa (garnish of manioc flour sautéed
with butter) and grated kale (cabbage), and
goes nicely with a caipirinha.

✕ Leblon

ARMAZÉM DO CAFÉ CAFE **$**
Map p240 (☑3874-5935; Rita Ludolf 87B; snacks
R$6-12; ⊘8am-11pm) Dark-wood furnishings
and the smell of fresh-ground coffee lend
authenticity to this Leblon coffeehouse. It
serves waffles, snacks and desserts, and
connoisseurs rate the aromatic roasts here
much more highly than at neighboring
cafes.

KURT PASTRIES **$**
Map p240 (General Urquiza 117B; desserts R$7-
12; ⊘8am-7pm Mon-Fri, 9am-6pm Sat) Extremely popular, Kurt spreads an array
of irresistible temptations: flaky strudels,
berry crumbles and palm-sized tortes with
strawberries and kiwifruit. There are a few
outdoor tables where you can nibble on
pastries and take in the street scene.

BIBI CREPES CREPERIE **$**
Map p240 (☑2259-4948; Cupertino Durão 81;
crepes R$13-28; ⊘noon-1am) This small, open-
sided restaurant attracts a young, garrulous
crowd who enjoy the more than two dozen
sweet and savory crepes available, as well
as design-your-own salads (choose from 40
different toppings). Come early to beat the
lunch crowds.

VEZPA PIZZERIA **$**
Map p240 (☑2540-0800; Av Ataúlfo de Paiva
1063; slices around R$10; ⊘noon-2am Sun-Thu,
to 5am Fri & Sat) Vezpa is a New York–style
pizza place, with brick walls and high ceilings, where you can order pizza by the slice.
The crusts are thin and crunchy and there
are decent selections on hand – try the
mozzarella with tomatoes and basil. Vezpa
also has locations in Ipanema (on Farme
de Amoedo) and Copacabana (on Djalma
Ulrich).

HORTIFRUTI SUPERMARKET **$**
Map p240 (Dias Ferreira 57; ⊘8am-8pm Mon-Sat,
to 2pm Sun) This popular grocer and produce market sells a wide variety of fruits
and vegetables, plus fresh juices and all the
supermarket essentials.

ZONA SUL SUPERMARKET SUPERMARKET **$**
Map p240 (Dias Ferreira 290; ⊘6am-11pm Mon-
Sat, 7am-10pm Sun) A Rio institution for
nearly 50 years, Zona Sul supermarket has
branches all over the city. This one is the

best of the bunch, with fresh-baked breads, imported cheeses and olives, wines, cured meats and other items. The adjoining pizza and lasagna counter serves decent plates. There's a handy **Ipanema branch** (Map p236; Prudente de Morais 49; ⊘24hr Mon-Sat, 7am-8pm Sun) near Praça General Osório.

YALLA
MIDDLE EASTERN $

Map p240 (⌨2540-6517; Dias Ferreira 45; mains R$20-35; ⊘11:30am-midnight) One of the few nonfancy options on this culinary street, Yalla is a small, quick-serving restaurant where you can pick up fresh tabbouleh or couscous salads, sandwiches on lavash bread (such as shawarma, falafel and shish kebab) or pasties filled with ricotta, beef or spinach. Don't miss the baklava for dessert.

TALHO CAPIXABA
SANDWICHES $

Map p240 (⌨2512-8760; Av Ataúlfo de Paiva 1022; sandwiches R$25-40; ⊘7am-10pm) This deli and gourmet grocer is one of the city's best spots to put together a takeout meal. In addition to pastas, salads and antipasti, you'll find excellent sandwiches (charged by weight) made from quality ingredients. You can also dine inside or at the sidewalk tables in front.

STUZZI
ITALIAN $$

Map p240 (⌨2274-4017; Dias Ferreira 48; sharing plates R$22-55; ⊘7pm-2am Mon-Sat, to midnight Sun) This buzzing, uberpopular Leblon spot specializes in creative Italian tapas (think roast lamb croquettes, and goat cheese, fig and honey bruschetta) and expertly mixed cocktails. The lively, candlelit tables on the sidewalk are the place to be; come early to score one.

VEGETARIANO SOCIAL CLUB
VEGETARIAN $$

Map p240 (⌨2294-5200; Conde Bernadotte 26L; buffet lunch R$41; ⊘noon-11pm Mon-Sat, to 5:30pm Sun; ⌖) Vegetarians interested in sampling Brazil's signature dish should visit this small charmer on a Wednesday or a Sunday when tofu *feijoada* is served. At other times, it serves a 10-dish lunch buffet, while the more elaborate evening à la carte menu features risottos, *yakisoba* (Japanese grilled noodles), heart-of-palm stroganoff and other inventive dishes.

PRIMA BRUSCHETTERIA
ITALIAN $$

Map p240 (⌨3592-0881; www.primab.com.br; Rainha Guilhermina 95; bruschetta R$9-17, mains R$41-53; ⊘noon-midnight) Prima showcases

an Italian delicacy not often seen in these parts, using imaginative ingredients such as goat's cheese, olive tapenade, prosciutto and smoked salmon to top its char-grilled bread. You'll also find fresh salads, antipasto plates and various risottos.

JUICE CO
INTERNATIONAL $$

Map p240 (⌨2294-0048; Av General San Martin 889; mains R$32-70; ⊘6pm-midnight Mon-Sat, noon-midnight Sun) This stylish two-story restaurant serves quite tasty, freshly squeezed juices. In an uberdesigned lounge-like setting, you can sample a wide range of fare – focaccia sandwiches, salads, risottos, grilled fish and roast meats, any of which can be paired nicely with one of 60 juice concoctions.

FELLINI
BUFFET $$

Map p240 (⌨2511-3600; General Urquiza 104; per kg R$75-85; ⊘11:30am-4pm & 7:30pm-midnight) One of Leblon's top buffet restaurants, Fellini has an enticing selection of dishes: salads, pastas, grilled fish and shrimp, a sushi counter and a hallowed roast-meat counter. The modest dining room attracts a mix of hungry patrons: tourists, neighborhood folk and the beautiful crowd included.

RÁSCAL
ITALIAN $$

Map p240 (⌨2259-6437; Shopping Leblon, Av Afrânio de Melo Franco 290; all-you-can-eat around R$70; ⊘noon-3pm & 7-10:30pm) This popular São Paulo chain arrived in Rio some years back and quickly earned top marks for its fantastic buffet. The huge spread of Italian cuisine includes salads, bruschetta, pizzas, pastas (six different kinds) and a few juicy grill choices.

★CT BOUCHERIE
FUSION $$$

Map p240 (⌨2529-2329; www.ctboucherie.com.br; Dias Ferreira 636; mains R$82-110; ⊘noon-4pm & 7pm-midnight Mon-Sat) Created by Claude Troisgros, Rio's most famous chef, this innovative Leblon restaurant takes the idea of the *churrascaria* (traditional barbecue restaurant) and turns it on its head. Instead of all-you-can-eat meat, you order a main course – say a beautifully turned out rack of lamb, duck breast or grilled fish – and you get as many sides as you wish, served *rodizio* style fresh from the kitchen.

Polenta with passion fruit, char-grilled vegetables, oven-roasted tomatoes, ratatouille with quinoa, and sweet-potato mash are among the many offerings. The setting is lively, and nicely designed (subway tiles, whimsical prints) with a welcome lack of pretension.

ZUKA
INTERNATIONAL $$$

Map p240 (☑3205-7154; Dias Ferreira 233; mains R$70-110; ⏱7pm-1am Mon, noon-4pm & 7pm-1am Tue-Fri, 1pm-1am Sat & Sun) One of Rio's best restaurants, Zuka prepares delectable, mouthwatering cuisine. Try zingy ceviche or the confection-like delicacy of Zuka's original foie gras to start, and follow with tender octopus over a roast potato crisp, honey-glazed duck breast with Moroccan couscous, grilled fish of the day with truffle sauce or many other outstanding dishes.

All the grilling happens at the open kitchen; you can sit at the counter and watch the chefs in action. The cocktails, particularly the lychee saketinis, and desserts are also excellent.

BRIGITE'S
BRAZILIAN $$$

Map p240 (☑2274-5590; Dias Ferreira 247; mains R$65-95; ⏱7pm-midnight Mon, noon-4pm & 7pm-midnight Tue-Sun) On restaurant-lined Dias Ferreira, Brigite's serves artfully prepared Franco-Italian fare in an inviting dining room with floor-to-ceiling windows, wood floors, white brick walls and a long reflective bar. Come for pasta with clams, lamb and creamy polenta with porcini mushrooms, and good wines by the glass. A festive air prevails as the weekend nears.

FORMIDABLE
BISTRO $$$

Map p240 (☑2239-7632; João Lira 148; mains R$80; ⏱noon-4pm & 7pm-midnight) The new hot spot in Leblon, Formidable is a charming bistro with only a handful of tables inside (and a few tables out front). It has a chalkboard menu with a small selection of changing daily specials, such as fresh fish of the day, couscous with vegetables, tuna niçoise, steak au poivre and a very tender roast pork.

This is French-style bistro cooking done to perfection. Come early to avoid a long wait.

SUSHI LEBLON
JAPANESE $$$

Map p240 (☑2512-7830; Dias Ferreira 256; mains R$60-90; ⏱noon-4pm & 7pm-1:30am Mon-Sat, 1pm-midnight Sun) Leblon's top sushi destination boasts a Zen-like ambience, with a handsome dark-wood sushi counter setting the stage for succulent cuisine. In addition to sashimi and sushi, you'll find grilled

namorado (a type of perch) with passion fruit *farofa*, sea-urchin ceviche and refreshing sake to complement the meal.

NAM THAI
THAI $$$

Map p240 (☑2259-2962; Rainha Guilhermina 95B; mains R$52-81; ⏱7pm-midnight Mon, noon-midnight Tue-Sat, noon-10:30pm Sun) Thai cuisine is a rarity in Rio, which makes charming Nam Thai even more of a star. The French-colonial interior is a cozy setting for the eclectic Thai cooking. Favorites include squid salad and spicy shrimp curry with pineapple. No less intoxicating are Nam Thai's tropical drinks, such as the *caipivodca de lychee* (lychee vodka caipirinha).

🍷🍸 DRINKING & NIGHTLIFE

Ipanema has a mix of stylish and classic bars attracting a 20- and 30-something crowd. For drinking alfresco, you will find peacefully set tables along the east side of Praça General Osório. Leblon has even more bars on offer than Ipanema, with venerable *botecos* (small, open-air bars) and a few lounges as well. A particularly good place to wander in search of a drink is toward the west end of Av General San Martin.

🍷 Ipanema

★CANASTRA
WINE BAR

Map p236 (Jangadeiros 42; ⏱6:30pm-1am Tue-Sat) At first glance, Canastra looks like any other casual *boteco* on the back streets of Rio: sidewalk tables with a crowd milling about with drinks and snacks. But the food here is outstanding, and the drink of choice is wine: perhaps unsurprising given that it's run by a trio of Frenchmen.

Their goal is to create a lively eating and drinking space without the pretension and high prices of so many other Rio locales. It's an admirable success. Come on Tuesdays for fresh oysters (a fine deal at R$40 a dozen).

★COMPLEX ESQUINA 111
COCKTAIL BAR

Map p236 (Maria Quitéria 111; ⏱noon-midnight Sun-Thu, to 3am Fri & Sat) This stylish, creative eating and drinking space has outdoor

THE GIRL FROM IPANEMA

Her name was Helô Pinheiro. Tall, tanned, young (she was 17 at the time) and quite lovely, she went frequently to the beach of Ipanema back in 1962. Her route from her home a few blocks away took her past the small Bar Veloso, where several men made overtures to her, though she hardly noticed them.

In August 1962 inside a cramped club in Copacabana, musician and composer Tom Jobim takes the stage along with João Gilberto. They play a song composed by Jobim and poet Vinícius de Moraes. It's a nostalgic, sorrowful tune, with unusual chord progressions and a jazzy beat, and titled 'Garota de Ipanema' (The Girl from Ipanema). The song becomes a smash hit and helps launch the sound of bossa nova, at the time a still-budding movement barely known even in Rio.

When Pinheiro later heard the tune, she never suspected that she was the inspiration for the song. She heard rumors, but didn't believe them – at least until 1965, when de Moraes declared in a press conference that Helô was indeed the inspiration behind the song, describing her as 'a golden girl, a mixture of flowers and mermaids, full of light and grace, but whose sight is also sad because it carries within it, on the way to the sea, the sense of youth that passes, of beauty that doesn't belong only to us.'

Pinheiro got to know de Moraes and Jobim – who both proposed to her. She was impressed with their musical gifts, but never became involved with either of them. In an interview with the *Guardian* in 2012, Pinheiro said, '...The two of them drank too much. They were always at the bar drinking whisky, caipirinhas, beer.' She shirked fame, marrying her high-school sweetheart and living a sedate life as a homemaker – there was pressure from her father, an army general, to settle down.

Years later, however, circumstances changed, and Pinheiro returned to the spotlight. She became a model, posing for *Playboy* (once alongside her daughter, in 2003), a radio host, a TV announcer and she wrote an autobiography in 1996. Although she never earned money directly from the song, it helped pave the way to success in a variety of enterprises, including a swimwear boutique (named Garota de Ipanema, naturally) located on the street next to the former Bar Veloso (now also called the Garota de Ipanema). The Rua Montenegro has been renamed as Vinícius de Moraes, in honor of the songwriter. Today Pinheiro lives in São Paulo, but for bossa nova fans she'll always be the girl from Ipanema.

candlelit tables in a tranquil corner of Ipanema. Try one of the signature sparkles (a champagne cocktail) while sharing a plate of tuna tartare, sliders or ceviche. It's a much-adored place by a good-looking neighborhood crowd, so come early to score an outdoor seat.

BAR ASTOR
BAR

Map p236 (www.barastor.com.br; Vieira Souto 110; ☺6pm-1am Mon-Thu, 1pm-3am Fri, noon-3am Sat, noon-10pm Sun) Won't make it to São Paulo? No problem. One of Sampa's best bars has now become a mainstay of post-beach revelry on prime real estate along the Ipanema shorefront. This gorgeous art deco bar does meticulously prepared caipirinhas, some 20 exotic flavors in all, and great food to help soak up the quality *cachaça* (sugarcane alcohol).

BARZIN
BAR

Map p236 (Vinícius de Moraes 75; ☺11am-3am Tue-Sun) Barzin is a popular spot for post-beach drinks; it's open-sided ground-floor bar fills with animated chatter at all hours. Upstairs you can catch a changing lineup of bands playing surf rock, hip-hop and other popular Brazilian music (cover charge from R$30 to R$80).

EMPÓRIO
BAR

Map p236 (☑3813-2526; Maria Quitéria 37; ☺8:30pm-late) A young mix of *cariocas* and gringos stirs things up over cheap cocktails at this battered old favorite in Ipanema. A porch out the front overlooks the street; it's a fine spot to stake out when the air gets too heavy with dubious '80s music. Don't come early; Empório doesn't get lively until after midnight.

DELIRIUM CAFE BAR

Map p236 (☑2502-0029; Barão da Torre 183; ⊘5pm-1am) This small and cozy pub has more than 300 varieties of brew, with labels from across Europe, the US, Australia and beyond. If you've been to the original Delirium in Brussels, you might be a bit disappointed by their modest sister enterprise. You also have to be mindful of the cost. Nevertheless, it's a great destination for beer lovers.

BARTHODOMEU BOTECO

Map p236 (☑2247-8609; Maria Quitéria 46; ⊘noon-2am) Barthodomeu is a friendly bar that has *boteco* charm. It's open-sided with wooden tables, minimal decor and waiters that bustle about under trays of *chope*, *feijoada,* grilled meats and piping-hot appetizers.

DEVASSA BOTECO

Map p236 (☑2540-8380; Visconde de Pirajá 539; ⊘noon-2am) Devassa makes its own creamy brews and offers them up to chatty *cariocas* at this bar and restaurant; it's one of seven in the Rio chain. The choices: *loura* (pilsner), *sarará* (wheat beer), *ruiva* (pale ale), *negra* (dark ale) and *Índia* (India pale ale; IPA). The food menu features well-prepared pub fare: burgers, steak, pastas, grilled fish and lots of appetizers.

GAROTA DE IPANEMA BAR

Map p236 (☑2522-0340; Vinícius de Moraes 49; ⊘noon-2am) During its first incarnation, this small, open-sided bar was called the Bar Veloso. Its name and anonymity disappeared once two scruffy young regulars – Tom Jobim and Vinícius de Moraes – penned the famous song, 'The Girl from Ipanema' (see p67). It changed history, and the name of the street, too.

Today you'll find a mix of tourists and *cariocas* here, as well as sizzling platters of grilled steak.

LORD JIM PUB

Map p236 (☑2294-4881; Paul Redfern 44; admission R$10-15; ⊘6pm-2am Mon-Sat, from noon Sun) Something of a novelty for *cariocas,* Lord Jim is one of several English-style pubs scattered about the Zona Sul. Darts, English-speaking waiters and a few expat beers – Guinness, Harps, Bass etc – are on hand to complete the ambience. The R$40 all-the-beer-and-caipirinhas-you-can-drink

nights (currently Wednesdays from 6pm to 10pm) get messy.

Unlike many bars, there's always a cover charge, though drink specials lessen the hurt.

BARETTO-LONDRA LOUNGE

Map p236 (☑3202-4000; Av Vieira Souto 80; ⊘8pm-2am Thu-Sat) You'll find one of Rio's most glam bars here inside the Hotel Fasano, and it offers a vision of decadence matched by few of the city's night spots. The intimate space, designed by Philippe Starck, has an enchantingly illuminated bar, leather armchairs and divans, and a DJ spinning world electronica.

The crowd is A-list; the drinks are pricey (cocktails cost around R$35); and unless you're a model (or have one on your arm), be prepared for a long wait at the door.

BLUE AGAVE BAR

Map p236 (Vinícius de Moraes 68; ⊘noon-2am) On a lively bar-lined street, this small bar gathers a largely gringo crowd who come for margaritas, bottles of Sol and a small selection of Tex-Mex fare (tacos, enchiladas and burritos). TVs over the bar show the latest NFL games.

SHENANIGAN'S BAR

Map p236 (Visconde de Pirajá 112A; admission R$5-25; ⊘6pm-1am Mon-Sat, from 4pm Sun) Overlooking the Praça General Osório, Shenanigan's is an English-style pub with exposed-brick walls, imported beers and a couple of tiny balconies perched above the street. Sunburnt gringos and the odd working girl mix it up over games of pool and darts to the backdrop of major games (Brazilian football, American NFL, NBA etc).

BIBI SUCOS JUICE BAR

Map p240 (☑2259-4298; www.bibisucos.com.br; Av Ataúlfo de Paiva 591A; juices R$6-15; ⊘8am-1am) Among Rio's countless juice bars, Bibi Sucos is a longstanding favorite. Here you'll find more than 40 different varieties, and a never-ending supply of the favorite *açaí*. Sandwiches (from R$10 to R$14) will quell greater hunger pangs.

POLIS SUCOS JUICE BAR

Map p236 (☑2247-2518; Maria Quitéria 70; juices R$8; ⊘7am-midnight) One of Ipanema's favorite spots for a dose of fresh-squeezed vitamins, this juice bar facing the Praça NS de Paz has dozens of flavors. You can pair those tangy beverages with sandwiches or *pão de queijo* (balls of cheese-stuffed tapioca bread).

TÔ NEM AÍ
GAY, BAR

Map p236 (📞2247-8403; cnr Farme de Amoedo & Visconde de Pirajá; ☺noon-3am) Located on Rua Farme de Amoedo, Ipanema's most gay-friendly street, this popular bar is a great after-beach spot.

GALERIA CAFÉ
GAY, BAR

Map p236 (📞2523-8250; www.galeriacafe.com.br; Teixeira de Melo 31; ☺11pm-4am Wed-Sat) This bar has a very mixed crowd and lovely decor.

🍸 Leblon

BREWTECO
BAR

Map p240 (Dias Ferreira 420; ☺11am-1am) A clear sign that the microbrew scene has arrived in Rio, Brewteco has scores of unique craft beers by the bottle from around the globe. California IPAs from Ballast Point, German hits such as Weihenstephaner, Belgian ales and unique Brazilian options including Fraga Weiss, a wheat beer from Rio, draw the crowds.

There are also two beers on tap, which are rotated constantly. Note that Brewteco is tiny, and has no seating. The 'bar' is essentially the sidewalk in front of the place, where the beer-sipping crowds gather.

ACADEMIA DA CACHAÇA
BAR

Map p240 (📞2529-2680; Conde Bernadotte 26G; ☺noon-1am) Although *cachaça* has a sordid reputation in some parts, at this bar the fiery liquor is given the respect it (nearly) deserves. Along with dishes of traditional Brazilian cooking, this pleasant indoor-outdoor spot serves more than 100 varieties of *cachaça;* you can order it straight, with honey and lime, or disguised in a fruity caipirinha.

BELMONTE
BAR

Map p240 (Dias Ferreira 521; ☺11am-3am) An icon in Leblon, Belmonte always draws huge crowds: it's pretty much a massive street party every night, with beer-drinking revelers spilling onto the sidewalk from 8pm onward. If you can score a table, don't miss the delicious, well-priced *pasteis* (dough that's filled then deep-fried) stuffed

with crab, jerked beef and cheese, shrimp, heart of palm and other tasty ingredients.

JOBI
BOTECO

Map p240 (📞2274-0547; Av Ataúlfo de Paiva 1166; ☺9am-5am) A favorite since 1956, Jobi has served a lot of beer in its day, and its popularity hasn't waned. The unadorned *botequim* (bar with table service) still serves plenty; grab a seat by the sidewalk and let the night unfold. If hunger beckons, try the tasty appetizers; the *carne seca* (jerked beef) and the *bolinhos de bacalhau* (codfish croquettes) are tops.

COBAL DO LEBLON
BAR

Map p240 (📞2239-1549; Gilberto Cardoso; ☺6pm-1am Tue-Sun) Leblon's flower-and-produce market is home to this popular outdoor bar hidden on the large back terrace. It draws groups of friends and young families, and is particularly lively on game days. There's also an eatery: Pizza Park.

BRACARENSE
BOTECO

Map p240 (📞2294-3549; José Linhares 85B; ☺9am-midnight Mon-Sat, 10am-10pm Sun) Opened in 1948, Bracarense is a classic *carioca* watering hole, famous for its simple, unpretentious ambience and its heavenly *salgados* (bar snacks). A steady stream of neighborhood regulars enjoy more than 20 varieties of the snacks to the accompaniment of ice-cold *chope*. Try the *aipim com camarão* (cassava with shrimp).

PIZZARIA GUANABARA
BAR

Map p240 (📞2294-0797; Av Ataúlfo de Paiva 1228; ☺noon-6am) One of the pillars of Baixo Leblon, this popular drinking spot serves lousy pizza, but that hasn't stopped patrons from packing it out at all hours of the night. Expect simple ambience and a young, flirtatious, beer-drinking crowd.

BAR VELOSO
BOTECO

Map p240 (📞2274-9966; Aristides Espínola 44; ☺11am-1am) Named after the original bar (now Garota de Ipanema) where Tom Jobim and Vinícius de Moraes penned the famous song 'The Girl from Ipanema,' the open-sided Bar Veloso attracts a young, good-looking crowd, who spill out onto the sidewalk on busy weekends. Upstairs there's a quieter, air-conditioned retreat where (mostly) men watch the game in peace.

USINA
LOUNGE

Map p240 (☑2249-9309; www.usina47.com.br; Rita Ludolf 47; admission R$25-50; ☺7pm-2am Mon-Sat, 6pm-midnight Sun) Usina gathers a young, attractive crowd, who sip brightly colored elixirs in its sleek and stylish mainfloor lounge. Upstairs, DJs break beats over the dance floor, and the occasional band makes an appearance.

🍷 Vidigal

ALTO VIDIGAL
BAR

(☑98741-3036; www.altovidigal.com; Armando de Almeida Lima 2; ☺2pm-2am Tue-Sun) In the heights of the Vidigal favela this rustic, open-sided bar draws a fun, bohemian crowd to its weekend DJ fests (admission ranges from R$15 to R$60). Live bands sometimes play on Thursdays. Other nights of the week it's a fairly sedate spot for taking in that great hilltop view. You can take a taxi here, or catch a mototaxi or van up from the Vidigal entrance.

Alto Vidigal also runs a hostel, which is a good option if you need to stay the night.

⭐ ENTERTAINMENT

★VINÍCIUS SHOW BAR
LIVE MUSIC

Map p236 (☑2523-4757; www.viniciusbar.com. br; 2nd fl, Prudente de Morais 34, Ipanema; admission R$35-50) Billing itself as the 'temple of bossa nova,' this place has been an icon in the neighborhood since 1989. The intimate space makes a fine setting to listen to firstrate bossa nova, and occasional Música Popular Brasileira (MPB) and samba. Shows typically start between 9:30pm and 11pm.

TEATRO DO LEBLON
PERFORMING ARTS

Map p240 (☑2529-7700; Conde Bernadotte 26, Leblon) This nicely located theater shows a mix of drama, cutting-edge and children's performances on three different stages. In the same complex is an assortment of lively eating and drinking spots.

CASA DA CULTURA
LAURA ALVIM
CULTURAL CENTER

Map p236 (☑2332-2016; Av Vieira Souto 176, Ipanema) Across from the beach in Ipanema, this small center stages plays, screens films and hosts art exhibitions; the atrium cafe is a pleasant spot for a bite.

ESTAÇÃO NET IPANEMA
CINEMA

Map p236 (☑2279-4603; Visconde de Pirajá 605, Ipanema) On the 1st floor of a small shopping complex in Ipanema, this cinema screens popular contemporary films from Brazil and abroad. Its single theater seats 140.

CINEMA LEBLON
CINEMA

Map p240 (☑2461-2461; Av Ataúlfo de Paiva 391, Leblon) Leblon's popular theater has two screens showing the latest Hollywood releases.

SHOPPING

Ipanema and Leblon are the best hunting grounds for top fashion designs, both home-grown and foreign labels. You'll also find curio and novelty stores, galleries, bookshops, liquor stores and plenty of cafes for refueling along the way. There's a lot going on along the main thoroughfares of Rua Visconde de Pirajá in Ipanema and Av Ataúlfo de Paiva in Leblon.

🛍 Ipanema

★HIPPIE FAIR
MARKET

Map p236 (Praça General Osório; ☺9am-6pm Sun) The Zona Sul's most famous market, the Hippie Fair (aka Feira de Arte de Ipanema) has artwork, jewelry, handicrafts, clothing and souvenirs for sale. Stalls in the four corners of the plaza sell tasty plates of *acarajé* (croquettes made from mashed black-eyed peas, with a sauce of *vatapá* – manioc paste, coconut and *dendê* oil – and shrimp; R$9), plus excellent desserts (R$4). Don't miss it.

GILSON MARTINS
ACCESSORIES

Map p236 (☑2227-6178; Visconde de Pirajá 462; ☺9am-8pm Mon-Sat) Designer Gilson Martins transforms the Brazilian flag and silhouettes of Pão de Açúcar and Corcovado into eye-catching accessories in his flagship store in Ipanema. This is the place for one-of-a-kind glossy handbags, wallets, passport covers, key chains and iPad covers. Products are durable and use recycled and sustainable materials – and are not available outside of Rio.

Gilson also has several other branches, including a spacious Copacabana (p97) showroom.

TOCA DO VINÍCIUS · MUSIC

Map p236 (☑2247-5227; www.tocadovinicius. com.br; Vinícius de Moraes 129; ☺11am-7pm Mon-Fri, 10am-6pm Sat, 3-6pm Sun) Bossa nova fans shouldn't miss this store. In addition to its ample CD and vinyl selection (starting at R$40) of contemporary and old performers, it also sells music scores and composition books. Around the store you'll find memorabilia from great songwriters, including Vinícius de Moraes and Chico Buarque.

10AQUIM · SWEETS

Map p236 (☑2523-5009; Garcia d'Ávila 149; ☺10am-6pm Mon-Sat) 🍴 This artisanal chocolatier carefully sources its cacao from a single environmentally conscious grower in Bahia, and has garnered international awards for its high-quality (and delicious!) products. Stop by this jewel-box-sized store for rich truffles, macarons, chocolate cakes and mini tarts that look almost too lovely to eat.

FORUM · CLOTHING

Map p236 (☑2267-2487; www.forum.com.br; Barão da Torre 422; ☺10am-6pm Mon-Fri, to 2pm Sat) Much-touted Brazilian designer Tufi Duek reigns over this curiously designed flagship store. You'll find stylish polos, snug-fitting button-downs and one-of-a-kind graphic T-shirts for the guys, along with a women's collection of boldly patterned skirts, dresses and blouses.

LIVRARIA DA TRAVESSA · BOOKS, MUSIC

(☑3205-9002; Visconde de Pirajá 572; ☺9am-midnight Mon-Sat, 11am-midnight Sun) One of several branches around town, Livraria da Travessa has a small selection of foreign-language books and periodicals, and some CDs upstairs. The buzzing 2nd-floor cafe (a branch of Bazzar) serves salads, sandwiches, quiches and desserts. There's an even larger Livraria da Travessa inside the Shopping Leblon (p72) mall.

LIDADOR · WINE

Map p236 (☑2227-0593; Vinícius de Moraes 120; ☺9am-8pm Mon-Fri, 10am-6pm Sat, to 3pm Sun) Lidador stocks Brazilian, Chilean and Argentinean wines as well as vintages from Europe and beyond. You'll also find a growing selection of craft brews from around the world as well as cachaças, rums and other spirits. There are other branches around town, including a Leblon location at Av Ataúlfo de Paiva 1079.

CASA IPANEMA · SHOES

Map p236 (Garcia d'Ávila 77; ☺10am-8pm Mon-Fri, 11am-6pm Sat) This stylish, open-sided boutique sells one-of-a-kind flip-flops (thongs) from a host of Brazilian designers. Prices are in the range of R$20 to R$120. It's a creative space with an upstairs gallery where you can catch the occasional art exhibition, workshop, and book and CD launches.

OSKLEN · CLOTHING

Map p236 (☑2227-2911; Maria Quitéria 85; ☺9am-8pm Mon-Fri, 10am-7pm Sat, 11am-5pm Sun) One of Brazil's best-known fashion labels outside the country, Osklen is notable for its stylish and well-made beachwear (particularly men's swim shorts and graphic T-shirts), sneakers and outerwear. The company was started in 1988 by outdoor enthusiast Oskar Metsavaht, the first Brazilian to scale Mont Blanc.

REDLEY · CLOTHING

Map p236 (☑2267-1573; Maria Quitéria 99; ☺9am-8pm Mon-Sat) In the heart of Ipanema, this multilevel fashion store is a fine place to browse for couture beach duds and streetwear. Unlike most other Ipanema boutiques, this one's aimed at the men, and it has an excellent assortment of T-shirts, shorts and swimsuits.

CATHERINE LABOURÉ · VINTAGE

Map p236 (☑2227-3375; 2nd fl, Visconde de Pirajá 207; ☺12:30-6:30pm Tue-Fri, 11am-4pm Sat) Tucked away inside an otherwise humdrum shopping center, this intriguing shop sells vintage dresses, skirts, silk scarves, handbags, shoes and sunglasses, with labels by top international designers. There's a smaller selection for men – mostly T-shirts and button-downs – as well as a few small antiques and collectibles for the home.

GAROTA DE IPANEMA · CLOTHING, ACCESSORIES

Map p236 (☑2521-3168; Vinícius de Moraes 53; ☺10am-7pm Mon-Sat) Located next to the famous bar of the same name, this tiny boutique is an excellent place to browse for attractive, reasonably priced bikinis and beachwear. There are also eye-catching T-shirts (for men and women), trucker hats, bags and other accessories.

WÖLLNER OUTDOOR · CLOTHING, ACCESSORIES

Map p236 (☑2512-6531; Visconde de Pirajá 511; ☺10am-9pm Mon-Fri) The great outdoors, and the shirt and shorts you'll need to enjoy it, seem to be the inspiration for Wöllner. Clothes and accessories are ruggedly styled, not unlike Abercrombie and American Eagle.

HAVAIANAS
SHOES

Map p236 (☑2267-7395; Farme de Amoedo 76; ⊙9am-8pm Mon-Sat, 10am-6pm Sun) This small shop is a great place to stock up on Brazil's iconic rubber sandals. You'll find a colorful variety of Havaianas for men, women and children, covering all price points (from R$26 to R$75).

ANTONIO BERNARDO
JEWELRY, ACCESSORIES

Map p236 (☑2512-7204; Garcia d'Ávila 121; ⊙10am-7pm Mon-Fri, to 4pm Sat) Designer-goldsmith Antonio Bernardo has garnered attention for his lovely bracelets, earrings and necklaces. The designs here are unique and artfully done, and Bernardo uses high-quality materials.

AMSTERDAM SAUER
JEWELRY

Map p236 (☑3539-0165; www.amsterdam sauer.com; Visconde de Pirajá 484; ⊙9am-7pm Mon-Fri, to 4pm Sat) Well known for its impressive collection of precious stones, Amsterdam Sauer also sells finely crafted jewelry. Watches, pens, wallets and other accessories are available, too. Check out its museum (p59) on Garcia d'Ávila while in the area.

H STERN
JEWELRY, ACCESSORIES

Map p236 (☑2274-3447; www.hstern.com.br; Visconde de Pirajá 490; ⊙9:30am-6:30pm Mon-Fri, 10am-4pm Sat) The famous jeweler H Stern has an array of finely crafted jewelry, watches and other accessories for sale. At the company's headquarters you can also take a tour of the H Stern gem museum (p59).

🏠 Leblon

MARIA OITICICA
JEWELRY

Map p240 (☑3875-8025; Shopping Leblon, Av Afrânio de Melo Franco 290; ⊙10am-10pm Mon-Sat, 1-9pm Sun) 🖉 Using native materials found in the Amazon, Maria Oiticica has created some lovely handcrafted jewelry inspired by indigenous art. Seeds, plant fibers and tree bark are just some of the ingredients of her bracelets, necklaces, earrings and sandals. There are even sandals and handbags made from fish 'leather.'

Maria Oiticica has a partnership with several indigenous tribes in the Amazon, which gather raw materials and even handcraft some of her pieces. The shop is located on the main floor of the Shopping Leblon mall.

SHOPPING LEBLON
SHOPPING CENTER

Map p240 (☑2430-5122; www.shoppingleblon. com.br; Av Afrânio de Melo Franco 290; ⊙10am-10pm Mon-Sat, 1-9pm Sun) This glittering multistory shopping center packed with top-name Brazilian and foreign labels is the best shopping destination in Leblon. It has plenty of tempting stores that will drain your vacation funds, as well as good restaurants and a cinema.

ESPAÇO FASHION
CLOTHING

Map p240 (☑2294-0526; Shop 112, Shopping Leblon, Av Afrânio de Melo Franco 290; ⊙10am-10pm Mon-Sat, 1-9pm Sun) This boutique has a decor and aesthetic aimed to attract a young, hip, somewhat fashion-forward group of shoppers with its form-fitting skirts, dresses and tops, its flashy sneakers and its one-of-a-kind jewelry.

ARGUMENTO
BOOKS, MUSIC

Map p240 (☑2239-5294; Dias Ferreira 417; ⊙9am-midnight Mon-Sat, 10am-11pm Sun) One of Leblon's fine neighborhood bookstores, Argumento stocks a small but decent selection of foreign-language books and magazines. The charming cafe in the back is the perfect place to disappear with a book.

ESCH CAFÉ
CIGARS

Map p240 (☑2512-5651; Dias Ferreira 78; ⊙3pm-midnight Mon, from noon Tue-Sat, 2-10pm Sun) This restaurant-bar is also the 'House of Havana,' which means if you have a taste for Cuban cigars, this is your place. The humidor is stocked with a decent selection, which you can enjoy there over a glass of port, or a few blocks away on the beach. It also has a Centro branch.

🏃 SPORTS & ACTIVITIES

FRUIT BRAZIL
TOUR

(www.fruitbrazil.com; tours per person US$25) This outfit focuses on the tropical fruits of Brazil, taking visitors on an in-depth 90-minute tasting tour through a local market in Ipanema. The market varies depending on the day of the week.

DIVE POINT   DIVING
Map p240 (☎96429-0895; www.divepoint.com. br/english; Shop 04, Av Ataúlfo de Paiva 1174, Leblon) Scuba divers can rent equipment or take classes from Dive Point. It also offers diving courses, and dive tours around Rio's main beaches and Ilha Cagarras (the island in front of Ipanema), as well as the premier dive spots in Arraial do Cabo, west of Rio.

ESCOLINHA DE VÔLEI   VOLLEYBALL
Map p236 (☎99702-5794; near Garcia d'Ávila, Ipanema Beach) Those interested in improving their volleyball game, or just in meeting some *cariocas,* should pay a visit to Escolinha de Vôlei. Pelé, who speaks English, has been hosting volleyball classes for more than 10 years. Lessons range from one to two hours. His students are a mix of *cariocas* and expats, who then meet for games after honing the fundamentals.

Look for Pelé's large Brazilian flag on the beach near Rua Garcia d'Ávila.

SPA MARIA BONITA   SPA
Map p236 (☎2513-4050; www.spamariabonita. com.br; Level P, Prudente de Morais 729, Ipanema) Although better known for its lush spa resort in Friburgo, Maria Bonita does offer a full range of treatments for those who'd rather not trek out to the countryside. Options here include aromatherapy baths, deep-tissue massage, shiatsu and acupuncture. There is also an organic and raw-food restaurant on-site.

BODY TECH   GYM
Map p240 (☎2529-8898; General Urquiza 102, Leblon; day/2-week pass from R$65/$330; ☺6am-11pm Mon-Fri, 9am-8pm Sat, 9am-2pm Sun) Body Tech has gyms all over the Zona Sul. It offers a full range of services: swimming pool, free weights and cardio machines, and classes such as dance, gymnastics and spinning.

This three-story branch is the best of the bunch, but there are also a couple of Body Techs in Ipanema (at Barão de Torre 577 and Gomes Carneiro 90), and one in Copacabana (at Av NS de Copacabana 801). If you're in town for a week or so, the staff will usually negotiate a discounted rate.

BLYSS YÔGA   YOGA
Map p236 (☎98291-0211; www.blyss.com.br; Suite 211, Visconde de Pirajá 318, Ipanema; per class R$50; ☺Mon-Sat) Near Praça NS da Paz, this peaceful center offers a full schedule of morning, afternoon and evening classes in Vinyasa, Hatha and power yoga. Some instructors speak English.

IPANEMA & LEBLON SPORTS & ACTIVITIES

IAN TROWER / ROBERT HARDING / GETTY IMAGES ©

1. Ipanema Beach (p58) **2.** Surfer, Ipanema Beach (p58)
3. *Futevôlei* (no-hands volleyball), Copacabana Beach (p87)

Beach Life

The beaches of Rio are the city's wondrous and carefree backyard. It's where *cariocas* (residents of Rio) from all walks of life – rich and poor, young and old, black and white, model-thin and beer-bellied – come to play and socialize against a backdrop of crashing waves and the ever-present green peaks towering over the city.

The Perfect Crowd

Although the mix is incredibly democratic, *postos* (posts) subdivide the beach into different sections, with each subculture drawn to its particular *posto*, whether drawing favela kids, volleyballers, well-heeled families or the beauty crowd.

Seaside Sport

Sports are a big seaside draw, and entail surfing, stand-up paddle boarding, jogging, cycling and skating the beachside path, football, volleyball and *futevôlei* – that uniquely Brazilian combination of volleyball played with football-style rules (no hands allowed!). There's also *frescobol*, a simple game where two players with wooden rackets stand 10m apart and pound a rubber ball back and forth.

Sit Back & Relax

Many beachgoers, however, would rather just relax and enjoy the scene. For sun-lovers, there's much to take in: the sand, the sea, the food and drink vendors, the passing people parade and much more.

3

BEACH ETIQUETTE

➡ Leave valuables back at the hotel. Take only the cash you need for the beach.

➡ Don't use a towel on the beach – instead, sit on a chair or a *kanga* (sarong); Brazilian men stand or sit on the sand.

➡ Choose your spot; find a *barraca* (stall) you like, hire chairs and sunshades from it.

➡ Don't bother bringing food or drink to the beach; support the local vendors.

Gávea, Jardim Botânico & Lagoa

Neighborhood Top Five

❶ Hiring a bike and going for a spin around the **Lagoa Rodrigo de Freitas** (p78).

❷ Taking a stroll through the lush and flower-filled **Jardim Botânico** (p79).

❸ Looking for monkeys on the forested paths of **Parque Lage** (p80), followed by lunch in the open-air restaurant.

❹ Sipping cocktails in an alfresco setting while admiring the view from **Palaphita Kitch** (p83).

❺ Checking out the latest exhibit at the **Instituto Moreira Salles** (p79).

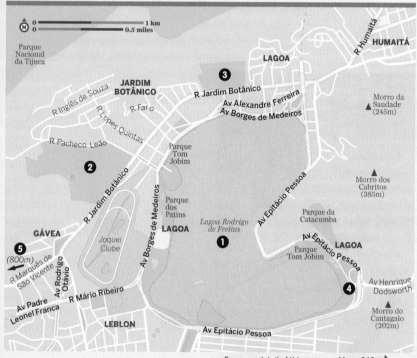

For more detail of this area, see Map p242 ➡

Explore Gávea, Jardim Botânico & Lagoa

Rio's picturesque lake is the focal point of these well-heeled neighborhoods. The Lagoa Rodrigo de Freitas is actually a saltwater lagoon and is much utilized by *cariocas* (residents of Rio). Joggers and cyclists zip along the shoreline trail by day, while the lakeside restaurants fill with people enjoying a meal and live music in the open air by night. This area includes the north, east and west sides of the lake. The streets on the south side of Lagoa are generally considered part of Ipanema and Leblon.

West of the lake are the botanical gardens for which the neighborhood, Jardim Botânico, is named. Here you'll find stately palms and a variety of flowering plants. South of the gardens is Gávea, home to Rio's premier horse-racing track and a planetarium. Aside from their natural attractions, these neighborhoods also have some excellent restaurants, lively nightlife and one of the Zona Sul's best cultural centers, the Instituto Moreira Salles.

Much of the development of this area is linked to the lake, which is named Rodrigo de Freitas in honor of the Portuguese settler who made his fortune off the sugarcane fields surrounding the lake in the 16th century. Factories blighted the landscape in the 1900s, and it took much of the 20th century for the area to recover. Although the lake is still too polluted for swimming, some wildlife has returned, and visitors might see egrets on the lookout for fish in the lake.

Local Life

➡ **Walks** For a scenic hike, you can take the uphill trail to Cristo Redentor (Christ the Redeemer) in Parque Lage (p80). A shorter trail offers great views from Parque da Catacumba (p80).

➡ **Markets** Praça Santos Dumont hosts an antiques market on Sundays and a fruit market on Fridays.

➡ **Nightlife** Bars near Praça Santos Dumont attract a young, festive crowd during the week.

Getting There & Away

➡ **Gávea buses** Centro, Flamengo and Catete (170); Ipanema and Copacabana (571, 572 and 574); and Leblon (432, 435 and 593).

➡ **Jardim Botânico buses** Centro, Flamengo and Catete (170); Copacabana and Ipanema (162, 570 and 584); and Leblon (512, 574 and 584).

➡ **Metro** Gávea (by early 2017).

➡ **Metrô na Superfície** Metro buses connect Botafogo station with Jardim Botânico.

Lonely Planet's Top Tip

One of Rio's often over-looked attractions, the Instituto Moreira Salles is well worth a visit. It has a picturesque setting and the museum stages first-rate exhibitions. If you have kids in tow, Saturdays are a good time to visit, as there are special (free) activities such as crafts, music and the like.

Best Places to Eat

➡ Volta (p81)
➡ PLage Cafe (p81)
➡ Olympe (p82)
➡ Bráz (p81)
➡ CT Trattorie (p82)

For reviews, see p80

Best Places to Drink

➡ Palaphita Kitch (p83)
➡ Hipódromo (p82)
➡ 00 (Zero Zero) (p82)
➡ Palaphita Gávea (p82)

For reviews, see p82

Best Places to Shop

➡ Dona Coisa (p83)
➡ Gabinete (p83)
➡ O Sol (p83)

For reviews, see p83

TOP SIGHT
LAGOA RODRIGO DE FREITAS

Rio is blessed with mountains, beaches and rainforest, so it's perhaps a little unfair that it would also have a picturesque lake – surrounded by highly desirable neighborhoods, no less. *Cariocas*, **however, take it in their stride and make ample use of the watery expanse by running the lakeside path, dining near the water's edge or simply admiring the view from almost any vantage point.**

No matter the time of year, you'll always find runners and cyclists making good use of the 7.2km path that encircles the lake (see Map p242). If you'd like to join them, there are various places to hire bikes, including the Parque dos Patins on the west side.

For an even better view over the lake, book a seat on a scenic helicopter flight that departs from a helipad on the west side of the lake. A much cheaper way to admire the view is to hike to the top of Parque da Catacumba.

Another way to experience the lake is to get out on the surface. Pollution makes swimming a bad idea, but you can hire pedal boats from the eastern side near the Parque do Cantagalo.

For those who prefer caipirinhas to plastic swan boats, the kiosks scattered along the lakeshore make a memorable setting for a sundowner. You can also dine in the open air at one of a dozen or so kiosks serving sushi, bistro fare, Brazilian and Middle Eastern dishes. Many places have live music on weekends, making it a popular draw with couples. You'll find kiosks near Parque do Cantagalo and Parque dos Patins. There's also the lakeside complex Lagoon, which houses restaurants, a cinema and a live-music venue.

One of the major events in the city's calendar is the lighting of the floating Christmas tree on the lake each year. If you're around in December, don't miss a visit by night.

Keep an eye out for capybaras, which can sometimes be spotted munching (or swimming) near the shoreline. Dusk is the best time to find them.

DON'T MISS...

➡ Cycling around the lake

➡ Skimming over the surface on a pedal boat

➡ Drinks and live music at a lakeside kiosk

⊙ SIGHTS

⊙ Gávea

★ INSTITUTO
MOREIRA SALLES   CULTURAL CENTER
(IMS; ☑3284-7400; www.ims.com.br; Marquês de São Vicente 476; ⊙11am-8pm Tue-Sun; 🛜) **FREE** This beautiful cultural center hosts impressive exhibitions, often showcasing the works of some of Brazil's best photographers and artists. The gardens, complete with artificial lake and flowing river, were designed by Brazilian landscape architect Roberto Burle Marx. There's also a craft shop and a quaint cafe that serves lunch and afternoon tea.

On display there's usually at least one Rio-focused exhibition, which taps into the extensive archive here: the IMS has more than 80,000 photographs, many portraying old streets of Rio as well as the urban development of other Brazilian cities over the last two centuries. Check the website to see what's on when you're in town.

PARQUE DA CIDADE   PARK
(☑2512-2353; www.rio.rj.gov.br/cultura; Estrada de Santa Marinha 505; ⊙8am-5pm Tue-Sun) On the outer reaches of Gávea, this lush park of native Mata Atlantica rainforest and replanted secondary forest provides a refreshing escape from the heavy traffic on nearby Rua Marquês de São Vicente. Local residents come to jog here, to go for long walks with their dogs and to let their kids run about at the large playground.

A hiking trail connects the park with Solar da Imperatriz, an 18th-century colonial building that is today part of a school for horticultural studies, near Jardim Botânico; it's best to go with a local who knows the way, as the path isn't well marked, and the danger of assault is an unlikely but serious consideration. The trail starts near the small waterfall. The park also has a small chapel, and a 19th-century colonial mansion and museum that remain closed for renovations.

PLANETÁRIO   PLANETARIUM
Map p242 (☑2274-0046; www.planetariodorio.com.br; Av Padre Leonel Franca 240; adult/child R$12/6, incl cúpula session R$24/12; ⊙9am-noon & 2-5pm Mon-Fri, 2:30-5pm Sat & Sun) Gávea's stellar attraction, the Planetário features a museum, a *praça dos telescópios* (telescopes' square) and a couple of state-of-the-art operating *cúpulas* (domes), each capable of projecting more than 6000 stars onto its walls. Forty-minute sessions in the domes take place on weekends and holidays. Visitors can also take a peek at the night sky through the telescopes on Wednesdays from 7:30pm to 8:30pm (6:30pm to 7:30pm from June to August).

The modern Museu do Universo (Universe Museum) houses sundials, a Foucault pendulum and other permanent exhibitions, plus temporary displays.

⊙ Jardim Botânico

JARDIM BOTÂNICO   GARDENS
Map p242 (☑3874-1808; www.jbrj.gov.br; Jardim Botânico 920; admission R$9; ⊙9am-5pm) This exotic 137-hectare garden, with more than 8000 plant species, was designed by order of the Prince Regent Dom João (later to become Dom João VI) in 1808. The garden is quiet and serene on weekdays and blossoms with families on weekends. Highlights of a visit here include the row of palms (planted when the garden first opened), the Amazonas section, the lake containing the huge Vitória Régia water lilies and the enclosed **orquidário**, home to 600 species of orchids.

There's an outdoor snack bar on the grounds (near a kid's playground) and an appealing cafe just outside the main entrance. The new visitor center shows films (in English and Portuguese) that give the history of the gardens, and has a gift shop that sells unique crafts and souvenirs, such as shirts made of bamboo and bowls with pre-Columbian designs made from banana fibers.

ESPAÇO TOM JOBIM   CULTURAL CENTER
Map p242 (www.jbrj.gov.br; Jardim Botânico 1008; ⊙noon-5pm Mon, 9am-5pm Tue-Sun) Bossa nova legend Tom Jobim was a big admirer of the botanical gardens. This Jardim Botânico concert venue and art space was created as a memorial to him in 2008. The 378-seat hall hosts concerts, plays and dance performances, and you can learn more about Jobim at the on-site museum, which holds photographs, personal objects and videos of the great composer.

CATACUMBA

Lagoa is one of the few neighborhoods in Rio that doesn't have a neighboring favela. This wasn't always the case: the Parque da Catacumba was once the site of a favela, and home to more than 10,000 residents at its height in the 1960s. According to historical records, the area was part of an estate belonging to a wealthy landowner in the 19th century. Upon her death, she left the lands to her slaves, though the first constructions didn't begin to appear until the 1930s. According to some former favela residents, the name Catacumba predates the favela, and refers to an indigenous burial ground – although no remains were ever found on the site.

Under the strong-armed government of Francisco Negrão de Lima, the *favelados* were removed in 1970 and their houses razed, in large part owing to the commercial value of the occupied lands. The expelled residents went on to form the Complexo da Maré, a favela near the airport that later became known as the 'Gaza Strip' because of its high murder rate.

Catacumba was subsequently reforested and turned into a public park. You can still see a few vestiges of the old favela on a hike to the Mirante do Sacopã lookout.

MUSEU DO MEIO AMBIENTE   MUSEUM
Map p242 (Environmental Museum; ☑2294-6619; Jardim Botânico 1008; ☺9am-5pm Tue-Sun) **FREE** Situated just outside the entrance to the botanical gardens, the Museu do Meio Ambiente houses temporary environmentally focused exhibits.

PARQUE LAGE   PARK
Map p242 (☑3257-1800, guided visits 3257-18721; www.eavparquelage.rj.gov.br; Jardim Botânico 414; ☺9am-7pm) This beautiful park lies at the base of Floresta da Tijuca, about 1km from Jardim Botânico. It has English-style gardens, little lakes and a mansion that houses the **Escola de Artes Visuais** (School of Visual Arts), which hosts free art exhibitions and occasional performances. The park is a tranquil place and the cafe here offers a fine setting for a coffee or a meal.

Native Atlantic rainforest surrounds Parque Lage, and you can sometimes see monkeys and toucans among the foliage. This is the starting point for challenging hikes up Corcovado.

⊙ Lagoa

LAGOA RODRIGO DE FREITAS   LAKE
See p104.

FUNDAÇÃO EVA KLABIN   MUSEUM
Map p242 (☑3202-8551; www.evaklabin.org.br; Av Epitácio Pessoa 2480; adult/child R$10/free, Sun free; ☺2-6pm Tue-Sun) An old mansion full of antiques, the former residence of Eva Klabin houses the works of art she collected

for 60 years. Reflecting Eva's diverse interests, the collection has 1100 pieces from ancient Egypt, Greece and China, including paintings, sculptures, silver, furniture and carpets.

PARQUE DA CATACUMBA   PARK
Map p242 (☑2247-9949; www.parquedacata cumba.com.br; Av Epitácio Pessoa; ☺8am-5pm Tue-Sun) On the edge of the Lagoa Rodrigo de Freitas, across a busy road, this park and sculptural garden has a short but steep trail to the Mirante do Sacopã lookout, which offers memorable views from a height of 130m above Lagoa. It's a 15-minute walk along a 600m forest-lined path. For a bit more excitement, you can scale a rock-climbing wall, go rappelling (abseiling) or take a tree-top walk offered by Lagoa Aventuras (p84).

 EATING

The open-air restaurants around the peaceful Lagoa Rodrigo de Freitas are big draws. On warm evenings music fills the air as diners eat, drink and enjoy the views across the water. The hot spots for drinking and dining are at the Parque dos Patins on the west side, where some places host live music, and Parque do Cantagalo on the east side. Gávea has a few dining and drinking spots around Praça Santos Dumont, while Jardim Botânico's thickest concentration of eateries is on Rua JJ Seabra and Rua Pacheco Leão.

✗ Gávea

BRASEIRO DA GÁVEA   BRAZILIAN $$
Map p242 (🖉2239-7494; www.braseirodagavea.
com.br; Praça Santos Dumont 116; sandwiches
around R$20, mains for 2 people R$50-110;
⊙noon-1am Sun-Thu, to 3am Fri & Sat) This
family-style eatery serves large portions
of its popular *linguiça* (garlicky pork sau-
sage) appetizers, *picanha* (rump steak) and
galetos (grilled chicken). On weekends the
open-air spot fills with the din of conversa-
tion and the aroma of freshly poured *chope*.
As the evening wanes, a younger crowd
takes over drinking late into the night.

GUIMAS   BRAZILIAN $$
Map p242 (🖉2259-7996; José Roberto Macedo
Soares 5; mains R$55-80; ⊙noon-1am) An up-
scale *carioca boteco* (small, open-air bar)
with a creative flair, Guimas has been going strong for more than 30 years. Winning
dishes include the *bacalhau à bras* (codfish
mixed with potatoes, eggs and onions),
shrimp risotto and the juicy *picanha wes-
sel* (grilled rump steak). There's outdoor
seating in front.

✗ Jardim Botânico

★VOLTA   BRAZILIAN $$
Map p242 (🖉3204-5406; www.restaurantevolta.
com.br; Visconde de Carandaí 5; mains R$40-
60; ⊙noon-midnight Mon-Sat, to 6pm Sun) Set
in a classy old villa with an outdoor patio
in a peaceful corner of Jardim Botânico,
Volta serves up playful, contemporary fare
inspired by Brazilian comfort food. Start
off with creative appetizers such as the
sardine-topped tapioca crisp or the *coxin-
ha* (cornmeal balls filled with chicken) with
creamy Minas cheese, before moving on to
sweet-potato gnocchi with pumpkin cream
or a perfectly tender filet mignon.

The kitchen is helmed by two
20-something identical twins, complete
with matching tattoos. Book ahead for
Tuesday nights, when there's live jazz.

PLAGE CAFE   CAFE $$
Map p242 (🖉2535-7336; off Jardim Botânico 414;
mains R$26-54; ⊙9am-6pm; 🔊🖉) Inside the
lush Parque Lage, this beautifully sited cafe
serves a few hearty dishes, such as rich pork
belly with lentils, plus salads, quiches, pastas such as eggplant lasagna and changing

daily specials like vegetarian cassoulet. On
weekends it's a popular gathering spot for
young families who come for brunch (R$27
to R$32), which features eggs Benedict,
yogurt with granola and fruit plates.

BRÁZ   PIZZERIA $$
Map p242 (🖉2535-0687; Maria Angélica 129;
pizzas R$50-80; ⊙6pm-midnight) The much-
touted pizzeria from São Paulo has had a
huge *carioca* following since opening in
Rio in 2007. Perfect crusts and superfresh
ingredients are two of the components that
make Bráz the best pizza place in town.
This is no secret, so arrive early and plan
on having a few quiet *chopes* on the front
patio before scoring a table.

LA BICYCLETTE   FRENCH $$
Map p242 (Jardim Botânico 1008; sandwiches
R$18-33; ⊙8:30am-6pm Tue & Wed, to 8pm Thu-
Sun; 🔊🖉) Just outside the entrance to the
botanical gardens (but inside the gates off
the busy roadway), La Bicyclette whips up
creative sandwiches (named after French
neighborhoods), hearty quiches, salads and
desserts. It's set in a lovely colonial building and has outdoor seating on a peaceful
veranda.

There's a second **location** (Map p242;
Pacheco Leão 320; ⊙8:30am-8pm; 🔊) on the
north side of the botanical gardens.

JOJÖ   CAFE $$
Map p242 (🖉3565-9007; www.jojocafe.com.br;
Pacheco Leão 812; mains R$35-55; ⊙6pm-2am
Tue-Fri, 1pm-1am Sat, to 8pm Sun) This small,
charming neighborhood cafe and bistro in
a peaceful corner in Jardim Botânico serves
up delectable salads, pastas and Asian-
inspired dishes such as Thai chicken curry.
There are a handful of sidewalk tables.
Oyster lovers should come on Thursdays
during happy hour, when oysters arrive
fresh from Santa Catarina.

BOROGODÓ   BRAZILIAN $$
Map p242 (🖉3495-0836; Pacheco Leão 836;
mains R$30-65; ⊙noon-4pm Tue-Thu, to 11:30pm
Fri & Sat, to 6pm Sun) In a charming yellow
colonial house, the two-story Borogodó is
a great neighborhood destination for bistro
fare: duck risotto with mushrooms, seafood
spaghetti, steak with fries and other unfussy but delicious dishes. The open doors
and windows let in the breeze, and the back
side of the botanical gardens are just across
the street.

✕ Lagoa

LAGOON   BRAZILIAN **$$**

Map p242 (✆2529-5300; www.lagoon.com.br; Av Borges de Medeiros 1424; mains R$35-75; ◷noon-2am) This lakefront eating and entertainment complex houses a handful of restaurants, a cinema and a bar and live-music venue. The best tables are on the 2nd floor, and offer photogenic views over the lake. Italian, seafood, bistro fare and traditional Brazilian cooking are among the options. No matter where you sit, you can order from any of the menus.

LA CARIOCA CEVICHERIA   PERUVIAN **$$**

Map p242 (✆2226-8821; Maria Angélica 113; sharing plates R$30-37; ◷6:30pm-1am Mon-Fri, from 1pm Sat & Sun) On a peaceful tree-lined street, La Carioca is an excellent spot for ceviche and other Peruvian hits. It has another, equally charming, branch in Ipanema (p62).

ARAB DA LAGOA   MIDDLE EASTERN **$$**

Map p242 (✆2540-0747; www.restaurantearab.com.br; Av Borges de Medeiros, Parque dos Patins; mains R$35-60; ◷9am-1:30am) This is one of the lake's most popular outdoor restaurants. It serves up traditional Middle Eastern specialties such as hummus, baba ghanoush, tabbouleh, kibbe and tasty thin-crust pizzas. The large platters for two or more are good for sampling a tasty variety.

During the day it's a peaceful refuge from the city, while at night you can hear live samba, *choro* (romantic, intimate samba) or jazz from 9pm on weekdays, and 7pm on Saturdays and Sundays.

CT TRATTORIE   ITALIAN **$$$**

Map p242 (✆2266-0838; Av Alexandre Ferreira 66; mains R$68-98; ◷noon-4pm & 7-11pm) This outstanding restaurant brought to you by top chef Claude Troisgros serves exquisite pasta dishes and northern Italian cuisine with Brazilian influences. Recent favorites: tender octopus carpaccio, fish with a cream sauce of *azedinha* (sorrel) and a rich spaghetti carbonara with *carne seca* (pulled dried beef). It has a classy design, with tile floors, oversized lights and black-and-white photos on the walls. Good wine selection.

OLYMPE   FUSION **$$$**

Map p242 (✆2539-4542; Custódio Serrão 62; mains R$90-125; ◷noon-4pm Mon-Fri, 7:30pm-midnight Mon-Sat) Claude Troisgros, one of

Rio's top chefs, and his son Thomas dazzle guests with unforgettable meals at this award-winning restaurant set in a peaceful villa on a quiet, tree-lined street. Originally from France, Troisgros mixes the old world with the new in dishes such as duck with passion fruit, endive and foie gras or shrimp risotto with white-truffle oil and mushroom foam.

🍷 🍸 DRINKING & NIGHTLIFE

Gávea has one of Rio's liveliest drinking spots for young people: Baixo Gávea, near Praça Santos Dumont. The bars here almost always draw in a crowd, with imbibers spilling onto the plaza most nights. Jardim Botânico has a youthful population that comes out en masse to the bars along Rua JJ Seabra. Meanwhile, the lakeside kiosks offer a more sedate experience, with couples gathering for live music to the backdrop of Lagoa and Cristo Redentor.

🍸 Gávea

PALAPHITA GÁVEA   BAR

Map p242 (Bartolomeu Mitre 1314; ◷6pm-4am) Overlooking the Joquei Clube (horse-racing track; p84), this sprawling open-air bar and party space is a wonderful mess of rustic wooden structures, thatch-roofed bars and scattered-about handmade furniture. It draws a young, animated crowd most nights and is a great place at which to end the night. On racing days, you can even place bets here and watch the horses thunder past.

HIPÓDROMO   BAR

Map p242 (Praça Santos Dumont 108; ◷noon-1am) In an area more commonly referred to as Baixo Gávea, Hipódromo is one of several bars responsible for the local residents' chronic lack of sleep. Most nights you'll find a college-age and twentysomething crowd celebrating here, with patrons spilling onto the facing Praça Santos Dumont.

00 (ZERO ZERO)   LOUNGE, CLUB

Map p242 (✆2540-8041; Av Padre Leonel Franca 240; cover R$40-80; ◷11pm-5am Tue & Thu-Sat) Housed in Gávea's planetarium, 00 starts the evening as a stylish restaurant and transforms into a lounge and nightclub around 1am. DJs spin at rotating parties held here, and on Tuesday nights, party promoter Bem Brasil (www.bembrasilrio.com.br) throws a bash for the hostel crowd, making it a good place to be if you want to mingle with other travelers.

Jardim Botânico

BAR DO HORTO   BAR
Map p242 (☑3114-8439; Pacheco Leão 780; ☺noon-2am Tue-Sun) Colorful Bar do Horto is one of Jardim Botânico's most charming bars. The decor is festive and kitsch: walls covered with shimmering fabric and an interior festooned with brightly hued paper lanterns, butterfly appliqués, bottle-cap curtains and other recycled ephemera. At night the sidewalk tables gather a convivial crowd that comes for cocktails and good cheer.

Lagoa

★PALAPHITA KITCH   LOUNGE
Map p242 (☑2227-0837; www.palaphitakitch.com.br; Av Epitácio Pessoa s/n; ☺6pm-1am) A great spot for a sundowner, Palaphita Kitch is an open-air, thatched-roof wonderland with rustic bamboo furniture, flickering tiki torches and a peaceful setting on the edge of the lake. This is a popular spot with couples, who come for the view and the creative (but pricey) cocktails: the caipirinhas, made from unusual fruits from the Northeast and Amazonia, are a hit.

BAR LAGOA   BOTECO
Map p236 (☑2523-1135; Av Epitácio Pessoa 1674; ☺noon-2am) With a view of the lake, past a busy road, Bar Lagoa is one of the neighborhood's classic haunts. Founded in 1935, this open-air spot hasn't changed all that much since then: the bar still has surly waiters serving excellent beer to ever-crowded tables and, in spite of its years, a youthful air pervades.

☆ ENTERTAINMENT

MIRANDA   LIVE MUSIC
Map p242 (☑2239-0305; www.mirandabrasil.com.br; Av Borges de Medeiros 1424, Lagoa; admission R$50-80) Situated on Lagoa Rodrigo de Freitas, Miranda is a classy but inviting bar and live-music venue that hosts a range of shows and events. These include *feijoada* (bean-and-meat stew served with rice) and live samba on Sundays (R$70), Música Popular Brasileira (MPB) groups and well-known Brazilian artists such as Mart'nália and BossaCucaNova (a group that blends bossa nova with electronica).

It's located inside the Lagoon complex.

🛍 SHOPPING

Aside from a few scattered shops, there isn't much of a shopping scene in Jardim Botânico or Lagoa. Residents from the neighborhood typically head to Ipanema, Leblon or to the huge Shopping da Gávea mall to satisfy their retail cravings. On weekends, however, an interesting market on the Praça Santos Dumont makes a journey here worthwhile.

DONA COISA   FASHION
Map p242 (☑2249-2336; www.donacoisa.com.br; Lopes Quintas 153, Jardim Botânico; ☺11am-8pm Mon-Fri, 10am-6pm Sat) One of Rio's premier boutiques, Dona Coisa sells top labels by Brazilian and international designers, including one-of-a-kind pieces you won't find elsewhere (such as snakeskin Converse by Missoni). The multiroom design house also has original objects for the home – delicate ceramics by Heloisa Galvão and engraved wineglasses, for instance – in addition to skin and beauty products by Phebo and Granado.

GABINETE   HOMEWARES
Map p242 (☑3173-8828; Lopes Quintas 87, Jardim Botânico; ☺11am-8pm Mon-Fri, 10am-6pm Sat) On a street with a growing number of shops and cafes, Gabinete is a fun place to browse for unusual items – decorative brass moose heads, vintage glassware, illuminated teapot lamps, wind-up circus miniatures and earth-toned pottery – which line the artfully lit display shelves of this intriguing curiosity cabinet.

O SOL   HANDICRAFTS
Map p242 (☑2294-6198; Corcovado 213, Jardim Botânico; ☺9am-6pm Mon-Fri, to 1pm Sat) O Sol is run by Leste-Um, a nonprofit social-welfare organization. This delightful store displays the works of regional artists and

sells Brazilian folk art in clay, wood and porcelain. It also sells baskets, hammocks and woven rugs.

SHOPPING DA GÁVEA
SHOPPING CENTER

Map p242 (☑2294-1096; Marquês de São Vicente 52, Gávea; ☺10am-10pm Mon-Sat, 2-9pm Sun) Shopping da Gávea touts itself as the preferred mall of artists and intellectuals, which may or may not matter to you when you're laying down serious cash for those sneakers. It's home to 200 stores, a five-screen cinema, several theaters and numerous restaurants, including La Pastaciutta, which serves tasty pastas and appetizers.

ISABELA CAPETO
CLOTHING

Map p242 (☑2537-3331; Alberto Ribeiro 17, Jardim Botânico; ☺10am-6pm Mon-Fri) One of Brazil's fashion stars, Isabela Capeto creates beautifully made clothing with seductive lines. Many of her pieces are embroidered and feature add-ons of vintage lace, sequins or fabric trims. This shop is a good place to see dresses and skirts that have earned her accolades from *O Globo, Vogue* and other publications.

🏃 SPORTS & ACTIVITIES

LAGOA AVENTURAS
ADVENTURE SPORTS

Map p242 (☑4105-0079; www.lagoaaventuras.com.br; Av Epitácio Pessoa 3000; zipline R$20, climbing wall R$25, treetop walk R$35, rappelling R$130; ☺9:30am-4:30pm Tue-Sun; ♿) Located in the Parque da Catacumba, across from Lagoa, this is a fine place to come for outdoor adventures. You can get a workout scaling a 7m rock-climbing wall, take a zipline ride, rappel (abseil) down a rock face or take a canopy walk through the treetops. Kids aged four years and up are welcome.

NIRVANA
SPA

Map p242 (☑2187-0100; www.enirvana.com.br; Joquei Clube, Jardim Botânico 1003, Gávea; ☺10am-9pm Mon-Fri, to 6pm Sat) Inside the Jockey Club, this sunny, full-service spa offers an enticing array of relaxing treatments, and you can also use the sauna. If you want to make a day of it, book a day-spa package, which includes a yoga class, lunch, exfoliating treatment, a selection of various treatments (reflexology, reiki, hot-rock massage etc) and an aromatherapy bath.

Nirvana also has a huge range of yoga, pilates and dance classes.

JOQUEI CLUBE
HORSE RACING

Map p242 (☑3534-9000; www.jcb.com.br; Jardim Botânico 1003, Gávea; ☺6-10pm Mon & Fri, 2-9pm Sat & Sun) One of the country's loveliest racetracks, with a great view of the mountains and Corcovado, the Joquei Clube (Jockey Club) seats 35,000. It lies on the Gávea side of the Lagoa Rodrigo de Freitas, opposite Praça Santos Dumont. Local race fans are part of the attraction – it's a different slice of Rio life.

Tourists are welcome in the members' area, which has a bar overlooking the track. Races are held on Mondays, Fridays, Saturdays and Sundays. The big event is the Brazilian Grand Prix (the first Sunday in August).

Copacabana & Leme

Neighborhood Top Five

1 Soaking up the sunshine on **Copacabana Beach** (p87), followed by a meal at an oceanfront eatery.

2 Exploring the **Forte de Copacabana** (p88) and taking in the view across the beach.

3 Walking to mountaintop heights along a forested trail inside the **Forte Duque de Caxias** (p88).

4 Admiring the breathtaking sea views from the **Bar do Alto** (p89) in Babilônia favela.

5 Listening to samba jam sessions at **Bip Bip** (p96).

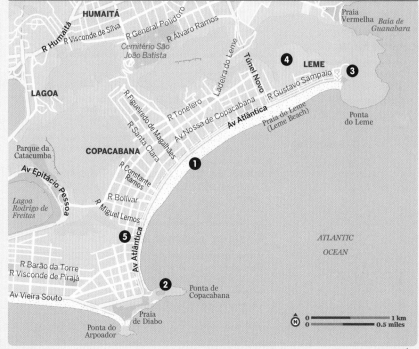

For more detail of this area, see Maps p244 and p248 ➡

COPACABANA & LEME

✖ Best Places to Eat

➡ Churrascaria Palace (p92)
➡ Bar do David (p89)
➡ El Born (p90)
➡ TT Burger (p90)
➡ Boulangerie Guerin (p88)
➡ Joaquina (p93)

For reviews, see p88 ➡

🍷 Best Places to Drink

➡ Escondido (p93)
➡ Estrelas da Babilônia (p89)
➡ Ponto da Bossa Nova (p93)
➡ Sindicato do Chopp (p96)
➡ Mais Que Nada (p96)
➡ As Melhores Cervejas do Mundo (p96)

For reviews, see p93 ➡

🔒 Best Places to Shop

➡ Brecho de Salto Alto (p97)
➡ Bossa Nova & Companhia (p97)
➡ Galeria River (p97)
➡ Loja Fla (p97)

For reviews, see p97 ➡

Explore Copacabana & Leme

With the construction of the neoclassical Copacabana Palace hotel in 1923, Copacabana – and Rio – became South America's most elegant destination, one frequented by international celebrities. Copacabana remained Rio's untarnished gem until the 1970s, when the area fell into decline. Today's Copa is a chaotic mix of discount stores and noisy traffic-filled avenues, with a humming red-light district and slightly edgy streets. While paradise it clearly is not, the beach remains beautiful. Framed by mountains and deep blue sea, the magnificent curve of shoreline stretches more than 4km.

Packing the beach are sun-worshippers of every age and background, from favela (slum, informal community) kids to aging socialites, from tourists to families from the Zona Norte. Copacabana's democratic mix, old-school *botecos* (small, open-air bars), eclectic restaurants and nightclubs, myriad shops and of course the handsome shoreline still entrance many visitors. While the cool kids cling to Ipanema and Leblon, Copacabana seems poised on the edge of a renaissance. Its glassy kiosks have brought class to the neighborhood, while Baixo Copa has become a nightlife destination.

The small neighborhood of Leme, just northeast of Copacabana (Av Princesa Isabel divides the two), has a village feel, with its mix of old-timers, upper-middle-class families and favela residents. The lack of major roads through Leme creates a more peaceful vibe, and the oceanfront restaurants make for a more relaxing setting for a drink than the buzzing Copacabana strip.

Local Life

➡ **Markets** Copacabana has a handful of weekly produce markets held at various locales. Our favorite happens in peaceful Bairro Peixoto (p88).
➡ **Hangouts** One of Copacabana's liveliest areas for a drink is Baixo Copa, a bar- and restaurant-lined strip just back from Av Atlântica around Rua Domingos Ferreira and Barão de Ipanema.
➡ **Arts** Little frequented by tourists, Espaço SESC (p97) often hosts an excellent lineup of dance and theater performances.

Getting There & Away

➡ **Bus** Ipanema (161 and 573), Leblon (161, 511 and 583), Gávea (161 and 583), Jardim Botânico (161, 573 and 583) and Centro (121, 123 and 124).
➡ **Metro** Cardeal Arcoverde, Siqueira Campos, Cantagalo and Ipanema/General Osório.

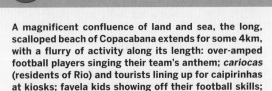

TOP SIGHT
COPACABANA BEACH

A magnificent confluence of land and sea, the long, scalloped beach of Copacabana extends for some 4km, with a flurry of activity along its length: over-amped football players singing their team's anthem; *cariocas* (residents of Rio) and tourists lining up for caipirinhas at kiosks; favela kids showing off their football skills; and beach vendors shouting out their wares among the tanned beach bodies.

Each group stakes out its stretch of sand. The area between the Copacabana Palace hotel and Rua Fernando Mendes is the gay and transvestite section, known as the Stock or Stock Market – easily recognized by the rainbow flag. Young football and *futevôlei* (soccer volleyball) players hold court near Rua Santa Clara. *Postos 5* and 6 are a mix of favela kids and *carioca* retirees, while the spot next to Forte de Copacabana is the *colônia dos pescadores* (fisher's colony). As Copacabana Beach curves north you get to the quieter sands of Leme (Av Princesa Isabel forms the demarcation between the two neighborhoods). Here you'll find a mix of older Leme residents as well as kids from the nearby favelas of Babilônia and Chapéu Mangueira.

Aside from frolicking in the waves and people-watching, the main attraction for visitors to the beach is running or cycling the beach path; the beachside lane closes to traffic on Sundays. Early risers can greet the sunrise while exercising. Another way to get physical is to have a go on a stand-up paddleboard, which you can hire from the south end of the beach. Hire outfits also offer lessons. By afternoon and nightfall, the beach kiosks are a great place to relax, rehydrate over *agua de côco* (coconut water), snack and have a few libations before the night begins. On weekends, there's also live music.

DON'T MISS...

➡ Stand-up paddle-boarding across the sea

➡ Evening drinks at a beachfront kiosk

➡ A Sunday run, walk or bike ride along the beach boulevard

PRACTICALITIES

➡ Map p244, E4

➡ Av Atlântica

◉ SIGHTS

COPACABANA BEACH
BEACH

See p87.

MUSEU DO IMAGEM E SOM
MUSEUM

Map p244 (www.mis.rj.gov.br; Av Atlântica, near Miguel Lemos) Copacabana finally has an outstanding rainy-day attraction, thanks to the stunning Museum of Image and Sound, which opened in 2016. The building, designed by celebrated New York firm Diller Scofidio + Renfro (who also designed NYC's High Line), features high-tech interactive galleries devoted to the great Brazilian music and film that has played such a pivotal role in the nation's culture. Performance halls and an open-air rooftop amphitheater (for outdoor films) are other highlights.

The museum also contains a gallery devoted to Carmen Miranda. You can peek at photographs, hear music, watch a few film clips and check out the over-the-top garments that once belonged to the famous starlet from Brazil (never mind that Miranda was actually born in Portugal).

FORTE DE COPACABANA
FORT

Map p244 (☑2521-1032; Av Atlântica & Rua Francisco Otaviano; adult/child R$6/free; ☉10am-7:30pm Tue-Sun) Built in 1914 on the promontory of the old Our Lady of Copacabana chapel, the fort of Copacabana was one of Rio's premier defenses against attack. You can still see its original features, including walls that are up to 12m thick, defended by Krupp cannons. Inside is a museum with several floors of exhibits tracing the early days of the Portuguese colony through to the mid-19th century. The views out across the full length of Copacabana are striking.

There are several cafes with fine vantage points, including Cafe Colombo (p91).

COLÔNIA DOS PESCADORES
MARKET

Map p244 (Av Atlântica, near Francisco Otaviano; ☉market 7:30am to 1pm) At the southern end of Copacabana Beach you'll see fishing folk at work, if you go early enough, mending lines and hauling in the catch. There's a small fish market here open to the public, and usually one vendor who sells and cooks up whole fresh fish on a small charcoal grill – a great deal at about R$15 for a decent-sized fish.

FORTE DUQUE DE CAXIAS
FORT

Map p248 (☑3223-5076; Praça Almirante Júlio de Noronha; adult/child R$4/free; ☉9:30am-4:30pm Tue-Sun) More commonly known as Forte do Leme, this military base is open to the public. Visitors can walk to the top of Morro do Leme (Leme Mountain) along a steep 800m trail that passes through Atlantic rainforest. At the top stands an 18th-century fort affording magnificent views of Pão de Açúcar (Sugarloaf Mountain) and the Cagarras Islands.

BAIRRO PEIXOTO
NEIGHBORHOOD

Map p244 (Anita Garibaldi) A world away from the bustle of Copacabana's busy avenues, the Bairro Peixoto is a peaceful enclave centered on the leafy Praça Edmundo Bittencourt. There you'll find a playground, park benches and tables where folks play dominoes and read the paper, all of which seem to lend the setting more of a village-like air than that of a big-city neighborhood. You might even see a few marmosets up in the trees.

Wednesday's a good day to visit, when the weekly fruit market takes place.

EATING

Rio's most visited neighborhood has an enormous variety of restaurants, from award-winning dining rooms to charming old bistros from the 1950s, as well as creperies, *churrascarias* (traditional barbecue restaurants), sushi bars and other ethnic haunts. In general, you will encounter less experimentation, but if you're looking for excellent traditional cuisine – both Brazilian and international – you will find plenty of delectable options in Copacabana. The restaurant strip along Av Atlântica has fine views of the seaside, but generally unexceptional food. The narrow roads crisscrossing Av NS de Copacabana from Leme to Arpoador contain many fine establishments – and mediocre ones. Do some exploring; trust your instincts and *bom proveito* (happy eating).

✗ Copacabana

★BOULANGERIE GUERIN
BAKERY $

Map p244 (☑2523-4140; Av NS de Copacabana 920; pastries R$9-12; ☉8am-8pm) Serving Rio's best croissants, *pains au chocolat*

MORRO DA BABILÔNIA

Scattered across the hillsides above Leme are two small favelas that lie side by side: **Babilônia** to the west (left side) and **Chapéu Mangueira** to the east (right side). These informal communities, home to about 4000 residents, have become a magnet for visitors since pacification arrived in 2009. Today in the area there are more than half-a-dozen hostels, simple bars and eateries with amazing views (and great cocktails), and a mountaintop rainforest preserve.

As you walk up to the favelas, you can also check out the **Mural de Babilônia**, a breathtaking Gaudi-esque mosaic that covers a long, sweeping wall (140 sq meters) near the bottom of the hill. The work was created by two artists from the Czech Republic who go by the names of X-Dog and Plebe, along with the help of dozens of volunteers.

To make the most of a visit to Babilônia favela, you can take a walking tour offered by Jungle Me (p49) or Rio by Bike (p205).

Access to the favelas is via Ladeira Ary Barroso, off Rua General Ribeiro da Costa, in Leme. If you don't feel like hoofing it, you can also take a mototaxi from here to the top.

A few favorite favela locales for eating and drinking:

Bar do David (Map p248; Ladeira Ary Barroso 66; appetizers R$20-30, mains around R$35; ⏱8am-10pm Tue-Sun) Located in Chapéu Mangueira favela, this simple open-sided eatery serves excellent snacks. The chef and owner David Vieira Bispo was formerly a fisherman, and his seafood *feijoada* (stew with rice) is outstanding – but available weekends only. At other times, you can nibble on seafood *croquetes*, garlic shrimp, sausage with manioc, and other hits that go nicely with a caipirinha or two.

Bar do Alto (Map p248; Ladeira Ary Barroso 57; ⏱1-10pm Wed-Sun) High up in the Babilônia favela, this friendly place has jaw-dropping views over Copacabana. It's an open-sided affair, with cool breezes, flickering candles on the tables, and a small menu with standouts such as fish or mixed-seafood *moqueca* (Bahian fish stew cooked in a clay pot with *dendê* oil, coconut milk and spicy peppers; around R$40), and *feijoada*-stuffed rolls – good for sharing. You'll also find some intriguing cocktails such as the *caipichopp*, a bubbly caipirinha that goes down smoothly – never mind the green color.

Estrelas da Babilônia (Map p248; Ladeira Ary Barroso; ⏱5-11pm Tue-Thu & Sun, to 3am Fri & Sat) In the uppermost reaches of the Babilônia favela, Estrelas da Babilônia has a picturesque open-air setting with an unrivaled view of the mountains and sea, with the cityscape of Copacabana wedged between the two. It's a fun and welcoming spot, run by a Colombian-Belgian couple, with a lineup of live music, film screenings and other events. It's worth coming for the view alone.

(chocolate-filled pastries) and eclairs, this French patisserie was an instant success upon opening in 2012. Prices for those delectable raspberry-covered tarts and creamy mille-feuilles are high, but so is the quality. You can also enjoy baguette sandwiches and thick slices of quiche if you're craving something more substantial.

GALETO SAT'S
BRAZILIAN $

Map p244 (☏2275-6197; Barata Ribeiro 7; mains R$18-26; ⏱noon-5am) One of Rio's best roast-chicken spots, laid-back Galeto Sat's has earned many fans since its opening back in 1962. Grab a seat along the mirrored and tiled wall, order a *chope* (draft beer) and enjoy the scent of grilled spit-roasted birds be-

fore tucking into a filling meal. Price-wise you can't beat the R$50 feast for two.

NONNA RIDOLFI
CAFE $

Map p244 (Ronald de Carvalho 161; sandwiches R$19-22; ⏱11am-9pm Tue, Wed, Fri & Sat, 4-10pm Thu, 11am-7pm Sun) This small, quaint cafe serves up tasty sandwiches, cheese and charcuterie plates, desserts and craft beers amid wooden shelves that evoke a bygone era. There's outdoor seating in front, offering a fine vantage point to take in this peaceful corner of Copacabana.

ANTONIA CASA E CAFE
BRAZILIAN $

Map p244 (Dias da Rocha 9; mains R$17-32; ⏱7:30am-10pm; 🛜) Though it's just a short stroll from Copacabana's busiest thoroughfare, this little cafe (which shares space with a home-design store) maintains a peaceful air, particularly if you sit at one of the tables on the small plaza in front. Stop in for sandwiches, *empadas* (meat or shrimp-filled pasties), desserts and coffee.

CERVANTES
BRAZILIAN $

Map p244 (2275-6147; Barata Ribeiro 7; sandwiches R$15-30; noon-4am Tue-Thu & Sun, to 6am Fri & Sat) A Copacabana institution, the late-night Cervantes gathers *cariocas* who come to feast on the trademark steak and pineapple sandwiches. This popular branch on busy Barata Ribeiro attracts a mostly standing-room-only crowd. For the sit-down restaurant, head a few steps around the corner to Av Pradio Junior 335.

BRASEIRO
BRAZILIAN $

Map p244 (Domingos Ferreira 214; mains R$17-35; 11am-midnight) Follow the scent of char-grilled chicken to this unfussy, open-sided favorite for a satisfying meal that won't drain the wallet. It's a jovial spot, with counter seating only.

RESTAURANTE NATURALEVE
VEGETARIAN $

Map p244 (Travessa Cristiano Lacorte; per kg R$50; 11am-4pm Mon-Sat) Set just off Rua Miguel Lemos, this tidy, health-conscious restaurant cooks up a reasonably priced lunch buffet, with vegetarian black beans, *moqueca* with salmon, grilled tofu, various baked dishes and fresh salads.

BIBI SUCOS
BRAZILIAN $

Map p244 (2255-5000; Santa Clara 36; mains R$18-36; 8am-1am Sun-Thu, to 2am Fri & Sat) Offering much the same recipe for success as its Leblon branch (p68), Bibi serves dozens of juices, along with savory and sweet crepes, sandwiches, burgers, pastas, quiches and build-your-own salads. It has outdoor tables and a bustling vibe. Go early or late to beat the lunchtime crowds.

FARAJ
MIDDLE EASTERN $

Map p244 (Francisco Sá 35; mains around R$27; 9am-10pm Tue-Sun) A much-loved neighborhood favorite, Faraj has a snack counter up front where you stop by for quick *kibe* (meat croquette), *esfiha* (triangular spinach or meat pastry) or juice, while the tables in back are the place to linger over plates of tabbouleh, hummus and daily lunch specials such as lamb kebabs with rice and lentils.

KONI STORE
JAPANESE $

Map p244 (Constante Ramos 44; hand rolls around R$16; 11am-2am Sun-Thu, to 6am Fri & Sat) This popular spot serves tasty *temaki* (seaweed hand rolls filled with tuna, salmon and other bites). It stays open late, making it ideal for a postbar snack.

O REI DAS EMPANADAS
SNACKS $

Map p244 (3258-3003; Barata Ribeiro 48; empanadas R$4-6; 9am-11:30pm Mon-Sat, to 8:30pm Sun) 'The king of empanadas' serves up piping-hot pasties, baked fresh throughout the day. There are more than a dozen varieties, including *carne picante* (spicy beef), *camarão* (shrimp) and dessert options such as banana with chocolate.

★ EL BORN
SPANISH $$

Map p244 (3496-1780; www.barelborn.com.br; Bolívar 17; tapas R$15-40; 5pm-2am Mon-Fri, from 3pm Sat & Sun) Named after Barcelona's hippest, foodie-loving neighborhood, El Born fires up some of Rio's best tapas plates: think Galician-style octopus, spicy prawns and tender Iberian ham. The setting channels a bit of old-world Spain, with rustic stone and brick walls, outdoor tables on the sidewalk and ample bar seating – the latter is a fine spot for watching the dexterous bartenders in action.

Don't order too much. Waiters emerge from the kitchen and make the rounds with freshly cooked tapas plates; if you see something you like, take it!

TT BURGER
BURGERS $$

Map p244 (Francisco Otaviano 67; mains around R$30; noon-midnight Sun-Wed, to 4am Thu-Sat) The son of famed local chef Claude Troisgros runs this high-end Brooklyn-style burger outpost, and has gained a strong following for his delicious burgers (the guava ketchup is outstanding), crispy fries and milkshakes. It's a charming spot, with subway tiles, framed photos, wood floors and a small front deck. There's a second location on Leblon's main drag (Av Ataúlfo de Paiva).

ARAB
MIDDLE EASTERN $$

Map p244 (Av Atlântica 1936; mains R$38-80; noon-1am) On the oceanfront road, Arab is a laid-back spot where you can linger at an outdoor table over delicious platters of tabbouleh, hummus, baba ghanoush, falafel, shawarma and other treats. There's also a lunch buffet.

SANTA SATISFAÇÃO
BRAZILIAN $$

Map p244 (☎2255-9349; www.santasatisfacao.com; Santa Clara 36C; mains R$27-46; ☺10am-10:45pm Mon-Sat) Oozing farmhouse charm, this always-packed bistro is worth forking out a bit extra for outstanding daily lunch specials of upscale Brazilian comfort food and sophisticated sandwiches. Among the favorites: pasta with Gorgonzola and sliced filet mignon, caprese salad, and an open-faced ham and Brie sandwich.

AMIR
MIDDLE EASTERN $$

Map p244 (☎2275-5596; Ronald de Carvalho 55C; mains R$43-58, sandwiches R$19-32; ☺noon-midnight Mon-Sat, to 11pm Sun) Step inside Amir and you'll enter a world of delicate aromas and handsomely dressed waiters in embroidered vests. Daytime crowds come for the buffet (R$70 on weekdays, R$80 weekends), while at night the à la carte menu features all the favorites, including delicious platters of hummus, *kaftas* (spiced meat patties), falafel, kibbe and salads.

There's a belly dancer on Friday nights at 8:30pm. Other nights you can smoke from a hookah if you snag a balcony seat.

LE BLÉ NOIR
FRENCH $$

Map p244 (☎2267-6969; Xavier da Silveira 19A; crepes R$40-70; ☺7:30pm-midnight) Flickering candles, art-filled walls and chattering crowds set the scene for feasting on Rio's best crepes. Le Blé Noir offers more than 50 different varieties, pairing rich ingredients such as shrimp and artichoke hearts or Brie, honey and toasted almonds. The wait can be long (45 minutes on average).

CAFE COLOMBO
CAFE $$

Map p244 (☎3201-4049; Forte de Copacabana, Praça Coronel Eugênio Franco; mains R$24-38; ☺10am-8pm Tue-Sun) Far removed from the hustle and bustle of Av Atlântica, this cafe has magnificent views of Copacabana Beach. At the outdoor tables you can sit beneath shady palm trees, enjoying cappuccino, omelets, waffles, salads or sandwiches as young soldiers file past. To get here, you'll have to pay admission (R$6) to the Forte de Copacabana (p88).

BAKERS
CAFE $$

Map p244 (☎3209-1212; www.thebakers.com.br; Santa Clara 86; mains R$25-45, desserts R$7-10; ☺9am-9pm; 🛜) The Bakers is a fine spot for flaky croissants, banana Danishes, apple strudels and other treats. There are

also waffles, omelets, salads, gourmet sandwiches (such as prosciutto and mozzarella on ciabatta), quiches (including ricotta with sun-dried tomatoes) and filling lunch specials such as grilled salmon or penne pasta.

DEVASSA
BRAZILIAN $$

Map p244 (☎2236-0667; Bolívar 8; mains R$35-65; ☺11am-2am) The popular Rio chain of upscale *botecos* is well known for its excellent beers. Devassa also serves tasty pub fare, including juicy burgers, veggie quesadillas, seafood pastas and the usual bar food. The open-sided restaurant enjoys a good location on the edge of Av Atlântica.

LA TRATTORIA
ITALIAN $$

Map p244 (☎2255-3319; Fernando Mendes 7A; mains R$38-70; ☺noon-midnight) Old photos, simple furnishings, hearty dishes and the constant din of conversation have made this trattoria a neighborhood favorite since 1976. Shrimp dishes are the Italian family's specialty: many diners have been won over by the *espaguete com camarão e óleo tartufado* (spaghetti with shrimp and truffle oil).

ARATACA
AMAZONIAN $$

Map p244 (☎2548-6624; Domingos Ferreira 41D; mains R$32-65; ☺10am-9pm) The casual, no-nonsense Arataca serves exotic cuisine of the Amazon. There's *moqueca* (a freshwater fish), *pirarucu* (a freshwater fish), *pato no tucupi* (roast duck flavored with garlic) or *vatapá* (a seafood dish with a thick sauce of manioc paste and coconut), all of which go nicely with real guaraná juice.

CAPRICCIOSA
PIZZERIA $$

Map p244 (☎2255-2598; Domingos Ferreira 187; pizzas R$50-85; ☺6pm-2am) Like its better-known version in Ipanema (p63), Capricciosa serves excellent thin-crust pizzas.

MÔNACO
SEAFOOD $$

Map p244 (☎2521-0195; Miguel Lemos 18; mains R$50-100, for 2 people R$70-160; ☺8am-2am) The casual Bar Mônaco is the neighborhood destination for sizzling plates of grilled squid, fresh cherne (grouper), shrimp and a mean bowl of Leão Veloso (a rich seafood soup). Sidewalk tables provide a relaxing place for a meal or a drink on a fairly untrafficked street.

ZOT
INTERNATIONAL $$

Map p244 (☎3489-4363; Bolívar 21; mains R$44-62; ☺6pm-midnight Tue-Sat, from noon Sun; 🖉)

THE KIOSKS OF COPACABANA

The *quiosque* (kiosk) has long been a presence on the beachfront of Rio. It's where cold drinks and snacks are doled out to *cariocas* (residents of Rio) on the move, and where plastic tables and chairs provide a fine vantage point for contemplating the watery horizon. In recent years Copacabana Beach has seen a new crop of flashy kiosks replacing the old-fashioned wooden ones. Now it's possible to get a decent meal (the kitchens are cleverly concealed underground), an ice-cold draft beer or gourmet snacks without ever leaving the sand.

The new kiosks are sprinkled all along Copacabana Beach, with most options roughly between Rua Siqueira Campos and the Copacabana Palace hotel. Here are a few current favorites:

Globo (Map p244; Copacabana Beach, near Miguel Lemos; snacks R$8-15; ⊘9am-midnight) Run by Brazil's major media network, Globo has a brightly illuminated kiosk with colorful seats near the new Museu do Imagem e Som. Aside from snacks and drinks, you can sometimes catch live programming here, such as mini concerts, televised interviews and public debates.

Cantinho Cearense (Map p244; near Duvivier; appetizers R$13-35, mains for 2 people R$63-100; ⊘9am-midnight) A popular gathering spot, Cantinho Cearense serves up cold *chope* (draft beer) and plenty of satisfying snacks, as well as heartier fare from the state of Ceará, including grilled seafood with fried cassava.

Espetto Carioca (Map p248; near Praça Julio de Noronha; snacks R$12-20; ⊘8am-midnight) At the northeast end of Leme, elevated over the beach, this peacefully set kiosk serves *espettos* (kebabs or skewers) of vegetables, meats and cheeses, which go nicely with drinks. Nearby, you can watch fearless *carioca* kids diving off the sea-wall. There's usually live music on weekends.

Set amid the bars of Baixo Copa, Zot is a sleek and stylish gastrobar featuring an inventive menu that showcases Brazilian ingredients and an excellent drink selection, including dozens of wines by the glass. Start off with a sharing plate (steak tartar with truffle oil, duck croquettes with aioli) before dining on shrimp linguine or vegetarian risotto.

★ CHURRASCARIA PALACE
CHURRASCARIA $$$

Map p244 (☑2541-5898; Rodolfo Dantas 16; all you can eat R$110; ⊘noon-midnight) Hands down, this is one of the best *churrascarias* in town. You'll find high-quality cuts of meat and attentive service at this elegantly set dining room. Waiters make frequent rounds with the goods; don't be shy about saying no, otherwise you'll end up with more than you could possibly eat.

AZUMI
JAPANESE $$$

Map p244 (☑2541-4294; Ministro Viveiros de Castro 127; meals R$80-180; ⊘7pm-midnight Tue-Sun) Some claim Azumi is the bastion of traditional Japanese cuisine in the city. This laid-back sushi bar certainly has its fans – both in the Nisei community and from abroad. Azumi's *sushiman* (sushi chef) masterfully prepares delectable sushi and sashimi, and the tempuras and soups are also excellent. Be sure to ask what's in season.

DON CAMILLO
ITALIAN $$$

Map p244 (☑2549-9958; Av Atlântica 3056; pastas R$40-110; ⊘noon-1am) This handsomely appointed Italian restaurant has flavorful pastas and lasagnas, as well as some excellent seafood dishes. Antique tile floors, distressed-wood beams and black-and-white photos make a nice setting, though it's hard to top the outdoor tables facing the beach. For pure decadence, try the linguine with lobster, crayfish and cherry tomatoes.

SIMON BOCCANEGRA
ITALIAN $$$

Map p244 (☑3269-4366; Aires Saldanha 98; mains R$60-88; ⊘noon-1am Tue-Sat, to 10pm Sun) Named after an Italian opera, this overly polished wine bar and *osteria* is set with reflective chandeliers, tall ceilings and a long wall lined with wine bottles. Come for ingredient-rich bruschettas, creative pastas and nicely prepared grilled meat or fish plates. You can also stop in for a drink, and relax in one of the velvet armchairs in front.

✖ Leme

JOAQUINA
BRAZILIAN $$

Map p248 (☑2275-8569; Av Atlântica 974; mains R$34-46; ⏱11:30am-midnight; 🔊) Joaquina has much to recommend it: a great ocean-facing location with outdoor seating; excellent caipirinhas that don't stint on the fresh fruit; and tasty Brazilian fare served up at fair prices. On Sundays Joaquina serves *feijoada* (R$34); on Saturdays it's oxtail rice (also R$34). Arrive early before it runs out. Other hits: *moqueca* for one, shrimp risotto and vegetarian stroganoff.

GALERIA 1618
BISTRO $$

Map p248 (☑2295-1618; Gustavo Sampaio 840; mains R$48-62; ⏱noon-midnight) Opened by two French expats in 2006, the art-filled Galeria 1618 offers tender grilled meats, shrimp linguine and fresh bruschetta plates. Inside, the design is elegant, if a little on the formal side, so you may prefer to eat at one of the sidewalk tables in front.

SHIRLEY
SPANISH $$

Map p248 (☑2275-1398; Gustavo Sampaio 610; mains R$46-60; ⏱noon-1am) The aroma of succulent paella hangs in the air as waiters hurry to and from the kitchen bearing platefuls of fresh seafood. Shirley, opened in 1954, was one of the first Spanish restaurants in town, and attracts a local following in its small Leme dining room.

In addition to paella, the mussel-vinaigrette appetizer and the oven-baked snapper in white-wine sauce are also recommended. Most seafood plates serve two (priced from R$96 to R$130).

LA FIORENTINA
ITALIAN $$$

Map p248 (☑2543-8395; Av Atlântica 458A; mains R$42-98; ⏱11:30am-midnight) One of Leme's classic Italian restaurants, La Fiorentina attracted Rio's glitterati in the 1960s. Today its beach-facing outdoor tables draw a loyal, mostly neighborhood crowd, who come to feast on oysters, seafood risottos and thin-crust pizzas.

🍷 DRINKING & 🍸 NIGHTLIFE

Despite being overshadowed by younger, hipper Ipanema to the south, Copacabana has seen marked improvement in its nightlife offerings, boosted in part by its ocean-fronting kiosks, which make a great spot for a late-afternoon drink. On the other side of the busy road are the open-air restaurants and bars of Av Atlântica, which are generally – with a few exceptions – overpriced tourist traps. More authentic is the emerging nightlife area that some have dubbed Baixo Copa (Lower Copa), where a dozen or so lively bars and restaurants are sprinkled along a quiet street just back from Av Atlântica. To explore this area, head along Rua Aires de Saldanha and Rua Domingos Ferreira, between Rua Almirante Gonçalves and Rua Constante Ramos. For something more upscale, the best options are at high-end hotel bars, some of which have million-dollar views.

ESCONDIDO
BAR

Map p244 (Aires de Saldanha 98, Copacabana; ⏱6pm-1am Tue-Sun) One of the top beer bars in Copacabana, Escondido has a rotating selection of microbrews such as American pale ales, stouts and ciders, including about two dozen on draft at any one time. It's a laid-back spot to head to with friends to sample a few brews and nibble on pub grub (including huge burgers).

PONTO DA BOSSA NOVA
BAR

Map p244 (☑2235-4616; Domingos Ferreira 215, Copacabana; ⏱noon-1am Sun & Mon, to 3am Tue-Sat) On a lively street sprinkled with bars, this boxy, wood-lined space has a tiny outdoor patio that makes a peaceful spot for sampling appetizers such as *carne seca com aipim* (jerked beef with fried cassava) and well-made caipirinhas. True to its name, there's live bossa nova – and Música Popular Brasileira (MPB) – from time to time.

SINDICATO DO CHOPP
BAR

Map p244 (☑2523-4644; Av Atlântica 3806, Copacabana; ⏱8am-2am) A Copacabana institution, this open-air bar looks out on wide Av Atlântica, with the beach in the background. Owing to its breezy location, it attracts a varied mix of people, all of whom play a part in Copa's inimitable street theater. The food isn't so hot here,

1. Rio Scenarium (p144), Lapa **2.** Outdoor bars, Baixo Gávea (p82)
3. Garota de Ipanema (p63) **4.** Al fresco dining, Centro (p128)

LONELY PLANET / GETTY IMAGES ©

Nightlife

By night, the energy on Rio's streets is electric. All-night street parties in Lapa, old-school *gafieiras* (dance halls), impromptu jam sessions at outdoor bars, riotous dance floors presided over by celebrated DJs – Rio's nightlife is all this and much more. The only thing you have to do is show up.

Lapa

Epicenter of Rio's samba scene, there's always something afoot in this atmospheric neighborhood on the edge of Centro. On weekends the party takes over, and the city closes the streets to traffic.

Nightclubs

Lapa aside, some of the best spots for dancing are in the Zona Sul, with trendy places like 00 (Zero Zero; p82) bringing in the well-dressed club kids.

Botecos

A much-loved institution in Rio, the *boteco* is a casual open-sided bar where *cariocas* (residents of Rio) gather over ice-cold *chopes* (draft beer) and snacks. Eating is an essential part of Rio's drinking culture.

Al Fresco

Cariocas make good use of the warm nights, with open-air drinking spots all around town. Try the Travessa do Comércio (p126) in Centro for colonial flavor, Bar Urca (p105) for great views, or the Copacabana kiosks for afternoon cocktails on the beachfront.

Lagoa

The pretty lagoon (p78) behind Ipanema and Leblon is a favorite spot among couples at night. Lakeside kiosks serve up cocktails and live music (as well as food) in tranquil open-air settings.

but the beers are icy cold and the ocean is, well, right there.

A second **branch** (Map p248; Av Atlântica 514) enjoys an equally peaceful beach-fronting view in Leme.

MAIS QUE NADA   CLUB

Map p244 (www.maisquenada-rio.com.br; Xavier da Silveira 34, Copacabana; ⊙7pm-2am Wed-Sun) This small, festive club draws an equal mix of *cariocas* and gringos who come for a dance-loving lineup of samba, salsa and rock. Cover charge varies from R$10 to upwards of R$25. Wednesday nights (samba) are free.

AS MELHORES CERVEJAS DO MUNDO   BAR

Map p244 (Ronald de Carvalho 154, Copacabana; ⊙3-11pm Mon-Sat) This friendly new spot looks more like a bottle shop than a bar, but beer lovers shouldn't miss it. You'll find an impressive selection of brews from around the globe here, and there's always some-thing going on: beer tastings, quiz nights, courses on beer and food pairings, and even a day (Saturday) when home brewers share their produce with one another.

Our favorite night is Thursday, when it breaks out the vinyl and spins records to the IPA-swilling crowd.

PAVÃO AZUL   BAR

Map p244 (Hilário de Gouveia, Copacabana; ⊙noon-midnight) A Copacabana classic, Pavão Azul is a simple open-sided bar that draws huge crowds, which gather on the sidewalk out front drinking ice-cold *chope* and chatting late into the night. It's been so successful in fact that the owners have opened a similar *boteco*, Pavãzinho, across the street. Don't miss the good, inexpensive *pataniscas* (codfish balls).

MUD BUG   BAR

Map p244 (☑3547-8527; www.mudbug.com.br; Rudolfo Dantas 16, Copacabana; ⊙5pm-3am) Mud Bug is a buzzing, warmly lit sports bar that has a rustic, all-wood interior where *cariocas* and foreigners mingle over football games, bar bites and a broad beer selection. There's also live music – typically classic rock – on weekends. A second, small-er Copacabana location is a few blocks west on Rua Paula Freitas, just north of NS de Copacabana.

BOTEQUIM INFORMAL   BOTECO

Map p244 (☑3816-0909; Domingos Ferreira 215, Copacabana; ⊙noon-1am) Botequim In-formal is a lively drinking spot with an el-evated open-sided deck, frothy drafts and appetizers that include a good fried polenta with Gorgonzola sauce. There are 10 other branches of Botequim Informal in Rio. This one lies amid half-a-dozen festive bars in the Baixo Copa subneighborhood.

FOSFOBOX   CLUB

Map p244 (☑2548-7498; www.fosfobox.com.br; Siqueira Campos 143, Copacabana; admission R$15-60; ⊙11pm-4am Wed-Sat) This subter-ranean club is hidden under a shopping center near the metro station. Good DJs spin everything from funk to glam rock, and the crowd here is one of the more eclec-tic in the club scene.

LE BOY   GAY, CLUB

Map p244 (☑2513-4993; www.leboy.com.br; Raul Pompéia 102, Copacabana; cover R$10-30; ⊙11pm-5am Tue-Sun) Open since 1992, Le Boy is Rio's gay temple. There are theme nights with drag shows and go-go boys.

TV BAR   GAY, BAR

Map p244 (www.bartvbar.com.br; Shopping Cas-sino Atlântico, Av NS de Copacabana 1417, Copa-cabana; cover R$15-50; ⊙10pm-5am Thu-Sat, to 3am Sun) The trendy favorite in town, with DJs spinning amid an audiovisual assault in the space of a former TV station.

☆ ENTERTAINMENT

★BIP BIP   LIVE MUSIC

Map p244 (☑2267-9696; Almirante Gonçalves 50, Copacabana; ⊙6pm-midnight Sun-Fri) For years Bip Bip has been one of the city's fa-vorite spots to catch a live *roda de samba* (informal samba played around a table), despite it being just a storefront with a few battered tables. As the evening progresses the tree-lined neighborhood becomes the backdrop to serious jam sessions, with mu-sic and revelers spilling into the street.

The musical lineup features samba on Thursdays, Fridays and Sundays, *choro* (short for *chorinho;* a romantic, intimate samba) on Mondays and Tuesdays, and bossa nova on Wednesdays. Music kicks off around 8pm.

BECO DAS GARRAFAS   LIVE MUSIC

Map p244 (http://becodasgarrafas.mus.br; Duvivier 37, Copacabana; admission R$30-40) Come to this club to connect to a small part of Brazilian history – and a big part of musical lore. It was on this lane where Tom Jobim and other innovators first unveiled bossa nova in the 1960s. Shuttered for years, the bar was brought back to life in 2014 and today hosts an excellent lineup of bossa and MPB singers.

It's a small and intimate space, and a must-see for music fans.

ESPAÇO SESC   PERFORMING ARTS

Map p244 (☎2548-1088; www.sescrj.org.br; Domingos Ferreira 160, Copacabana) Hosting an excellent assortment of theater and dance performances, Espaço SESC is a bulwark of the Copacabana arts scene. The repertoire tends toward the experimental and avant-garde, particularly during annual dance and theater festivals.

SALA MUNICIPAL
BADEN POWELL   PERFORMING ARTS

Map p244 (☎2548-0421; Av NS de Copacabana 360, Copacabana; admission R$20-80) One of the few music halls in the Zona Sul, the 500-seat Sala Municipal Baden Powell hosts a broad range of concerts throughout the year, with MPB and jazz figuring prominently.

 SHOPPING

Copacabana's shops, just like its local residents, are a diverse bunch, with everything from *cachaça* (sugarcane alcohol) to football jerseys on hand, as well as shoe stores, surf shops and record stores thrown in the mix. Fashion hunters will find more lower-tier labels than in neighboring Ipanema, along with lower prices to match. Between Copa and Ipanema is the Galeria River, a low-rise shopping mall lined with surf and swimwear shops.

★ BRECHO DE SALTO ALTO   VINTAGE

Map p244 (Siqueira Campos 143, Copacabana; ⊙10am-7pm Mon-Fri, to 4pm Sat) Head to the upstairs level of Shopping Siqueira Campos, and pass through the beaded curtain into this fun and welcoming shop that sells a range of vintage-inspired clothing and accessories for men and women. Many pieces are actually recent creations, but made from vintage fabrics – meaning you can find nicely cut shirts (no butterfly collars) and skirts in one-of-a-kind designs.

BOSSA NOVA & COMPANHIA   MUSIC

Map p244 (☎2295-8096; Duvivier 37A, Copacabana; ⊙9am-7pm Mon-Fri, to 5pm Sat) Here you'll find a decent assortment of bossa, *choro* and samba CDs and LPs, as well as musical instruments, coffee-table books, sheet music and biographies of top Brazilian composers.

GALERIA RIVER   SHOPPING CENTER

Map p244 (Francisco Otaviano 67, Arpoador; ⊙9am-8pm Mon-Sat) Surf shops, skateboard and rollerblade outlets, and shops selling beachwear and fashions for young nubile things fill this shopping gallery in Arpoador. Shorts, bikinis, swim trunks, party attire and gear for outdoor adventure are here in abundance. You can also rent surfboards (though for short rentals it's easier hiring on the beach).

LOJA FLA   CLOTHING, ACCESSORIES

Map p244 (☎2541-4109; Av NS de Copacabana 219, Copacabana; ⊙10am-6pm Mon-Fri, to 4pm Sat) With more than 30 million fans worldwide, Flamengo is one of the most-watched football (soccer) teams in all of Brazil. This shop sells all the Flamengo goods, including jerseys, logo-emblazoned socks and soccer balls, posters, iPhone covers and other memorabilia. The prices aren't cheap (jerseys run from R$90 to R$200), but that hasn't dented the popularity of this often-packed little store.

GILSON MARTINS   ACCESSORIES

Map p244 (Av Atlântica 1998, Copacabana; ⊙9am-9pm Mon-Sat, 10am-4pm Sun) Like its flagship store in Ipanema (p70), this colorful shop sells well-crafted wallets, bags, keychains and other items with images of Cristo Redentor (Christ the Redeemer), the Brazilian flag and other iconic designs.

OSKLEN SURFING   CLOTHING

Map p244 (Francisco Otaviano 67, Arpoador; ⊙9am-8pm Mon-Fri, from 10am Sat, 11am-5pm Sun) The famous Brazilian beachwear brand sells its well-made board shorts, T-shirts, *sungas* (Speedo-sized swimsuits) and a few bikinis from this attractive store in Arpoador. You can even buy a very beautiful Kronig design surfboard here, if you have a spare R$1600.

HAVAIANAS   SHOES

Map p244 (☎2267-2418; Xavier da Silveira 19, Copacabana; ⊙9am-8pm Mon-Sat, 10am-6pm

Sun) If you're out of ideas for gifts to take home, head to this sizeable Havaianas shop, where the ubiquitous Brazilian rubber sandal comes in all different styles, and sporting the flags of Brazil, Argentina, Portugal, England and Spain. There are snazzy designs for women, and even logo-bearing bags, key chains and beach towels.

SHOPPING SIQUEIRA
CAMPOS   SHOPPING CENTER

Map p244 (☑2549-0650; Siqueira Campos 143, Copacabana; ☺10am-9pm Mon-Fri, to 6pm Sat, to 4pm Sun) One of Rio's first malls, this quirky shopping center packs an intriguing mix of stores in a no-nonsense, parking-garage-like interior. Scattered across two floors, you'll find numerous antique shops, used-book and record stores, internet cafes, art galleries and dozens of other surprising finds.

DRACO STORE   CLOTHING

Map p244 (☑2227-7393; Francisco Otaviano 55, Arpoador; ☺9am-8pm Mon-Sat, to 6pm Sun) This menswear store specializes in stylish beachwear, including well-made swim shorts. You'll also find jeans, button-downs and T-shirts (in the R$50 to R$90 range) – the best of which bear the names of Rio neighborhoods (Copacabana, Ipanema, Arpoador etc).

ZIMPY   CLOTHING

Map p244 (Santa Clara 50, Copacabana; ☺9am-8pm Mon-Fri, to 6pm Sat) Along boutique-lined Santa Clara, this Copacabana-born brand sells colorful, reasonably priced skirts, dresses and accessories – including eye-catching silver jewelry. Free-flowing and attractively cut, Zimpy garments are ideal for summer wear.

MUSICALE   MUSIC

Map p244 (☑2267-9607; Av NS de Copacabana 1103C, Copacabana; ☺10am-7pm Mon-Fri, to 4pm Sat) Musicale has a small but well-curated selection of used CDs (and a few new titles), most of which cost under R$35. Albums run the gamut between samba, MPB and regional sounds. There's also US and British rock and indie as well as world music such as French pop and *nueva cancion*. You can listen to used discs on one of several CD players scattered around the store.

MUNDO VERDE   FOOD

Map p244 (☑2135-4415; www.mundoverde. com.br; Av NS de Copacabana 1171, Copacabana;

☺9am-8pm Mon-Fri, to 4:30pm Sat) Brazil's largest health-food retailer, Mundo Verde sells organic products including snacks, such as *salgados* (bar snacks), jams made from Amazonian fruits, and other assorted goods. The sun-care products are usually cheaper here than in pharmacies, and probably better for your skin.

SPORTS & ACTIVITIES

SURF RIO   WATER SPORTS

Map p244 (www.surfrio.com.br; Posto 6, Copacabana Beach; per hr R$50-60; ☺7:30am-5pm) The latest sporting novelty on the beaches of Rio is stand-up paddleboarding, a sport that's been around since the 1960s but has only recently attracted a worldwide following. Near the southern end of Copacabana, Surf Rio is one of several places on the beach where you can hire gear.

If you've never tried stand-up paddling before, Surf Rio also offers classes (R$40 per person for a half-hour lesson) where you can learn the basics.

SPIRIT SURFBOARDS   WATER SPORTS

Map p244 (Galeria River, Francisco Otaviano 67, Arpoador; surfboard hire per 1/2 days R$40/50; ☺10am-6pm Mon-Sat) This surf shop rents out surfboards, but you'll need to put down a hefty deposit as security (R$450).

RIO SAMBA DANCER   DANCE

Map p244 (☑98202-9810; www.riosambadancer. com; Barata Ribeiro 261A, Copacabana; group/private classes R$70/150) English-speaking dance instructor Hélio Ricardo offers private and group dance classes in samba or *forró*, a popular music of the Northeast. To try out your new moves, sign up for a samba-class and night-tour combo: you'll take a one-hour crash course, then head out to Lapa for a night of dancing in a club (R$100 per person; cover charge not included).

YOGA BHUMI   YOGA

Map p244 (☑3201-1355; www.yogabhumi.com. br; Room 202, Francisco Sá 31, Copacabana) This recommended yoga studio offers Hatha, Vinyasa and Iyengar yoga, and offers a range of workshops, retreats and meditation courses on the side. Individual classes cost R$40, with discounts available for longer commitments.

Botafogo, Humaitá & Urca

Neighborhood Top Five

1 Gliding up to the top of **Pão de Açúcar** (p101) by cable car for the awe-inspiring view of Rio at your feet.

2 Learning about Brazil's many indigenous cultures at the interactive **Museu do Índio** (p102).

3 Walking between forest and sea on the peaceful **Pista Cláudio Coutinho** (p102).

4 Checking out works by some of Rio's most talented street artists at **GaleRio** (p102).

5 Basking on the sands of **Praia Vermelha** (p103), one of Rio's prettiest little beaches.

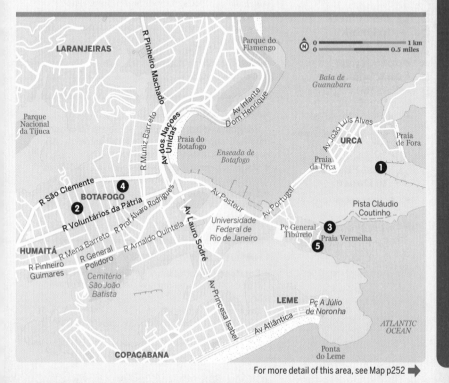

For more detail of this area, see Map p252 ➡

BOTAFOGO, HUMAITÁ & URCA

Lonely Planet's Top Tip

Although Urca is home to one of Rio's top attractions, few visitors venture into the neighborhood beyond Pão de Açúcar. Its quiet tree-lined streets (such as Rua Otávio Correia) make for some intriguing exploring, and there are picturesque views from the bayside roads (such as Av João Luís Alves).

Best Places to Eat

→ Lasai (p105)
→ Meza Bar (p103)
→ Oui Oui (p103)
→ Emporium Pax (p103)
→ Miam Miam (p103)

For reviews, see p115 ➡

Best Places to Drink

→ Comuna (p105)
→ Caverna (p105)
→ Bar Urca (p105)
→ Champanharia Ovelha Negra (p106)
→ Espírito do Chopp (p106)

For reviews, see p117 ➡

☆ Best Places to Dance

→ Cabaret Lounge (p106)
→ Bar Bukowski (p106)
→ Casa da Matriz (p106)

For reviews, see p117 ➡

Explore Botafogo, Humaitá & Urca

Traditional, middle-class Botafogo and neighboring Humaitá, may not have the beaches of their neighbors to the south, but they don't lack for much else, with intriguing museums, movie theaters, quaint bookshops, a shopping center, and festive, open-air bars on tree-lined backstreets. There are also a few nightclubs and a boulevard dotted with old mansions.

To the east, Urca is even more idyllic, with shaded, quiet streets. Its eclectic architecture includes art deco and modernist houses backed by manicured gardens. Along the seawall, which forms the northwestern perimeter of Pão de Açúcar, fisherfolk cast for dinner as couples lounge beneath palm trees, taking in views of Baía de Guanabara (Guanabara Bay) and Cristo Redentor (Christ the Redeemer). Tiny Praia Vermelha in the south marks the beginning of a pleasant walking trail and has one of Rio's finest beach views.

Botafogo is named after the Portuguese settler João Pereira de Souza Botafogo and grew in importance following the arrival of the Portuguese court in the late 1800s. Dona Carlota Joaquina, the wife of Dom João VI, had a country villa here, and she used to bathe in the Baía de Guanabara. With royalty established in the area, arriving aristocrats built many mansions, some of which still stand as schools, theaters and cultural centers.

In the 19th century, development was spurred by the construction of a tram that ran to the Jardim Botânico (botanical garden), linking the bay with Lagoa Rodrigo de Freitas. This artery still plays a vital role in Rio's traffic flow, though Botafogo's main streets are now extremely congested.

Local Life

→ **Hangouts** At Bar Urca (p106), locals sip beers and munch on appetizers along the seawall across the street, while taking in the pretty views.
→ **Markets** Browse the produce stands of Cobal do Humaitá (p106) by day and sample the bars by night.
→ **Shopping** Botafogo Praia Shopping (p107) has colorful shops, a cinema and upper-floor restaurants with great views.

Getting There & Away

→ **Botafogo buses** Ipanema, Leblon and Copacabana (161 and 573); Jardim Botânico and Gávea (170, 176 and 592).
→ **Urca buses** Centro (107); Ipanema, Leblon and Copacabana (511); Jardim Botânico and Gávea (512).
→ **Metro** Botafogo.

MARIA SWARD / GETTY IMAGES ©

TOP SIGHT
PÃO DE AÇÚCAR

One of Rio's dazzling icons, Pão de Açúcar (Sugarloaf Mountain) offers a vision of Rio at its most disarming. Following a steep ascent to the mountain, you'll be rewarded with superb views of Rio's gorgeous shoreline, and the city planted among the green peaks. From the summit, 395m above Rio and the Baía de Guanabara, it's quite clear why Rio is called the Cidade Maravilhosa (Marvelous City).

The most traditional way to reach the top is to board the two-stage cable car that departs from Urca every 20 minutes or so. The glass-and-steel cars are good fun in themselves, and ascend 215m to Morro da Urca. From here, you can see Baía de Guanabara and along the winding coastline; on the ocean side of the mountain is Praia Vermelha, in a small, calm bay. Morro da Urca has a restaurant, souvenir shops, a playground, outdoor theater and a helipad. In the summer, concerts are sometimes staged in the amphitheater.

The second cable car goes up to Pão de Açúcar. At the top, the city unfolds beneath you, with Corcovado mountain and Cristo Redentor off to the west, the twinkling lights of Niteroi across the bay to the east, and the long curve of Copacabana Beach to the south. If the breathtaking heights unsteady you, a cafe is on hand to serve caipirinhas and other drinks. There's also a restaurant, an ice-cream shop and the obligatory souvenir shop.

Those who'd rather take the long way to the top should sign up with one of the granite-hugging climbing tours offered by various outfits in Rio. Morro da Urca is much easier to climb, and you can do it on your own. The short but steep path takes about 30 minutes to the top. You'll find the unmarked trail along the Pista Cláudio Coutinho (p102).

For prime views of the Cidade Maravilhosa, go around sunset on a clear day.

DON'T MISS...

➡ Drinking caipirinhas while watching planes land beneath you

➡ Summer concerts up top

➡ The walking trail up Morro da Urca

PRACTICALITIES

➡ Map p252, G2

➡ ☏2546-8400

➡ www.bondinho.com.br

➡ Av Pasteur 520, Urca

➡ adult/child R$62/31

➡ ☉8am-7:50pm

◉ SIGHTS

◉ Botafogo & Humaitá

GALERIO   GALLERY

Map p252 (São Clemente 117; ⊙10am-6pm Mon-Fri) **FREE** Set in a grand 19th-century mansion on busy São Clemente, GaleRio is a showcase of cutting-edge urban street art. You'll find a changing array of paintings, installations, sculptures and repurposed objects (such as stop signs turned into panoramic backdrops or payphone booths transformed into furniture).

This is also the home of **EixoRio**, a city-sponsored institute that aims to create the largest open-air urban art gallery in the world. Some 130 different graffiti artists will create works along 40km of walls that border line 2 of Rio's metro through the Zona Norte (northern district).

MUSEU CASA DE RUI BARBOSA   MUSEUM

Map p252 (☑3289-4600; www.casaruibarbosa. gov.br; São Clemente 134; admission R$4, Sun free; ⊙9am-5:30pm Tue-Fri, 2-6pm Sat & Sun) The former mansion of famous Brazilian journalist and diplomat Rui Barbosa is now a museum housing his library and personal belongings. Barbosa played a pivotal role in shaping the country's socioeconomic development in the early 20th century.

MUSEU DO ÍNDIO   MUSEUM

Map p252 (☑3214-8700; www.museudoindio.org. br; Rua das Palmeiras 55; ⊙9am-5:30pm Tue-Fri, 1-5pm Sat & Sun) **FREE** Featuring multimedia exhibitions on Brazil's northern tribes, the small Museu do Índio provides an excellent introduction to the economic, religious and social life of Brazil's indigenous people. Next to native food and medicinal plants, the four life-size dwellings in the courtyard were actually built by four different tribes.

As a branch of Funai (the National Indian Foundation), the museum contains an excellent archive of more than 14,000 objects, 50,000 photographs and 200 sound recordings. Its indigenous ethnography library containing 16,000 volumes by local and foreign authors is open to the public during the week.

PRAIA DE BOTAFOGO   BEACH

Map p252 (Av dos Naçoes Unidas) Although the waters of the bay are too polluted for swimming, the beach overlooking the Enseada de Botafogo (Botafogo Inlet) makes a photogenic setting for a run or bike ride. Hopeful football stars play pick-up games along the shore, against the backdrop of sailboats bobbing on the water and Pão de Açúcar off in the background.

MIRANTE DO PASMADO   LOOKOUT

Map p252 (Bartolomeu Portela) Sweeping views of Enseada de Botafogo, Pão de Açúcar and Corcovado await visitors who make the journey up Pasmado. It's best reached in the early morning or late afternoon, when the light is at its best for capturing the postcard panorama. Visitors will also be able to see details of a favela from above. The overlook is best reached by taxi via Rua General Severiano.

MUSEU VILLA-LOBOS   MUSEUM

Map p252 (☑2266-3845; Sorocaba 200; ⊙10am-5pm Mon-Fri) **FREE** Housed in a century-old building, this modest museum is dedicated to the memory of Brazil's greatest classical composer and founder of the Brazilian Academy of Music, Heitor Villa-Lobos. In addition to scores, musical instruments – including the piano on which he composed – and personal items, the museum contains an extensive sound archive. Classical concerts are sometimes held in the adjoining courtyard.

◉ Urca

PÃO DE AÇÚCAR   MOUNTAIN

See p101.

PISTA CLÁUDIO COUTINHO   WALKING TRAIL

Map p252 (⊙6am-sunset) Everyone loves this paved 2km trail winding along the southern contour of Morro da Urca. It's a lush treed area, with the waves crashing on the rocks below. Look out for families of marmosets with their gray fur, striped tails and tiny faces. To get here, walk 100m north along the edge of Praia Vermelha (with your back to the cable-car station) and you'll see the entrance to the path straight ahead, just past the beach.

About 300m along the path, there's a small trail leading off to Morro da Urca. From there you'll have a fine view over the city that won't cost a thing (except plenty of sweat – the path up is steep!). Pão de Açúcar can also be climbed – but it's not recommended without an experienced guide and climbing gear.

PRAIA DA URCA
BEACH
Map p252 (Av João Luís Alves) This tiny beach is popular with neighborhood kids who gather here for pick-up football games when school is not in session (and sometimes when it is). A small restaurant, Garota da Urca (p105), lies near the beach.

PRAIA VERMELHA
BEACH
Map p252 (Praça General Tibúrcio) Beneath Morro da Urca, narrow Praia Vermelha has superb views of the rocky coastline from the shore. Its coarse sand gives the beach the name *vermelha* (red). Because the beach is protected by the headland, the water is usually calm.

EATING

The dining scene has exploded here recently, with some of Rio's most creative restaurants opening up on the tree-lined backstreets of Botafogo and Humaitá. A great street for browsing is Rua Nelson Mandela (right next to the Botafogo metro station), which is lined with casual, open-air eating and drinking spots. For higher-end dining, Rua Conde de Irajá, 12 blocks west in Humaitá, has excellent restaurants. Urca, largely residential, has only a few choices.

Botafogo & Humaitá

BOUA KITCHEN & BAR
BISTRO $
Map p252 (www.theboua.com.br; Nelson Mandela 102, Botafogo; burgers R$26-38) Behind the Botafogo metro station, this lively gastropub is one of more than a dozen eating and drinking spots along this lane. The microbrew selection is outstanding (with a rotating lineup of Belgian, German, US and Brazilian beers). You can sit outside and nosh on thick burgers, appetizers or steak and Gorgonzola risotto while watching the passing people parade.

MEZA BAR
TAPAS $$
Map p252 (☑3239-1951; www.mezabar.com.br; Capitão Salomão 69, Humaitá; tapas R$12-30; ☺6pm-1am) Humaitá's see-and-be-seen hot spot serves up delectable, Brazilian-slanted tapas to a sophisticated and trendy crowd. Creative cocktails and delightful staff round out the fun.

MIAM MIAM
CONTEMPORARY $$
Map p252 (☑2244-0125; www.miammiam.com. br; General Goés Monteiro 34, Botafogo; mains around R$60; ☺7pm-midnight Tue-Fri, 8pm-1am Sat) Exposed-brick walls and a mishmash of retro furnishings set the scene for dining in style at Botafogo's culinary darling. Chef Roberta Ciasca serves up her own brand of comfort food, which means smoked trout with roasted potatoes, pork with basmati rice and pineapple, eggplant lasagna with sheep's milk yogurt, and other unique dishes.

OUI OUI
FRENCH, BRAZILIAN $$
Map p252 (☑2527-3539; www.restauranteouioui. com.br; Conde de Irajá 85, Humaitá; small plates R$35-42; ☺noon-3pm & 7pm-midnight Mon-Fri, 8pm-1am Sat) On a tranquil street, elegantly set Oui Oui serves innovative tapas plates designed for sharing – carmelized ribs with pumpkin puree, duck risotto, haddock croquettes, and zesty quinoa salad with truffle oil are perennial favorites.

LIVRARIA PREFÁCIO
BRAZILIAN $$
Map p252 (☑2527-5699; Voluntários da Pátria 39, Botafogo; mains R$22-49; ☺10am-10pm Mon-Fri, 2-10pm Sat & Sun) This charming restaurant scores high on novelty: it's hidden in the back of a bookshop, with stone walls, low-lit lamps and bookshelves. Atmosphere aside, the food is quite good, with nicely presented pastas, sandwiches, salads and more creative fare such as Indian samosas.

LE DEPANNEUR
CAFE $$
Map p252 (Voluntários da Pátria 86, Botafogo; sandwiches R$22-32; ☺8am-10:30pm; ☎) This buzzing cafe and deli serves up juices, waffles, crepes, salads, antipasti plates and specialty sandwiches. On weekends the large plant-trimmed front patio fills with brunching locals and makes a good people-watching perch. There's also a self-serve bakery with croissants and other goodies, and plenty of other provisions for picnickers.

EMPORIUM PAX
BRAZILIAN $$
Map p252 (☑3171-9713; www.emporiumpax.com. br; Botafogo Praia Shopping, 7th fl, Praia de Botafogo 400, Botafogo; lunch buffet R$44-65; ☺noon-midnight) One of many eateries at Botafogo Praia Shopping, Emporium Pax is a more polished affair than the adjoining food court and offers spectacular views of Pão de Açúcar and Baía de Guanabara. The big draw is the extensive lunch buffet, though

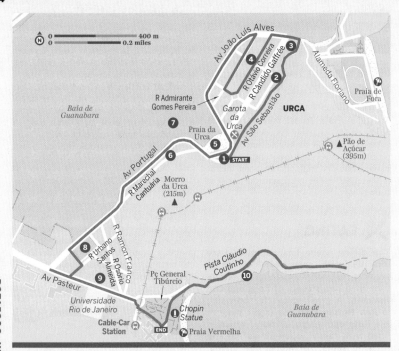

🏃 Neighborhood Walk
Urca, the Village by the Sea

START RUA MARECHAL CANTUÁRIA
END PRAIA VERMELHA
LENGTH 5KM, THREE HOURS

One of Rio's most charming neighborhoods is also one of its least explored. Our walk begins where Rua Marechal Cantuária meets Av São Sebastião. On your left, you'll see the former **1 Cassino da Urca**, a once-popular gambling and nightspot, where Carmen Miranda and Josephine Baker both performed.

Veer to the right along Av São Sebastião, following the road uphill. You'll pass **2 Carmen Miranda's former residence** at No 131 and soon reach the wall that separates the military fort from the neighborhood.

At the end of the street, take the steps down to Av João Luís Alves. Stop for a cold drink at **3 Bar Urca** (p106), where you can admire the views.

Explore the tree-lined backstreets by heading down **4 Rua Otávio Correira**
and looping back along Rua Admirante Gomes Pereira.

Cut back to Av João Luís Alves and follow it to **5 Praia da Urca** (p103), a tiny beach with more fine views of the bay.

Stay on the bay side as the road forks. Peek inside **6 Igreja de Nossa Senhora do Brasil** (the chapel is on the ground floor; the church upstairs), noting the small Brazilian flag on the Madonna's cloak.

Facing the church is the floating **7 statue of São Pedro no Mar**. On June 29, St Peter's feast day, the fisherfolk process across the bay, past the statue, scattering flowers across the water.

Go along what is now Av Portugal to a bridge. On the left is **8 Quadrado da Urca**, a harbor.

Follow **9 Av Pasteur** southeast past majestic buildings such as Companhia de Pesquisa de Recursos Minerais (Av Pasteur 404), guarded by a lion and a winged creature.

Follow **10 Pista Cláudio Coutinho** (p102) out and back to Praia Vermelha.

for something lighter you can order salads, sandwiches and quiches, plus tasty desserts.

★LASAI   FUSION $$$

Map p252 (✆3449-1834; www.lasai.com.br; Conde de Irajá 191, Humaitá; prix fixe R$185-245; ⏱7:30-10:30pm Tue-Fri, 1pm-10:30pm Sat) Inside an elegant early 20th-century house in Humaitá, Lasai has dazzled critics and foodies for its deliciously inventive cuisine. The *carioca* chef Rafa Costa e Silva earned his chops in some of the world's best dining rooms (including Mugaritz in Spain), and he puts his skills to brilliant use here. Reservations essential.

There's no set menu: dishes are based on whatever is fresh for the day (and some ingredients are grown in the chef's own garden).

✗ Urca

JULIUS BRASSERIE   EUROPEAN $$

Map p252 (✆3518-7117; Av Portugal 986; mains R$45-75; ⏱noon-midnight Tue-Sun) This elegant Dutch-Brazilian-run restaurant in Urca turns out a creative mix of grilled meats, seafood, pastas and risottos in a quiet location on the edge of Praia da Urca. It makes a great lunch or dinner spot, followed by a stroll around the neighborhood.

GAROTA DA URCA   BRAZILIAN $$

Map p252 (✆2541-8585; João Luís Alves 56; mains R$35-68; ⏱noon-1am Sun-Thu, to 2:30am Fri & Sat) Overlooking the small Praia da Urca, this neighborhood restaurant serves good-value weekday lunch specials, and you can enjoy views over the bay from the open-air veranda. By night, a more garrulous crowd converges for steak and *chope* (draft beer).

BAR URCA   BRAZILIAN $$$

Map p252 (✆2295-8744; Cândido Gaffrée 205; mains R$52-136; ⏱noon-3pm & 7-11pm) Near the end of Urca, you'll find an elegantly set dining room with big windows letting in the breeze (not to mention lovely views over the bay). The seafood is first-rate, with scrumptious *caldeirada* (seafood stew), *moqueca* and grilled octopus on the menu.

Bar Urca is better known, however, for its popular snack stand on the street level, where you can order appetizers and drinks, and assemble a satisfying feast to enjoy on the seawall across the street.

⬤ DRINKING & ⬤ NIGHTLIFE

Botafogo is the place to go for lively, authentic *carioca* bars, with fun, mixed crowds and little of the pretense you might encounter in bars further south. Rua Visconde de Caravelas is a good place to browse the pub scene.

⬤ Botafogo & Humaitá

COMUNA   BAR

Map p252 (✆3029-0789; www.comuna.cc; Sorocaba 585, Botafogo; ⏱6pm-2am Tue-Sun) This creative space is equal parts bar, art gallery and independent bookseller (and indie publishing house). There's always something afoot in the delightfully off-the-beaten-path locale, with workshops, music sessions, readings, exhibitions and fashion shows. It's also just a great spot for a bite (try one of the award-winning burgers) and a local microbrew.

CAVERNA   BAR

Map p252 (✆3507-5600; www.espacocaverna. com; Assis Bueno 26, Botafogo; ⏱6pm-1am Mon-Fri, 7pm-2am Sat) Yet another reason why Botafogo may be surpassing Ipanema in the cool factor these days, this always buzzing rock-and-roll-loving bar and bistro serves up microbrews and juicy burgers amid a fun and festive atmosphere (though the music rocks a little loud some nights).

CRAZY CATS   BAR

Map p252 (www.facebook.com/crazycatsbistro; Sorocaba 19, Botafogo; ⏱7pm-1am Wed & Thu, 8pm-2am Fri & Sat, 5-11pm Sun) Vintage lovers shouldn't miss this imaginatively configured space in Botafogo. The owners must have raided every antique shop in Rio to assemble this curious collection, named after their four *gatos* (cats). Great sparkling cocktails, tasty snacks (such as ceviche) and a classic rock-leaning soundtrack (plus the odd live band) all add to the appeal.

CABARET LOUNGE   LOUNGE

Map p252 (✆2226-4126; www.cabaretlounge. com.br; Voluntários da Pátria 449, Humaitá; cover R$15-40; ⏱7pm-3am Tue-Thu, 9pm-5am Fri & Sat) The cozy Cabaret Lounge channels the look of an old-fashioned Parisian dance hall, with red walls, glittering chandeliers, velvet couches and armchairs, and gilt frames (containing video screens rather than sepia prints). Champagne and cocktails are the drinks of choice. As the evening progresses, it becomes more of a dance spot, with DJs spinning overhead.

CALAVERA BAR

Map p252 (☎3734-5461; Capitão Salomão 14, Humaitá; ☺6pm-midnight Mon-Thu, to 2am Fri & Sat) Opened in 2015, Calavera is the newest gastropub to open in Humaitá. You'll find creative snacks, craft beer and a hipster-leaning crowd that raise glasses inside the small but artfully designed space.

CHAMPANHARIA OVELHA NEGRA BAR

Map p252 (☎2226-1064; www.champanharia ovelhanegra.com.br; Bambina 120, Botafogo; ☺5:30-11:30pm Mon-Fri) One of Rio's best happy-hour scenes, Ovelha Negra draws a mostly local crowd who come for the lively conversation and the 40 different varieties of champagne and prosecco – the specialties of the house.

ESPÍRITO DO CHOPP BAR

Map p252 (☎2266-5599; Cobal do Humaitá, Voluntários da Pátria 446, Humaitá; ☺11am-midnight Sun-Thu, to 2am Fri & Sat) One of many open-air venues in the Cobal, Espírito do Chopp fills up its plastic tables most nights with a festive, low-key crowd. The beer flows in abundance and there's always music nearby – either here or at one of the neighboring bars.

O PLEBEU BAR

Map p252 (☎2286-0699; Capitão Salomão 50; ☺noon-2am Mon-Sat, to 7pm Sun) In the liveliest stretch of Botafogo, O Plebeu is a welcoming, open-sided, two-story bar with tables spilling onto the sidewalk and a 2nd-floor balcony. Neighborhood regulars pack this place, drawn by ice-cold bottled beer, codfish balls and an unpretentious crowd befitting the name (The Commoner).

COBAL DO HUMAITÁ BAR

Map p252 (Voluntários da Pátria 446, Humaitá; ☺8am-2am) A large food market in Humaitá, the Cobal transforms into a festive nightspot when the sun goes down, complete with open-air eating and drinking.

BAR BUKOWSKI CLUB

Map p252 (☎2244-7303; Álvaro Ramos 270, Botafogo; admission R$50; ☺9pm-6am Fri & Sat) Paying homage to the bohemian American

writer, this club has a downstairs dance floor and bar, and an upstairs level for live bands playing rock, pop and blues. It's a great scene, and usually attracts a fun crowd. There's also a pool table, darts and you can have a go at one of the water pipes.

CASA DA MATRIZ CLUB

Map p252 (☎2266-1014; www.facebook.com/casadamatriz; Henrique de Novaes 107, Botafogo; admission R$20-40; ☺11pm-5am Wed-Sat) Artwork lines this space in Botafogo. With numerous rooms to explore (lounge, screening room, dance floors), this old mansion embodies the creative side of the *carioca* (resident of Rio) spirit. It usually attracts a student crowd. Check the Facebook page for party listings.

🍷 Urca

BAR URCA BAR

Map p252 (☎2295-8744; Cândido Gaffrée 205; ☺8am-11pm) This much-loved neighborhood bar and restaurant has a marvelous setting near Urca's bayside waterfront. At night, young and old crowd along the seaside wall to enjoy cold drinks, appetizers and fine views.

GAROTA DA URCA BAR

Map p252 (☎2541-8585; João Luís Alves 56; ☺noon-1am Sun-Thu, to 2:30am Fri & Sat) A neighborhood crowd gathers over *chope* and *salgados* (snacks) in the evening at this low-key spot.

☆ ENTERTAINMENT

TERRA BRASILIS LIVE MUSIC

Map p252 (☎2275-4651; Praça General Tibúrcio, Urca; ☺noon-midnight Mon-Fri, 1-5pm Sat & Sun) Just beside Praia Vermelha, Terra Brasilis has gorgeous views of Pão de Açúcar looming overhead. Jazzy Música Popular Brasileira (MPB) bands play from about 8pm on weeknights (and at 1pm on weekends), making for a delightful open-air setting. The food (mains R$40 to R$76) is less spectacular; it's best to stick to drinks and appetizers. It's located in the building marked Circulo Militar da Praia Vermelha.

ESTAÇÃO NET RIO CINEMA

Map p252 (☎2226-1986; Voluntários da Pátria 35, Botafogo) This two-screen cinema in Botafogo shows a range of films – Brazilian, foreign, independent and the occasional Hollywood film. It has a lovely cafe inside, as well as a shop selling used records and books with a number of works focusing on film arts.

ESTAÇÃO NET BOTAFOGO
CINEMA

Map p252 (☑2226-1988; Voluntários da Pátria 88, Botafogo) One block from Estação Net Rio, this small three-screen theater shows a mix of local and foreign films. The cafe in front is a good place to grab a quick *cafézinho* (small black coffee) before the movie.

SHOPPING

Shopping in Botafogo usually means heading to the high-rise mall overlooking the bay. There are, however, other options, such as the Museu do Índio's small handicrafts shop (with all pieces made by Brazilian tribes) as well as a cozy bookshop near the cinemas with a backroom cafe. Urca, quiet old soul that she is, has nothing in the way of shopping.

BARATOS DE RIBEIRO
MUSIC, BOOKS

Map p252 (Paulino Fernandes 15, Botafogo; ⊙11am-8pm Mon-Sat) Vinyl fans and bookworms flock to this cabinet of musical and literary curiosity with its extensive collection of unusual albums combined with secondhand art books, novels and other intrigue – including strange titles in English (spotted when last we passed through: the cowboy novel *Wyatt Earp* and an autobiography of Katharine Hepburn).

LIVRARIA DA TRAVESSA
BOOKS

Map p252 (Voluntários da Pátria 97, Botafogo; ⊙10am-10pm) Part of Rio's best-loved bookstore chain, this branch has an appealing cafe, a music section (CDs, vinyl reprints) and a small but decent foreign-language section (English, French, Spanish), it's a fine place to while away a rainy day.

COMPARSARIA
SHOES, ACCESSORIES

Map p252 (Voluntários da Pátria 45; ⊙9am-8pm Mon-Fri, 10am-7pm Sat, 3-8pm Sun) This boutique stocks handsomely crafted shoes and sandals, leather bags and satchels, hats, wallets and other accessories. Production runs are limited and styles veer between timeless, avant-garde and utterly unwearable.

ÍNDIO E ARTE
HANDICRAFTS

Map p252 (☑3214-8719; Museu do Índio, Rua das Palmeiras 55, Botafogo; ⊙9am-5:30pm Mon-Fri, 1-5pm Sat & Sun) Inside the grounds of the Museu do Índio, this shop sells a variety of indigenous handicrafts, including masks, musical instruments, toys, pots, baskets and weapons. Regional artists, mostly from northern tribes, create objects crafted from native materials such as straw, clay, wood and feathers.

BOTAFOGO PRAIA SHOPPING
SHOPPING CENTER

Map p252 (☑3171-9872; Praia de Botafogo 400, Botafogo; ⊙10am-10pm Mon-Sat, 2-9pm Sun; 🖳) Botafogo's large shopping center has dozens of stores, featuring Brazilian and international designers to suit every style – and clothe every part of the body. The 3rd floor's the best for top designers: check out stores such as Maria Filó, Reserva and Hope. The mall also has a cinema and several top-floor restaurants, such as Emporium Pax (p103), with great panoramic views.

RIO SUL SHOPPING
SHOPPING CENTER

Map p252 (☑2545-7200; www.riosul.com.br; Lauro Müller 116, Botafogo; ⊙10am-10pm Mon-Sat, 3-10pm Sun) The biggest shopping center you can reach without heading to Barra da Tijuca, Rio Sul has more than 400 shops, featuring both the prominent and the obscure, plus cinemas and restaurants.

The mall offers free transport to/from its Rio Sul kiosk on Copacabana Beach (near Siqueira Campos) and from other points in Ipanema and Leblon to the shopping center. Check the website for departure times.

SPORTS & ACTIVITIES

You can hire a stand-up paddleboard (around R$30 per 30 minutes) or a two-person kayak (around R$15 per person per 30 minutes) from one of the informal rental outfits at Praia Vermelha.

CASA DE DANÇA CARLINHOS DE JESUS
DANCE

Map p252 (☑2541-6186; www.carlinhosdejesus.com.br; Álvaro Ramos 11, Botafogo) At this respected dance academy in Botafogo, Carlinhos and his instructors offer evening classes in samba, *forró*, salsa and tango. On some Friday nights, open dance parties for students and guests are held. One of Botafogo's colorful *bloco* parties, Dois Pra Lá, Dois Pra Cá, begins from here during Carnaval.

SAMBAPHOTO / LEONARDO PAPINI / GETTY IMAGES©

1. Rock climbing, Pão de Açúcar (p101) **2.** Hiking, Corcovado (p112)
3. Hang gliding over Rio **4.** Surfer, Praia da Barra da Tijuca (p157)

EDUARDO AZEREDO FOTOGRAFIAS / GETTY IMAGES ©

Outdoor Adventures

Blessed with tropical rainforest, towering peaks and sparkling seaside, the Cidade Maravilhosa (Marvelous City) offers some captivating ways to spend a sun-drenched afternoon. You can go hang gliding, surfing, biking, hiking, running and rock climbing amid spectacular scenery without leaving the city limits.

Hang Gliding

Although it will cost you a fair bit, hang gliding off Pedra Bonita (p50) is an unforgettable experience: just the pilot and you, soaring high over treetops and landing near the sea.

Rock Climbing

Sure, you can take the cable car to the top of Pão de Açúcar (Sugarloaf Mountain), but for an adrenaline rush and mesmerizing scenery, sign up for a rock-climbing trip (p49) to the top. The view will be all the sweeter.

Surfing

Superb waves (p51) are all around Rio. For a quick fix, you can join the locals off Arpoador. More serious surfers should get a ride on the surf bus and head west to Macumba or Prainha.

Hiking

Rio's tropical rainforest makes a fine setting for a hike (p49). Head to Floresta da Tijuca for hikes through lush forest, followed by a dip in a waterfall.

Cycling

The beachside bike path is great anytime for cyclists, and you can plot a route from Leblon up through Flamengo, riding waterside for most of the journey. You can also take a scenic spin around Lagoa.

Flamengo & Around

FLAMENGO | COSME VELHO | CATETE | GLÓRIA | LARANJEIRAS

Neighborhood Top Five

1 Taking the steep cog train up Corcovado for a panoramic view beneath Rio's open-armed **Cristo Redentor** (p112).

2 Exploring Rio's past days of demagogues and political intrigue in the **Museu da República** (p114).

3 Admiring the colorful works of talented but little-known artists at the **Museu Internacional de Arte Naïf do Brasil** (p114).

4 Making the short but steep climb up to the 18th-century **Igreja de Nossa Senhora da Glória do Outeiro** (p115).

5 Taking a bike ride through the expansive **Parque do Flamengo** (p114).

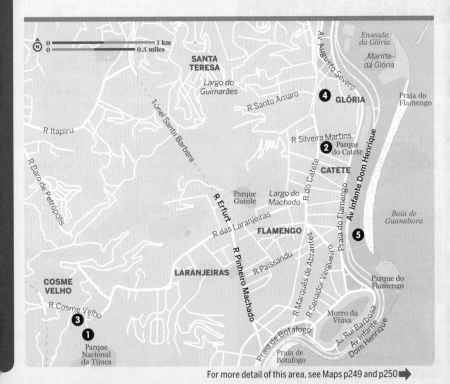

For more detail of this area, see Maps p249 and p250 ➡

Explore Flamengo & Around

Running east from the bay out to Corcovado, the residential neighborhoods of Flamengo, Laranjeiras, Catete, Glória and Cosme Velho have much history hidden in their old streets. The Parque do Flamengo dominates the region. Also known as the *aterro* (landfill), this beach-fronting green space is one of the world's largest urban parks, and includes a nationally recognized art museum, biking and running trails, sports fields and thousands of trees and flowering plants. Inland from the park, the shaded streets of Flamengo are sprinkled with a few cafes, historic *botecos* (small, open-air bars) and gossip-filled juice bars.

West of Flamengo, Laranjeiras is a tightly woven community with a small-town feel. Charming plazas such as the Praça São Salvador are great spots for taking in the neighborhood. Cosme Velho lies beyond Laranjeiras and is the key access point for those heading up to the statue of Cristo Redentor (Christ the Redeemer) by cog train.

The aging buildings of bustling Catete and Glória have seen better days. These twin districts flourished in the mid-19th century when their locations on the city outskirts made them desirable places to live. Nobles and merchants built homes in this district, including the Barão de Novo Friburgo, who built the stately Palácio do Catete. By the end of the century, however, the wealthy began moving further out as the inner city expanded.

Local Life

→ **Outdoors** Parque do Flamengo (p114) draws locals, especially on Sundays, when the main road through the park closes to traffic. Parque Guinle (p115) and Parque do Catete (p115) are peaceful escapes from the bustling city.

→ **Folk art** The Museu de Folclore Edison Carneiro (p115) has beautiful pieces from around Brazil. One-of-a-kind works of art make fine gifts at Pé de Boi (p118).

→ **Hangouts** Centro Cultural Oi Futuro (p114) hosts cutting-edge exhibits, and stages plays and concerts.

Getting There & Away

→ **Flamengo buses** Leblon, Ipanema and Copacabana (571 and 573).

→ **Express bus** 580 from Largo do Machado metro station.

→ **Laranjeiras and Cosme Velho buses** Leblon (570 and 583), Ipanema and Copacabana (569 and 583).

→ **Metro** Flamengo, Largo do Machado, Catete and Glória.

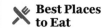

Best Places to Eat

→ Ferro e Farinha (p116)
→ Prana Vegetariano (p116)
→ Tacacá do Norte (p115)
→ Sírio Libaneza (p116)
→ Luigi's (p116)

For reviews, see p115 ➡

Best Places to Drink

→ Devassa (p117)
→ Bar do Zé (p117)
→ Adega Portugália (p117)
→ Belmonte (p117)
→ Herr Brauer (p117)

For reviews, see p117 ➡

Best Live Music

→ Severyna de Laranjeiras (p118)
→ Cariocando (p116)

For reviews, see p118 ➡

FLAMENGO & AROUND

TOP SIGHT
CRISTO REDENTOR

One of Rio's most identifiable landmarks, the magnificent 38m-high Cristo Redentor (Christ the Redeemer) looms large atop the granite mountain of Corcovado. From here, the statue has stunning views over Rio, which probably explains the contented expression on his face. There are various ways to reach the statue, but the traditional way is via a steep cog train, which ascends through tropical forest and adds a touch of excitement to the experience.

The Views

Corcovado, which means 'hunchback,' rises straight up from the city to a height of 710m, and at night the brightly lit statue is visible from nearly every part of the city. When you reach the top, you'll notice the Redeemer's gaze directed at Pão de Açúcar (Sugarloaf Mountain), with his left arm pointing toward the Zona Norte; Maracanã football stadium crowds the foreground. You can also see the international airport on Ilha do Governador just beyond and the Serra dos Órgãos mountain range in the far distance. Beneath Christ's right arm you can see Lagoa Rodrigo de Freitas, Hipódromo de Gávea, Jardim Botânico, and over to Ipanema and Leblon.

Getting to the Statue

Corcovado lies within the Floresta da Tijuca. The most popular way up is to take the red narrow-gauge train that departs every 30 minutes from the cog station. It takes approximately 20 minutes to reach the top. To reach the cog station, take any 'Cosme Velho' bus; from Copacabana, Ipanema or Leblon bus 583 will get you there.

DON'T MISS...

→ The hike up Corcovado from Parque Lage
→ The splendid views along the way (sit on the right side of the train for the best scenery)
→ Other nearby sites in Cosme Velho

PRACTICALITIES

→ Map p250, A4
→ ☎2558-1329
→ www.corcovado.com.br
→ cog station: Cosme Velho 513
→ adult/child R$62/40
→ ◷8am-7pm

There's also a road going up to the base of the monument. A private car or taxi will take you only as far as Paineiras parking lot, from which you must transfer to an authorized van to continue the 2km to the top (at a cost of R$35 per person). You can also travel by van from Corcovado train station. Vans also depart from Copacabana in front of Praça do Lido from 8am to 4pm (adult/child R$62/40) and Largo do Machado from 8am to 5pm (adult/child R$62/40).

The most challenging way to reach the statue is on foot. You'll need a moderate level of fitness and plenty of water. It's a 2½-hour walk, with a few tough sections. The trail starts at Parque Lage near Jardim Botânico and goes through rainforest to the heights of Corcovado. At the end of the trail you'll need to pay the admission (R$35), which includes the van ride a further 1km to the site.

Historical Background

Named one of the world's Seven New Wonders in 2007, Cristo Redentor is Brazil's largest and most recognized monument. The Redeemer, which opened in 1931, is considered to be the world's largest art deco statue. It's not a gift from the French, as is popularly believed. However, chief sculptor Paul Landowski was of French-Polish origin and carried out much of the construction in France. He collaborated with the Rio architect-engineer Heitor Silva Costa (1873–1947). Many organizations helped make the statue a reality, including several individuals who went door-to-door asking for contributions.

The idea of the statue originated in 1921 when a group called Círculo Carioca held a competition for a religious monument to commemorate Brazil's upcoming 100 years of independence. Heitor's winning project, which took 10 years to build, was considered particularly ambitious at the time – naysayers doubted whether it could be accomplished at all. Heitor's original idea depicted Christ as a vertical form with a long cross held against his side but the committee wanted something recognizable from a great distance, so the crosslike outstretched arms were chosen instead. Today it's one of Brazil's most frequented attractions, welcoming more than one million visitors a year.

When to Go

Or rather...when *not* to go: avoid going on weekends when the crowds are thickest. Obviously, keep an eye on the sky and don't bother going on cloudy or overcast days. Your best bet for beating the crowds is to go first thing in the morning.

CRISTO ON FILM

The benign savior has played a supporting role in a few Hollywood films. It has appeared in *Now, Voyager* (1942) starring Bette Davis, and in Alfred Hitchcock's *Notorious* (1946), with Cary Grant and Ingrid Bergman. More recently the disaster film *2012*, which depicted the end of the world in vivid, unadulterated glory, showed Cristo crumbling as a giant tidal wave destroys the city of Rio. As an aside, the archdiocese of Brazil didn't take kindly to the depiction and sued Columbia Pictures for copyright infringement (for using the image without permission).

If you visit the statue by cog train you can also visit a couple of nearby sites that make a good add-on to the day's exploring. A short stroll west of the cog-train station is the Museu Internacional de Arte Naïf do Brasil (p114), which has a unique collection of works from around the world (and discounted admission if you show your Corcovado ticket). A bit further along is the Largo do Boticário (p114), a curious slice of Rio that seems straight out of the 1800s.

◉ SIGHTS

◉ Flamengo

PARQUE DO FLAMENGO
PARK

Map p250 Officially called Parque Brigadeiro Eduardo Gomes, Parque do Flamengo was the result of a landfill project that leveled the São Antônio hill in 1965. It now spreads all the way from downtown Rio through Glória, Catete and Flamengo, and around to Botafogo. The 1.2 sq km of land reclaimed from the sea now stages every manner of *carioca* (resident of Rio) outdoor activity.

Cyclists and rollerbladers glide along the myriad paths, while the park's many football fields and sports courts are framed against the sea. On Sundays and holidays, the avenues through the park are closed to vehicle traffic from 7am to 6pm.

Designed by famous Brazilian landscaper Burle Marx (who also landscaped Brasília), the park features some 170,000 trees of 300 different species. There are two indoor attractions in the park: the **Museu de Arte Moderna** and the **Monumento Nacional aos Mortos da II Guerra Mundial**.

CENTRO CULTURAL OI FUTURO
ARTS CENTER

Map p250 (✆3131-3060; www.oifuturo.org.br; Dois de Dezembro 63; ⊘11am-8pm Tue-Sun) **FREE** One of Rio's most visually exciting additions is this futuristic space on the edge of Flamengo. Within 2000 sq meters of exhibition area spread across six floors the center features temporary multimedia installations that run the gamut from architecture and urban design to pop art, photojournalism and eye-catching video art.

There's also a permanent exhibition on the history of telecommunications in Brazil. The top floor houses an auditorium, where visitors can attend concerts and plays, or catch a documentary.

◉ Cosme Velho

CRISTO REDENTOR
MONUMENT

See p112.

MUSEU INTERNACIONAL DE ARTE NAÏF DO BRASIL
MUSEUM

Map p250 (✆2205-8612; www.museunaif.com; Cosme Velho 561; adult/child R$12/6; ⊘10am-6pm Tue-Fri, to 5pm Sat & Sun; ☐180, 184, 583, 584) A short walk west from the Corcovado cog-train station, this small museum has a fascinating collection of colorful paintings made by artists working well outside of the establishment. Also known as primitivist, *arte naïf* paintings often deal with marginalized peoples – Roma, sharecroppers, ghetto dwellers – and although small, the collection has pieces from 100 countries, giving a truly global reach to the exhibition.

Highlights here include a massive, much-reproduced painting by Lia Mittarakis, which depicts a vibrant Rio with Cristo Redentor as the focal point. Circling the room above it, *Brasil, 5 Séculos* (Brazil, 5 Centuries) is one long canvas showing key points in Brazil's history from 1500 to the 1960s. Visitors receive a 50% discount by showing a ticket stub from the Corcovado cog train.

LARGO DO BOTICÁRIO
HISTORIC SITE

Map p250 (Cosme Velho 822) The brightly painted but sadly dilapidated houses on this picturesque plaza date from the early 19th century. Largo do Boticário was named in honor of the Portuguese gentleman – Joaquim Luiz da Silva Souto – who once ran a *boticário* (apothecary) utilized by the royal family. The sound of a brook coming from the nearby forest adds to the plaza's charm. Occasional art and cultural events are hosted here.

◉ Catete

MUSEU DA REPÚBLICA
MUSEUM

Map p249 (✆2127-0324; museudarepublica. museus.gov.br; Rua do Catete 153; admission R$6, Wed & Sun free; ⊘10am-5pm Tue-Fri, 2-6pm Sat & Sun) The Museu da República, located in the **Palácio do Catete**, has been wonderfully restored. Built between 1858 and 1866 and easily distinguished by the bronze condors on its eaves, the palace was home to the president of Brazil from 1896 until 1954, when President Getúlio Vargas committed suicide here. The museum has a good collection of art and artifacts from the Republican period, and also houses a good restaurant for lunch, an art-house cinema and a bookstore.

Vargas made powerful enemies in the armed forces and the political right wing, and was attacked in the press as a communist for his attempts to raise the minimum wage and increase taxes on the middle and upper classes. Tensions reached a critical level when one of Vargas' bodyguards fired shots at a journalist. Although the journalist was unharmed, an air-force officer guarding him was killed, giving the armed forces the pretext they needed to demand the resignation of Vargas. In response, Vargas committed suicide, and his emotional suicide note read: 'I choose this means to be with you [the Brazilian people] always...I gave you my life; now I offer my death.' The 3rd-floor bedroom in which the suicide occurred is eerily preserved.

PARQUE GUINLE PARK

Map p249 (Paulo Cesar de Andrade 407) This handsomely landscaped park is a pleasant refuge from busy Rua das Laranjeiras outside its sphinx-guarded gates. It has a small wooded area, a tiny lake with ducks and there are always a few *cariocas* lounging on the grass.

Designed by French landscape architect Gochet (with later flourishes by Roberto Burle Marx), the park is also home to the dramatic **Palácio das Laranjeiras**, the state governor's residence (currently closed to visitors). The palace overlooks the west side of the park and is partially hidden by the thicket of trees.

MUSEU DE FOLCLORE
EDISON CARNEIRO MUSEUM

Map p249 (☑3826-4434; www.cnfcp.gov.br; Rua do Catete 179; ☺11am-6pm Tue-Fri, 3-6pm Sat & Sun) FREE Created in 1968, this museum is an excellent introduction to Brazilian folk art, particularly that from the northeast. Its permanent collection comprises 1400 pieces, and includes Candomblé costumes, ceramic figurines and religious costumes used in festivals. The museum also features a folklore library and a small shop that sells handicrafts, books and folk music. The museum is located next door to the Palácio do Catete.

PARQUE DO CATETE PARK

Map p249 (Rua do Catete) The small landscaped park on the grounds of the Palácio do Catete provides a quiet refuge from the city. Its pond and shade-covered walks are popular with neighborhood strollers and children. Special performances in the park include concerts and plays.

◉ Glória

IGREJA DE NOSSA SENHORA
DA GLÓRIA DO OUTEIRO CHURCH

Map p249 (☑2557-4600; www.outeirodagloria. org.br; Praça NS da Glória 135; ☺9am-noon & 1-4pm Mon-Fri, 9am-noon Sat & Sun) This tiny church atop Ladeira da Glória commands lovely views out over Parque do Flamengo and the bay. Considered one of the finest examples of religious colonial architecture in Brazil, the church dates from 1739 and became the favorite of the royal family upon their arrival in 1808.

Some of the more fascinating features of the church are its octagonal design, its single tower (through which visitors enter), the elaborately carved altar (attributed to the Brazilian sculptor Mestre Valentim) and its elegant 18th-century tiles.

✖ EATING

Flamengo has a mix of longtime local favorites and stylish newcomers. Rua Marquês de Abrantes is one of the best streets on which to see old and new vying for attention. Laranjeiras doesn't have much of a restaurant scene, but the neighborhood has several charming options for those wanting to get off the beaten path. Catete and Glória are dotted with inexpensive juice bars and lunch counters, making them good areas for those eating on a dime. Most places are along Rua do Catete, with a couple of standouts hidden along the backstreets.

✖ Flamengo

TACACÁ DO NORTE AMAZONIAN $

Map p250 (☑2205-7545; Barão do Flamengo 35; tacacá R$22, juices R$8-17; ☺9am-11pm Mon-Sat) In the Amazonian state of Pará, people order their *tacacá* late in the afternoon from their favorite street vendor. In Rio, you don't have to wait until the sun is setting. The fragrant soup of manioc paste, lip-numbing jambu leaves (a Brazilian herb), and fresh and dried shrimp isn't for everyone. But then again, neither is the Amazon.

This simple lunch counter also serves savory bowls of *açaí*, which is how folks in the Amazon eat it; it's quite different from the sweet juice versions served everywhere else in Rio.

SÍRIO LIBANEZA MIDDLE EASTERN $

Map p250 (www.rotisseriasl.com.br; Largo do Machado 29, Loja 16-19; snacks R$8-24; ☺8am-11pm Mon-Sat; 🔊) Always packed, this bustling place serves up tasty and cheap Syrian-Lebanese cuisine and great juices. Try the hearty *kibe de forno* (oven-baked ground-beef dish with spices), a hummus platter or *kafta* (spiced meat patty), followed by baklava and other sweets. It's inside the Galleria Condor on Largo do Machado.

RESTAURANTE KIOTO JAPANESE $$

Map p250 (☎2225-5705; 3rd fl, Ministerio Tavares Lira 105; all-you-can-eat lunch/dinner R$55/70; ☺noon-midnight) Hidden on a street behind Largo do Machado, this simple, well-concealed restaurant (it's above a pool hall) is worth seeking out when you're craving a sushi feast that won't break the bank. There's an enormous variety of rolls available at the buffet, and you can take pride in dining at a restaurant known to only a handful of *cariocas*.

INTIHUASI PERUVIAN $$

Map p250 (☎2225-7653; Barão do Flamengo 35D; mains R$60-80; ☺noon-3pm & 7-11pm Tue-Sat, 12:30-5pm Sun) Colorfully decorated with Andean tapestries and artwork, this tiny Peruvian restaurant serves mouthwatering ceviches, *papas rellenas* (meat-filled potatoes), seafood soups and other classic dishes from the Andes. For a break from caipirinhas, try a pisco sour or a nonalcoholic *chicha morada* (a sweet concoction made from purple corn).

NANQUIM BUFFET $$

Map p250 (☎2556-5119; www.restaurante nanquim.com.br; Rua do Pinheiro 10; per kg R$87; ☺noon-3:30pm) Hidden inside the Instituto dos Arquitetos on a quiet street, this inviting restaurant has a small but excellent self-service lunchtime buffet. Pastas, seafood, risotto, quiches, vegetarian dishes and salads are among the options. The 19th-century building is a mix of rustic and modern, with designs and sketches by Oscar Niemeyer adorning the walls.

Another branch in Jardim Botânico offers the same mix of contemporary design and good food.

✖ Laranjeiras & Cosme Velho

PRANA VEGETARIANO VEGETARIAN $

Map p250 (Ererê 11, Cosme Velho; mains R$30; ☺noon-7pm Mon-Fri, to 3pm Sat; 🍴) A short stroll from the cog train up Corcovado, this very friendly vegetarian restaurant has garnered quite a following for its deliciously healthy meat-free plates. The small menu changes daily, and features creative and filling lunch combinations, plus sandwiches served after 4pm. Great juices and smoothies.

LUIGI'S ITALIAN $$

Map p250 (☎2205-5331; Senador Corrêia 10, Laranjeiras; mains R$36-54; ☺noon-midnight Tue-Sun) Well off the beaten path, Luigi's is a casual Italian restaurant set in an old villa in Laranjeiras. Join neighborhood regulars for a drink on the small, covered courtyard or head inside to blessed air-conditioning for homemade pastas, authentic pizzas (available after 6pm) fired in the wood-burning oven and creamy tiramisu.

✖ Catete

★FERRO E FARINHA PIZZERIA $$

Map p249 (Andrade Pertence 42; pizzas R$30-40; ☺7-11:30pm Wed-Sat, from 6:30pm Sun) Sei Shiroma, an expat from NYC, and a dexterous team of dough handlers serve up Rio's best pizza at this atmospheric and delightfully ramshackle spot in Catete. Seats are few, with just a handful of bar stools crowding around the pizza makers and oven at center stage, plus a few outdoor tables, so go early to try to beat the crowds.

CARIOCANDO BRAZILIAN $$

Map p249 (☎2557-3646; http://barcariocando. com.br/site; Silveira Martins 139; per kg R$40-60; ☺noon-3pm & 7pm-midnight Mon-Sat) This atmospheric pay-by-weight restaurant serves up a good selection of Brazilian dishes by day, and transforms to a live-music spot with a menu of mostly drinks and appetizers by night (cover charge around R$20). Saturday afternoons, which feature *feijoada* (a bean-and-meat stew served with rice) and live *choro* (romantic, improvised samba-related music) or samba, are a great time to stop in (per person R$60).

CATETE GRILL
BUFFET $$

Map p249 (☑2285-3442; Rua do Catete 239; per kg R$62; ⏰11am-11pm) The Catete Grill has an excellent buffet with a wide range of seafood (including langoustine), grilled meats, sushi, pastas, salads, appetizers and baked dishes.

✖ Glória

TABERNA DA GLÓRIA
BRAZILIAN $$

Map p249 (☑2265-7835; Rua do Russel 32; mains R$40-72; ⏰noon-1am) On a small plaza in the heart of Glória, this large outdoor eatery serves decent Brazilian staples – and in abundance; most dishes here serve two. Next door is a roast-chicken restaurant and both are fine spots to enjoy an ice-cold *chope* (draft beer) and open-air ambience.

CASA DA SUÍÇA
SWISS $$$

Map p249 (☑2252-5182; Cândido Mendes 157; mains R$63-115, fondue around R$85; ⏰noon-3pm Sun-Fri & 7pm-midnight daily) Tucked inside the Swiss embassy, this cozy restaurant serves top-notch steak tartare, and specializes in flambés and fondues. The Casa da Suíça creates an almost tangible aura of sensuality, perhaps due to those open fires flaring inside.

🍷🍸 DRINKING & NIGHTLIFE

Few tourists visit the bars in Flamengo, which are mostly low-key neighborhood hangouts that are popular around happy hour. Rua Marquês de Abrantes is the best street to take in the scene, with bars and restaurants attracting a drinking crowd. Laranjeiras is best known for Rua Alice, which sports a couple of traditional *botecos*.

DEVASSA
BOTECO

Map p250 (☑2556-0618; Senador Vergueiro 2, Flamengo; ⏰noon-1am) A particularly inviting branch of the growing Devassa network, this bar is set on a shaded square, and serves the usual Devassa hits, including great drafts.

BAR DO ZÉ
BAR

Map p249 (Barão de Guaratiba 59, Catete; ⏰5pm-midnight Mon-Sat) Hidden down a narrow cobblestone side street off Rua do Catete, Bar do Zé has bohemian charm and remains little known to most *cariocas*. You'll find just a few tables inside among the old bottle-lined shelves, low-playing samba on the radio and groups of friends gathered on the street out front.

ADEGA PORTUGÁLIA
BAR

Map p249 (Largo do Machado 30, Catete; ⏰11am-midnight) Overlooking leafy Largo do Machado, Adega Portugália has an ideal location for enjoying a bit of open-air drinking and eating in an untouristy corner of Rio. In addition to a garrulous crowd and ice-cold *chope*, you'll find classic bar snacks such as *bolinhos de bacalhau* (codfish croquettes) and Portuguese-style sardines.

BELMONTE
BOTECO

Map p250 (☑2552-3349; Praia do Flamengo 300, Flamengo; ⏰9am-2am) One of the classic *botecos* in Rio, Belmonte is a vision of Rio from the '50s. Globe lights hang overhead as patrons down ice-cold drafts from the narrow bar. Meanwhile, unhurried waiters make their way across the tile floors, carrying plates of *pasteis de camarão* (shrimp pasties) or steak sandwiches. This hugely successful chain, born here, is now widespread across Rio.

HERR BRAUER
BAR

Map p250 (☑2225-4359; Barão do Flamengo 35, Flamengo; ⏰noon-midnight Mon-Sat) Dedicated to the great beers of the world, this cozy drinking den serves some 80 labels in all: Belgian beers, such as Duvel and Deus; German labels, including Erdinger and Warsteiner; English brews Abbot Ale and Newcastle; plus Guinness, Brazilian microbrews and dozens of other offerings. Stop in for happy hour from 6pm to 8pm, when you can get a first-rate pint for R$19.

BAR DO SERAFIM
BAR

Map p250 (☑2225-2843; Alice 24A, Laranjeiras; ⏰11am-midnight Mon-Sat, to 6pm Sun) On a lively stretch of Rua Alice, the Bar do Serafim is a simple, convivial *boteco* serving tasty Portuguese appetizers and plenty of *chope*. It's been around since 1944, and remains an institution and a popular happy-hour spot among neighborhood regulars.

ARMAZÉM DO CHOPP
BAR

Map p250 (☎2225-1796; Marquês de Abrantes 66, Flamengo; ☺11am-2am) On a bar-sprinkled stretch of Flamengo, this wooden, barn-like bar has outdoor seating on the raised veranda in front and cooler (air-conditioned) seating inside. It's a lively local meeting spot, particularly in the early evenings, and there's a good-value selection of dishes including appetizers and grilled meats to accompany the cold beers.

ENTERTAINMENT

SEVERYNA DE LARANJEIRAS
LIVE MUSIC

Map p250 (☎2556-9398; www.severyna.com. br; Ipiranga 54, Laranjeiras; admission R$15-25; ☺11:30am-1am) At night this broad, rustically decorated dining hall forms the backdrop to Brazilian rhythms, and there's a broad menu of Northeastern fare. Groups perform *forró*, a popular music of the Northeast (on Mondays from 9pm); samba (Fridays from 10pm); and rock (Saturdays from 10pm).

MAZE INN
LIVE MUSIC

Map p249 (☎2558-5547; www.jazzrio.info; Casa 66, Tavares Bastos 414, Catete; admission R$25-50; ☺10pm-3am, 1st Fri of month) Also known as the 'Casa do Bob' after owner Bob Nadkarni, this once-a-month event is well worth attending. It's set in the guesthouse of the same name high up in Tavares Bastos (one of Rio's safest favelas). There's a fun mix of *cariocas* and expats, with live jazz and fantastic city views.

CENTRO CULTURAL OI FUTURO
PERFORMING ARTS

Map p250 (☎3131-3060; www.oifuturo.org.br; Dois de Dezembro 63, Catete) This hypermodern cultural center and gallery space also stages dance performances and concerts. The fare is generally not mainstream.

ESPAÇO MUSEU DA REPÚBLICA
CINEMA

Map p249 (☎3826-7984; Museu da República, Rua do Catete 153, Catete) The screening room located behind the dramatic Museu da República shows contemporary and vintage films of indie and world cinema. Entrance is via the Parque do Catete.

SHOPPING

While not a traditional shopping destination, this area offers some worthwhile exploring, particularly if you stop in at the whimsical vintage shop on Rua Alice and the art-gallery-handicrafts emporium known as Pé de Boi in Laranjeiras.

PÉ DE BOI
HANDICRAFTS

Map p250 (☎2285-4395; www.pedeboi.com. br; Ipiranga 55, Laranjeiras; ☺9am-7pm Mon-Fri, to 1pm Sat) Although everything is for sale here, Pé de Boi feels more like an art gallery than a handicrafts shop, owing to the high quality of the wood and ceramic works, and the tapestries, sculptures and weavings. This is perhaps Rio's best place to see one-of-a-kind pieces by artists from Bahia, Amazonia, Minas Gerais and other parts of Brazil.

Don't miss the upstairs area, which has photos of some of the artists whose work is on sale.

MARACATU BRASIL
MUSIC

Map p250 (☎2557-4754; www.maracatubrasil .com.br; Ipiranga 49, Laranjeiras; ☺11am-8pm Mon-Sat) You can't miss the lime-green building that houses this small percussion store and workshop. Inside, you can buy an *afoxê* (a gourd shaker with beads strung around it), conga and bongo drums, tambourines and other Brazilian percussion instruments. Upstairs there's a drum clinic, where you can study with local instructors.

SPORTS & ACTIVITIES

MARACATU BRASIL
COURSE

Map p250 (☎2557-4754; www.maracatubrasil. com.br; 2nd fl, Ipiranga 49, Laranjeiras; ☺10am-6pm Mon-Sat) This is the best place in Rio to study percussion, and students have the opportunity to perform in music events throughout the city. Instructors here offer courses in a number of different drumming styles: Amazonian rhythms, samba, conga drums, Candomblé and much more, plus private lessons in guitar and other instruments.

If you plan to stick around in Rio a while, you can sign up for group classes (from

R$165 per month) or hire an instructor for private classes. On the 1st floor of the building, Maracatu sells instruments.

MAR DO RIO DIVING
Map p249 (☑2225-7508; www.mardorio.com.br; Shop 16, Marina da Glória, Av Infante Dom Henrique, Glória) One of several dive operators in the Marina da Glória, Mar do Rio offers two-tank dives for around R$200 (gear hire costs extra) on Saturdays and Sundays, departing at 8:30am and returning at 2:30pm. It also offers night dives twice a month. Less-experienced divers can opt for one of the courses, including a five-day PADI-certified basic course.

SAIL IN RIO BOAT TOUR
Map p249 (☑99998-3709; www.sailinrio. com; Marina da Glória, Glória; 2/4/6hr private sailing tours from US$240/300/400) This recommended outfit offers excellent private sailing tours around Rio. You can arrange anything from a two-hour sail around the bay to a six-hour trip out to the Cagarras Islands in front of Ipanema.

Centro & Praça Mauá

CINELÂNDIA | PRAÇA TIRADENTES | PRAÇA XV | PRAÇA MAUÁ

Neighborhood Top Five

❶ Pondering the future while browsing interactive exhibits in the beautifully designed **Museu do Amanhã** (p128).

❷ Peering back through hundreds of years of Brazilian history at the **Museu Histórico Nacional** (p122).

❸ Taking in first-rate art installations and rooftop views at the **Museu de Arte do Rio** (p127).

❹ Going eye-to-eye with fish, sharks and rays in **AquaRio** (p128).

❺ Watching a show inside the lavish **Theatro Municipal** (p123).

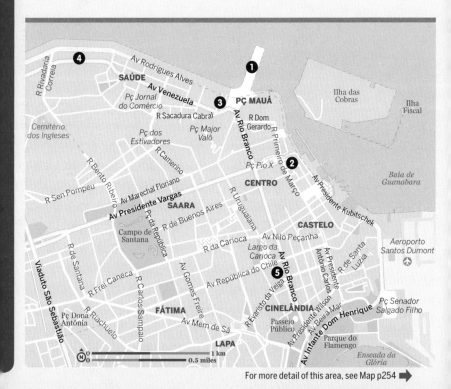

For more detail of this area, see Map p254 ➡

Explore Centro & Praça Mauá

Rio's downtown is an architectural medley of old and new, with striking baroque churches and narrow colonial streets juxtaposed against looming office towers and wide, traffic-filled boulevards. During the week it's all fuss and hurry as Rio's lawyers, secretaries and clerks jostle on the crowded streets. But despite the pace, it's worth joining the fray; Centro has some of the city's best museums and its most intriguing historical sights, including avant-garde art galleries and 18th-century cathedrals.

The southern focal point of downtown is Cinelândia, which has a wide plaza framed with grand buildings, a historic theater, an old cinema and several outdoor cafes. Near the waterfront, Praça XV is another pivotal sight, home to a former royal residence turned into a museum and some cafes. A short stroll from here leads to the Travessa do Comércio, one of the oldest intact parts of Rio. Lined with colonial architecture, the narrow cobblestone streets here buzz with life on weekday evenings, as *cariocas* (residents of Rio) pack the outdoor bars and cafes.

Many pedestrian-only areas crisscross Centro, and for the urban wanderer, there's no better destination in Rio. In addition to Praça XV and Cinelândia, it's worth exploring the streets around picturesque Praça Tiradentes. A handful of galleries, old dance halls and historic sites lie nearby. A few blocks north of here is Saara, a giant street bazaar crammed with discount stores and sprinkled with Lebanese restaurants.

North of Centro is Praça Mauá, a waterfront plaza that has become the symbol of Rio's renaissance. The once derelict streets here have been revitalized with new museums, an aquarium and towering office buildings, and there are yet new restaurants, cafes and bars in the works.

Local Life

➡ **Arts** There are several key concert halls in the area, including Theatro Municipal (p123) and Teatro Rival Petrobras (p133).

➡ **Hangouts** Open-air bars along Travessa do Comércio and nearby streets draw festive after-work crowds.

➡ **Shopping strips** The narrow, pedestrian-packed streets of Saara are intriguing for browsing.

Getting There & Away

➡ **Bus** From the Zona Sul look for the following destinations printed in the window: 'Rio Branco,' 'Praça XV' and 'Praça Tiradentes.'

➡ **Metro** Cinelândia, Carioca, Uruguaiana and Presidente Vargas.

Lonely Planet's Top Tip

Centro provides good value for money. There are lots of museums in the area that have free admission, and stiff competition helps keep lunch prices down – particularly at the many decent pay-by-weight restaurants. For an inexpensive cruise on the bay, hop on the ferry to Niterói (p127).

 Best Places to Eat

➡ Brasserie Rosário (p129)
➡ L'Atelier du Cuisinier (p130)
➡ AlbaMar (p130)
➡ Cais do Oriente (p130)
➡ Govinda (p128)
➡ Imaculada (p130)

For reviews, see p128 ➡

Best Places to Drink

➡ Samba Caffe (p132)
➡ Jazz In Champanheria (p132)
➡ Amarelinho (p132)

For reviews, see p130 ➡

◉ **Best Historic Sites**

➡ Igreja São Francisco da Penitência & Convento de Santo Antônio (p124)
➡ Ilha Fiscal (p127)
➡ Mosteiro de São Bento (p128)
➡ Igreja de Nossa Senhora do Carmo da Antiga Sé (p125)
➡ Paço Imperial (p125)

For reviews, see p123

CENTRO & PRAÇA MAUÁ

TOP SIGHT
MUSEU HISTÓRICO NACIONAL

Home to one of the most important collections in Brazil, the National History Museum has a treasure trove of artifacts dating back to the early days of the Portuguese presence in the New World. The extensive collection, containing more than 250,000 items, is set inside a sprawling 18th-century complex that was once part of the Forte de Santiago, a strategic point for the city's defense.

The collection begins with a survey of Brazil's pre-Columbian cultures in the hall titled 'Oreretama,' meaning 'Our Land' in Tupi. From there, it continues to the Portuguese maritime empire of the 15th century, with exquisite porcelain and objects from trading in the Far East, and moves on to the colonization of Brazil. Exhibits depict early life through models, such as the curious mechanized model of a sugar mill, and they don't shy away from the horrors of slavery.

There are also some fine pieces documenting the presence of the Portuguese royal family, from when the entire court packed up and sailed to Rio, ahead of Napoleon's invasion; displays from the bloody war of the Triple Alliance; a reconstructed 1840s pharmacy; and a fascinating collection of imperial carriages.

The 20th century receives less attention, and for an understanding of the Vargas period, you'll have to pay a visit to the former presidential palace of President Getúlio Vargas, the Museu da República (p114), in Catete.

The best way to get to the Museu Histórico Nacional is by metro to Cinelândia station and then walking 15 minutes northeast to the museum. Allow about two hours to view the whole collection.

DON'T MISS...

➡ Pre-Columbian exhibits portraying indigenous culture, myths and everyday tools

➡ The full-size recreation of a 19th-century pharmacy

➡ The gilded imperial carriages

PRACTICALITIES

➡ Map p254, G4

➡ ☑3299-0311

➡ www.museuhistorico nacional.com.br

➡ off General Justo, near Praça Marechal Âncora

➡ admission R$8, Sun free

➡ ◷10am-5:30pm Tue-Fri, 2-6pm Sat & Sun

◉ SIGHTS

◉ Cinelândia & Around

PRAÇA FLORIANO   PLAZA
Map p254 (Rio Branco) The heart of modern Rio, the Praça Floriano (known to *cariocas* simply as Cinelândia) comes to life at lunchtime and after work when the outdoor cafes are filled with a beer-swilling office crowd. The square is also Rio's political marketplace and is a major meeting point for protestors. Most city marches and rallies culminate here on the steps of the old Câmara Municipal in the northwestern corner of the plaza.

THEATRO MUNICIPAL   THEATER
Map p254 (☎2332-9220; www.theatromunicipal. rj.gov.br; Av 13 de Maio, Praça Floriano; guided tours R$10) Built in 1905 in the style of the Paris Opera, the magnificent Municipal Theater is the home of Rio's opera, orchestra and ballet. Its lavish interior contains many beautiful details – including the stage curtain painted by Italian artist Eliseu Visconti, which contains portraits of 75 major figures from the arts, including Carlos Gomes, Wagner and Rembrandt.

Guided multilingual tours lasting 45 minutes are offered from Tuesday to Friday (at noon, 2pm and 4pm) and Saturday (at noon). It's also well worth coming for a performance.

MUSEU NACIONAL DE
BELAS ARTES   MUSEUM
Map p254 (☎3299-0600; www.mnba.gov.br; Rio Branco 199; adult/student R$8/4, Sun free; ☺10am-6pm Tue-Fri, noon-5pm Sat & Sun) Rio's fine-arts museum houses more than 18,000 original paintings and sculptures, some of which date back to works brought over from Portugal by Dom João VI in 1808. One of its most important galleries is the **Galeria de Arte Brasileira**, which includes 20th-century classics such as Cândido Portinari's *Café*. Other galleries display Brazilian folk art, African art and furniture, as well as contemporary exhibits. Audio guides are available (R$8).

BIBLIOTECA NACIONAL   HISTORIC BUILDING
Map p254 (☎2220-9484; Rio Branco 219; ☺9am-5pm Mon-Fri, 10am-3pm Sat) **FREE** Inaugurated in 1910, Rio's neoclassical national library is the largest in Latin America. It's home to more than nine million volumes, including many rare books and manuscripts. Among the treasure trove are original letters written by Princess Isabel, the first newspapers printed in the country and two copies of the precious Mainz Psalter Bible, printed in 1492. Free guided tours in English depart at 1pm.

CENTRO CULTURAL
JUSTIÇA FEDERAL   CULTURAL CENTER
Map p254 (☎3261-2550; Rio Branco 241; ☺noon-7pm Tue-Sun) **FREE** The stately building overlooking the Praça Floriano served as the headquarters of the Supremo Tribunal Federal (Supreme Court) from 1909 to 1960. Following a restoration project completed in 2001, it opened as a cultural center. It features exhibitions on photography and Brazilian art, and some fascinating shows from abroad sometimes make their way here.

PASSEIO PÚBLICO   PARK
Map p254 (Rua do Passeio; ☺9am-5pm) The oldest park in Rio, the Passeio Público was built in 1783 by Mestre Valentim, a famous Brazilian sculptor, who designed it after Lisbon's botanical gardens. In 1860 the park was remodeled by French landscaper Glaziou. The park features some large trees, a pond with islands and an interesting crocodile-shaped fountain. The entrance gate was built by Valentim. Before neighboring Parque do Flamengo was created from landfill, the sea came right up to the edge of this park.

MUSEU DE ARTE MODERNA   MUSEUM
Map p254 (MAM; ☎3883-5600; www.mamrio. org.br; Infante Dom Henrique 85, Parque do Flamengo; adult/child R$14/free; ☺noon-6pm Tue-Fri, 11am-6pm Sat & Sun) At the northern end of Parque do Flamengo, the MAM is recognizable by its striking postmodern edifice designed by Alfonso Eduardo Reidy. The landscaping by Burle Marx is no less impressive. Inside, the design feels a bit dated, but it's still worth a visit for the superb collection of Brazilian artists, which includes works by Bruno Giorgi, Di Cavalcanti and Maria Martins.

Curators often bring excellent photography and design exhibits to the museum, and the cinema hosts regular film festivals throughout the year. After a devastating fire in 1978 that consumed 90% of its collection, the MAM is finally back on its feet, and it now houses 11,000 permanent works.

PORTO MARAVILHA

Rio's docklands, located north of Centro in the neighborhoods of Gamboa and Barrio Saúde (and also stretching into Centro, São Cristóvão and Cidade Nova), have been transformed into the Porto Maravilha (Marvelous Port; www.portomaravilha.com.br), the most exciting and ambitious of the city's transformations in the run-up to hosting the 2016 Olympic Games. The massive urban waterfront revitalization project, clocking in at an area of five million sq meters and costing an estimated R$8 billion, has turned a historic but underused and dilapidated port into one of Rio's showcase attractions, with new cultural spaces such as the Museu de Arte do Rio (p127), the Museu do Amanhã (p128) and the massive AquaRio (p128) aquarium; plus 17km of bike paths, numerous parks, and squares dotted with 15,000 new trees. A flashy new light rail (the VLT; p126) connects the area with other parts of downtown. As the traditional birthplace for samba and *choro* (romantic, improvised, samba-related music), Rio's port is once again singing following the dramatic transformation.

◎ Praça Tiradentes & Around

IGREJA SÃO FRANCISCO DA PENITÊNCIA & CONVENTO DE SANTO ANTÔNIO
CHURCH

Map p254 (☑2262-0129; Largo da Carioca 5; ☺church 8am-6pm Mon-Fri, 8-11am Sat) Overlooking the Largo da Carioca is the baroque Igreja São Francisco da Penitência, dating from 1726. Restored to its former glory, the church's sacristy, which dates from 1745, has blue Portuguese tiles and an elaborately carved altar made out of jacaranda wood. It also has a roof panel by José Oliveira Rosa depicting St Francis receiving the stigmata.

The church's **statue of Santo Antônio** is an object of great devotion to many *cariocas* in search of a husband or wife.

A garden on the church grounds leads to the catacombs, used until 1850. Visits must be arranged in advance.

Next door, the Convento de Santo Antônio was built between 1608 and 1615. It contains the chapel of Nossa Senhora das Dores da Imaculada Conceição. Fabiano de Cristo, a miracle-working priest who died in 1947, is entombed here.

CENTRO DE ARTE HÉLIO OITICICA
MUSEUM

Map p254 (☑2242-1012; Luís de Camões 68; ☺noon-8pm Mon, Wed & Fri, 10am-6pm Tue, Thu & Sat) FREE This avant-garde museum is set in a 19th-century neoclassical building that originally housed the Conservatory of Music and Dramatic Arts. Today the center displays permanent works by the artist, theoretician and poet Hélio Oiticica, as well as bold contemporary art exhibitions, well-tuned to Oiticica's forward-leaning aesthetics.

REAL GABINETE PORTUGUÊS DE LEITURA
HISTORIC BUILDING

Map p254 (☑2221-3138; Luís de Camões 30; ☺9am-6pm Mon-Fri) FREE Built in the Portuguese Manueline style in 1887, the gorgeous Portuguese Reading Room houses more than 350,000 works, many dating from the 16th, 17th and 18th centuries. It also has a small collection of paintings, sculptures and ancient coins.

CENTRO CARIOCA DE DESIGN
CULTURAL CENTER

Map p254 (Praça Tiradentes 48; ☺10am-7pm Mon-Sat) FREE In a historic building overlooking Praça Tiradentes, this multifloor cultural space showcases a changing array of exhibitions related to design, urbanism and architecture. Depending on what's on, works here can be a fascinating window into the major ideas and challenges shaping the ever-growing cities of today.

IGREJA DE NOSSA SENHORA DO ROSÁRIO E SÃO BENEDITO
CHURCH

Map p254 (Uruguaiana 77; ☺7am-5pm Mon-Fri, to 1pm Sat) Sadly, a fire in 1967 destroyed much of the elaborate interior of this historic church, leaving only the unadorned walls that date back to the early 1700s. Dedicated to Our Lady of the Rosary as well as the black St Benedict, the church has been an important icon for Afro-Brazilians, serving a congregation of mostly black and mulatto Catholics over the years.

Penitents leave offerings to the black martyr Anastasia (venerated as a saint, but

ILHA DE PAQUETÁ

This **tropical island** (⌨ferry 0800-721-1012; www.grupoccr.com.br/barcas) in the Baía de Guanabara was once a very popular tourist spot and is now frequented mostly by families from the Zona Norte. There's a certain dirty, decadent charm to the colonial buildings, unassuming beaches and businesses catering to local tourism. The place gets crowded on weekends.

There are no cars on the island. Transport is by foot, bicycle (with literally hundreds for rent) or horse-drawn cart. Go to Paquetá for the boat ride through Rio's famous bay and to see *cariocas* at play – especially during the Festa de São Roque, which is celebrated with fireworks, a procession and music on the weekend following August 16.

Boats leave from near the Praça XV (Quinze) de Novembro in Centro. The ferry takes 70 minutes and will cost you R$10 for a return trip. There are 12 departures daily; boats leave roughly every 90 minutes from about 7am.

not recognized officially by the Catholic church) in a candlelit room next to the entrance. A huge crowd gathers every May 13, to commemorate the end of slavery.

CAMPO DE SANTANA
PARK

Map p254 (Praça da República & Rua Frei Caneca) Campo de Santana is a pleasant green space that, on September 7, 1822, was the scene of the proclamation of Brazil's independence from Portugal by Emperor Dom Pedro I of Portugal. The landscaped park with an artificial lake and swans is a fine place for a respite from the chaotic streets, and you're likely to see a few wild *agoutis* (hamster-like rodents native to Brazil) scuttling about.

MORRO DA PROVIDÊNCIA
VIEWPOINT

Map p261 (⌚aerial tram 7am-7pm Mon-Fri, 8am-2pm Sat) Rio's oldest favela (slum, informal community) lies just north of Estação Dom Pedro II, the central train station. A free *teleférico* (aerial tram) connects the train station with the favela, and continues to a station on the north side (close to Gamboa). The views are excellent, and it's worth stopping at the top, but it's not advisable to wander around the favela on your own. If you plan to explore, go with a local who knows the area.

◎ Praça XV & Around

MUSEU HISTÓRICO NACIONAL
MUSEUM

See p122.

PRAÇA XV (QUINZE) DE NOVEMBRO
HISTORIC SITE

Map p254 (near Primeiro de Março) The first residents on this historic site were Carmelite

fathers who built a convent here in 1590. It later came under the property of the Portuguese crown and became Largo do Paço, which surrounded Paço Imperial, the royal palace. The square was later renamed Praça XV (Quinze) de Novembro after Brazil declared itself a republic on November 15, 1822.

A number of historic events have taken place here: the coronation of Brazil's two emperors (Pedro I and Pedro II), the abolition of slavery and the overthrow (deposition) of Emperor Dom Pedro II in 1889.

PAÇO IMPERIAL
HISTORIC BUILDING

Map p254 (⌨2215-2622; Praça XV (Quinze) de Novembro 48; ⌚noon-6pm Tue-Sun) FREE The former imperial palace was originally built in 1743 as a governor's residence. Later it became the home of Dom João and his family when the Portuguese throne transferred the royal seat of power to the colony. In 1888 Princesa Isabel proclaimed the Freedom from Slavery Act from the palace's steps. The building was neglected for many years but has been restored and today it hosts excellent changing exhibitions and concerts. There's also a good cafe and several restaurants here.

IGREJA DE NOSSA SENHORA DO CARMO DA ANTIGA SÉ
CHURCH

Map p254 (Sete de Setembro 14; ⌚8:30am-3:30pm Mon-Fri, 9:30am-noon Sat) This beautifully restored church and former cathedral dates back to the 1770s, and it played an important role in the imperial days of Rio. The elaborately gilded rococo-style interior witnessed royal baptisms, weddings and funeral rites. Several kings were crowned here – including Pedro I in 1822 and his son

VLT: A NEW DOWNTOWN RAIL LINE

Rio's new light rail – the **VLT** (Light Rail Vehicle; www.vltcarioca.com.br) – is part of a massive urban-renewal project helping to transform Centro. Slated to launch in 2016, the VLT will have 32 stations in Rio, running about half-a-dozen routes throughout downtown. For visitors, handy lines include the route from Cinelândia to Praça Mauá and from Praça XV to Praça Tiradentes. There will also be links to Aeroporto Santos Dumont, Rodoviária Novo Rio bus station and the train station.

Pedro II in 1841; it is the only place in the New World where this occurred. The royal family used to sit in the balcony boxes overlooking the altar.

TRAVESSA DO COMÉRCIO   STREET
Map p254 (near Praça XV (Quinze) de Novembro) Beautiful two-story colonial town houses line this narrow cobblestone street leading off Praça XV (Quinze) de Novembro. The archway, called **Arco de Teles**, leading into the area was once part of an old viaduct running between two buildings. Today, Travessa do Comércio contains half-a-dozen restaurants and drinking spots that open onto the streets. It's a favorite spot for *cariocas* after work.

CENTRO CULTURAL
BANCO DO BRASIL   CULTURAL CENTER
Map p254 (CCBB; ☑3808-2020; www.culturabancodobrasil.com.br; Primeiro de Março 66; ⊙9am-9pm Wed-Mon) **FREE** Housed in a beautifully restored 1906 building, the CCBB hosts some of Brazil's best exhibitions. Facilities include a cinema, two theaters and a permanent display of the evolution of currency in Brazil. There is always something going on, from exhibitions and lunchtime and evening concerts to film screenings, so look at *O Globo's* entertainment listings or the *Veja Rio* insert in *Veja* magazine before you go.

IGREJA DE NOSSA SENHORA
DE CANDELÁRIA   CHURCH
Map p254 (☑2233-2324; Praça Pio X; ⊙8am-4pm Mon-Fri, 9am-noon Sat, to 1pm Sun) Built between 1775 and 1894, NS de Candelária was the largest and wealthiest church of imperial Brazil. The interior is a combination of baroque and Renaissance styles. The ceiling above the nave reveals the origin of the church. The cupola, fabricated entirely from limestone shipped from Lisbon, is one of its most striking features.

The construction of the original church, dating from the late 16th century was credited to a ship's captain who was nearly shipwrecked at sea. Upon his safe return he vowed to build a church to NS de Candelária. A later design led to its present-day grandeur.

Mass is said at 7am daily except Monday and Saturday, and at 9am and 11am on Sunday. Be sure to watch out for traffic as you cross to the church.

CENTRO CULTURAL
CORREIOS   CULTURAL CENTER
Map p254 (☑2253-1580; Visconde de Itaboraí 20; ⊙noon-7pm Tue-Sun) **FREE** In a grand edifice dating from the 1920s, this cultural center houses three spacious floors that host a creative lineup of changing exhibitions, mostly focusing on Brazilian artists, writers and architects. Take the old-fashioned elevator to the top floor and work your way down.

CASA FRANÇA-BRASIL   BUILDING
Map p254 (☑2332-5120; www.casafrancabrasil.rj.gov.br; Visconde de Itaboraí 78; ⊙10am-8pm Tue-Sun) **FREE** In a neoclassical building dating from 1820, the Casa França-Brasil sponsors changing exhibitions that often deal with political and cultural facets of *carioca* society. The classical revival building once served as a customs house. There's a restaurant (p129) attached.

MUSEU NAVAL   MUSEUM
Map p254 (☑2104-5506; Dom Manuel 15; ⊙noon-5pm Tue-Sun) **FREE** Chronicling the history of the Brazilian navy from the 16th century to the present, the museum also has exhibitions of model warships, maps and navigational instruments.

Naval enthusiasts should also visit the nearby **Espaço Cultural da Marinha**, on the waterfront near the eastern end of Av Presidente Vargas. It contains the *Riachuelo* submarine, which you can wander through, the *Bauru* (a WWII torpedo boat) and the royal family's large rowboat. Boat tours to Ilha Fiscal palace leave from the docks here.

ILHA FISCAL HISTORIC BUILDING

(☏2233-9165; tours R$25; ⊗tours 12:30pm, 2pm & 3:30pm Thu-Sun) This eye-catching lime-green neo-Gothic palace sitting in the Baía de Guanabara looks like something out of a child's fairy-tale book. It was designed by engineer Adolfo del Vecchio and completed in 1889. Originally used to supervise port operations, the palace is famous as the location of the last Imperial Ball on November 9, 1889. Today it's open for guided tours, which leave from the dock near Praça XV (Quinze) de Novembro. Purchase tickets from the Museu Naval.

PALÁCIO TIRADENTES HISTORIC BUILDING

Map p254 (☏2588-1251; Primeiro de Março; ⊗10am-5pm Mon-Sat, noon-5pm Sun) FREE The stately Tiradentes Palace houses the seat of the legislative assembly. Exhibits on the 1st and 2nd floors relate the events that took place here between 1926 and the present. One of its darkest hours was when the National Assembly was shut down in 1937 under the Vargas dictatorship; it later served

as the Department of Press and Propaganda. Most information is in Portuguese, though you can listen to a rundown of history in English at the interactive machine in the foyer.

The statue in front, incidentally, is not a likeness of Russian mystic Rasputin, but rather that of martyr Tiradentes, who led the drive toward Brazilian independence in the 18th century. He was imprisoned in one of the former holding cells beneath the building.

◉ Praça Mauá & Around

MUSEU DE ARTE DO RIO MUSEUM

Map p254 (MAR; www.museudeartedorio.org.br; Praça Mauá 5; adult/child R$8/4, Tue & last Sun of month free; ⊗10am-6pm Tue-Sun) Looming large over Praça Mauá, the MAR is an icon for the rebirth of Rio's once derelict port. The huge museum hosts wide-ranging exhibitions that focus on Rio in all its complexity – its people, landscapes, beauty,

---

WORTH A DETOUR

NITERÓI

A short ferry ride across the bay from Rio, Niterói is a midsized city (population around 500,000) with some impressive modern architecture near the bay front, and pretty beaches further out.

Niterói's principal attraction is the famous **Museu do Arte Contemporânea** (MAC; ☏2620-2400; www.macniteroi.com.br; Mirante da Boa Viagem; admission R$10; ⊗10am-6pm Tue-Sun). Designed by Brazil's most famous architect, Oscar Niemeyer, the MAC has a wild curvilinear design that blooms like a flower (or more prosaically, a flying saucer) against sweeping bay views. Unfortunately the exhibits inside the museum are less inspiring. It's about 1.5km from the Niterói ferry terminal; to get here, turn right as you leave the terminal and walk about 50m across to the bus stop in the middle of the road; a 47B minibus will drop you at the museum door.

A handful of other Niemeyer-designed buildings are also located bayside in Niterói; they're part of the so-called 'Caminho de Niemeyer' (Niemeyer Way). A good starting point is the **Teatro Popular** (www.teatropopularoscarniemeyer.art.br; Av Jornalista Rogério Coelho Neto), located just a short stroll north of the ferry terminal.

The **Ponte Rio-Niterói** (Ponte Pres Costa E Silva) offers spectacular views of the Baía de Guanabara. The bridge is 15.5km long, 60m high and 26.6m wide, with two three-lane roads. There's a tollbooth 3km from the Niterói city center.

The **ferry** (Map p254; ☏0800-721-1012; www.grupoccr.com.br/barcas; one way/return R$5/10) to Niterói leaves from Praça XV (Quinze) de Novembro in Centro every 20 minutes; it's usually packed with commuters. Once you reach the dock in Niterói, there isn't much to see in the immediate area. From here, catch a bus to the MAC or to one of the beaches – or just turn around and return by ferry.

The cruise back across the bay is perhaps just as valid a reason for leaving Rio. Out on the water, you'll have impressive views of downtown, Pão de Açúcar and the other green mountains rising up out of the city; you'll also see planes (quite close) landing and taking off at Aeroporto Santos Dumont. Try to be on the water at sunset, when Centro glows with golden light.

challenges and conflicts. Start off by taking the elevator to the top (6th) floor, and absorbing the view over the bay. There's also an excellent restaurant here. Then work your way down through the galleries, taking in a mix of international and only-in-Rio exhibitions.

MUSEU DO AMANHÃ   MUSEUM

Map p254 (www.museudoamanha.org.br; Rodrigues Alves 1) Designed by famed Spanish architect Santiago Calatrava, this beautifully conceived science museum has interactive exhibitions on outer space, Earth and its biodiversity, humans (and our impact on the world), and the major global trends and challenges that lie in the future. In all, the museum takes a rather philosophical, and not entirely pessimistic, look at the human species and its long-ranging impact on everything around it.

The underlying question: what will the future look like? And can new ideas and technologies solve the impending crises facing an increasingly warming and quite overpopulated planet?

AQUARIO   AQUARIUM

(☑2558-3735; www.aquariomarinhodorio.com.br; Rodrigues Alves 379; admission R$40; ☉9am-6pm) The largest aquarium in South America is Rio's newest major downtown attraction. You can get an up-close look at some 350 different species (there are more than 8000 animals in all), spread among two dozen different tanks. The highlight is a 3.3-million-liter aquarium with a tunnel through the middle that gives the impression of walking right through the depths of a rich aquatic zone.

Sharks, rays, sea turtles and many fish found in Brazil's coastal waters are among the star attractions. There are also hands-on areas for kids.

MOSTEIRO DE SÃO BENTO   CHURCH

Map p254 (☑2206-8100; Dom Gerardo 68; ☉7am-5:30pm) This is one of the finest colonial churches in Brazil. Built between 1617 and 1641 on Morro de São Bento, the monastery has an excellent view over the city. The simple facade hides a baroque interior richly decorated in gold. Among its historic treasures are wood carvings designed by Frei Domingos da Conceição and made by Alexandre Machado, and paintings by José de Oliveira Rosa.

On Sundays the High Mass at 10am includes a choir of Benedictine monks singing Gregorian chants; early risers can also hear Mass on weekdays at 7:30am. To reach the monastery from Rua Dom Gerardo, go to No 40 and take the elevator to the 4th floor.

MORRO DA CONCEIÇÃO   HISTORIC SITE

Map p254 One of Rio's oldest neighborhoods, this pretty area feels like a tiny slice of Portugal, with its old shuttered houses, quiet cobblestone streets and twittering birds. While there isn't a lot to do here (it's really just one long winding street), there are a few galleries open to visitors (look for 'atelier' signs) and a good local restaurant. There's also a hostel if you want to stay overnight. Saturday is the liveliest time to visit.

To get here on foot, take the narrow uphill lane Ladeira João Homem, reachable just off Praça Mauá.

✕ EATING

Rio's busiest neighborhood has everything from greasy lunch counters to French bistros. Most restaurants open only for lunch on weekdays. Many pedestrian-only areas throughout Centro (such as Rua do Rosário) are full of restaurants, some spilling onto the sidewalk, others hidden on upstairs floors. Restaurant hunting here is something of an art.

✕ Cinelândia & Around

GOVINDA   VEGETARIAN $$

Map p254 (☑3549-9108; 2nd fl, Rodrigo Silva 6; lunch R$32; ☉11:30am-3:30pm Mon-Fri; ☑) Amid artwork and decorations from India, the always-welcoming Hare Krishnas whip up tasty vegetarian dishes made with care. Govinda is tucked down a narrow lane just off Rua São José and is always packed, so arrive early to get a seat.

DA SILVA   PORTUGUESE $$

Map p254 (☑2524-1010; 4th fl, Graça Aranha 187; all you can eat R$60, after 2pm R$50; ☉noon-4pm Mon-Fri) Hidden inside the Clube Ginástico Português, this large, simply decorated restaurant spreads one of Rio's best lunch buffets. Portuguese in flavor, Da Silva has delicious salads, steaks and seafood, along with an enormous variety of addictive *ba-*

calhau (cod) dishes and dozens of other items.

✖ Praça Tiradentes & Around

CONFEITARIA COLOMBO
BRAZILIAN $

Map p254 (☑2505-1500; www.confeitaria colombo.com.br; Gonçalves Dias 34; pastries around R$9, sandwiches R$18-40; ⊘9am-7pm Mon-Fri, to 5pm Sat) Stained-glass windows, brocaded mirrors and marble countertops create a lavish setting for coffee or a meal. Dating from the late 1800s, the Confeitaria Colombo serves desserts – including a good *pastel de nata* (custard tart) – befitting its elegant decor. The restaurant overhead, **Cristóvão** (buffet per person R$87; ⊘noon-4pm), spreads an extensive buffet of Brazilian dishes for those wanting to further soak up the splendor.

CASA PALADINO
BRAZILIAN $

Map p254 (Uruguaiana 224; mains R$18-30; ⊘7am-8:30pm Mon-Fri, 8am-noon Sat) Going strong since 1906, this frozen-in-time delicatessen is lined with bottles, canned goods and other preserves. Find the hidden restaurant in the back for Paladino's famed sandwiches, such as the *triplo* (pastrami, egg and melted cheese), and fluffy omelets with ingredients including cod, squid and octopus. It all goes nicely with an ice-cold draft beer.

CEDRO DO LÍBANO
LEBANESE $$

Map p254 (☑2224-0163; Senhor dos Passos 231; mains R$38-60; ⊘11am-4pm Mon-Sat) If you can get past the wedding-reception-like decor – white tablecloths with plastic chairs and tables – you can enjoy some excellent traditional Lebanese cooking at this long-running institution (opened in 1948). Kibbe, *kaftas* (spiced meat patties) and lamb are served tender and cooked to perfection.

CAFÉ DO BOM CACHAÇA DA BOA
CAFE $$

Map p254 (☑2509-1018; Rua da Carioca 10; mains R$34-40; ⊘10am-8pm Mon-Fri, 10:30am-2pm Sat) With a professorial air, this wood-lined cafe and bookshop doles out sandwiches, salads, crepes and coffees, but it's best known for its *cachaça* (sugarcane alcohol) menu, which includes more than 100 varieties.

✖ Praça XV & Around

BISTRÔ DO PAÇO
CAFE $

Map p254 (☑2262-3613; Praça XV (Quinze) de Novembro 48, Paço Imperial; mains R$17-38; ⊘noon-7pm) On the ground floor of the Paço Imperial, this informal restaurant offers a tasty assortment of quiches, salads, soups and other light fare. Save room for the delicious pies and cakes.

BRASSERIE ROSÁRIO
FRENCH $$

Map p254 (☑2518-3033; Rua do Rosário 34; mains R$26-73; ⊘11am-9pm Mon-Fri, to 6pm Sat) Set in a handsomely restored 1860s building, this atmospheric bistro has a hint of old Europe about it. The front counters are full of croissants, *pains au chocolat* (chocolate-filled pastries) and other baked items, while the restaurant menu features roast meats and fish, soups, baguette sandwiches, quiche, cheese plates and the like.

AL FARABI
BRAZILIAN $$

Map p254 (www.alfarabi.com.br; Rua do Rosário 30; mains R$30-36; ⊘10am-10pm Tue-Fri, to 5pm Mon & Sat) On one of Rio's most picturesque pedestrian lanes, Al Farabi doles out Brazilian standards in an atmospheric old dining room surrounded by books. You can also dine on the cobblestones out the front. There's live music Wednesday to Friday (jazz and Música Popular Brasileira) from around 6:30pm.

CREPE NOUVEAU ART
FRENCH $$

Map p254 (☑2233-3571; Visconde de Itaboraí 78, Casa França-Brasil; crepes R$29-38; ⊘10am-8pm) Inside the Casa França-Brasil, this charming restaurant serves savory galettes, sweet crepes and hearty lunch specials. The veranda has a lovely view of Igreja da Candelária and is a fine anytime destination for coffee, snacks and desserts.

CAFÉ ARLEQUIM
CAFE $$

Map p254 (☑2220-8471; Praça XV (Quinze) de Novembro 48, Paço Imperial; mains R$27-44; ⊘9am-8pm Mon-Fri, 10am-6pm Sat) In the middle of a shop selling books and CDs, this small, lively, pleasantly air-conditioned cafe is a fine spot to refuel, with Italian coffee, sandwiches, salads, quiches, lasagna and desserts.

RANCHO INN
INTERNATIONAL $$

Map p254 (☑2233-6144; 2nd fl, Rua do Rosário 74, Centro; mains R$35-50; ⊘11:30am-3:30pm Mon-Fri) Exposed brick and tall windows lend a vaguely Parisian air to this charming upstairs lunchtime spot. The menu changes daily and features specials like risotto with duck and shiitake mushrooms, and farfalle with smoked salmon. If you're particularly hungry, you may want to opt for the less fancy, fixed-price lunch buffet (R$28 to R$34).

L'ATELIER DU CUISINIER — FRENCH $$$

Map p254 (☑3179-0024; Theophilo Otoni 97; mains R$60-70, 3-course lunch R$78; ⊘noon-3pm Mon-Fri) Set in a 19th-century building just off busy Av Rio Branco, this small 24-seat eatery serves some of the best cuisine in Centro. The menu is tiny (just a few options each day), but beautifully executed, with David Jobert creating recipes with fresh-from-the-market Brazilian ingredients.

ALBAMAR — SEAFOOD $$$

Map p254 (☑2240-8378; Praça Marechal Âncora 186; mains R$78-132; ⊘noon-8pm) AlbaMar has long been one of Rio's best seafood destinations. Top picks are fresh oysters, grilled seafood with vegetables and *moqueca* (seafood stew cooked in coconut milk). The old-fashioned green gazebo-like structure offers excellent views of the Baía de Guanabara and the area of Niterói over the bay.

CAIS DO ORIENTE — BRAZILIAN $$$

Map p254 (☑2233-2531; www.caisdooriente.com.br; Visconde de Itaboraí 8; mains R$55-85; ⊘noon-4pm Sun & Mon, to midnight Tue-Sat) Brick walls lined with tapestries stretch high to the ceiling in this almost-cinematic 1870s mansion. Set on a brick-lined street, hidden from the masses, Cais do Oriente blends elements of Brazilian and Mediterranean cooking in dishes such as duck breast with Brazil-nut *farofa* (garnish of manioc flour sautéed with butter) and açaí sauce. There's a back courtyard and an upstairs space that hosts periodic concerts.

✖ Praça Mauá & Around

ANGU DO GOMES — BRAZILIAN $

Map p254 (Sacadura Cabral 75; mains R$19-26; ⊘11am-10pm Mon-Thu, to 2am Fri, to 6pm Sat) Set in a weather-beaten colonial building in Saúde, Angu do Gomes is a much-loved *carioca* eating spot. Opened in 1955, the restaurant is best known for its iconic *angu,* a kind of polenta topped with sausage, chicken, vegetables or seafood. It's a

fine destination when visiting the sights of Praça Mauá or catching live music at Pedra do Sal (p132) samba street party.

IMACULADA — BRAZILIAN $$

Map p254 (Ladeira do João Homem 7; mains R$25-40; ⊘11am-4pm Mon, to 10pm Tue-Sat; 🐾) In the old neighborhood of Morro da Conceição, Imaculada is a Rio classic. The walls are adorned with artwork and the food is good. Come for daily lunch specials – *bobó de camarão* (manioc paste with dried shrimp, coconut milk and cashew nuts) on Thursdays or *feijoada* (bean and meat stew) on Fridays and Saturdays – and beer and appetizers at day's end.

MIRONGA — BRAZILIAN $$

Map p254 (☑2518-7727; Av Rio Branco 19; mains R$28-39; ⊘8am-10am & 11:30am-3:30pm Mon-Fri, noon-5pm Sun; 🐾) With its tall ceilings, exposed Edison bulbs, lounge-like music and chunky wood tables, Mironga channels a Brooklyn vibe, which is unsurprising given the owner has deep NYC connections. Aesthetics aside, the food is excellent, with the focus on grilled dishes (picanha, salmon and chicken breast) and burgers, with salads, ceviche and codfish snacks for those looking for something lighter.

DRINKING & NIGHTLIFE

Rio's working folks have some fine choices when it comes to joining the happy-hour fray. One of the most magical settings for a sundowner is along the historic Travessa do Comércio. The sidewalk tables on this narrow, cobbled lane are packed on weekday nights, particularly as the weekend nears – Thursday is always a good bet. Places see a bit of action during the day on Saturdays (several restaurants along Rua do Rosário serve *feijoada*), but close the rest of the weekend. Another choice after-work spot is Praça Floriano, which has a handful of bars.

SAMBA CAFFE — BAR

Map p254 (Rua do Ouvidor 23, Centro; ⊘3:30pm-midnight Mon-Fri, noon-8pm Sat) Hidden in a lane leading off Praça XV (Quinze) de Novembro, Samba Caffe is one of many photogenic open-air bars tucked into Rio's old colonial center. The narrow pedestrian lane

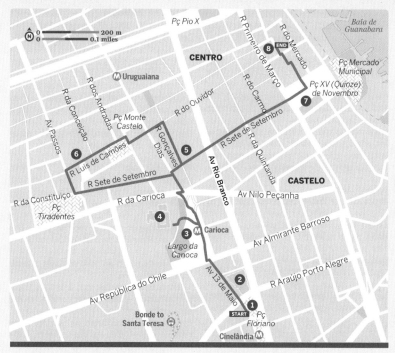

🏃 Neighborhood Walk
Historic Centro

START PRAÇA FLORIANO
END TRAVESSA DO COMÉRCIO
LENGTH 3KM; FOUR HOURS

A mélange of historic buildings and skyscrapers, Centro is a fine place to experience the city away from its beaches and mountains. Do this tour during the week, as the area is deserted (and unsafe) on weekends.

Start at ❶ **Praça Floriano** (p123), a scenic plaza set with several outdoor cafes. On the north side, the neoclassical ❷ **Theatro Municipal** (p123) is one of Rio's finest buildings, particularly after its recent R$65-million renovation. If you time your visit right, take one of the guided tours.

Stroll north along Av 13 de Maio. You'll pass through the ❸ **Largo da Carioca**, a bustling area with a small market. On the hill is ❹ **Igreja São Francisco da Penitência** (p124), an 18th-century church with a jaw-dropping gilded interior. Reach it via stairs or elevator near the Carioca metro station.

After taking in the views, walk over to narrow Rua Gonçalves Dias to reach ❺ **Confeitaria Colombo** (p129) for caffeine, pastries and art nouveau.

From Rua Gonçalves Dias, turn left on Rua do Ouvidor, following it to Largo de San Francisco de Paula. One block further is the ❻ **Real Gabinete Português de Leitura** (p124), a historic reading room that seems straight out of 19th-century Portugal.

Turn right when exiting and pass Praça Tiradentes, before heading left over to Rua Sete de Setembro. Follow it until it ends near the ❼ **Paço Imperial** (p125). Once the seat of the Portuguese rulers in Brazil, the building today houses intriguing art exhibitions, and cafes.

Leaving the Paço, cross Praça XV (Quinze) de Novembro and take the narrow lane beneath the arch. You'll walk along one of Centro's oldest lanes, ❽ **Travessa do Comércio** (p126), full of open-air restaurants and bars. It's a fitting ending to a day's wander.

is a popular meeting spot, and a festive air arrives at workday's end as *cariocas* fill the tables spilling onto the street.

JAZZ IN CHAMPANHERIA
BAR

Map p254 (Sacadura Cabral 63, Centro; ⊙6pm-1am Tue-Fri, 11pm-5am Sat) Set in a restored colonial building across from Praça Mauá, Jazz In draws a buzzing crowd that mingles among the art-covered walls, sipping bubbly (champagne and prosecco) and nibbling on bruschetta, sandwiches and other light fare. It's a lively after-work spot that morphs into a dance club as the evening progresses.

AMARELINHO
BOTECO

Map p254 (☎3549-8434; Praça Floriano 55, Cinelândia; ⊙10am-1am) Easy to spot by its bright *amarelo* (yellow) awning, Amarelinho has a splendid setting on the Praça Floriano, with the Theatro Municipal in the background. Waiters serve plenty of *chope* (draft beer) here as they wander among the crowded tables. Amarelinho is a popular lunch spot but packs in even bigger crowds for that ever-important after-work brew.

WEEK
GAY

Map p254 (☎2253-1020; www.theweek.com.br; Sacadura Cabral 135, Centro; 10pm-5am Sat) Rio's best gay dance club has a spacious dance floor, excellent DJs and lots of go-go dancers. Saturday nights are when the big parties are held. On other nights, there might not be anything on, so check online before heading out.

⭐ ENTERTAINMENT

★ GINGA TROPICAL
DANCE

Map p254 (☎3588-6857; www.gingatropical.com.br; Praça Tiradentes 79, Centro; admission R$160; ⊙10pm Sun, Mon, Thu & Fri) For a look at Brazil's rich folkloric dances, book a ticket to an evening performance of Ginga Tropical. Some 16 different dance styles are represented, including a somewhat spooky Orixás performance, lightning-fast *frevo,* and a stunning acrobatically inclined capoeira group. Other highlights: twirling Amazonian *carimbó,* sultry Northeastern *forró,* and a wild and very rarely performed *boleadeira* from Rio Grande do Sul.

Shows take place in the old dance hall Estudantina. Ticket prices are high, but there's a lot of talent on stage, and few places where you can see all these dances at once.

TRAPICHE GAMBOA
SAMBA

Map p254 (☎2516-0868; Sacadura Cabral 155, Gamboa; admission R$15-25; ⊙6:30pm-1am Tue-Fri, 8:30pm-2am Sat) A charming live samba joint, Trapiche Gamboa is set in a multi-story colonial edifice in Gamboa (just north of Centro) and has a friendly, mixed crowd and decent appetizers. It's a casual affair, with samba musicians gathering around a table on the ground floor, and dancers spilling out in front of them. It's best reached by taxi (R$40 or so from the Zona Sul).

PEDRA DO SAL
SAMBA

Map p254 (Largo João da Baiana, Gamboa; ⊙8pm-midnight Mon & Fri) The Monday- and Friday-night street parties are major draws for lovers of samba, whether they be Brazilian or foreign, rich or poor. The lively *samba da mesa* features a handful of changing players who belt out well-known songs to swaying, joyful crowds surrounding the tiny plaza.

The atmospheric but run-down setting is rich in history – samba was born in the Bahian community that once flourished here. Because the action happens outdoors, the music is canceled on days of heavy rain. It's best to take a taxi here (around R$40 from Copacabana).

ESTUDANTINA MUSICAL
SAMBA

Map p254 (Praça Tiradentes 79, Centro; admission R$15-40; ⊙10pm-3:30am Tue) This old dance hall packs large crowds on Tuesday nights, when lovers of *forró* descend en masse for an evening of dancing to first-rate bands. The open-air veranda provides a nice spot to cool off if you've danced yourself into a sweat.

ODEON PETROBRAS
CINEMA

Map p254 (☎2240-1093; Praça Floriano 7, Cinelândia) Rio de Janeiro's landmark cinema is a remnant of the once-flourishing movie-house scene that gave rise to the name Cinelândia. The restored 1920s film palace shows independent films, documentaries and foreign films, and sometimes hosts the gala for prominent film festivals.

CENTRO CULTURAL CARIOCA
SAMBA

Map p254 (☎2252-6468; www.centroculturalcarioca.com.br; Rua do Teatro 37, Centro; admission R$20-40; ⊙7pm-1am Mon-Thu, 8:30pm-2am Fri & Sat) This carefully restored 19th-century building hosts an excellent musical lineup throughout the week, and it is a good option for those wanting to escape the crowds in Lapa, Rio's popular music district. The scene here is slightly more staid, which makes it a good choice for couples.

THEATRO MUNICIPAL
THEATER
Map p254 (⏍2332-9191; www.theatromunicipal. rj.gov.br; Av 13 de Maio, Praça Floriano) This gorgeous art nouveau theater provides the setting for Rio's best opera, ballet and symphonic concerts. The theater seats 2400, and sight lines are generally quite good.

TEATRO RIVAL PETROBRAS
LIVE MUSIC
Map p254 (⏍2240-4469; www.rivalpetrobras. com.br; Álvaro Alvim 33, Cinelândia; admission R$30-80; ⏍box office 3-9pm Mon-Fri, 4-9pm Sat) This place stages MPB, samba, *chorinho* (informal instrumental music) and *forró* groups – both up-and-comers as well as veteran musicians such as Tania Alves and Mart'nália. The setup is dinner-theater style, and you can order food and drink throughout the show. The samba and *feijoada* feast on the last Saturday of every month (from 1pm to 5:30pm) is a highlight.

 SHOPPING

For a break from the chrome and glass of the Zona Sul, check out the old-school shops of historic Centro. Bargains abound in the narrow pedestrian streets around Saara, where shops peddle everything from clothes and cosmetics to toys, jerseys and all the fabric and sequins you'd ever need to make your own Carnaval costume. Nearby streets offer a little of everything, including discounted record stores, secondhand bookshops and percussion stores, often set behind century-old shop fronts.

GRANADO
BEAUTY
Map p254 (⏍3231-6747; Primeiro de Março 14, Centro; ⏍8am-8pm Mon-Fri, 10am-2pm Sat) A classic-looking apothecary with a name that's been around since 1870, Granado incorporates Brazilian ingredients in its all-natural products. Favorites include the Castanha do Brasil (made from chestnuts from the Amazon) line of moisturizers, shampoos and conditioners.

You'll also find bright, sweet-smelling soaps and bath gels (even for pets and babies), scented candles, perfumes, shaving products and retro-looking bags. There are other locations in Lapa, Ipanema and Leblon.

SOBRAL
JEWELRY, SOUVENIRS
Map p254 (Gonçalves Dias 5, Centro; ⏍9am-8pm Mon-Fri, to 2pm Sat) This small, colorful shop sells chunky, eye-catching necklaces and earrings, along with picture frames and minimalist forms of Pão de Açúcar and Cristo Redentor. All items are made of resin and come in an array of colors, from richly saturated hues to clear transparent.

ARLEQUIM
BOOKS, MUSIC
Map p254 (⏍2220-8471; Praça XV (Quinze) de Novembro 48, Paço Imperial, Centro; ⏍10am-8pm Mon-Fri, to 6pm Sat) Bossa nova plays overhead at this charming cafe, bookstore and music shop. As well as new books (including foreign-language titles), Arlequim sells CDs covering bossa, samba and other styles. The cafe menu features salads, sandwiches and other light fare (mains R$20 to R$37).

LIVRARIA DA TRAVESSA
BOOKS, MUSIC
Map p254 (⏍3231-8015; Sete de Setembro 54, Centro; ⏍9am-8pm Mon-Fri, to 2pm Sat) Livraria da Travessa offers a peaceful refuge from the people-packed sidewalks out front. There are some books in English, and an array of colorful coffee-table books. There's another Centro branch on Av Rio Branco 44, which also has an in-store cafe.

GALERIA MONIQUE PATON
ARTS
Map p254 (⏍2268-0506; www.galeriamonique paton.com; 2nd fl, Rua do Rosário 38, Centro; ⏍11am-5pm Mon-Sat) One of a handful of new galleries on this colonial street, Galeria hosts intriguing mixed-media shows from up-and-coming artists in Rio and beyond.

CASA OLIVEIRA
MUSIC
Map p254 (⏍2508-8539; Rua da Carioca 70, Centro; ⏍9am-7pm Mon-Fri, to 1pm Sat) One of several excellent music shops on Rua da Carioca, Casa Oliveira sells all the pieces that make up the rhythm section of Carnaval *baterias* (percussion sections). Unique souvenirs for the musically minded include *cavaquinos* (ukulele-sized guitars), which start at around R$200, and *pandeiros* (tambourines), starting at R$50.

BERINJELA
MUSIC, BOOKS
Map p254 (⏍2532-3646; Av Rio Branco 185, Centro; ⏍9am-7pm Mon-Fri, 10am-1pm Sat) Berinjela is a fine place to hunt for old records and classic samba CDs, and there's also a selection of used books (though only a handful in English). It's hidden in a small shopping center, down a spiral ramp.

PEETER VIISIMAA / GETTY IMAGES ©

1. Santa Marta favela 2. Hillside favela 3. Cable cars, Complexo do Alemão (p152)

Favelas

In recent years, many of Rio's favelas (slums, informal communities) have been transformed. Although controversial, the pacification plan – police invasions to drive out drug traffickers followed by the installation of security posts – has been largely successful. Public investment has poured into these safe harbors, helping to unite them with the rest of the city.

Traveling in Style

New transportation has been installed at some favelas, including cable cars at sprawling Complexo do Alemão (p152), elevators whisking residents up to Cantagalo (p59) and Pavão/Pavãozinho, and a tram to the top of Santa Marta. As part of the port beautification (Porto Maravilha), plans are underway to add a cable car to Morro da Providência, considered Rio's oldest favela, and one of its most crime-ridden until recently.

Artful Intentions

Favelas have attracted artists. The rainbow-colored hues painted across residences overlooking Praça Cantão in Santa Marta have helped show the world that a favela is more than a backdrop of poverty and hopelessness. The giant photographs by French artist JR have raised awareness of marginalized communities. In Morro da Providência, his oversized portraits plastered on homes, show the human, individual face of the favela rather than the faceless million-plus who live in Rio's shanty towns.

FAVELA EXPERIENCES

➡ Marcelo Armstrong and Paulo Amendoim lead recommended tours around Rocinha (see p207).

➡ Take in the aerial views over Complexo do Alemão or Morro do Cantagalo in Ipanema.

➡ Spend the night in a favela guesthouse; it's a great way to see beyond the stereotypes.

Santa Teresa & Lapa

Neighborhood Top Five

① Photographing the **Escadaria Selarón** (p138), a moving work of art created by an artist who made the mosaic-covered staircase his life's work.

② Riding the **bonde** (p139) over the Arcos da Lapa and up to village-like Santa Teresa.

③ Watching sunlight play through the dazzling stained-glass windows at the **Catedral Metropolitana** (p140).

④ Surveying the exquisite modern-art collection at **Museu Chácara do Céu** (p139).

⑤ Taking in the fine views over Rio and Baía de Guanabara from the **Parque das Ruínas** (p139).

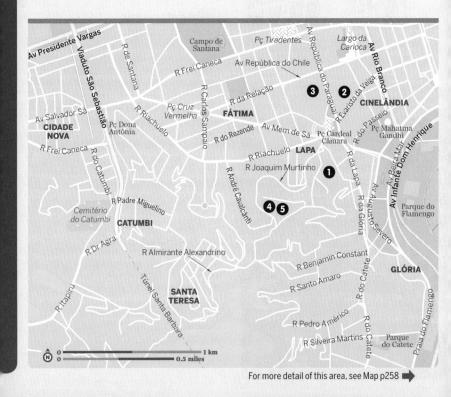

For more detail of this area, see Map p258 ➡

Explore Santa Teresa & Lapa

Icons of bohemian Rio, Santa Teresa and Lapa are two rough-and-tumble neighborhoods that have contributed considerably to the city's artistic and musical heritage. On a hill overlooking the city, Santa Teresa has an impressive collection of 19th-century mansions set along winding lanes. Many beautiful colonial homes stretch skyward, their manicured gardens hidden behind gabled fences.

Today Santa Teresa is the buzzword for a vibrant arts scene. Throughout the year, the sounds of impromptu festivals and street parties fill the air, ranging from Afro-Brazilian *maracatu* drumming along Rua Joaquim Murtinho to live jazz at the Parque das Ruínas, and the annual Portas Abertas event sees dozens of artists open their studios and cover the streets with living installations.

The streets of Lapa lie down the hill from Santa Teresa and south of Cinelândia. Formerly a residential neighborhood of the wealthy, Lapa became a red-light district in the 1930s. Although it is still a gritty area, it's also one of the music capitals of Brazil. At night, revelers from all over the city mingle among its samba clubs and music-filled bars. The music scene has brought some gentrification to the area, including new restaurants, hostels and even a luxury hotel.

Lapa's landmark aqueduct, Arcos da Lapa, is one of the neighborhood's most prominent features. Coursing over the 64m-high structure are narrow tracks that carry the photogenic *bonde* (tram) to and from Santa Teresa.

Local Life

➡ **Markets** Lapa's excellent Feira do Rio Antigo (p146) features antiques, crafts, food and live music.

➡ **Hangouts** Santa Teresa has some fine local haunts, including the Bar do Gomes (p143) and the Bar do Mineiro (p141).

➡ **Shopping strips** The Rua do Lavradio is dotted with antique shops and cafes, plus samba clubs by night.

Getting There & Away

➡ **Santa Teresa buses** Centro (206 and 214) from Carioca metro station.

➡ **Lapa buses** Leblon, Ipanema and Copacabana (161); Gávea and Jardim Botânico (158 and 161).

➡ **Metro** Cinelândia.

Lonely Planet's Top Tip

Santa Teresa is fringed by favelas (slums, informal communities). Be cautious when walking around, and avoid deserted streets. The best time to explore is on Saturdays or Sundays, when the neighborhood is at its liveliest.

Despite signs of renewal, Lapa still has its share of crime. Take care when strolling around the neighborhood, and be mindful of pickpocketing on busy weekend nights.

SANTA TERESA & LAPA

 Best Places to Eat

➡ Rústico (p140)

➡ Espírito Santa (p141)

➡ Casa Momus (p142)

➡ Aprazível (p141)

➡ Térèze (p141)

For reviews, see p140 ➡

Best Places to Drink

➡ Bar dos Descasados (p142)

➡ Leviano Bar (p143)

➡ Antônio's (p143)

➡ Anexo Bar (p143)

For reviews, see p142 ➡

☆ Best Live Music

➡ Rio Scenarium (p144)

➡ Semente (p144)

➡ TribOz (p144)

➡ Democráticos (p144)

➡ Carioca da Gema (p144)

➡ Circo Voador (p144)

For reviews, see p144 ➡

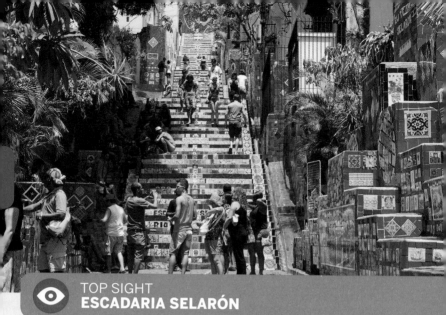

TOP SIGHT
ESCADARIA SELARÓN

Created by the Chilean-born artist Jorge Selarón, the staircase bearing his name boasts colorful mosaics that cover the 215 steps leading up into the hilltop enclave of Santa Teresa. Situated in the heart of Rio's vibrant samba district, the *escadaria* has come to symbolize Lapa's creative and bohemian spirit, and its rebirth from a worn and battered former red-light district to a musical powerhouse.

Sadly, Selarón died at the age of 65 in early 2013 – his body was found on the same steps to which he'd devoted the last 20 years of his life. Selarón was a well-known figure in the neighborhood, having moved to Rio in 1983 and settled in a house right off the stairway. What started out as a whim in 1990 evolved into an obsession; he was often spotted at work in Lapa and rarely left the neighborhood.

The mosaics started out as a homage to the Brazilian people by utilizing green, yellow and blue, the colors of the flag. Later he added mirrors and unusual colors and patterns to illustrious effect. As the media began to cover his unusual contribution to the urban landscape, his fame spread, and soon travelers began arriving with ceramics from their own countries to donate, which he later incorporated into his ever-evolving installation. The stairs' tiles hail from more than 60 countries. After he completed the stairs, he began covering other surfaces in need of cosmetic attention, including mosaics near the Arcos da Lapa.

The stairs have been named a city landmark, and have been featured in numerous magazines, and photo and film shoots. Snoop Dogg's 'Beautiful' features the steps, as well as U2's 'Walk On.' Rio's stirring bid for the 2016 Olympics, 'The Passion that Unites Us,' also showcases the steps.

A hand-painted sign in English and Portuguese explains Selarón's vision.

DON'T MISS...

➔ The plaque describing Selarón's work

➔ Mosaics of pregnant women, including one with Selarón's own face!

➔ Depictions of the steps in music videos

PRACTICALITIES

➔ Map p258, F4

➔ stairway btwn Joaquim Silva in Lapa & Pinto Martins in Santa Teresa

◉ SIGHTS

◉ Santa Teresa

BONDE
CABLE CAR

(⊙departures every 30min) The *bonde* that travels up to Santa Teresa from Centro is the last of the historic streetcars that once crisscrossed the city. Its romantic clatter through the cobbled streets has made it the archetype for bohemian Santa Teresa. Currently the *bonde* travels from the cable-car station in **Centro** (Map p254; Lélio Gama 65) over the scenic Arcos da Lapa and up as far as Largo do Guimarães in the heart of Santa Teresa.

After a tragic accident in 2011, the *bonde* was taken out of commission, while much-needed improvements to the tracks were made. After more than four years, the line opened again – but only traveling 1.7km of the 10km of tracks. Work continues on the route, with full completion expected by 2017 at the earliest.

MUSEU CHÁCARA DO CÉU
MUSEUM

Map p258 (☑3970-1126; www.museuscastro maya.com.br; Murtinho Nobre 93; adult/child R$2/free, Wed free; ⊙noon-5pm Wed-Mon) The former mansion of art patron and industrialist Raymundo Ottoni de Castro Maya contains a small but diverse collection of modern art, formerly Ottoni's private collection, which he bequeathed to the nation. In addition to works by Portinari, Di Cavalcanti and Lygia Clark, the museum displays furniture and Brazilian maps dating from the 17th and 18th centuries, and also hosts temporary exhibitions.

Beautiful gardens surround the building, and a panoramic view of Centro and Baía de Guanabara awaits visitors.

PARQUE DAS RUÍNAS
VIEWPOINT

Map p258 (☑2215-0621; Murtinho Nobre 169; ⊙10am-8pm Tue-Sun) **FREE** This park contains the ruins – exterior brick walls and a newly built staircase – of the mansion belonging to Brazilian heiress Laurinda Santos Lobo. Her house was a meeting point for Rio's artists and intellectuals for many years until her death in 1946. There's a small gallery on the ground floor, but the real reason to come here is for the excellent panorama from the viewing platform up top.

There's also a small outdoor cafe-kiosk and terrace where open-air concerts are sometimes held.

CASA DE BENJAMIN CONSTANT
HISTORIC BUILDING

Map p258 (☑3970-1177; Monte Alegre 255; admission R$2, Sun free; ⊙10am-5pm Wed-Fri, 1-5pm Sat & Sun) This tranquil estate served as the residence for one of Brazil's most influential politicians in the founding of the young republic. Benjamin Constant (1837–91) was an engineer, military officer and professor before taking an active role in the Provisional Government. He is also remembered for founding a school for blind children. Painstakingly preserved, his house provides a window into his life and times.

The lush gardens provide a fine view over Centro and Santa Teresa.

CENTRO CULTURAL LAURINDA SANTOS LOBO
CULTURAL CENTER

Map p258 (☑2215-0618; Monte Alegre 306; ⊙10am-6pm Tue-Sun) **FREE** Built in 1907, this large mansion once served as a salon for artists from Brazil and abroad, as the location of parties hosted by socialite Laurinda Santos Lobo. Guests included Brazilian composer Heitor Villa-Lobos and American dancer Isadora Duncan. Today, as a cultural center, the building still plays an active role in the neighborhood by hosting exhibitions and open-air concerts throughout the year.

LARGO DO GUIMARÃES
SQUARE

Map p258 (Almirante Alexandrino) The plaza named after Joaquim Fonseca Guimarães (a local resident whose house became Hotel Santa Teresa, just up the road) now forms the center of bohemian Santa Teresa. A festive Carnaval street party originates here, and a number of restaurants, handicrafts and thrift shops lie within a short distance. This is a key cable-car stop on the *bonde*.

LARGO DAS NEVES
SQUARE

Map p258 (end of Progresso) A slice of village life in the city, this small plaza is one of Santa Teresa's most picturesque little squares. While empty by day, at night the bars surrounding the square come alive, with revelers crowding the walkways. At times, Música Popular Brasileira (MPB) bands perform to a young crowd here.

Largo das Neves is the cable-car terminus of the Paula Matos *bonde* line.

⊙ Lapa

ESCADARIA SELARÓN
LANDMARK

See p138.

ARCOS DA LAPA
AQUEDUCT

Map p258 (near Av Mem de Sá) A much-photographed symbol of Lapa, the arches date back to the mid-1700s, when the structure served as an aqueduct to carry water from the Carioca River to downtown Rio. In a style reminiscent of ancient Rome, the 42 arches stand 64m high. Today it carries the *bonde* (p139) on its way between Centro and Santa Teresa.

CATEDRAL METROPOLITANA
CHURCH

Map p258 (☑2240-2669; www.catedral.com.br; Av República do Chile 245; ☉7am-5pm) This enormous cone-shaped cathedral was inaugurated in 1976 after 12 years of construction. Among its sculptures, murals and other works of art, the four vivid stained-glass windows, which stretch 60m to the ceiling, are breathtaking. The cathedral can accommodate up to 20,000 worshippers.

The **Museu de Arte Sacra** (Museum of Sacred Art; Map p258; admission R$2; ☉9am-noon & 1-4pm Wed, 9am-noon Sat & Sun) in the basement contains a number of historical items, including the baptismal font used at the christening of royal princes and the throne of Dom Pedro II.

FUNDIÇÃO PROGRESSO
ARTS CENTER

Map p258(☑3212-0800;www.fundicaoprogresso.com.br; Rua dos Arcos 24; ☉9am-6pm Mon-Fri) Once a foundry for the manufacturing of safes and ovens, Fundição Progresso today hosts avant-garde exhibitions, concerts and samba performances throughout the year. It is one of the few buildings in the area that survived the 1950s neighborhood redistricting project to widen Av República do Paraguai.

If you're sticking around Rio for a while, you can sign up for classes in capoeira, dance, yoga and theater arts.

✕ EATING

Great views, a diverse crowd and a scenic atmosphere among late 19th-century buildings set the stage for a great night out in bohemian Santa Teresa. Most restaurants are within a short stroll of Largo do Guimarães. Although Lapa is known more for its samba than its cuisine, more and more restaurants are opening in the area, catering to the young crowds heading to the dance halls.

✕ Santa Teresa

CAFECITO
CAFE $

Map p258 (☑2221-9439; www.cafecito.com.br; Paschoal Carlos Magno 121; sandwiches R$14-26; ☉9am-10pm Thu-Tue; 🛜) A few steps above street level, this open-air cafe attracts a mix of foreigners and neighborhood regulars; the Argentine owner is a longtime Santa Teresa resident. You'll find imported beers, desserts, cocktails (caipirinhas and mojitos), tapas plates and tasty ciabatta sandwiches with ingredients such as artichoke hearts, Gorgonzola and prosciutto.

ALQUIMIA
CREPERIE $

Map p258 (Largo das Neves 11; crepes R$12-22; ☉5pm-midnight Thu-Sun) Beautifully set on tranquil Largo das Neves, Alquimia is a friendly Franco-Brazilian-run place that fires up delicious crepes, and it's also a charming spot to come for a drink in the evening. There's live music, and occasional art exhibitions are held here.

NEGA TERESA
BRAZILIAN $

(Almirante Alexandrino 1458; mains around R$10; ☉5-10pm Thu-Sun) Bringing her Bahian delicacies to the people of Rio, Nega Teresa serves up scrumptious *acarajé* (a fritter filled with shrimp and spices) from a simple stand in the outer reaches of Santa Teresa, about 1km southwest of Largo do Guimarães. Connoisseurs rate Nega's street food among the city's best.

LARGO DAS LETRAS
CAFE $

Map p258 (☑2221-8992; Almirante Alexandrino 501; snacks R$4-8; ☉2-10pm Tue-Sat, to 8pm Sun) Directly above the Largo do Guimarães *bonde* stop, this bookstore and cafe has shaded outdoor tables that make for a fine break when out exploring. The cafe is set back from the street and up a flight of steps.

RÚSTICO
BRAZILIAN $$

Map p258 (☑3497-3579; Paschoal Carlos Magno 121; mains R$45-65; ☉6pm-midnight Mon, Thu & Fri, 1pm-midnight Sat, 1-10pm Sun; ☑) In an old mansion overlooking the *bonde* tracks,

Rústico is a local favorite in Santa Teresa for its romantic outdoor terrace and first-rate cooking. A creative menu is designed by the Argentine owners. Among the crowd-pleasers: hearty salads with sun-dried figs, nuts and smoked salmon; boar leg in a white-wine sauce with caramelized apple and ginger; and vegetarian *moqueca* (traditionally a Bahian fish stew).

BAR DO MINEIRO
BRAZILIAN $$

Map p258 (☏2221-9227; Paschoal Carlos Magno 99; mains R$51-75; ☉noon-2am Tue-Sat, to midnight Sun) Black-and-white photographs of legendary singers cover the walls of this old-school *boteco* (small, open-air bar) in the heart of Santa Teresa. Lively crowds have been filling this spot for years to enjoy traditional Minas Gerais dishes. The *feijoada* (bean-and-meat stew with rice) is tops, and served every day, along with appetizers, including *pasteis* (savory pastries). Strong caipirinhas will help get you in the mood.

CAFE DO ALTO
BRAZILIAN $$

Map p258 (☏2507-3172; Paschoal Carlos Magno 143; mains R$30-45; ☉noon-8pm Mon, to 10pm Tue-Fri, 9am-10pm Sat & Sun) Conveniently located a few steps from Largo do Guimarães (the epicenter of Santa Teresa), Cafe do Alto whips up filling Northeastern dishes. The wide-ranging menu features *tapiocas* (crepes made from manioc flour), *casquinha de siri* (pulled crab), *xinxim de galinha* (chicken and dried shrimp with coconut, ginger and spices over rice) and other unique dishes, plus some lighter fare such as sandwiches.

It's a lively spot that draws crowds, though Brazilians tend to give higher marks for the cooking than do foreigners.

MIKE'S HAUS
GERMAN $$

Map p258 (☏2509-5248; Almirante Alexandrino 1458A; mains R$34-65; ☉noon-midnight Tue-Sun) Mike's Haus has a pub-like atmosphere with traditional German cooking and cold glasses of imported Weizenbier. The only downside is that it's a long way from the center of Santa Teresa. It has a smaller, better-located branch (but with a simplified menu) closer to Largo do Guimarães.

★ESPÍRITO SANTA
AMAZONIAN $$$

Map p258 (☏2507-4840; Almirante Alexandrino 264; mains R$50-88; ☉noon-midnight Wed-Mon) Espírito Santa is set in a beautifully restored building in Santa Teresa. Take a seat on the back terrace with its sweeping views or inside the charming, airy dining room, and feast on rich, expertly prepared meat and seafood dishes from the Amazon and the Northeast.

Top picks include the *moqueca,* made with a delicious river fish (pintado), and the slow-roasted pork ribs served with sweet potato. Don't miss the creative cocktails, some of which feature juices from Amazonian fruits.

★APRAZÍVEL
BRAZILIAN $$$

Map p258 (☏2508-9174; Aprazível 62; mains R$70-110; ☉noon-11pm Tue-Sat, to 6pm Sun) Hidden on a windy road high up in Santa Teresa, Aprazível offers beautiful views and a lush garden setting. Grilled fish and roasted dishes showcase the country's culinary highlights of land and sea. Standouts include orange-infused grilled fish with coconut rice, cashews and roasted plantains.

This place is a bit out of the way, so call ahead (sometimes the restaurant is booked up by groups). Take a taxi and have your map handy, as drivers don't always know the spot.

TÉRÈZE
FUSION $$$

Map p258 (☏3380-0220; Felicio dos Santos, Hotel Santa Teresa; mains R$80-130; ☉noon-3:30pm & 7:30-11pm) Under the command of French chef Philippe Moulin, Térèze provides a memorable dining experience. All the elements are there, from the decadent menu to the suggested wine pairings and the superb views over the city. Choose from the likes of creamy codfish risotto with lobster bisque, suckling pig with mashed sweet potatoes and truffles, and eggplant gnocchi with cashew pesto.

Tables and artwork are made from reclaimed lumber and recycled materials.

✗ Lapa

ESPAÇO LAPA CAFE
BRAZILIAN $

Map p258 (☏3971-6812; www.espacolapa-cafe.com.br; Gomes Freire 457; mains R$15-36; ☉10am-6pm Mon, to 11pm Tue-Fri) This creative eat, drink and live-music space serves up good three-course lunch specials, plus sandwiches, snacks and a huge beer selection from across the globe (more than 400 varieties, though not all are always available). Several nights a week live bands playing rock, pop and salsa take to the small stage at the back.

★CASA MOMUS MEDITERRANEAN **$$**

Map p258 (☑3852-8250; www.casamomus.com.br; Rua do Lavradio 11; mains R$40-60; ⊘11:30am-5pm Mon, to midnight Tue & Wed, to 2am Thu-Sat) One of the best and loveliest restaurants in Lapa, Casa Momus has a small, but well-executed menu of Mediterranean-influenced dishes. Start with prawn croquettes, fried polenta with spicy Gorgonzola, or Moroccan lamb *kafta* (spiced meat patty) with tabbouleh and yogurt sauce; then feast on oxtail risotto with watercress, sesame-crusted tuna, pork tenderloin saltimbocca and other rich main courses.

Casa Momus is set in a beautifully decorated 19th-century building on a pedestrian-only stretch of Rua do Lavradio, with outdoor tables on the cobblestones.

SANTO SCENARIUM BRAZILIAN **$$**

Map p258 (☑3147-9007; www.santoscenarium.com.br; Rua do Lavradio 36; mains R$40-50; ⊘11:30am-5pm Mon, to midnight Tue-Sat) Angels, saints and other sacred images adorn the exposed-brick walls of this marvelously atmospheric restaurant on Lapa's antique row. Grilled meats and other Brazilian staples are on offer at lunchtime, while at night *cariocas* (residents of Rio) gather for cold beer, appetizers and sandwiches (such as the popular filet mignon with mozzarella and sliced pineapple). There's live music most nights.

ERNESTO GERMAN **$$**

Map p258 (☑2509-6455; Largo da Lapa 41; sandwiches R$20-25, mains R$40-70; ⊘11am-midnight Mon-Sat) With high ceilings and exposed-brick walls, there's an old-time feel to this restaurant and drinking spot that's just a short stroll from the samba clubs in Lapa. Ernesto has an extensive menu, though its grilled meats, codfish dishes and German-inspired plates such as sausage with lentils are standouts. There's live music – MPB or samba – on Wednesdays (from 8pm; R$7) and Fridays (from 10pm; R$13).

MANGUE SECO CACHAÇARIA BAHIAN **$$**

Map p258 (☑3852-1947; Rua do Lavradio 23; mains R$40-60; ⊘11am-midnight Mon-Thu, to 2am Fri & Sat) Part of the Rio Scenarium nightspot empire, Mangue Seco serves a mix of seafood and Bahian fare, with hearty *moquecas* and *caldeirada de frutos do mar* (seafood stews). Upstairs, there's a bar with more than 100 types of *cachaça*

(sugarcane alcohol), and there's live music (often samba) from Tuesdays through Thursdays.

NOVA CAPELA PORTUGUESE **$$**

Map p258 (☑2552-6228; Av Mem de Sá 96; mains R$34-58; ⊘11am-4am) This classic, old-time eating and drinking spot opened in 1967 and is a well-known draw for neighborhood bohemians: a noisy mix of artists, musicians and party kids fill the place till early into the morning. Legendarily bad-tempered waiters serve up big plates of traditional Portuguese cuisine.

Start off with the excellent *bolinhos de bacalhau* (codfish balls), before moving onto the famous *cabrito* (goat) dishes.

BAR BRASIL GERMAN **$$**

Map p258 (☑2509-5943; Av Mem de Sá 90; mains R$42-62; ⊘11:30am-midnight Mon-Sat) According to legend, this German restaurant went by the name Bar Adolf until WWII. Although the name has been Brazilianized, the cuisine is still prepared according to the same prewar tradition. Sauerkraut, *wurst* (sausage), lentils and an ever-flowing tap quench the appetite and thirst of the sometimes-rowdy Lapa crowd.

🍷 DRINKING & NIGHTLIFE

Santa Teresa and Lapa are two of Rio's most atmospheric neighborhoods, but are still rough around the edges, so take care when visiting. Lapa is at its wildest during the weekends, when *cariocas* from all over the city head to the neighborhood's samba clubs. Santa Teresa's bar scene is sprinkled along the main street near Largo do Guimarães, though Largo das Neves, with its tiny plaza and open-sided bars, is also a draw. Take a taxi when visiting these neighborhoods at night.

🍷 Santa Teresa

BAR DOS DESCASADOS LOUNGE

Map p258 (☑3380-0200; Almirante Alexandrino 660; ⊘noon-midnight) Inside Hotel Santa Teresa, this stylish bar with outdoor seating has lovely views over the city (looking north). You can enjoy decadent cocktails (including a caipirinha made with tangerines grown on the property) and savory snacks such as salmon tartare while pondering the A-list crowd. The bar is fairly empty during the week but becomes a livelier destination, mostly for couples, on weekends.

The bar has an intriguing history: the building was once a hotel for the recently divorced, and before that the bar functioned as the slave quarters of a working coffee plantation.

BAR DO GOMES   BOTECO

Map p258 (☑2232-0822; Áurea 26; ☺noon-1am Mon-Sat, to 10pm Sun) Although the sign says 'Armazém do São Thiago,' everyone calls the place Bar do Gomes. Regardless, this simple hole-in-the-wall has long been a favorite gathering spot, particularly on weekends, when young and old pack the few standup tables and bar front, and spill onto the sidewalk.

GOYA-BEIRA   BAR

Map p258 (☑2232-5751; Largo das Neves 13; ☺6pm-midnight Sun-Thu, to 2am Fri & Sat) Small but charming Goya-Beira is one of Santa Teresa's gems, and has a peaceful view onto Largo das Neves. Owner Rose Guerra prepares intriguing *cachaça* infusions as well as pizzas and appetizers. Things are liveliest on weekends.

🍸 Lapa

LEVIANO BAR   BAR

Map p258 (☑2507-5967; www.levianobar.com. br; Av Mem de Sá 49; ☺6pm-late) Near the entrance to Mem de Sá, the Leviano Bar is part of a new crop of slightly more upscale drinking and dance spots. Watch the passing people parade – and take in the great view of the Arcos da Lapa – from the outdoor area before heading to the upstairs dance floor, where DJs mix house, electrosamba, soul and reggae.

ANTÔNIO'S   BOTECO

Map p258 (☑2224-4197; Av Mem de Sá 88; ☺4pm-3am Mon-Fri, from noon Sat & Sun) Antônio's in Lapa has lots of old-school charm with its hanging lamps, wrought-iron trim work and simple wooden tables. There are a few seats on the sidewalk for taking in the pulsing street scene. There are also plenty of other drinking spots nearby, if you feel like wandering.

SARAU   BAR

Map p258 (Av Mem de Sá 64; ☺6pm-4am Tue-Sun) Just past the Arcos da Lapa and tucked inside a building covered with an enormous mural, this place is hard to miss. There's live music (samba and *forró*, popular music of the Northeast) from 7:30pm. It's also a great spot for having a few drinks at one of the many outdoor tables on the plaza in front and taking in the vertiginous street scene.

ANEXO BAR   BAR

Map p258 (Rua do Rezende 52; ☺7pm-3am Tue-Sun) Tucked down a side street away from the Lapa mayhem, Anexo is an alternative space where you can find *boa gente* (good people). It's a friendly mixed crowd that comes for cocktails, good music and conversation within an art-filled interior. Owner Luiz and his crew make great drinks and tasty snacks (try the sausage and cheese sandwich).

VACA ATOLADA   BAR

Map p258 (Gomes Freire 533; ☺8pm-2am Tue-Sat) For an authentic samba experience, head to this simple, brightly lit, tile-covered eating and drinking den. You'll find a *samba de roda* (table with samba-playing musicians) and a local crowd that squeezes up and joins in with the songs and dance (when space allows). This is old-school Lapa: friendly, ungentrified and full of life.

LA PAZ   CLUB

Map p258 (Rua do Rezende 82; admission R$10-30; ☺11pm-6am Wed-Sat) For a break from samba, this popular nightspot provides a fine antidote, with a groove-loving dance floor provided by DJs spinning hip-hop, house and funk. It's a small and intimate club with an underground vibe; it has two dance floors, and a band that takes the stage on Friday and Saturday nights.

BURACO DA LACRAIA   GAY

Map p258 (☑2242-0446; André Cavalcante 58; admission R$40-45; ☺10pm-5:30am Fri & Sat) Going strong since the 1980s, Buraco da Lacraia always makes for a riotous night out. You'll find glamorous and trashy visitors, bizarre drag shows, karaoke, a dark room and other amusements. Admission includes free drinks – beer and certain well drinks – all night long.

SANTA TERESA & LAPA DRINKING & NIGHTLIFE

⭐ **ENTERTAINMENT**

RIO SCENARIUM
SAMBA

Map p258 (www.rioscenarium.com.br; Rua do Lavradio 20, Lapa; cover R$25-50; ⊙7pm-4am Tue-Sat) One of the city's most photogenic nightspots, Rio Scenarium has three floors, each lavishly decorated with antiques. Balconies overlook the stage on the 1st floor, where dancers keep time to the jazz-infused samba, *choro* or *pagode* (popular samba music) filling the air. Rio Scenarium receives much press outside of Brazil, and attracts at least as many foreigners as locals.

SEMENTE
SAMBA

Map p258 (☑9781-2451; Evaristo da Veiga 149, Lapa; admission R$20-40; ⊙8pm-2am) One of the few venues in Lapa that holds court on Sunday and Monday nights, Semente has longevity. Although it has closed and reopened a few times, it was one of the first places to bring samba back to the city. Its current incarnation is small and intimate, with good bands and a crowd that comes for the music rather than the Lapa mayhem.

TRIBOZ
JAZZ

Map p258 (☑2210-0366; www.triboz-rio.com; Conde de Lages 19, Lapa; cover around R$30; ⊙6-8pm & 9pm-1am Thu-Sat) Not for lazy ears, this avant-garde jazz house, a little hidden gem among the sonic cognoscenti, is unique in Rio for its serious approach to performances. Run by an Australian ethnomusicologist, it sits in a shadier part of old Lapa in a signless mansion, which transforms into a beautiful showcase space for Brazil's most cutting-edge artists.

The crowd skews to over thirties and/or music aficionados, who come for the evening's three 45-minute sets and good-value, Oz-inspired grub. Reservations are essential two days in advance by phone only.

DEMOCRÁTICUS
SAMBA

Map p258 (☑2252-1324; Rua do Riachuelo 93, Lapa; admission R$25-50; ⊙10pm-3am Wed-Sat) Murals line the foyer of this 1867 mansion. The rhythms filter down from above. Follow the sound up the marble staircase and out into a large hall filled with tables, an enormous dance floor and a long stage covered with musicians. A wide range of *cariocas* gathers here to dance, revel in the music and soak up the splendor of the samba-infused setting.

If you come to just one *gafieira* (dance hall) in Lapa, Democráticus is a good choice.

CARIOCA DA GEMA
SAMBA

Map p258 (www.barcariocadagema.com.br; Av Mem de Sá 79, Lapa; cover R$25-40; ⊙7pm-2am Mon-Fri, from 9pm Sat & Sun) Although it's now surrounded by clubs, Carioca da Gema was one of Lapa's pioneers when it opened in 2000. This small, warmly lit club still attracts some of the city's best samba bands, and you'll find a festive, mixed crowd filling the dance floor most nights.

Monday nights (when most samba clubs are closed in Lapa) are particularly popular.

CIRCO VOADOR
CONCERT VENUE

Map p258 (☑2533-0354; www.circovoador.com. br; Rua dos Arcos, Lapa; admission R$40-90) In a curvilinear building behind the Arcos da Lapa, Circo Voador hosts big-name Brazilian and international artists. The acoustics here are excellent, and after a show you'll find plenty of other musical options in the area. Check the website to see what's on. You can also take classes in capoeira (Afro-Brazilian martial arts), dance, percussion and yoga.

LAPA 40 GRAUS
LIVE MUSIC

Map p258 (☑3970-1338; www.lapa40graus.com. br; Rua do Riachuelo 97, Lapa; admission R$10-50; ⊙6pm-5am Wed-Sat) This impressive multistory music venue and pool hall has space for lounging on the 1st floor, more than a dozen pool tables on the 2nd floor, and a small stage and dancing couples on the top floor. There are usually two shows nightly. Pop, rock, samba and *choro* kick off around 7pm and 11pm.

SACRILÉGIO
SAMBA

Map p258 (☑3970-1461; Av Mem de Sá 81, Lapa; admission R$25-40; ⊙7pm-2am Tue-Thu, to 6am Fri, 9pm-6am Sat) A short stroll past the Arcos da Lapa, you'll find Sacrilégio, a key spot for catching live samba bands in an intimate setting. The outdoor garden makes a fine spot for imbibing a few cold *chopes* while the music filters through the windows. In addition to samba, Sacrilégio hosts *choro*, *forró* and MPB bands.

THE DANCE HALLS OF OLD

If you're interested in Brazilian music and dance, shine up your dancing shoes and head for some of Rio's old-school-style dance halls, known as *gafieiras*. Originally established in the 1920s as dance halls for Rio's urban working class, *gafieiras* nowadays attract an eclectic combination of musicians, dancers, *malandros* (con men) and, of course, the radical chic from Zona Sul. Modern and sleek they are not. Typically held in the ballrooms of old colonial buildings in Lapa, the locations are magnificently Old World. Bow-tied waiters serve ice-cold *cerveja* (beer) under low, yellow lights and, while the setup initially looks formal, give it a few rounds and it will dissolve into a typically raucous Brazilian evening.

Before *gafieiras* were established, Rio's different communities were polarized by their places of social interaction: opera and tango for the Europeans; street *choro* (romantic, intimate samba) for the Africans. Responding to a social need and in tandem with the politics of the time, *gafieiras* quickly became places where musicians and audiences of black and white backgrounds alike could mix and create new sounds. Through the *gafieiras*, the street-improvised *choro* formations became big-band songs and a new Brazilian sound was born. The best and oldest dance halls are Democráticus (p144), attracting a young yet fashionably bohemian crowd on Wednesdays, and Estudantina Musical (p132), which has a much-loved night of revelry on Tuesdays.

The standard of dancing is outstanding in Brazil, so expect to see couples who would be considered professional in Europe or the US dancing unnoticed across the polished floors. While just about anything goes in Rio, it's an opportunity for *cariocas* to dress up a little, so you will see quite a few dresses and smart shoes. Don't be intimidated by the other dancers. Unlike in Buenos Aires, where the tango is for experts only, Brazilians are pretty relaxed about newcomers dancing. For those traveling solo, *gafieiras* are fantastic places to meet some intriguing locals and learn a few steps. Dance around the edge of the dance floor with the rest of the dancers to get a closer look at how the dance works – if you are a woman, you won't wait long before someone asks you to dance. Alternatively you can take a lesson and perhaps meet some fellow beginners to dance with. There are a number of places where you can sign up for a group or private lesson.

By Carmen Michael

SANTA TERESA & LAPA ENTERTAINMENT

BECO DO RATO LIVE MUSIC
Map p258 (☑2508-5600; http://becodorato.com.br; Joaquim Silva 11, Lapa; ⊙6pm-3am Tue, Thu & Fri) One of Lapa's classic bohemian spots, this tiny bar has excellent live groups playing to a samba-loving crowd. The outdoor seating and informal setting are an unbeatable mix. Marcio, the friendly owner, hails from Minas Gerais; to get the night started, ask him for a tasty *cachaça* from his home state.

Friday nights are some of the best nights to go, though there's also live music on Tuesdays and Thursdays. It's located on a battered stretch of Lapa; Beco do Rato, incidentally, means 'Alley of the Rat.'

PAIOL 08 LIVE MUSIC
Map p258 (☑2524-2950; Rua dos Arcos 10, Lapa; admission R$25-60; ⊙10pm-4am Fri-Sun) Right next to the Arcos da Lapa, this multilevel

bar and live-music venue has an upstairs open-air terrace with great views of the old aqueduct. The stage inside hosts an eclectic lineup of DJs, live samba, MPB, jazz, rock and cabaret performances.

TEATRO ODISSÉIA SAMBA
Map p258 (☑2226-9691; Av Mem de Sá 66, Lapa; admission R$25-40; ⊙11pm-6am Wed-Sat, 2pm-midnight Sun) This spacious three-story Lapa club features live-music shows and DJs, with a relaxed area upstairs if you need a break from the sounds. There's also a terrace with views of the Arcos da Lapa. You'll find plenty of samba, and MPB and rock make an occasional appearance.

FUNDIÇÃO PROGRESSO CONCERT VENUE
Map p258 (☑3212-0800; www.fundicaoprogresso.com.br; Rua dos Arcos 24, Lapa; admission R$25-50) This former foundry in Lapa hides one

of Rio's top music and theater spaces. A diverse range of shows is staged here: big-name acts such as Manu Chao and Caetano Veloso, plus theater, video arts and ballet. The foundation is one of Lapa's premier arts institutions, and you can study dance, capoeira and circus arts here.

SALA CECÍLIA MEIRELES   PERFORMING ARTS
Map p258 (☑2332-9223; www.salaceciliameireles .com.br; Largo da Lapa 47, Lapa) Lapa's splendidly restored early-20th-century gem hosts orchestral concerts throughout the year. Lately the repertoire has included contemporary groups, playing both *choro* and classical music.

CINE SANTA TERESA   CINEMA
Map p258 (☑2222-0203; www.cinesanta.com.br; Paschoal Carlos Magno 136, Santa Teresa) This small, single-screen theater is well located on Largo do Guimarães. Befitting the art-loving 'hood, the cinema screens a selection of independent and Brazilian films.

 SHOPPING

Stomping ground for Rio's bohemian crowd, Santa Teresa has a growing number of handicraft shops and vintage stores, with some enticing restaurants and cafes that add to the appeal. In Lapa you'll find Rua do Lavradio, the city's best antiques street. It's at its liveliest on the first Saturday of the month.

LA VEREDA HANDICRAFTS   HANDICRAFTS
Map p258 (☑2507-0317; Almirante Alexandrino 428, Santa Teresa; ⊙10am-8pm) La Vereda stocks a colorful selection of handicrafts from local artists and artisans in a spot near Largo do Guimarães. Hand-painted clay figurines by Pernambuco artists, heavy Minas ceramics, delicate sterling silver jewelry and loosely woven tapestries cover the interior of the old store.

Other cool gift ideas: T-shirts bearing a *bonde* image, block prints by local artist Erivaldo and vibrant *arte naïf* canvases by various Santa artists. There are several other handicraft shops and galleries also on this street.

TUCUM   HANDICRAFTS
Map p258 (☑2242-5860; Paschoal Carlos Magno 100, Santa Teresa; ⊙2-8pm Sun-Wed, from 11am Thu-Sat) This small but welcoming shop

specializes in crafts and artwork from the Amazon. You'll find woven baskets, organic jewelry made from Amazonian seeds and fibers, hammocks, small wood carvings, pottery, wall hangings and more.

SCENARIUM ANTIQUE   ANTIQUES
Map p258 (☑3147-9014; Rua do Lavradio 28, Lapa; ⊙9am-6pm Mon, 10am-7pm Tue-Fri, 10am-2pm Sat) One of Lavradio's best antique shops, this place is packed with glass- and dishware, furniture, iron kettles, lamps, oil paintings and a variety of other displays that make for a curious glimpse into the past.

LAPA DECOR   ANTIQUES
Map p258 (☑2221-1878; Rua do Lavradio 158, Lapa; ⊙9am-6pm Mon-Fri, to 3pm Sat) This old colonial edifice hides an intriguing selection of antiques, from tables and chairs to chandeliers, glassware, ceramics and old oil paintings. Although many objects for sale here won't fit in your suitcase, it's still a fun place to browse.

FEIRA DO RIO ANTIGO   MARKET
Map p258 (☑2224-6693; Rua do Lavradio, Lapa; ⊙10am-6pm 1st Sat of month) Although the Rio Antiques Fair happens just once a month, don't miss it if you're in town. The colonial buildings become a living installation as the whole street fills with antiques, clothing and craft vendors, and food stalls. Samba bands add to the festive air.

SPORTS & ACTIVITIES

EAT RIO FOOD TOURS   WALKING TOUR
(www.eatrio.net; per person US$90) On these highly recommended small-group tours, you'll visit markets, snack bars and other foodie hot spots to taste a wide range of exotic fruits, juices and street food little known outside of Brazil. The English-speaking guides are excellent and provide culinary as well as cultural insight. The cost of the tour includes all foods and snacks, including a big meal at the end.

Tours begin in Lapa or Santa Teresa.

FUNDIÇÃO PROGRESSO   DANCE
Map p258 (☑2220-5070; www.fundicaoprogresso .com.br; Rua dos Arcos 24, Lapa) This cultural center offers a wide range of courses, including classes in dancing: African styles, salsa, tango and samba. Those seeking

something different can sign up for classes in percussion, acrobatics (run by the respected dance-theater-circus outfit Intrépida Trupe) or capoeira. Percussion and circus arts courses typically cost R$200 for twice-weekly classes for a month. Capoeira costs R$100 for a month.

You can also take a drop-in yoga class (R$30), currently held on Tuesdays and Thursdays at 12.30pm.

NÚCLEO DE DANÇA
RENATA PEÇANHA   DANCE
Map p258 (☏2221-1011; www.renatapecanha.com.br; Rua dos Inválidos 129, Lapa) A large upstairs studio on the edge of Lapa, this dance academy offers classes in *forró,* salsa, *zouk* (a slow and sensual dance derived from the lambada) and samba. Twice-weekly classes cost about R$140 per month.

Zona Norte

Neighborhood Top Five

1 Hearing the roar of the crowds as some of the world's best players take to the field inside hallowed **Maracanã Football Stadium** (p150).

2 Browsing handicrafts, snacking on Northeastern dishes and partner-dancing to live *forró* in the **Feira Nordestina** (p152).

3 Exploring relics from Brazil's early-19th-century past at the neoclassical **Museu do Primeiro Reinado** (p152).

4 Taking a stroll amid the greenery of the once im-perial **Quinta da Boa Vista** (p152).

5 Perusing pre-Columbian artifacts inside the **Museu Nacional** (p152), a former royal palace.

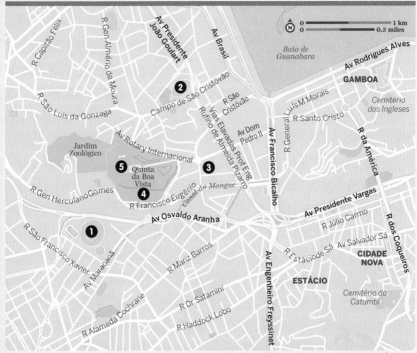

For more detail of this area, see Map p261 ➡

Explore Zona Norte

Vast Zona Norte sprawls many kilometers toward the Baixada Fluminense. It boasts fewer attractions than the Zona Sul and Centro, but there are still excellent reasons to visit, including soccer rowdiness at Maracanã, great views from little-visited landmarks and historical intrigue at former palaces.

The Zona Norte is home to many distinct neighborhoods and favelas (slums, informal communities), including several with pivotal roles in the competitive Carnaval parade. Rehearsals at samba schools are a worthwhile draw, and attract huge crowds as Carnaval draws nearer. Some favelas are receiving dramatic makeovers, including Complexo do Alemão, a collection of communities that is slowly becoming a tourist attraction, courtesy of a *teleférico* (cable car) that glides over the favela hillsides.

In the 19th century the Zona Norte was the home of the nobility, including Dom João VI. The area saw dramatic transformation as mangrove swamps were cleared to make way for stately homes. In the 20th century, the wealthy moved out and exploding urbanism transformed the landscape into a gritty, heavily populated, working-class suburb. A visit is recommended for those who want to see how the rest of Rio lives. You'll escape the tourist crowds and experience an authentic slice of Rio far removed from the picture-postcard sights of the Zona Sul.

Although the area is spread out, several sites are fairly close together and are easily reached by metro, lying just west of Centro. Other places are best reached by taxi.

Local Life

➡ **Nightlife** Dust off your dance shoes and join *forró*-loving crowds at a long night of live music and dancing in the Feira Nordestina (p152).

➡ **Markets** CADEG (p153) is Rio's largest market and a fine place to browse the endless rows of produce, meats and fish; it's also home to great-value restaurants, with a festive air (and live music) on weekends.

Getting There & Away

➡ **Maracanã buses** From Copacabana, Ipanema and Leblon (464); to Copacabana and Ipanema (456 and 457); to Leblon (464).

➡ **Maracanã metro** Maracanã.

➡ **Quinta da Boa Vista buses** Copacabana, Ipanema and Leblon (474).

➡ **Quinta da Boa Vista metro** São Cristóvão (for Museu Nacional and Jardim Zoológico).

Lonely Planet's Top Tip

The best time to visit this area is on weekends, when you'll find the markets, parks and other attractions at their liveliest.

 Best Places to Eat

➡ Aconchego Carioca (p153)
➡ Barsa (p153)
➡ Da Gema (p154)

For reviews, see p153 ➡

 Best Views

➡ Sambódromo (p153)
➡ Complexo do Alemão (p152)
➡ Igreja da Penha (p153)

For reviews, see p152 ➡

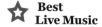 **Best Live Music**

➡ Renascença Clube (p154)
➡ Feira Nordestina (p152)

For reviews, see p154 ➡

 ZONA NORTE

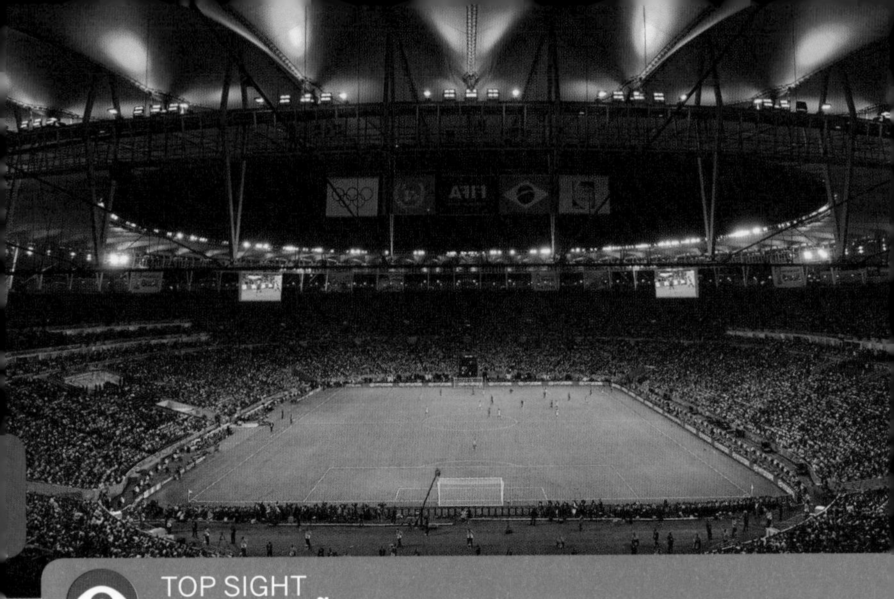

TOP SIGHT
MARACANÃ FOOTBALL STADIUM

CHRIS BRUNSKILL LTD / CONTRIBUTOR / GETTY IMAGES ©

Rio's Maracanã stadium is hallowed ground among football lovers. The massive arena has been the site of legendary victories and crushing defeats (such as Brazil's gut-wrenching loss in the final game of the 1950 World Cup to Uruguay). More recently, Maracanã played a starring role in the 2014 World Cup when it hosted major games, including Brazil's opener. The stadium will also host the opening and closing ceremonies of the 2016 Summer Olympics, as well as the football final. But no matter who takes the field, the 78,800-seat open-air arena comes to life in spectacular fashion on game day.

DON'T MISS...

- A match between any of Rio's hometown rivals.
- Peering behind the scenes on a stadium tour.

PRACTICALITIES

- Map p261, A3
- ☎8871-3950
- www.suderj.rj.gov.br/maracana.asp
- Av Maracanã, São Cristóvão
- admission R$40-80
- Ⓢ Maracanã

The Spectacle

A game at Maracanã is a must-see. Matches here rate among the most exciting in the world, and the fans among the most colorful. The devoted pound huge samba drums, spread vast flags across great swaths of the stadium, dance in the aisles, and detonate smoke bombs in team colors. You'll hear – and feel – the deafening roar when the home team takes the field, and the wall of sound and palpable air of near hysteria will surround you when a player pounds the ball into the back of the net. Things are only slightly calmer since alcohol was banned inside the stadium back in 2003 – though with pressure from FIFA, an exception to the law was put in place for the 2014 World Cup.

Going to a Game

Games take place year-round and generally happen on Saturday or Sunday (starting at 4pm or 6pm) or on Wednesday and Thursday (around 8:30pm). Seating at the stadium is by sector, A through F. The north (E and F) and south (B and C) seats are behind the goals and are generally the cheapest and liveliest sections. East (D) and west (A) sectors have better sight lines and are pricier; these have numbered seats and are not as rowdy as the goal seats. Maracanã Mais is part of the west sector, with buffet service included in the ticket price. The ticket price is R$40 to R$80 for most games.

Although buses run to and from the stadium, on game days the metro is generally faster and less crowded.

The Redesign

Maracanã remains Brazil's largest sports arena, seating nearly 79,000 fans (78,838 to be exact) – which is not as many as in years past. It underwent a massive R$1 billion renovation before the 2014 World Cup. During renovations, all seats were replaced in the arena, the lower level was demolished to improve visibility, access ramps were expanded and the stadium added a new roof, which now covers all seats. It's also sustainably designed – complete with a rainwater collection system. The facade, which is a protected landmark under the National Institute of Historical & Artistic Heritage, has remain unchanged.

In 2016 the stadium takes the spotlight once again as the setting for the opening and closing ceremonies of the Summer Olympics and Paralympic Games. It will also host the football finals. After the Olympics, Maracanã will continue serving as the staging post for matches between Rio's league teams – Flamengo, Fluminense, Vasco da Gama and Botafogo.

Maracanã Tour

For a behind-the-scenes look at the stadium, take a tour. A must for football fans, the tour takes you through the press box, the grandstand, into the locker rooms and then through the tunnel out onto the field. You'll also visit a room that pays tribute to Brazilian legends who made history here such as Pelé and Garrincha. Tours (around $40) take place from 9am to 5pm; on game days the last tour starts four hours before kick-off.

GAME-DAY TOURS

If you prefer to go in a group, a number of English-speaking tour operators organize game-day outings, including transportation. Leading big-group tours are **Brazil Expedition** (☎99998-2907; www. brazilexpedition.com; per person R$120-150) and Be a Local (p208). For something more personalized, independent guide Sergio Manhães (p50) takes small groups with him (via metro) on game day.

The first time Brazil hosted the World Cup was in 1950, when the final game took place inside Maracanã stadium, which had been built in preparation for the big tournament. Brazil made it all the way to the finals, and more than 170,000 fans packed the stadium to watch the last match against Uruguay. With the match tied at 1–1, Uruguay scored a goal with just 11 minutes left to play. The victory stunned the crowd and left a deep scar on the nation's psyche – this crippling defeat on home soil is still in parlance today and referred to as the *maracanaço*, roughly translated as 'that God-awful thing that happened in Maracanã!'

ZONA NORTE MARACANÃ FOOTBALL STADIUM

⊙ SIGHTS

MARACANÃ FOOTBALL STADIUM STADIUM
See p150.

FEIRA NORDESTINA MARKET
Map p261 (☏2580-5335; www.feiradesaocristo
vao.org.br; Campo de São Cristóvão; admission
R$4, Tue-Thu free; ⊘10am-6pm Tue-Thu, 10am
Fri-9pm Sun) This enormous fair (32,000
sq meters with over 600 stalls) is not to
be missed. It showcases the culture from
the Northeast, with *barracas* (food stalls)
selling Bahian dishes as well as beer and
cachaça (sugarcane alcohol), which flows
in great abundance here. The best time to
go is on the weekend, when you can catch
live bands playing *forró*, plus samba groups
and comedy troupes, MPB (Música Popular
Brasileira) and *rodas de capoeira* (capoeira
circles).

The vibrant scene runs nonstop from Friday morning through to Sunday evening. In
addition to food and drink, you can browse
music CDs (*forró*, of course), hammocks
and a wide assortment of handicrafts.

QUINTA DA BOA VISTA PARK
Map p261 (☏2562-6900; ⊘9am-5pm) Quinta
da Boa Vista was the residence of the Portuguese imperial family until the Republic
was proclaimed. Today it's a large and busy
park with gardens and lakes. On weekends
it's crowded with football games and families from the Zona Norte. The former imperial mansion houses the Museu Nacional
and Museu da Fauna. The Jardim Zoológico, Rio's zoo, is 200m away.

MUSEU NACIONAL MUSEUM
Map p261 (☏3938-1100; Quinta da Boa Vista;
adult/child R$6/3; ⊘noon-5pm Mon, 10am-
5pm Tue-Sun) There are many interesting
exhibits housed in the former imperial
mansion: dinosaur fossils, saber-toothed
tiger skeletons, beautiful pieces of pre-
Columbian ceramics from the littoral and
high plains of Peru, a huge meteorite, hundreds of stuffed birds, mammals and fish,
gruesome displays of tropical diseases, and
exhibits on the peoples of Brazil.

This museum and its imperial entrance
are still stately and imposing, and the view
from the balcony to the royal palms is majestic. However, the weathered buildings
and unkempt grounds have clearly declined
since the fall of the monarchy.

**MUSEU DO PRIMEIRO
REINADO** NOTABLE BUILDING, MUSEUM
Map p261 (☏2332-4513; Av Dom Pedro II 293;
⊘11am-5pm Tue-Fri) FREE A 1km walk east of
the Quinta da Boa Vista, this former mansion of the Marquesa de Santos depicts the
history of the First Reign (the reign of bumbling Dom Pedro I before he was driven
out of the country). The collection includes
documents, furniture and paintings, but
the main attraction is the building and its
interior, with striking murals by Francisco
Pedro do Amaral.

JARDIM ZOOLÓGICO ZOO
Map p261 (Rio Zoo; ☏3878-4200; Quinta da
Boa Vista; admission R$10; ⊘9am-4:30pm Tue-
Sun) Covering over 12 hectares, the zoo at
Quinta da Boa Vista has a wide variety of
reptiles, mammals and birds, mostly indigenous to Brazil. Special attractions include
the large walk-through aviary and the night
house, which features nocturnal animals.
The monkey house is also a crowd favorite.
Some animal enclosures are cramped,
though overall the reproduced habitats are
fairly well done.

COMPLEXO DO ALEMÃO NEIGHBORHOOD
(teleférico R$5; ⊘teleférico 6am-8pm Mon-Fri,
8am-6pm Sat) This sprawling collection of
makeshift communities has gotten a new
lease on life since the inauguration of a
teleférico in 2011. With five stations set
on the hills of this 70,000-strong community, the once arduous journey in and out
of the favela is now a breeze. Tourists are
slowly discovering one of Rio's newest un-
sung attractions, which has splendid views
over the hillsides. Disembark at Palmeiras
(the uppermost station) for a poke around.
There are snack stands here and occasional
live music on weekends.

The easiest way to get to the lowest gondola station, Bonsucesso, is by taxi, though
if you're confident moving about Rio, you
can take a commuter train from Central
Station to Bonsucesso, which connects to
the *teleférico* (and save yourself a R$50
one-way taxi fare). Be aware that although
security has improved dramatically in the
last few years, there are still occasional outbreaks of violence, with the rare shootout
between police and drug traffickers every
now and again.

CIDADE DO SAMBA
CULTURAL SITE

Map p261 (Samba City; ☎2213-2503; http://cid adedosambarj.globo.com; Rivadávia Correa 60, Gamboa; ☺10am-5pm Tue-Sat) Located north of Centro, near the port, Samba City is actually made up of 14 large buildings where the top schools assemble the Carnaval floats. It's an intriguing place for those who want a behind-the-scenes look at those massive and wildly imaginative creations. You can catch occasional samba shows here, though these are mostly put on for visiting tour groups.

CADEG
MARKET

Map p261 (Centro de Abastecimento do Estado da Guanabara, Supply Center of Guanabara State; www.cadeg.com.br; Capitão Félix 110, Benfica; ☺1am-5pm Mon-Sat, to 2pm Sun) While the Centro de Abastecimento do Estado da Guanabara doesn't have quite the same ring to it as 'Ipanema beach,' this voluminous market packs a treasure trove of fruits, vegetables, meats, fish, cheeses, flowers and spices. And while the 350-plus shops are mostly a wholesale affair (hence the 1am opening time), the real reason to come here is for lunch, with a number of good and decidedly unfussy restaurants spread around the four-story building.

IGREJA DA PENHA
CHURCH

(☎3219-6262; Largo da Penha 19, Penha; ☺7am-6pm) Rio's most dramatically set church in a 17th-century, double-steepled confection offers dramatic 360-degree views from its clifftop perch. A recently renovated tram whisks visitors up to the top (free of charge), though the faithful prefer to ascend the 382 steps on their own power – and some even do it on their knees. The church is surrounded by favelas and best reached by taxi.

SAMBÓDROMO
STADIUM

Map p261 (www.sambadrome.com; Marques do Sapucaí) The epicenter of Rio's Carnaval, the Sambódromo was designed by Oscar Niemeyer and completed in 1984. During the big parades, come for the fantastic views from the stands across elaborate floats, whirling dancers and pounding drum corps. The open-air arena received a makeover for the 2016 Olympics, with improved sight lines and a more symmetrical design in keeping with Niemeyer's original vision.

WORTH A DETOUR

BEACHES OF EAST RIO

A number of beaches lie just east of Niterói. The ones closest to town are too polluted for swimming, but as you continue out you'll reach some pristine beaches – **Piratininga**, **Camboinhas**, **Itaipu** and finally **Itacoatiara**, the most fabulous of the bunch. Framed by two looming hills on either side of the shore and backed by vegetation, the white sands of Itacoatiara seem a world away from the urban beaches of Rio. *Barracas* (food stalls) sell scrumptious plates of fish, and there are also food stands overlooking the beach. The surf is strong here – evidenced by the many surfers jockeying for position – so swim with caution. To get here, you can take bus 38 or any bus labeled 'Itacoatiara' from the ferry terminal (R$4, 50 minutes). If you're traveling in a group, you can negotiate a return fare with a taxi driver.

 EATING

ACONCHEGO CARIOCA
BRAZILIAN $$

Map p261 (☎2273-1035; Barão de Iguatemi 379, Praça da Bandeira; mains for 2 people R$70-100; ☺noon-11pm Tue-Sat, to 5pm Sun) Aconchego Carioca consistently ranks as one of the best places in town to eat traditional Brazilian cuisine. The setting, cozy and welcoming, has a casual neighborhood vibe, but attracts diners from across the city who come for *bobó de camarão* (shrimp and coconut-milk stew), pork ribs with guava sauce, and a *cachaça*-tinged flan for dessert.

BARSA
PORTUGUESE $$

Map p261 (☎2585-3743; 4th fl, Capitão Félix 110, Benfica; mains for 2 people R$50-120; ☺noon-4pm Mon-Thu, to 5pm Fri-Sun) Inside the massive CADEG market, Barsa serves mouthwatering dishes using the freshest ingredients imaginable (not surprising, since Rio's largest produce market surrounds the place). The most famous dish is their roast suckling pig and all the fixings, which serves four and costs about R$300 – though half servings are also available. On Sunday there's live *chorinho* (a kind of instrumental music).

ZONA NORTE ENTERTAINMENT

DA GEMA BRAZILIAN **$$**

(☎3549-1480; Barão de Mesquita 615, Tijuca; snacks R$6-28; ☺5pm-midnight Tue-Fri, from 1pm Sat, 1-6pm Sun) Well off the beaten path, this humble-looking *botequim* (bar with table service) dishes up mouthwatering *petiscos* (appetizers). It was begun by three culinary graduates who have elevated simple bar ingredients into high art in dishes such as *pastel de feijao-preto* (black-bean pasties), house-made *linguiça* (sausage) and *fondue da gema* (polenta with crunchy pork rinds and sweet peppers, served with pork ribs and sausage).

Its location near Salgueiro Escola de Samba (400m away) makes it a good pre-party spot on Saturday nights.

RESTAURANTE QUINTA DA BOA VISTA PORTUGUESE **$$**

Map p261 (☎2589-4279; Parque da Quinta da Boa Vista; mains R$45-70; ☺11am-6pm) Inside the 1822 chapel of the former royal palace, this place serves up excellent *bacalhau ao forno* (oven-baked codfish), *caldeirada de frutos de mar* (seafood stew) and other Portuguese classics. The *picanha* (rump-steak) is also top-notch. The servers, dressed in period costume, add a whimsical touch to the proceedings.

ENTERTAINMENT

RENASCENÇA CLUBE LIVE MUSIC

(☎3253-2322; www.renascencaclube.com.br; Rua Barão de São Francisco 54, Andaraí; ☺5-10pm Mon & Sat) For an authentic slice of Rio, head to one of the massive open-air samba parties that happen several times a week in Andaraí. The set-up is simple: a handful of musicians gathered around a table playing samba, while huge dance-loving crowds (that join in on many of the songs) gather around. Monday nights (*samba do trabalhador*, or samba for the worker), which are lead by maestro Moacyr Luz, are excellent.

If you like samba, don't mind big crowds and are up for a bit of adventure, then this place is for you – it's well off the tourist circuit.

Barra da Tijuca & Western Rio

Neighborhood Top Five

❶ Hiking through tropical rainforest, enjoying memorable views from rocky lookouts and recovering beneath cool waterfalls in the **Floresta da Tijuca** (p161).

❷ Basking on the wide golden sands of **Praia da Barra da Tijuca** (p157).

❸ Exploring the lushly decadent gardens of **Sítio Burle Marx** (p157).

❹ Delving into Brazil's rich folk-art traditions at the impressive **Casa do Pontal** (p157).

❺ Looking for wildlife on the peaceful trails of the **Parque Ecológico Chico Mendes** (p157).

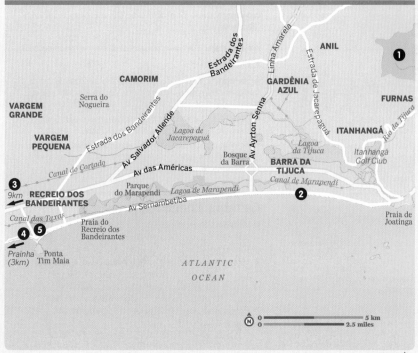

For more detail of this area, see Map p262 ➡

Best Places to Eat

➡ Laguna Restaurante (p157)

➡ Don Pascual (p160)

➡ Bira (p160)

For reviews, see p157 ➡

Best Places to Walk

➡ Floresta da Tijuca (p161)

➡ Bosque da Barra (p157)

➡ Parque Ecológico Chico Mendes (p157)

For reviews, see p157 ➡

Best Places to Shop

➡ Village (p161)

➡ Fashion Mall (p162)

➡ Barra Shopping (p162)

For reviews, see p161 ➡

BARRA DA TIJUCA & WESTERN RIO

Explore Barra da Tijuca & Western Rio

The Miami of Rio, Barra da Tijuca is a sprawling suburb with huge malls and entertainment complexes, long traffic corridors and very little pedestrian movement. Barra – as it's known locally – is also where much of the 2016 Summer Olympics will take place. The beach here is the real attraction, a wide and lovely 12km-long stretch of shoreline.

The commercial area feels quite different from other parts of Rio, as Barra's development happened relatively recently. The middle class first began moving here in the 1970s, when *cariocas* (residents of Rio) fled crowded, crime-ridden streets to live on an unpopulated stretch of beachfront. Today, the influx of new residents has created crowded, problematic conditions once again.

While first-time visitors to Rio don't always make it to Barra da Tijuca, there are some intriguing sights here, aside from the beach. The Sítio Burle Marx (p157) contains some of the city's most picturesque gardens, while the Casa do Pontal (p157) houses a fascinating collection of folk art.

Once you get beyond the development of Barra, the region gets less and less urban, and you'll soon feel like you're deep in the tropics. Some of Rio's best beaches lie out this way. There are also great restaurants in idyllic settings where you can feast on seafood while watching crashing waves, all of which seems a far cry from busy downtown Rio.

Local Life

➡ **Hangouts** Even party people from the Zona Sul will make the trip out to Nuth (p160), one of Rio's loveliest nightclubs.

➡ **Beaches** The western beaches are quite stunning, particularly Joatinga, Prainha and Grumari (p160).

➡ **Arts** Barra's architecturally striking Cidade das Artes (p160) is the go-to destination for concerts and performances.

Getting There & Away

➡ **Metrô na Superfície** The Barra Expresso metro bus connects Ipanema/General Osório metro station with points along Barra.

➡ **Metrô** The new *linha* 4 (line 4) connects Barra da Tijuca to Ipanema. It runs from Jardim Oceânico station (eastern Barra) to São Conrado, Antero de Quental (Leblon), Jardim de Alah (Leblon), NS da Paz (Ipanema) and General Osório (Ipanema and Copacabana).

⊙ SIGHTS

PRAIA DA BARRA DA TIJUCA   BEACH
Map p262 (Av Sernambetiba, Recreio dos Bandeirantes) The best thing about Barra is the beach. It stretches for 12km, with the lovely blue sea lapping at the shore. The first few kilometers of its eastern end are filled with bars and seafood restaurants.

The young and hip hang out in front of *barraca* (stall) No 1, in an area known as Praia do Pepê, after the famous *carioca* hang-gliding champion who died during a competition in Japan in 1991.

PARQUE OLÍMPICO   LANDMARK
Map p262 This is the epicenter of the 2016 Summer Olympics and the Paralympic Games. You'll find seven arenas here: the tennis center, the aquatics stadium, the velodrome and separate arenas for basketball, judo and wrestling, handball, and fencing and tae kwon do. After the Olympics, the city plans to convert some of the arenas into training facilities, while others will be dismantled and used to construct schools.

SÍTIO BURLE MARX   GARDENS
(☑2410-1412; visitas.srbm@iphan.gov.br; Estrada da Barra de Guaratiba 2019, Guaratiba; admission R$10; ⊙tours 9:30am & 1:30pm Tue-Sat) This 35-hectare estate was once the home of Brazil's most famous landscape architect, Roberto Burle Marx. The estate's lush vegetation includes thousands of plant species, some of which are rare varieties from different corners of the globe. A 17th-century **Benedictine chapel** also lies on the estate, along with Burle Marx's original farmhouse and studio, where you can see displays of paintings, furniture and sculptures by the talented designer. Tours are by advance appointment only.

On the downside, it's a very long drive to get out here (either take a costly taxi or go by private vehicle, making sure you have a good map or GPS); you're not allowed to wander on your own; and there's no food at the museum.

PARQUE ECOLÓGICO
CHICO MENDES   PARK
Map p262 (☑2437-6400; Km 17, Av Jarbas de Carvalho 679, Recreio dos Bandeirantes; ⊙8am-5pm Tue-Sun) This 40-hectare park was created in 1989 and named after the Brazilian ecological activist who was murdered for his work.

The park protects the remaining sand-spit vegetation from real-estate speculators. The facilities include a visitor center and ecological trails that lead to a small lake.

CASA DO PONTAL   MUSEUM
Map p262 (☑2490-4013; www.museucasadopontal.com.br; Estrada do Pontal 3295, Recreio dos Bandeirantes; admission permanent collection/temporary exhibits R$10/4; ⊙9:30am-5pm Tue-Fri, 10:30am-6pm Sat & Sun) Owned by French designer Jacques Van de Beuque, this impressive set of more than 5000 pieces is one of the best folk-art collections in Brazil. The assorted artifacts are grouped according to theme, including music, Carnaval, religion and folklore. The grounds of the museum are surrounded by lush vegetation.

BOSQUE DA BARRA   PARK
Map p262 (Av das Américas 6000, at Av Ayrton Senna, Barra da Tijuca; ⊙8am-5pm Tue-Sun) Covering 50 hectares of salt-marsh vegetation, this park is a refuge and breeding area for many small birds and animals. The woods have a jogging track and cycle path.

PARQUE DO MARAPENDI   PARK
Map p262 (Av Sernambetiba, Recreio dos Bandeirantes; ⊙8am-5pm) This biological reserve sets aside 70 hectares for study and has a small area for leisure, with workout stations and games areas.

✕ EATING

Far from the bustling streets of central Rio, one can find some of the city's more rustic dining experiences, such as open-air spots with beautiful views complemented by fresh seafood. Places in Barra and western Rio are best reached by private transport.

LAGUNA RESTAURANTE   BRAZILIAN $$$
Map p262 (☑2495-1229; www.restaurantelaguna.com.br; Ilha da Gigóia 34, Barra da Tijuca; mains for 2 people R$135-175; ⊙6pm-midnight Thu & Fri, 1pm-midnight Sat, 1-8pm Sun; 🚗) Located on an island near the eastern section of Barra, this charming spot serves excellent seafood dishes meant for sharing. Start off with *casquinha de siri* (pulled crab), then move to a platter of grilled seafood or a rich *moqueca* (Bahian fish stew). The lush setting – open-air tables with lake and mountain views – is a big part of the allure.

1. Jardim Botânico (p79) 2. *Maracujá* (passion fruit) flower
3. Floresta da Tijuca (p161)

Green Spaces

No matter where you are in the city, you won't have to travel far to get a dose of nature. Rio has abundant parks and green spaces, some quite small and manicured (Parque do Catete) and others veritable wildernesses (Floresta da Tijuca).

Floresta da Tijuca

Rio's wide rainforest-covered expanse (p161) is teeming with plant and animal life. You can take scenic or challenging walks, including rewarding scrambles up its 900m-high peaks.

Sítio Burle Marx

Far west of town, but worth the trip, the gardens (p157) of Rio's famous landscape architect bloom with thousands of plant species. The lush estate is full of history, which you'll discover on a guided tour.

Parque do Flamengo

The landfill-turned–green space (p114) is best on Sunday when through-streets close to traffic, and runners and cyclists claim the long curving paths skirting the bay.

Jardim Botânico

These stately royal gardens (p79) make for a fine break from the beach. Here you can take in rare orchids, see massive Vitória Régia lilies and other Amazonian flora and admire the royal palms planted when the Portuguese royals ruled from Rio.

Parque do Catete

Behind the former presidential palace, this small but elegant park (p115) is complete with a swan-filled pond and a gallery (and cinema) adjoining the green space.

WORTH A DETOUR

BEACHES WEST OF RIO

Although Copacabana and Ipanema are Rio's most famous stretches of sand, there are many inviting beaches in the area, some in spectacular natural settings.

The first major beach you'll reach heading west of Leblon is **Praia do Pepino** in São Conrado. It's near where the hang gliders land, and it's not the cleanest beach around. Further west is the small, lovely but well-concealed **Praia da Joatinga**, reachable by a steep path down a rocky hillside. Be aware of the tides, so you don't get stranded.

Although it gets crowded on weekends, **Praia do Recreio dos Bandeirantes** is almost deserted during the week. The large rock acts as a natural breakwater, creating a calm bay. The 2km-long stretch of sand is popular with families.

The secluded 700m-long **Praia da Prainha** lies just past Recreio. It's one of the best surfing beaches in Rio, so it's always full of surfers. Waves come highly recommended.

The most isolated and unspoiled beach close to the city, **Praia de Grumari** is quiet during the week and packed on weekends with *cariocas* looking to get away from city beaches. It is a gorgeous setting, surrounded by mountains and lush vegetation.

From Grumari, a narrow road climbs over a jungle-covered hillside toward **Praia de Guaratiba**. West of here you'll get a good view of the **Restinga da Marambaia** (the vegetation-rich strip between the beach and the mainland), closed off to the public by a naval base. *Cariocas* enjoy eating lunch at several of the seafood restaurants in the area.

It's very difficult to reach these beaches by public transport. It's best to go by private car or taxi. Traffic can be quite heavy, so allow plenty of time for the trip.

If you're driving, park your car at Shopping Barra Point, turn right at the exit and walk to the Unimed e Posto Shell fuel station. Behind this, you can board a small ferry that makes the short trip to the island of Ilha da Gigóia. Reserve ahead.

DON PASCUAL CONTEMPORARY $$$

Map p262 (☑2428-6237; www.donpascual.com. br; Estrada do Sacarrão 867, Vargem Grande; mains R$62-92; ☀noon-1am) Don Pascual has undeniable charm. Amid lush scenery you'll dine on open-sided wooden decks, listening to the sounds of birdsong and perhaps spying a toucan flitting past. Not surprisingly, by night it's all couples at the candlelit tables. The food is good – juicy *picanha* (beef rump), *moquequinha de frutas do mar* (seafood and coconut stew) and *ravioli de cordeiro* (lamb ravioli) – but not quite as dazzling as the ambience.

The only surprise is it's hard to get to; call ahead for specific directions. You can also spend the night, or simply arrive early and go for a dip in the pool.

BIRA SEAFOOD $$$

(☑2410-8304; Estrada da Vendinha 68A, Barra de Guaratiba; mains for 3 people R$190-300; ☀noon-5pm Thu-Sun) Splendid views await diners who make the trek to Bira. On a breezy wooden deck, diners can partake in the flavorful, rich seafood served in huge portions – big enough for three. It's located about 35km west of Rio in the marvelous seaside setting of Barra de Guaratiba, 45 to 80 minutes from the city, depending on traffic.

 DRINKING & NIGHTLIFE

NUTH CLUB

Map p262 (☑3575-6850; www.facebook.com/ nuthoficial; Av Armando Lombardi 999, Barra da Tijuca; admission R$30-80; ☀9pm-4am) This club (pronounced 'Nooch') is one of Barra's favorite dance spots. Expect a friendly, well-dressed crowd grooving to DJs spinning electro-samba, house and hip-hop. If you don't like the venue, or the price tag, there are other bars and restaurants nearby.

 ENTERTAINMENT

CIDADE DAS ARTES PERFORMING ARTS

Map p262 (☑3325-0102; www.cidadedasartes. org; Av das Americas 5300, Barra da Tijuca) Rio's grandest new arts complex is a R$500 million venture that houses an 1800-seat concert hall, as well as theaters, a chamber music hall, a cinema and a restaurant. It's home to the Brazilian Symphony Orchestra, and features a wide-ranging repertoire, including contemporary dance, puppet

FLORESTA DA TIJUCA – PARQUE NACIONAL DA TIJUCA

The Tijuca is all that's left of the Atlantic rainforest that once surrounded Rio de Janeiro. **Parque Nacional da Tijuca** (www.parquedatijuca.com.br; ⊘8am-5pm), a 120-sq-km tropical jungle preserve, is an exuberant green, with beautiful trees, creeks and waterfalls, mountainous terrain and high peaks. It has an excellent, well-marked trail system. Candomblistas (practitioners of the Afro-Brazilian religion of Candomblé) leave offerings by the roadside; families have picnics; and serious hikers climb the 1012m to the summit of Pico da Tijuca.

The heart of the forest is the **Alto da Boa Vista** area in the Floresta (Forest) da Tijuca, which has many lovely natural and human-made features. Among the highlights of this beautiful park are several **waterfalls** (Cascatinha de Taunay, Cascata Gabriela and Cascata Diamantina), a 19th-century **chapel** (Capela Mayrink) and numerous **caves** (Gruta Luís Fernandes, Gruta Belmiro and Gruta Paulo e Virgínia). Also in the park is a lovely **picnic spot** (Bom Retiro) and two **restaurants** – the elegant Restaurante Os Esquilos and Restaurante a Floresta near the Ruínas do Archer (Major Archer's House).

The park is home to many different bird and animal species, including iguanas and monkeys, which you might encounter on one of the excellent day hikes you can make here; the trails are well signed. Good, free trail maps are given out at the park entrance.

The entire park closes at sunset. It's best to go by car, but if you don't have a vehicle, numerous outfits lead hiking tours, including Jungle Me (p49), **Rio Adventures** (✆2705-5747; www.rioadventures.com; hiking/climbing/rafting tours from R$160/350/450) and **Rio Hiking** (p49).

The best route by car is to take Rua Jardim Botânico two blocks past the Jardim Botânico (heading east from Gávea). Turn left on Rua Lopes Quintas and then follow the Tijuca or Corcovado signs for two quick left turns until you reach the back of the Jardim Botânico, where you turn right. Then follow the signs for a quick ascent into the forest, past the picturesque lookout points of Vista Chinesa and Mesa do Imperador. As soon as you seem to come out of the forest, turn right onto the main road and you'll see the stone columns to the entrance of Alto da Boa Vista on your left after a couple of kilometers. You can also drive up to Alto da Boa Vista by heading out to São Conrado and turning right up the hill at the Parque Nacional da Tijuca signs. Coming from Barra da Tijuca, take Estrada da Barra da Tijuca north, which eventually turns into Rua da Boa Vista, from where there are entrances into the park.

shows, jazz, musicals, choral recitals and experimental ensembles.

CITIBANK HALL CONCERT VENUE
Map p262 (✆4003-5588; Av Ayrton Senna 3000, Barra da Tijuca) Rio's largest (6000-seat) concert house tends to change names every few years, but continues to host top international and Brazilian bands, as well as ballet, opera and Broadway shows. The hall is in Via Parque Shopping (p162). Purchase tickets through Tickets for Fun (p41).

UCI – NEW YORK CITY CENTER CINEMA
Map p262 (✆2461-1818; New York City Center, Av das Américas 5000, Barra da Tijuca) UCI – New York City Center is Brazil's largest megaplex, featuring 18 different screening rooms complete with large, comfortable chairs

and stadium seating. Films are screened constantly (every 10 minutes on weekends).

SHOPPING

Barra da Tijuca is a kingdom of shopping malls; each offers something slightly different than the one next door.

VILLAGE MALL
Map p262 (✆3003-4177; www.shopping-villagemall.com.br; Av das Américas 3900, Barra da Tijuca; ⊘11am-11pm Mon-Sat, 1-9pm Sun) This shopping behemoth is Rio's most extravagant mall, with high-end retailers such as Prada, Cartier, Tiffany, Miu Miu, Michael Kors and Burberry, as well as an Apple store.

FASHION MALL
MALL

(📞2111-4427; www.fashionmall.com.br; Estrada da Gávea 899, São Conrado; ◷10am-10pm Mon-Sat, 3-9pm Sun) This is not only Rio's most beautiful mall but it also features luxe retailers – Fred Perry, Rolex and others – plus all of Brazil's most recognizable brands. It's located in the upper-class neighborhood of São Conrado.

BARRA SHOPPING
MALL

Map p262 (📞4003-4131; Av das Américas 4666, Barra da Tijuca; ◷10am-10pm Mon-Sat, 1-9pm Sun) Rio's largest mall (and one of the biggest on the continent) is an easy place to shop away a few hours – or days – as do 30 million shoppers each year. More than 500 stores clutter this 4km-long stretch, plus five movie screens, a kids' parkland and a wealth of dining options.

RIO DESIGN CENTER
SHOPPING CENTER

Map p262 (📞2430-3024; www.riodesignbarra. com.br; Av das Américas 7777, Barra da Tijuca; ◷10am-10pm Mon-Sat, 3-9pm Sun) This architecturally rich center features a number of excellent home-furnishing stores selling designer lamps, vases, decorative pieces and furniture. It also has some very good restaurants and a few art galleries.

VIA PARQUE SHOPPING
SHOPPING CENTER

Map p262 (📞2430-5100; www.shoppingvia-parque.com.br; Av Ayrton Senna 3000, Barra da Tijuca; ◷10am-10pm Mon-Sat, 1-9pm Sun) With 200 stores, six movie theaters and an abundance of restaurants, this shopping center is the heart of Rio's thriving consumer culture. The center also houses one of the city's big, busy and diverse concert arenas, Citibank Hall (p161).

🏃 SPORTS & ACTIVITIES

BARRA WATER SHUTTLE
BOAT TOUR

Map p262 (📞3942-0209; www.bws.tur.br; 📶) For a different side of Barra, don't miss this fascinating boat tour that takes you through the lagoons of the region. Amid a lush watery landscape there are excellent wildlife-watching opportunities: many birds, plus the odd caiman and capybara. The English-speaking guide has a wealth of info to offer on the area.

🛏 Sleeping

Rio has a wide range of lodgings, including boutique B&Bs, trendy hostels and bohemian guesthouses; there are scores of luxury hotels, particularly in Copacabana. Prices remain steady and are comparable to what you'd expect in a North American oceanside city; an abundance of options keeps rates from going sky high, except during Carnaval and major events.

Hotels

Despite Rio's growing popularity, the city's hotel scene is lackluster. The majority of hotels are in glass and steel high-rises, with marble- and chrome-filled lobbies, and comfortable but uninspiring rooms. The best features will be the view (if there is one) and the door...to exit the room and explore this fascinating city. Amenities to look for include pools, wi-fi (usually free except in some luxury hotels, which charge exorbitant rates) and beach service (towels, chairs and attendants).

Hostels

With more than 200 hostels scattered around the city, Rio does not lack for budget lodging. Hostels are great settings for meeting other travelers. With more and more Brazilians traveling, your dorm mate is just as likely to be from Porto Alegre as they are from Perth. Rio's hostels range in price and style, and subcultures dominate. For a bohemian vibe, try Santa Teresa; for the nightlife scene, look around Lapa, Copacabana and Ipanema. And for something totally different, stay in a hostel located in a favela.

Apartment Rentals

The best way to save money in Rio is to rent an apartment. There are numerous rental outfits in Ipanema and Copacabana, though you can also go through Airbnb (www.airbnb.com). This site allows you to rent a whole apartment or simply a room in a shared flat, making it a good way to meet *cariocas* (residents of Rio).

If you book through an agency, nightly high-season rates start around R$200 for a small studio apartment in Copacabana and R$350 in Ipanema. Typically, you'll need to pay 30% to 50% up front; some agencies accept credit cards' others use PayPal. Make sure you ask whether utilities and cleaning fees are included in the price. Reputable outfits include Rio Spot Homes (p170), Ipanema for Rent (p167), Blame It on Rio 4 Travel (p170) and Rio Apartments (p170).

Prices & Reservations

Rooms with an ocean view cost about 30% to 50% more than rooms without. During the summer (December through March), hotel rates typically rise by about 30%, and many places book up well in advance, so it's wise to reserve ahead. There's no getting around it: prices double or triple for New Year's Eve, Carnaval and major events, such as the Olympics. Most accommodations, including hostels, will only book in four- or seven-day blocks around these times. It's never too early to book for Carnaval; better places fill up to a year in advance.

Breakfast

Nearly every guesthouse, hostel and hotel serves some form of *café da manhã* (breakfast). At cheaper places, this may only be a roll, some bread and instant coffee; better places serve fresh fruit, juices, strong coffee, yogurt, cheese, cured meats, fresh bread and perhaps cooked eggs. Oddly, Rio's most expensive lodgings often charge for breakfast.

SLEEPING

NEED TO KNOW

Price Ranges

Prices are for double rooms, except for hostels with only dorm beds, in which case the price is for one person in a dorm bed.

$	less than R$200
$$	R$200–500
$$$	more than R$500

Room Tax

Keep in mind that many hotels add between 5% and 15% in taxes and service charges. Cheaper places don't generally bother with this. Be sure to read the fine print when booking.

Websites

Airbnb (www.airbnb.com) Thousands of apartment listings across Rio.

Couchsurfing (www. couchsurfing.com) More than 10,000 hosts in Rio, and an active meet-up community.

Booking (www.booking. com) Generally the best deals for hotels and guesthouses.

Lonely Planet (lonelyplanet.com/ brazil/rio-de-janeiro/hotels) Extensive hotel reviews and online booking.

Lonely Planet's Top Choices

Casa Beleza (p173) Friendly hosts and an enticing pool in a villa guesthouse in Santa Teresa.

Hotel Santa Teresa (p175) Rio's finest boutique hotel, with a great restaurant and bar.

Pouso Verde (p169) Charming guesthouse in a peaceful Jardim Botânico location.

Maze Inn (p174) Unique English-run place with striking views in Tavares Bastos favela.

Copacabana Palace (p171) Gorgeous, historic hotel with great restaurants and top service.

Mirante do Arvrão (p174) Gorgeous views from this hilltop perch in Vidigal favela.

Best Guesthouses

Rio Guesthouse (p171) Top-floor high-rise B&B with jaw-dropping views.

Margarida's Pousada (p167) Easy-going option in an ideal Ipanema location.

Casa da Gente (p173) Eco-minded guesthouse above Lapa.

Casa Áurea (p173) Laid-back Santa Teresa guesthouse with a hammock-filled garden.

Best Boutique Lodging

Vila Galé (p175) Gorgeous new property in Rio's samba epicenter.

Casa Mosquito (p167) Beautifully designed boutique guesthouse above Ipanema.

Best Unusual Stays

Casa Caminho do Corcovado (p172) Idyllic B&B set amid rainforest surroundings.

Cama e Café (p173) Stay in a rented room up in bohemian Santa Teresa.

Utrópico (p176) Lush setting on a river island in Barra.

Rio Surf 'N Stay (p176) Get away from it all (and surf!) at this Recreio hostel.

Don Pascual (p176) Incredible setting amid tropical rainforest, with a lovely pool and restaurant.

Best by Budget

$

Rio Hostel (p173) Great Santa Teresa location and a charming atmosphere.

Cabana Copa (p169) Buzzing hostel in a peaceful location in Copacabana.

Vidigalbergue (p174) Fun hostel with unrivaled sea views.

$$

Casa Cool Beans (p175) Wonderfully welcoming villa with a pool in Santa Teresa.

Casa da Carmen e do Fernando (p173) A friendly art-filled guesthouse.

Rio Spot Homes (p170) Reliable rental outfit with apartment listings across the Zona Sul.

$$$

Marina All Suites (p169) Plush suites and jaw-dropping views in a perfect Leblon location.

Hotel Fasano (p168) Join the celebrity set in this Philippe Starck–designed hotel.

Porto Bay Rio Internacional (p171) A beachfront favorite in Copacabana.

Where to Stay

Neighborhood	For	Against
Ipanema & Leblon	Great location near the beach and the lake, with Rio's best restaurants and bars surrounding. Great views possible: ocean, lake or even Corcovado.	Pricier than other locations. Fewer options than Copacabana.
Copacabana & Leme	Wealth of lodging possibilities packed into a long, narrow, high-rise-lined neighborhood. Proximity to the beach. Good transport connections to other parts of the city. Good restaurants and bars.	Nightlife more limited than Ipanema or Botafogo. Very touristy; some *cariocas* avoid it. Sex tourism in some parts; tourist-trap restaurants along Av Atlântica.
Botafogo & Urca	Good neighborhood with restaurants, bars and nightclubs that attract a local crowd.	Not within walking distance of the beach. Noisy, traffic-clogged avenues. Few attractions.
Flamengo & Around	Better prices than the beachside districts.	Few options, mostly budget. Very few restaurants and bars, and very little nightlife.
Santa Teresa & Lapa	Santa Teresa is a charming bohemian district with great architecture and alternative, art-minded residents. Has a handful of good restaurants and drinking spots. Lapa is the epicenter of Rio's samba-fueled nightlife.	Santa Teresa is far from the beaches; poor transport links. Lapa is unappealing and gritty by day.
Barra da Tijuca & Western Rio	Great beaches with a laid-back vibe.	Long commutes into town. No neighborhood vibe; most locals use cars to get around.

SLEEPING

🛏 Ipanema

RIO HOSTEL – IPANEMA
HOSTEL **$**

Map p236 (📞2287-2928; www.riohostelipanema. com; Casa 1, Canning 18; dm/d from R$60/180; @🛜) This friendly hostel is in a small villa on a peaceful stretch of Ipanema. A mix of travelers stay here, enjoying the clean rooms, the airy top-floor deck with hammocks and the small front veranda. The location is fantastic: it's less than 10 minutes' walk to either Ipanema or Copacabana Beach.

The entrance is unsigned, behind a gate, so make sure the hostel knows you're coming.

HOSTEL HARMONIA
HOSTEL **$**

Map p236 (📞2523-4905; www.casadaharmonia. com; Casa 18, Barão da Torre 175; dm R$65-75; ❄ @🛜) Run by a Californian, Hostel Harmonia is a small but appealing hostel with a good traveler vibe. The lounge and rooms have two-toned wood floors, and quarters are clean and well maintained, with four to six beds in each room.

CHE LAGARTO IPANEMA
HOSTEL **$**

Map p236 (📞2512-8076; www.chelagarto.com; Paul Redfern 48; dm/d R$80/355; ❄ @🛜) Part of a small empire of hostels in South America, Che Lagarto's Ipanema location is a popular spot for those young travelers who want to be close to the beach. It's a five-story hostel, with basic rooms and not

---

LOVE AMONG THE CARIOCAS

Living in such a crowded city, *cariocas* (residents of Rio) can have a terrible time snatching a few moments of privacy. For those living with their parents or sharing a tiny apartment with roommates, an empty stretch of beach, a park bench or a seat in the back of a cafe are all fine spots to steal a few kisses, but for more...progressive action, *cariocas* take things elsewhere: to the motel, aka the *love* motel.

Love motels aren't so much a *carioca* oddity as they are a Brazilian institution. They're found in every part of the country, usually sprouting along the outskirts of cities and towns. Some are designed with lavish facades – they may be decked out to resemble medieval castles, Roman temples or ancient pyramids – while others blend in discreetly. Regardless of the exterior, the interiors are far removed from the 'less is more' design philosophy. Mirrors cover the ceilings and heart-shaped, vibrating beds stretch beneath them. Rose-tinted mood lights, Jacuzzis, televisions loaded with porn channels, dual-headed showers and a bedside room-service menu featuring sex toys: all these come standard in most love motels. Such places scream seediness in many other countries. In Brazil, however, they're nothing out of the ordinary. People need a place for their liaisons, so they might as well have a laugh and a bit of fun while they're at it. Motels are used by young lovers who want to get away from their parents; by parents who want to get away from their kids; and by couples who want to get away from their spouses. They are an integral part of the nation's social fabric, and it's not uncommon for *cariocas* to host parties in them.

The quality of motel varies. The most lavish are three-story suites with a hot tub beneath a skylight on the top floor, a sauna and bathroom on the 2nd floor, and a garage underneath (allowing anonymity). They come standard with all the other mood-enhancement features. For the best suites, expect to pay upwards of R$500 for eight hours, and more on weekends. *Cariocas* claim that an equally fine time can be had at standard rooms.

If you wish to check out this cultural institution, here are some options:

Shalimar (📞3322-3392; www.hotelshalimar.com.br; Av Niemeyer 218, Vidigal; r per 6hr R$78-420) Popular love motel with many themed rooms, located west of Leblon.

Vips (📞3322-1662; www.vipsmotel.com.br; Av Niemeyer 418, Vidigal; ste per 8hr R$180-600) A favorite love motel on the beachfront road west of Leblon.

Love Time (Map p249; 📞2558-1911; www.lovetimehotel.com.br; Rua do Catete 63, Glória; r per 4hr R$100-283) Centrally located love motel in Glória.

much common space, aside from a bar on the ground floor.

LIGHTHOUSE HOSTEL   HOSTEL $

Map p236 (⌨2522-1353; www.thelighthouse. com.br; No 20, Barão da Torre 175; dm/d/tr R$75/200/240; ❅@☎) Situated with a handful of other budget spots on a quiet lane, the Lighthouse has an easygoing vibe and clean, simple rooms that attract a good mix of backpackers. Accommodations consist of an eight-bed dorm room, and one private double with a fold-out sofa, sleeping three in total.

IPANEMA FOR RENT   APARTMENT $$

Map p236 (⌨99603-2109, 7822-4684; www. ipanemaforrent.com.br; Sobreloja 29, Visconde de Pirajá 318; apt from R$150) This apartment rental outfit has dozens of listings around Copacabana and Ipanema. You'll find everything from small, very basic and affordable options within walking distance to the beach to plush rentals with great views overlooking the ocean.

MANGO TREE   HOSTEL $$

Map p236 (⌨2287-9255; www.mangotreehostel. com; Prudente de Morais 594; dm R$80, d with/ without bathroom from R$270/230; ❅@☎) In a cheery yellow house in Ipanema, this popular hostel offers rooms with two-toned wood floors and a welcoming atmosphere. The front porch provides open-air space for unwinding, and there's also a lounge/ TV room.

IPANEMA BEACH HOUSE   HOSTEL $$

Map p236 (⌨3202-2693; www.ipanemahouse. com; Barão da Torre 485; dm R$75-95, d with/ without bathroom from R$290/230; @☎❆) The location is fabulous: it's set in a converted two-story house with a beautiful pool and yard, just a short stroll to the beach. The rooms and bathrooms, however, could use some upkeep, and space is tight in the six- and nine-bed dorms (in the form of three-tiered bunk beds). Prices are higher on weekends.

MARGARIDA'S POUSADA   POUSADA $$

Map p236 (⌨2239-1840; www.margaridaspou sada.com; Barão da Torre 600; d from R$300; ❅@☎) Those seeking something smaller and cozier than a high-rise hotel should try this superbly located Ipanema *pousada* (guesthouse). You'll find 11 pleasant, simply furnished rooms scattered about the low-rise building. Margarida also rents out several private, fully equipped apartments nearby.

BONITA   HOSTEL $$

Map p236 (⌨2227-1703; www.bonitaipanema. com; Barão da Torre 107; dm R$60, d with/without bathroom R$270/220; ❅@☎❆) This peacefully set converted house has history: it's where bossa nova legend Tom Jobim lived from 1962 to 1965 and wrote some of his most famous songs. Rooms are clean but simply furnished, and most open onto a shared deck overlooking a small pool and patio.

IPANEMA HOTEL
RESIDÊNCIA   APARTMENT $$

Map p236 (⌨3125-5000; www.ipanemahotel. com.br; Barão da Torre 192, Ipanema; d R$500, per month from R$7000; ❅☎❆) Set on one of Ipanema's lovely tree-lined streets, this high-rise has large apartments with kitchen units, lounge areas and pleasant bedrooms. Each apartment has a veranda; some are larger than others. There's also a sunny rooftop pool surrounded by artificial grass, a sauna and a tiny workout room.

IPANEMA INN   HOTEL $$

Map p236 (⌨2523-6092; www.ipanemainn. br; Maria Quitéria 27; d from R$535; ❅☎) Located just a short stroll from the beach, the Ipanema Inn is a simple hotel whose rooms have off-white ceramic tile floors and simple wood furnishings; some rooms are disappointingly small. *Superiores* (front-facing rooms) don't have ocean views, but if you lean far enough out the window, you get a glimpse of the beachfront.

ARPOADOR INN   HOTEL $$

Map p236 (⌨2523-0060; www.arpoadorinn.com. br; Francisco Otaviano 177; r with/without view R$690/510; ❅☎) Overlooking Praia do Arpoador (Arpoador Beach), this six-story inn is the only hotel in Ipanema and Copacabana that doesn't have a busy street between it and the beach. The rooms are small and basic, but the brighter 'deluxe' rooms have glorious ocean views. The hotel also has a good restaurant facing the beach.

CASA MOSQUITO   GUESTHOUSE $$$

Map p236 (⌨3586-5042; www.casamosquito. com; Saint Roman 222; r from R$650; ❅☎) Opened by two French expats, Casa Mosquito is a beautifully designed boutique guesthouse with luxuriously appointed rooms. The converted all-white 1940s mansion sits on a tranquil garden-filled property with scenic views of Pão de Açúcar (Sugarloaf Mountain) and the Pavão-Pavãozinho favela. It's located on a steep, winding street about 10 minutes' walk from Praça General Osório. Meals are available by request.

APARTHOTEL ADAGIO
HOTEL $$$

Map p236 (☎2114-8100; www.mercure.com; Av Rainha Elizabeth 440; d from R$590; ✱@🖥🌊) This hotel offers attractively designed suites with faux-wood floors, big windows and light, muted colors. Some rooms have balconies, and the upper two floors (eight and nine) have slightly better views (though you still won't see the ocean). All have small kitchen units including microwave, sink and mini-fridge. There's a pool, which is surrounded by tall buildings.

MAR IPANEMA
HOTEL $$$

Map p236 (☎3875-9191; www.maripanema.com.br; Visconde de Pirajá 539; d R$540-850; ✱) This reliable hotel has trim, modern rooms with decent beds, good lighting and a bright, clean layout. It's also in a great location, on Ipanema's lively shopping strip, just two blocks from the beach. There's also a relaxing rooftop bar. The downside is the lack of a view, which is a small loss if you plan to spend your day out enjoying the city.

VISCONTI
APARTMENT $$$

Map p236 (☎2111-8600; www.promenade.com.br; Prudente de Morais 1050; ste from R$525; ✱) The Visconti has stylish modern suites (wood floors, leather furniture, modular lamps) with living-dining rooms, balconies and bedrooms. It's on a tree-lined residential street a block from the beach.

SHERATON
HOTEL $$$

(☎2529-1122; www.sheraton-rio.com; Av Niemeyer 121, Vidigal; d from R$820; ✱@🖥🌊) The Sheraton is a true resort hotel, with large, peaceful grounds. Every room has a balcony, facing either Leblon and Ipanema or verdant greenery. The rooms are nicely furnished in a cozy, contemporary style. You'll enjoy a nearly private beach in front, plus tennis courts, swimming pools and a good health club. The main drawback is that it's far from the action.

GOLDEN TULIP
IPANEMA PLAZA
HOTEL $$$

Map p236 (☎3687-2000; www.goldentulip-panemaplaza.com; Farme de Amoedo 34; d from R$680; ✱🖥🌊) A top choice, the 18-story Plaza features nicely decorated rooms with tile floors, a muted color scheme and sizable windows to admit the tropical rays. You'll also find broad, comfortable beds, spacious bathrooms (with bathtubs) and a lovely rooftop pool. Some rooms overlook the ocean, others face the outstretched arms of Cristo Redentor (Christ the Redeemer).

SOL IPANEMA
HOTEL $$$

Map p236 (☎2525-2020; www.solipanema.com.br; Av Vieira Souto 320; r with/without ocean view from R$750/600; ✱@🖥🌊) Occupying prime real estate facing Ipanema Beach, the tall, slender Sol Ipanema features rooms decorated in creams and earth tones, with dark-wood furnishings and good lighting. Pricier rooms have magnificent, unobstructed ocean views but are otherwise identical to the standard rooms.

CAESAR PARK
HOTEL $$$

Map p236 (☎2525-2525; www.sofitel.com; Av Vieira Souto 460; d from R$780; ✱@🌊) Popular with business travelers, this well-located beachfront option has sizable rooms with a warm, inviting feel, artwork on the walls, and flat-screen TVs. The best rooms have ocean views.

HOTEL PRAIA IPANEMA
HOTEL $$$

Map p236 (☎2141-4949; www.praiaipanema.com; Av Vieira Souto 706; d from R$700; ✱@🌊) With a view of Ipanema Beach, this popular 16-story hotel offers trim, comfortable rooms, each with a balcony. The design is sleek and modern, with off-white tile floors, recessed lighting and artwork on the walls. Stretch out on the molded white lounge chairs next to the rooftop pool or, better yet, enjoy a meal: the penthouse restaurant, Espaço 7zero6 (p64), is excellent.

HOTEL FASANO
HOTEL $$$

Map p236 (☎3202-4000; www.fasano.com.br; Av Vieira Souto 80; d from R$1660; ✱@🖥🌊) Designed by Philippe Starck, the Fasano has 91 sleek rooms set with Egyptian-cotton sheets, goose-down pillows and high-tech fittings. The best rooms have balconies overlooking the crashing waves of Ipanema Beach, which lies just across the road. Rooms without a view simply don't justify the price. The lovely rooftop pool (open to guests only) is truly breathtaking – as are the room rates.

With stylish rooms, a great location and a much-touted seafood restaurant and bar, this is the top destination for the style set and celebrity crowd: Lady Gaga, Kate Moss, Will Smith and Madonna have all been guests.

⌂ Leblon

LEMON SPIRIT HOSTEL HOSTEL $
Map p240 (⌂2294-1853; www.lemonspirit.com; Cupertino Durão 56; dm R$70-90; ❋@☎) One of Leblon's only hostels, Lemon Spirit boasts an excellent location one block from the beach. The dorm rooms (four to six beds in each) are clean and simple without much decor. There's a tiny courtyard in front, and the attractive lobby bar is a good place to meet other travelers over caipirinhas.

LEBLON SPOT DESIGN HOSTEL HOSTEL $$
Map p240 (⌂2137-4310; www.leblonspot.com; Dias Ferreira 636; dm weekday/weekend R$62/110, d R$260-350; ❋@☎) The location is outstanding: you're within a short stroll to some of Rio's best restaurants and liveliest drinking spots. The setting is a former house, with bright but rather cramped rooms with wood floors, a small lounge and a tiny veranda. Unlike other Rio hostels, there isn't much socializing here, and the staff isn't the friendliest.

MARINA ALL SUITES BOUTIQUE HOTEL $$$
Map p240 (⌂2172-1100; www.hoteismarina.com.br; Av Delfim Moreira 696; ste from R$935; ❋@☎) You'll find beautifully decorated rooms, doting service and all the creature comforts here. As per the name, all rooms are suites, meaning that between the comfy bedroom and the living room you'll have plenty of space in which to stretch out. The best rooms in the oceanfront hotel have splendid views of the shoreline.

Other attractions include the first-rate Bar D'Hotel restaurant, the trendy open-sided Bar do Lado on the ground floor and the lovely top-floor pool.

RITZ PLAZA HOTEL APARTMENT $$$
Map p240 (⌂2540-4940; www.ritzhotel.com.br; Av Ataúlfo de Paiva 1280; r from R$620; ❋☎❄) In one of Rio's most desirable areas, this stylish low-key hotel has attractive, uniquely designed rooms and common areas that give the Ritz a boutique feel. The best rooms have kitchen units and balconies – some offering partial ocean views – and all are trimmed with artwork, good lighting and spotless bedrooms. Amenities include an elegant (if often empty) bar, a sauna, a pool and a spa.

MARINA PALACE HOTEL $$$
Map p240 (⌂2529-5700; www.bhghoteis.com.br/marina-palace; Av Delfim Moreira 630; r from R$555; ❋@☎❄) Occupying a privileged position overlooking Praia de Leblon, this 26-story hotel has contemporary rooms with artwork, sizable beds, flat-screen TVs, and DVD and CD players. Spacious deluxe rooms face the ocean. The Marina has first-rate service, and a top-floor bar and restaurant with 360-degree views.

After time at the beach, the main level Bar do Praia, with its open-sided deck and lateral beach views, is a fine place to head for drinks and snacks (and sushi!).

⌂ Jardim Botânico

★POUSO VERDE GUESTHOUSE $$
Map p242 (⌂2529-2942; www.pousoverde.com; Caminhoá 14; s/d R$240/300) On a quiet cobblestone street in a charming corner of Jardim Botânico, Pouso Verde has elegant, comfortably furnished rooms, the best of which have views of Cristo Redentor. The historic house (which dates back to the 1890s) is packed with artwork, and the owners go out of their way to make guests feel at home. Excellent breakfasts.

⌂ Copacabana & Leme

CABANA COPA HOSTEL $
Map p244 (⌂3988-9912; www.cabanacopa.com.br; Travessa Guimarães Natal 12, Copacabana; dm R$40-80, d R$180-250; ❋@☎) Top hostel honors go to this Greek-Brazilian-run gem in a colonial-style '50s house tucked away in a Copacabana cranny. Four- to 10-bed dorms prevail throughout the home, which is chock-full of original architectural details and a hodgepodge of funky floorings. There's a lively bar and common areas.

The hostel runs a brand-new all-suites building next door: a great option for travelers who want a private room without missing out on the social interaction of a hostel.

PURA VIDA HOSTEL $

Map p244 (☑2210-8885; www.puravidahostel. com.br; Saint Roman 20, Copacabana; dm R$40-60, d from R$180; @ 🛜) Pura Vida occupies a converted castle-like mansion (built in the 1920s) that was once the home of the Polish ambassador. It has huge dorm rooms sleeping four to 12, polished wood floors, and spacious common areas including an outdoor veranda with bar. Behind the building are 10 brightly painted but boxy chalets, surrounded by greenery: a great option for couples.

WALK ON THE BEACH HOSTEL HOSTEL $

Map p244 (☑2545-7500; www.walk-on-the-beach.com; Dias da Rocha 85, Copacabana; dm R$40-70; @ 🛜) Set in a two-story villa on one of Copacabana's quiet backstreets, this nicely designed hostel offers good-value, fan-cooled dorm rooms (that sleep three to 12 in each), though the metal, institutional-looking bed frames and thin mattresses lessen the appeal. It has a lounge and a small bar, and maintains a welcoming, low-key vibe.

CHE LAGARTO HOSTEL $

Map p244 (☑3209-0348; www.chelagarto.com; Barata Ribeira 111, Copacabana; dm R$37-60; ✳ @ 🛜 ≋) This popular full-service hostel has a friendly, party atmosphere. The small rooftop pool with adjoining bar is a good place to meet other travelers, and the hostel arranges loads of activities – boat parties, nights out in Lapa, BBQs and more. There are two other Che Lagartos in Copacabana and one in Ipanema.

RIO SPOT HOMES APARTMENT $$

Map p244 (☑3988-7613, 99188-3304; www. riospothomes.com; Office 214, Prado Junior 48, Copacabana) This reputable, well-run rental agency has scores of listings around the Zona Sul, with excellent-value apartments in Ipanema, Copacabana and Barra, from inexpensive crash pads to luxurious five-bedroom flats that can accommodate up to 15 people.

BLAME IT ON RIO 4 TRAVEL APARTMENT $$

Map p244 (☑3813-5510; www.blameitonrio4 travel.com; Xavier da Silveira 15B, Copacabana) Created by a kind, helpful expat from New York, this professional agency rents many types of apartments. It also has a travel agency, a few computers for internet use and a laundry next door.

RIO APARTMENTS APARTMENT $$

Map p244 (☑4042-6221; www.rioapartments. com; Santa Clara 98, Copacabana) A Swedish-run outfit with many apartment rentals in the Zona Sul.

CHE LAGARTO –
SUITES SANTA CLARA BOUTIQUE HOSTEL $$

Map p244 (☑3495-3133; www.chelagarto.com; Santa Clara 304, Copacabana; r with/without bathroom from R$220/170; ✳ @ 🛜) On a tree-lined street in Copacabana's Bairro Peixoto neighborhood, this converted house has clean, simple and well-maintained rooms (all private rooms, no dorms) and a small downstairs lounge where you can meet other travelers. The friendly staff gives out helpful advice, and can direct you to loads of activities.

EDIFICIO JUCATI HOSTEL, APARTMENT $$

Map p244 (☑2547-5422; www.edificiojucati.com. br; Tenente Marones de Gusmão 85, Copacabana; d/q from R$230/290; ✳ 🛜) Near a small park and on a tranquil street, Jucati has large, simply furnished serviced apartments with slate floors and small but serviceable kitchens. Have a look at the layout before committing. Most apartments have just one bedroom with a double bed and a living room with a bunk bed. The small, covered courtyard is a fine spot to unwind.

HOTEL SANTA CLARA HOTEL $$

Map p244 (☑2256-2650; www.hotelsantaclara. com.br; Décio Vilares 316, Copacabana; s/d/ tr from R$250/280/320; ✳ 🛜) Along one of Copacabana's most peaceful streets, you'll find this attractive three-story hotel, with a white stucco facade and blue shutters. The front-facing upstairs rooms are best, and well worth the extra money, with wood floors, antique bed frames, writing desks and balconies. The rooms in back are a little gloomy.

OLINDA RIO HOTEL $$

Map p244 (☑2159-9000; www.olindariohotel. com.br; Av Atlântica 2230, Copacabana; d with/ without ocean view from R$620/500; ✳ 🛜) Set in a handsome cream-colored building overlooking Copacabana Beach, the Olinda Rio is a classic. Its marble lobby, complete with chandeliers and grand piano, has an old-world charm, although its rooms are modern. The best of the bunch face the ocean and are worth the price.

RIO GUESTHOUSE   B&B $$

Map p244 (✆2521-8568; www.rioguesthouse. com; Francisco Sá 5, Copacabana; d R$380-590; ❄☎) The Australian-Brazilian hosts open up their home and rent out several comfortable rooms at this split-level penthouse overlooking Copacabana Beach. The highlight is undoubtedly the outdoor patio, which has gorgeous views over Copacabana.

RIO DESIGN HOTEL   BOUTIQUE HOTEL $$

Map p244 (✆3222-8800; www.riodesignhotel. com; Francisco Sá 17, Copacabana; r R$475-590; ❄@☎) This stylish 13-story hotel demonstrates real design smarts. Rooms have tile floors, artful lighting and big windows, and each floor is decorated in a different style. A new pool and restaurant were in the works when we last passed through.

ACAPULCO   HOTEL $$

Map p248 (✆3077-2000; www.acapulcohotel. com.br; Gustavo Sampaio 854, Leme; s/d from R$390/440; ❄@☎) The Acapulco lies just a short stroll (one block) from the immortalized Copacabana Beach. Renovations have made it an attractive option. Most rooms have a neat look to them, with laminate wood floors, and colorful duvets and curtains.

ORLA COPACABANA   HOTEL $$

Map p244 (✆2525-2425; www.orlahotel.com.br; Av Atlântica 4122, Copacabana; d R$460-630; ❄☎❆) The Spanish-owned Orla Copacabana has some attractive, understated rooms, but the beach-facing location is a real draw. The standard rooms are too dark and cramped, so it's not worth staying unless you book one of the deluxe rooms with their unobstructed ocean views.

COPACABANA PALACE   HOTEL $$$

Map p244 (✆2548-7070; www.belmond.com; Av Atlântica 1702, Copacabana; d from R$1500; ❄@☎❆) Rio's most famous hotel has hosted heads of state, rock stars and other prominent personalities – Queen Elizabeth once stayed here, as did the Rolling Stones. The dazzling white facade dates from the 1920s, when it became a symbol of the city. Today accommodations range from deluxe rooms to spacious suites with balconies.

The pool is the loveliest in Rio, and the restaurants are top-notch.

PORTO BAY RIO INTERNACIONAL   HOTEL $$$

Map p244 (✆2546-8000; www.portobay.com. br; Av Atlântica 1500, Copacabana; d from R$750; ❄@☎❆) One of Copacabana's top beachfront hotels, Porto Bay has stylish rooms with a light and airy feel that are painted in cool tones. Large white duvets, light hardwoods, elegant furnishings and simple artwork all complement each other nicely. Big windows let in lots of light, and most rooms have balconies.

PESTANA RIO ATLÂNTICA   HOTEL $$$

Map p244 (✆2548-6332; www.pestana.com; Av Atlântica 2230, Copacabana; r from R$700; ❄@☎❆) Beautifully located along Copacabana Beach, the Portuguese-owned Pestana has excellent amenities, decent service and a wide range of rooms. The best have wood floors, balconies and a bright, modern design scheme. Rooms at the lower end are rather bland and too small to recommend.

SOFITEL RIO DE JANEIRO   HOTEL $$$

Map p244 (✆2525-1232; www.sofitel.com; Av Atlântica 4240, Copacabana; d from R$880; ❄@☎❆) One of Rio's priciest hotels, the French-owned Sofitel does its best to impress. The excellent service, comfortable rooms, two lovely pools and the beachfront location have earned many fans. All rooms have balconies and are tastefully furnished. Deluxe rooms and suites have ocean views.

MERCURE ARPOADOR   HOTEL $$$

Map p244 (✆2113-8600; www.mercure.com; Francisco Otaviano 61, Copacabana; ste from R$550; ❄@☎❆) This dapper all-suites hotel is nicely located in Arpoador, giving easy access to both Ipanema and Copacabana. The suites have sleek white leather sofas that open into beds, modern kitchenettes, TVs with a stereo and a DVD player, ambient lighting and comfortable bedrooms. All of the rooms have balconies, although there is no view.

🏠 Botafogo & Urca

VILA CARIOCA   HOSTEL $

Map p252 (✆2535-3224; www.vilacarioca.com. br; Estácio Coimbra 84, Botafogo; dm R$35-60, d R$130-320; ✳@☎) On a peaceful tree-lined street, this low-key and welcoming hostel has four- to 15-bed dorms in an attractively decorated house. The common areas are a fine spot to mingle with other travelers.

ACE HOSTEL
HOSTEL $

Map p252 (✐2527-7452; www.acehostels.com.br; São Clemente 23, Botafogo; dm R$30-50; ✳@) One block from the metro, this small, friendly and well-run hostel has well-maintained rooms – all with private bathrooms – and a spacious lounge/TV room. Ace also operates a guesthouse a few doors down, which is good for those seeking a private room.

INJOY HOSTEL
GUESTHOUSE $$

Map p252 (✐3593-6662; www.injoyhostel.com; Estácio de Coimbra 80, Botafogo; d from R$250; ✳@☎) Despite the name, this place feels less like a hostel and more like a small guesthouse. Injoy has 18 private rooms set in a lovely house at the end of a tree-lined lane. Rooms are modern, very clean and well maintained, and each is named after a major city, with iconic photos from that destination decorating one wall. Friendly staff.

HOTELINHO URCA
GUESTHOUSE $$

Map p252 (✐3449-8867; www.hotelinho.com; Marechal Cantuária 10, Urca; r with/without bathroom from R$280/180; ✳☎☀) One of the few lodging options in Urca, this quiet, low-key guesthouse has a range of clean, well-equipped rooms with attractive wood floors. The sunny veranda has views over the bay and is the best feature; there's also a tiny dip pool. Hotelinho Urca also rents several apartments nearby. You'll score a 5% discount if paying in cash.

O VELEIRO
GUESTHOUSE $$

Map p250 (✐2554-8980; www.oveleiro.com; Mundo Novo 1440, Botafogo; r R$240-380; ✳☎☀) Surrounded by Atlantic rainforest, O Veleiro is a delightfully set guesthouse located on a cobblestone road uphill from Botafogo. The rooms are small and adequately furnished but the backyard is the real attraction, with hammocks, a small pool and pretty views (plus the occasional marmoset visitor).

On the downside, it's a bit of a trudge to get down to Botafogo (even more so on the way back uphill), but for a tranquil escape

that's still inside central Rio, this is a decent option.

IBIS
HOTEL $$

Map p252 (✐3515-2999; www.ibis.com; Paulino Fernandes 39, Botafogo; r from R$260; ✳☎) Like many other Ibis hotels around Brazil, this no-frills branch offers very clean, simple, modern rooms in a high-rise building at excellent prices. The rooms are small but functional with work spaces, big windows and bathrooms just large enough not to be considered cramped.

OZTEL
HOSTEL $$

Map p242 (✐3042-1853; www.oztel.com.br; Pinheiro Guimarães 91, Botafogo; dm R$45-75, d R$240-300; ✳@☎) Evoking a Warholian aesthetic, Rio's coolest and most colorful hostel is like sleeping in an art gallery. The artsy front deck and bar is an inviting hangout lounge but the real coup are the private rooms: with a garden patio under the nose of Cristo Redentor, you'll be hard-pressed to find a groovier room in Rio.

🛏 Flamengo & Around

BROTHERS HOSTEL
HOSTEL $

Map p250 (✐2551-0997; www.brothershostel.com.br; Farani 18, Flamengo; dm R$45-60, d R$125-175; ✳@☎) In a handsomely converted house, this hostel was started by four well-traveled Brazilian brothers. Some of the rooms are cramped, but the rock-loving bar is a good place to meet other guests.

DISCOVERY HOSTEL
HOSTEL $

Map p249 (✐3449-0672; www.discoveryhostel.com; Benjamin Constant 26, Catete; dm/d R$60/200; ✳☎) One of Rio's most socially minded hostels, Discovery is a great place to meet other travelers. While it's not on the beach, the attractive converted house is convenient for exploring the nightlife of Lapa, and it's an easy stroll to the metro. In addition to dorm rooms (a minus for the triple bunks), the hostel has a couple of colorful private rooms.

There's a bar, a lounge and a small plant-lined patio. The staff organizes many activities for guests.

CASA CAMINHO DO CORCOVADO
B&B $$

Map p250 (✐2557-2359; www.casacaminhodocorcovado.com.br; Filinto de Almeida 283, Cosme Velho; d R$240-390; ✳☎) On the Corcovado hillside, this idyllic place is surrounded by tropical rainforest, and feels like a peaceful escape from the city. Friendly, knowledgeable hosts offer just two attractive rooms and one bungalow overlooking the garden; it's in high demand so book early. Fine views, and a relaxing air pervades.

SOLAR DO COSME
GUESTHOUSE $$
Map p250 (📋3596-0585; www.solardocosme.com; Ladeira do Ascurra 124, Cosme Velho; s/d R$234/260) Nestled at the foothill of Corcovado, this tranquil guesthouse earns high marks from guests for the kindhearted hosts, who are happy to share tips on making the most of Rio. The rooms are tidy and well maintained, and the lush grounds add to the value.

On the downside, it's a long way from the beach, though it's a short walk to the railway station leading up to Cristo Redentor.

🛏 Centro & Praça Mauá

POP ART HOSTEL
HOSTEL $
Map p254 (📋2253-9069; www.poparthostel.com.br; Ladeira João Homem 56, Morro da Conceição; dm/d from R$40/130; ❄️🤶) Located in the pretty neighborhood of Morro da Conceição, this hostel has clean, modern rooms decorated with colorful artworks (though not necessarily pop art). The rooms lack windows, though there's a small, pleasant back terrace with views. It's a friendly spot, and it's on one of Rio's most picturesque cobblestone lanes, just a short stroll to the sights of Praça Mauá.

🛏 Santa Teresa

RIO HOSTEL
HOSTEL $
Map p258 (📋3852-0827; www.riohostel.com; Joaquim Murtinho 361; dm/s/d from R$35/80/120; ❄️@🤶) This Santa favorite provides travelers with a home away from home. The backyard patio with its pool is a great place to meet other travelers, and there's also a kitchen for guests. Rooms are clean, and there are attractive doubles, including private suites with fine views behind the pool.

CASA DA GENTE
GUESTHOUSE $
Map p258 (📋2232-2634; www.casadagente.com; Gonçalves Fontes 33, Santa Teresa; s/d from

R$125/185; 🤶) 🌿 A short stroll from the top of the Escadaria Selarón, the Casa da Gente is a welcoming French-Brazilian-run guesthouse with a strong interest in sustainability. Rainwater catchment, solar panels, composting and a green roof are all part of the ethos. The rooms themselves are bright, clean and simply furnished.

The grassy terrace is a pleasant place to relax after exploring the city. It's not a bad spot for cat lovers, as there are three felines in residence.

★CASA BELEZA
POUSADA $$
Map p258 (📋98288-6764; www.casabeleza.net; Laurinda Santos Lobo 311; r R$260-450; ❄️🤶🏊) This lovely property dates back to the 1930s and was once a governor's mansion. Tropical gardens overlook the picturesque pool, and you can sometimes spot toucans and monkeys in the surrounding foliage. It's a small and tranquil operation, with just four guestrooms and one peacefully set villa (complete with a rooftop deck offering panoramic views).

The kind, multilingual family that runs the *pousada* lives on-site.

CASA ÁUREA
GUESTHOUSE $$
Map p258 (📋2242-5830; www.casaaurea.com.br; Áurea 80; d R$300-340, s/d without bathroom R$170/220; ❄️🤶) Set in one of Santa Teresa's oldest homes (1871), the two-story Casa Áurea has rustic charm, simple but cozy rooms and a large covered garden where you can lounge on hammocks, fire up the barbecue or whip up a meal in the open-air kitchen. Very welcoming and kindhearted hosts.

CAMA E CAFÉ
HOMESTAY $$
Map p258 (📋2225-4366; www.camaecafe.com; Progresso 67; r R$196-300) A fine alternative to hotels and guesthouses, Cama e Café is a B&B network that allows travelers to book a room from local residents. There are several dozen options to choose from, with the majority of listings in Santa Teresa, and a few scattered options in Laranjeiras, the Zona Sul and Barra.

Accommodations range from modest to lavish. The best rooms are inside colonial homes that offer panoramic views and lush gardens.

CASA DA CARMEN E DO FERNANDO
GUESTHOUSE $$
Map p258 (📋2507-3084; www.bedandbreakfast rio.com.br; Hermenegildo de Barros 172; s/d from

SLEEPING CENTRO & PRAÇA MAUÁ

R$175/225; 🛜📺) This familiar eight-room guesthouse attracts a laid-back crowd that feels right at home in the century-old building. The colorfully decorated lounge is adorned with artwork (including paintings by one of the owners) and has a comfy, lived-in feel; it's a fine place to watch a film, play music or enjoy the view through the oversized picture window.

Out the back is a small pool and a rustic terrace, which have equally impressive views. Rooms are simply furnished but enlivened with bright colors and likewise come with views.

CASALEGRE   GUESTHOUSE $$

Map p258 (🖉98670-6158; www.casalegre.com.br; Monte Alegre 316; s R$150-250, d R$190-300; 🛜) Casalegre has a rustic, art-loving, bohemian vibe. Its rooms vary in size (the cheapest two share a bathroom), but all are decorated with different works of art and

---

FAVELA CHIC

Favela sleeps are nothing new. Intrepid travelers have been venturing into Rio's urban mazes for over a decade, but as more and more of Rio's favelas are pacified, hostels and *pousadas* (guesthouses) are popping up faster than the rudimentary constructions which make up the favelas themselves. Our favorites:

Maze Inn (Map p249; 🖉2558-5547; www.jazzrio.com; Casa 66, Tavares Bastos 414, Catete; dm R$90, s/d from R$175/225) Set in Tavares Bastos favela, the Maze Inn is a fantastic place to overnight for those looking for an alternative view of Rio. The rooms are uniquely decorated with original artworks by English owner and Renaissance man Bob Nadkarni, while the veranda offers stunning views of the bay and Pão de Açúcar (Sugarloaf Mountain). Don't miss the jazz parties held on the first Friday of every month.

Mirante do Arvrão (🖉3114-1868; www.mirantedoarvrao.com.br; Armando de Almeida Lima 8, Vidigal; dm/s/d from R$58/158/400; ❄🛜) A surprising find in Vidigal, the Mirante do Arvrão has beautifully set rooms, the best of which offer gorgeous views over the ocean. It's worth paying extra for a deluxe room with floor-to-ceiling windows and a private balcony. The hostel is built from sustainable materials and uses solar power to heat the showers.

Varandas do Vidigal (🖉3114-3661; www.varandasdovidigal.com.br; Casa 3, Madre Ana Coimbra, Vidigal; dm R$38-45, d R$110-130; ❄🛜) This friendly hostel has clean, zen-like, tile-floored dorm rooms with four to 12 top-quality beds as well as a private double. The ocean views are mesmerizing, particularly from the laid-back veranda-bar. The friendly owner, who speaks English and hails from Rio Grande do Sul, has a deep affection for Vidigal and a wealth of insight into the community.

Vidigalbergue (🖉3114-8025; www.vidigalbergue.com.br; Casa 2, Av Niemeyer 314, Vidigal; dm R$45-60; ❄@🛜) A 15-minute walk from Leblon brings you to this small hostel at the bottom of Vidigal favela, where these days there's even a tourist map to guide you around. The coup here is the stunning sea views from all the dorms and the hospitality of the two English-speaking best-friend owners, Luis and Andre.

Babilônia Rio Hostel (Map p248; 🖉3873-6826; www.babiloniariohostel.com.br; Ladeira Ary Barroso 50, Leme; dm R$40-50, d R$140-170) Uphill from Leme, this place has five dorm rooms and two private rooms, including one much-sought-after chamber (Quarto Vidigal) with air-conditioning and a sea view. It's a friendly place in a small, welcoming community and there are good eating and drinking options nearby. It's an easy 10-minute stroll downhill to the beach, but an uphill challenge on the return – take a mototaxi to save those hamstrings.

Pousada Favelinha (🖉98406-7764; www.favelinha.com; Almirante Alexandrino 2023, Santa Teresa; dm R$50, d R$110; @🛜) Located in the favela of Pereirão da Silva, Pousada Favelinha has four double rooms and a five-bed dorm, all with balconies that have stunning views over the city to Pão de Açúcar. There's also a terrace, a lounge and lots of insider info available from the welcoming Brazilian-German owners.

each is named after the artist whose work adorns its walls. There's a strong communal vibe here, and the owners often host parties, yoga classes and other activities.

It has an art gallery on the 1st floor and a small terrace in back.

CASA BIANCA
GUESTHOUSE $$

Map p258 (☑3233-1563; www.guesthousebianca .com; Murtinho Nobre 35; r from R$330; ✳🛜) This beautiful 1930s-era mansion down the road from Parque das Ruínas has lovely details: stained-glass windows, tall ceilings, a marble staircase and period furnishings. Rooms are attractively set with wood floors and antique fixtures; two have excellent views, one of which has a private veranda. It's a quiet place, with just three rooms, and the friendly owner lives on-site.

CASTELINHO 38
HOTEL $$

Map p258 (☑2252-2549; www.castelinho38.com. br; Triunfo 38; r from R$250; ✳@🛜) A Santa Teresa charmer, Castelinho offers spacious rooms with high ceilings, wood floors and a light, airy design. It's set in a mid-19th-century mansion and has an outdoor terrace with a garden and lounge space.

VILLA LAURINDA
GUESTHOUSE $$

Map p258 (☑3648-2216; www.villalaurinda.com; Laurinda Santos Lobo 98; r with/without bathroom from R$300/200; 🛜💦) In a converted 1888 Victorian, the Villa Laurinda presents a serene portrait of life in Santa Teresa. At the house entrance there is a lovely pool, ringed with tropical foliage and mango trees. The rooms are simply designed with wide plank floors and range from small to large; three of the rooms share a bathroom (others are en suite).

You'll also find classically furnished common areas, including a small library with a grand piano.

CASA COOL BEANS
GUESTHOUSE $$

Map p258 (☑2262-0552; www.casacoolbeans. com; Laurinda Santos Lobo 136; d R$250-400; ✳@🛜💦) Your expectations will easily be exceeded at this discreet 10-room B&B, where the American owner's mantra focuses on personalized service. Each colorful room in the renovated 1930s Spanish-style villa was designed by a different Brazilian artist; book room nine for the best views. It also has a spacious sun deck and an enticing pool. No children allowed.

★ **HOTEL SANTA TERESA**
BOUTIQUE HOTEL $$$

Map p258 (☑2222-2755; www.santa-teresa-hotel.com; Almirante Alexandrino 660; d from R$1000; ✳@🛜💦) What is probably the finest boutique hotel in Rio is set in a lavishly restored building that was part of a coffee plantation in the 19th century. It includes artfully designed rooms, an award-winning restaurant, a full-service spa, a stylish bar and a pool with fine views over the city.

The design incorporates a certain tropical elegance, with art and artifacts from across Brazil on display in common areas and in some rooms.

MAMA RUISA
HOTEL $$$

Map p258 (☑2508-8142; www.mamaruisa. com; Santa Cristina 132; r R$700-900; ✳🛜💦) French-owned Mama Ruisa aims for bohemian chic in its seven spacious, uniquely designed guest rooms. Every whim is catered for in this inspiring converted colonial mansion; guests can opt for massages and private tours or simply enjoy the spectacular view over the bay from the swimming pool.

🛏 Lapa

BOOKS HOSTEL
HOSTEL $

Map p258 (☑3437-3783; www.bookshostel.com; Francisco Muratori 10; dm R$50-70; ✳@🛜) In the heart of Lapa and true to the nature of the neighborhood, this party hostel is the appetizer for your crazy night out. Dorms have graffiti art and there's a sociable *barraca*-style bar (rooms overlooking it don't allow for much sleep). All bathrooms are shared, and only some rooms have air-conditioning.

VILA GALÉ
BOUTIQUE HOTEL $$$

Map p258 (☑2460-4500; www.vilagale.com; Riachuelo 124; r R$360-800; ✳🛜💦) Breathing new life into ragged Lapa, Vila Galé – a high-end luxury chain from Portugal – invested some €35 million in this beautiful property. The spacious, well-appointed rooms are good value, and the best of them are set in a 19th-century building overlooking a lovely pool. The rooms are quiet despite having the best of Rio's nightlife right outside the door.

🛏 Barra da Tijuca & Western Rio

Few foreign travelers stay in the neighborhoods west of Leblon, as you generally need a car to get around. However, you are close to some of Rio's best beaches, which get wilder the further west you go.

RIO SURF 'N STAY
HOSTEL **$**

Map p262 (☑3418-1133; www.riosurfnstay.com; Raimundo Veras 1140, Recreio dos Bandeirantes; dm/d from R$55/160; ❄ 🛜) Just a short stroll to the fine surf off Macumba Beach, this converted house, which is owned by a New Zealander and a Brazilian, is the go-to spot for anyone who has come to Rio to learn to surf. The dorm rooms (sleeping four or five people) and private doubles are comfortably furnished, and the hosts do their best to make everyone feel at home.

There is a kitchen for guest use and a grassy lawn with palm trees that is fine for lazing about on. Surf packages, which include lessons and accommodation, are available; a three-night package with two two-hour lessons and a shared room costs R$495. Rio Surf 'N Stay is about 30km west of Leblon.

UTRÓPICO
GUESTHOUSE **$$**

Map p262 (☑4042-1155; www.utropicoguesthouse.com.br; Ilha Primeira; r from R$300; ❄ 🛜 🏊) Utrópico has a stunning location on a river island in the Lagoa da Tijuca, toward the western end of Barra. The rooms are attractive, but the tropical-like surroundings fairly upstage everything else. Swim in the pool and admire the view of green mountains and the peaceful lagoon.

Access is by boat, which also takes you through the canals and within walking distance of Barra's lovely beach. By taxi it's about 30 minutes' drive to Ipanema; once the new metro lines open, access will be much faster (and cheaper).

DON PASCUAL
GUESTHOUSE **$$**

Map p262 (☑3417-0776; www.donpascual.com.br; Casa 12, Estrada do Sacarrão 867, Vargem Grande; r weekday/weekend from R$325/436; ❄ 🛜 🏊) Surrounded by lush vegetation, this hidden gem has attractive rooms with a rustic-chic allure. Some of the rooms are split-level and incorporate reclaimed lumber into the cabin-like design. There's an enticing swimming pool and a restaurant that invites lingering. The downside? It's a long drive from Ipanema, and you'll need a car and excellent directions to get here. Call ahead for specifics.

Understand Rio de Janeiro

RIO DE JANEIRO TODAY .178

Great changes are sweeping across Rio, with its revitalized waterfront and expanded metro, though crime, pollution and other problems remain.

HISTORY 180

Portuguese royals, authoritarian demagogues, repressive military dictatorships and socially minded visionaries have all played a role in Rio's complicated past.

THE SOUNDS OF RIO. 191

Rio's greatest hits feature bossa nova, *tropicália*, Música Popular Brasileira (MPB), hip-hop and, above all, samba.

FOOTBALL. 196

When it comes to the beautiful game, no other place quite compares: a look at Rio's extraordinary footballing legacy.

ARCHITECTURE 200

From baroque churches to postmodern concert halls, Rio has some surprising architectural treasures.

Rio de Janeiro Today

It's a pivotal moment for Rio de Janeiro. With major public works happening all across the city, Mayor Eduardo Paes is betting big. His wager: that a wealth of private and public investment showered on the city will pay off, much as it did for Barcelona after its Olympic Games. *Cariocas* (residents of Rio), meanwhile, are hopeful about the city's urban renaissance, while also leery of the rising crime, pollution and the ongoing recession that could herald darker days ahead.

Best on Film

Cidade de Deus (City of God; director Fernando Meirelles, 2002) Oscar-nominated film showing coexistence of brutality and hope in a Rio favela.

Orfeu Negro (Black Orpheus; director Marcel Camus, 1959) The Orpheus-Eurydice myth set during Rio's Carnaval with a groundbreaking bossa nova soundtrack.

Central do Brasil (Central Station; director Walter Salles, 1998) Epic journey through unglamorized Brazil, set in Rio and the Northeast.

Madame Satã (director Karim Aïnouz, 2002) Compelling portrait of Rio's gritty Lapa district during the 1930s.

Best in Print

Dancing With the Devil in the City of God (Juliana Barbassa, 2015) Portrait of the great changes happening now, plus a look at Rio's complex social challenges.

Rio de Janeiro Reader (Daryle Williams et al, 2015) Covers 450 years of history, culture and politics.

Brazil on the Rise (Larry Rohter, 2010) A journey through the culture, history and economic transformation of Brazil.

Bossa Nova (Ruy Castro, 2000) A fascinating look at the poets, composers and musicians behind the music.

A Revitalized Waterfront

After winning the right to host the 2014 World Cup and the 2016 Summer Olympics, Rio got straight to work. Back in 2009, the city unveiled Porto Maravilha (Marvelous Port), an ambitious project that aimed to revitalize an astounding 5 million sq meters of the city's derelict waterfront near downtown, with new museums, green spaces, office buildings and residences.

After more than US$1.7 billion of investment and seven years of construction, the project is nearing completion. For locals who haven't visited in a while, it will be a downtown transformed. The unsightly elevated highway that once marred the skyline has been torn down and replaced by tunnels, with new parks laid over the top. A new high-tech light rail will travel along 26km of rails through downtown, looping past the striking Praça Mauá, with its two grand museums – including a cutting-edge science museum designed by celebrated Spanish architect Santiago Calatrava.

Nearby stands the AquaRio, the largest aquarium in South America. Public and private investment has been pouring in. Even Donald Trump has gotten in on the action, opening five 38-story-high towers near the waterfront. Picturesque colonial-era buildings, forgotten for years beneath a layer of grime, are being restored, while new bike lanes (17km in all) and waterfront walking paths will connect it with other parts of downtown.

The Downtown Renaissance

Although the port is the focal point, other parts of downtown are also being restored, including the Praça Tiradentes, a historic part of downtown whose nearby streets had long since been abandoned to urban blight. A new five-star hotel (Le Paris) will open here, in what was once an infamous brothel. Further east, Morro da

Providência, Rio's oldest favela, has also benefited from public investment: a new *teleférico* (cable car) connects the uppermost reaches of the favela with Rio's Central Station. It's the second favela to receive this (after Complexo do Alemão). Although local residents benefit from the *teleférico*, not everyone is pleased. When the city government proposed the building of a similar cable-car system in Rocinha, Rio's largest favela, the community protested, saying the money would be better spent on improving basic sanitation.

Boom Days in Barra

Another beneficiary of Rio's lavish public spending is the district of Barra da Tijuca, which will be the epicenter of the 2016 Summer Olympics. Several of its massive, newly constructed sporting arenas will be used as high-tech training facilities for future athletes, others will be dismantled and used to build public schools. Parts of the Olympic Village and the Athletes Park will be transformed into luxury housing. Even more impressive is the whopping R$8 billion expansion of Rio's metro system: a 17km extension running from Ipanema to Barra that will carry an estimated 300,000 passengers a day. Engineers and laborers have been working around the clock to meet the 2016 deadline.

Ongoing Challenges

It isn't all good news in the *Cidade Maravilhosa* (Marvelous City). By 2015 Mayor Paes admitted the city would be unable to fulfill the promise to clean the polluted Baía de Guanabara (Guanabara Bay) before the Olympics. Alarmingly, an independent investigation by the Associated Press found dangerous levels of viruses in the bay – where many sailing events are to be held – though this is not surprising given that 70% of the city's sewage flows untreated into the bay. Unfortunately, pollution isn't limited to Guanabara. The lagoon (Lagoa Rodrigo de Freitas) also has disturbing levels of pollution (more than 60 tons of dead fish washed up on the shore in 2015, caused by a lack of oxygen owing to pollution). On the plus side, the Olympic spotlight has forced Rio to address its polluted waterways. Protests led by the fishing and boating community continue to put pressure on the city to clean up the sewage – and prevent officials from reneging on their promises once the Games are over.

Rio's other big problem: crime. With rising unemployment and a full-blown economic recession underway, violence is surging once again. A Reuters report found that street crime had risen by 25% in 2014, the biggest jump since 1991. Gun battles in previously pacified favelas (such as Dona Marta) and brazen beachfront robberies by groups of criminals in broad daylight have only added to the worry that the city is on a downward slide.

if Rio were 100 people

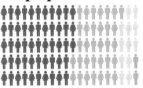

53 would be white
33 would be multiracial
12 would be black
2 would be other

belief systems

(% of population)

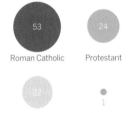

Roman Catholic 53

Protestant 24

Other 22

Spiritist 1

population per sq km

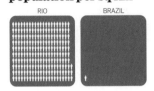

RIO   BRAZIL

⋔ ≈ 25 people

History

Discovered in the 1500s, Rio became a key settlement in Portugal's New World empire, particularly after the entire Portuguese court decamped here in the early 1800s. Magnificent churches and fine colonial-era streets still attest to the imperial wealth lavished on the city, though by the late 1800s Rio was already a divided city of haves and have-nots. The 20th century saw an influx of immigrants, explosive favela growth, the rise of a military dictatorship and a loss of prestige, when Brasília replaced Rio as the nation's capital. The last decade has seen boom days once again, with burgeoning financial growth.

Brazil is the only country in the New World that was both the seat of an empire (when the Portuguese king came over) and an independent monarchy (when Dom Pedro I declared independence).

The Portuguese Arrival

In the 15th century Portugal, ever infatuated with the sea, began its large-scale explorations that would eventually take Portuguese explorers to the coast of Brazil in 1500. A little over a year later, Gonçalo Coelho sailed from Portugal and entered a huge bay in January 1502. It was his chief pilot, Amerigo Vespucci, however, who would give the name to this bay. Mistaking it for a river (or possibly making no mistake at all since the old Portuguese 'rio' is another word for bay), he dubbed it Rio de Janeiro (River of January).

Noble Savages & Savage Nobles

Some believe that the indigenous Guanabara and Tupinambá (better known as the Tupi) inspired works such as Sir Thomas Moore's *Utopia* (1516) and Rousseau's Enlightenment-era idea of the 'noble savage.' This all started from the letters credited to Amerigo Vespucci on his first voyage to Rio in 1502. The idea common at the time was that there existed on earth an Eden, and that it lay undiscovered. Vespucci claimed to have found that Eden, from his cursory observations of the Tupi. They were described as innocent savages, carefree and well groomed, with the unusual custom of taking daily baths in the sea. The fact that native women were freely offered to the strange foreigners probably added to the enthusiasm with which they spoke about the region upon their return to Portugal.

TIMELINE	8000 BC	AD 1502	1565
	Descendents of hunter-gatherers who crossed the Bering Strait from East Asia between 10,000 BC and 12,000 BC settle along Baía de Guanabara.	Portuguese explorer Gonçalo Coelho sails into Baía de Guanabara. His chief pilot, Amerigo Vespucci (after whom 'America' is named), dubbed the lovely setting Rio de Janeiro.	After driving off the French and their indigenous allies, the Portuguese found the first permanent settlement, São Sebastião do Rio de Janeiro.

In fact, the honeymoon didn't last long. The conquerors soon came to see the forest-dwelling *índios* as raw manpower for the Portuguese empire, and enslaved them and set them to work on plantations. The *índios*, too, turned out to be different than the Europeans imagined. The Tupinambá were warlike and ate their enemies – through ritualistic cannibalism they believed they would receive the power and strength of the consumed opponent. They also didn't take to the work as the Portuguese had expected, and were dying off in large numbers from introduced diseases. By the 17th century the Tupinambá had been completely eradicated. To fulfill their growing labor demands, the Portuguese eventually turned to Africa.

Africans in Brazil

The Portuguese began bringing blacks, stolen from Africa, into the new colony shortly after Brazil's founding. Most blacks were brought from Guinea, Angola and the Congo and would constitute some three million people brought to Brazil over its three-and-a-half centuries of human trafficking. The port of Rio had the largest number of slaves entering the colony – as many as two million in all. At open-air slave markets these new immigrants were sold as local help or shipped to the interior, initially to work on the thriving sugar plantations, and later – when gold was discovered in Minas Gerais in 1704 – to work back-breaking jobs in the mines.

Although slavery was rotten anywhere in the New World, most historians agree that the Africans in Rio had it better than their rural brethren. Those who came to Rio worked in domestic roles as maids and butlers and out on the streets as dock workers, furniture movers, delivery boys, boatmen, cobblers, fishermen and carpenters. The worst job was transporting the barrels of human excrement produced in town and emptying them into the bay.

As Rio's population grew, so too did the number of slaves imported to meet the labor needs of the expanding coffee plantations in the Paraíba Valley. By the early 19th century African slaves made up two-thirds of Rio's population.

Lots of illicit liaisons occurred between master and slave, and children born into mixed backgrounds were largely accepted into the social sphere and raised as free citizens. This contributed considerably to creating Brazil's melting pot. While escape attempts were fewer in Rio than in the more brutal climate of the Northeast, there were attempts. Those seeking freedom often set their sights on *quilombos* (communities of runaway slaves). Some were quite developed – as was the case with Palmares, which had a population of 20,000 and survived

'Order and Progress,' the slogan on Brazil's flag, comes from French philosopher Auguste de Comte (1797–1857), whose elevation of reason and scientific knowledge over traditional beliefs was influential on the young Brazilian republic.

1550–80	1763	1807	1822
The Portuguese bring over 2000 slaves to the new colony. Over the next 300 years, more than three million people stolen from Africa will be relocated to Brazil.	With gold flowing from Minas Gerais through Rio, the city grows wealthy and swells in population to 50,000; the Portuguese court transfers the capital of Brazil from Salvador to Rio.	Napoleon invades Portugal and the Portuguese prince regent (later known as Dom João VI) and his entire court of 15,000 flee for Brazil. The royal family showers wealth upon Rio.	Left in charge of Brazil after his father Dom João VI returns to Portugal, Dom Pedro I declares independence from Portugal and crowns himself 'emperor' of Brazil.

through much of the 17th century before it was wiped out by federal troops.

Abroad, the country was receiving pressure to outlaw slavery, and trafficking in human cargo was eventually banned in 1830. This move, however, did nothing to improve the lives of slaves already in Brazil, who would have to wait another two generations to gain their freedom. Despite the ban, shipment of human cargo continued well into the 1850s, with 500,000 slaves smuggled into Brazil between 1830 and 1850. The British (out of economic self-interest) finally suppressed Brazil's trafficking with naval squadrons.

Pressure from home and abroad reached boiling point toward the end of the 19th century until, in 1888, from the steps of the Royal Palace overlooking Praça XV (Quinze) de Novembro, slavery was declared abolished. Brazil was the last country in the New World to end slavery.

Rio's Early Days

In order to get the colony up and running, the Portuguese built a fortified town on Morro do Castelo in 1567 to maximize protection from European invasion by sea and *índio* attack by land. They named their town São Sebastião do Rio de Janeiro, in honor of patron saint Sebastião – and namesake of King Sebastião of Portugal. Cobbled together by the 500 founding *cariocas* (residents of Rio), early Rio was a poorly planned town with irregular streets in the medieval Portuguese style. It remained a small settlement through the mid-17th century, surviving on the export of brazilwood and sugarcane. In Rio's first census (in 1600), the population comprised 3000 *índios*, 750 Portuguese and 100 blacks.

With its excellent harbor and good lands for sugarcane, Rio became Brazil's third most important settlement (after Salvador da Bahia and Recife-Olinda) in the 17th century.

The gold rush in Minas Gerais had a profound effect on Rio and caused major demographic shifts on three continents. The rare metal was first discovered by *bandeirantes* (explorers and hired slave-hunters) in the 1690s, and as word spread gold seekers arrived in droves. Over the next half-century an estimated 500,000 Portuguese arrived in Brazil and a million African slaves were imported. Rio served as the natural port of entry for this flow of people and commerce to and from the Minas Gerais goldfields.

In the 18th century Rio morphed into a rough-and-tumble place attracting a sturdy brand of European immigrant. Most of the settlement was built near the water, where Praça XV (Quinze) de Novembro stands today), beside rows of warehouses, with noisy taverns sprinkled along

In the half-century of gold fever, some 500,000 Portuguese immigrated to Brazil, and one million slaves were brought here. Rio served as the entry port for people and commerce flowing to and from the goldfields.

1831	1888	1889	1900
Brazil's first homegrown monarch, Dom Pedro I, proves incompetent and abdicates. In 1840, his son Pedro II takes the throne and ushers in a long period of growth and stability.	Slavery is abolished in Brazil, the last country in the New World to do so. The law is signed by Princesa Isabel, admired by many blacks as their benefactress.	A military coup, supported by Brazil's wealthy coffee farmers, overthrows Pedro II. The monarchy is abolished and the Brazilian Republic is born.	Mayor Pereira Passos ushers in a period of urbanization, creating grand boulevards, opening up Copacabana (via tunnel), and improving public health and sanitation.

the main streets. Rio was a rough city full of smugglers and thieves, tramps and assassins, and slaves on the run. Smuggling was rampant, with ships robbed and the sailors murdered, and bribes given over to the police. Gold flowing through the city created the constant menace of pirates. Adding a note of temperance to the place were the religious orders that came in small bands and built Rio's first churches.

Rio Under the King

In 1807 Napoleon's army marched on Lisbon. Two days before the French invasion, 40 ships carrying the Portuguese prince regent (later known as Dom João VI) and his entire court of 15,000 set sail for Brazil under the protection of British warships. After the initial landing in Bahia (where their unkempt state was met with bemusement), the royal family moved down to Rio, where they settled.

This had momentous consequences for the city as the king, missing the high culture of Europe, lavished his attention on Rio, envisioning a splendid European-style city for his new hometown. European artisans

HISTORICAL SITES

Paço Imperial (p125)	The former imperial palace was home to the royal family when they arrived from Portugal.
Praça XV (Quinze) de Novembro (p125)	Named after the date Brazil declared itself a republic (November 15, 1822), this plaza has witnessed a lot of historical action, including the crowning of two emperors and the abolition of slavery.
Travessa do Comércio (p126)	This narrow alley is a window into colonial Rio, with 18th-century buildings converted into bars and restaurants.
Museu Histórico Nacional (p122)	Set in the 18th-century royal arsenal, this museum houses Rio's best assortment of historical artifacts.
Jardim Botânico (p79)	Prince Regent Dom João ensured the city would have no shortage of green spaces, and ordered this verdant garden to be planted in 1808.
Museu da República (p114)	Formerly known as the Palácio do Catete, this mansion was Brazil's presidential home from 1896 to 1954. Getúlio Vargas was the last president to live here, and committed suicide in one of the upstairs rooms.
Praça Floriano (p123)	Centro's picturesque main square has long been the meeting ground for popular demonstrations, including student uprisings against the military dictatorship in the 1960s and victory celebrations following World Cup finals.
Garota de Ipanema (p63)	Famed spot where Tom Jobim and Vinícius de Moraes penned the 'Girl from Ipanema,' the international success of which was a major moment in the history of bossa nova.

1917	1923	1928	1930
Samba is officially born, with the first recording of the song 'Pelo Telefone.' This song and others soon get wide airplay on the radio.	The Copacabana Palace opens its doors. It becomes an icon of Rio's tropical glamor, with international jet-setters flying down during Rio's pre-Depression boom.	Deixa Falar becomes the first *escola de samba* (samba school; called a 'school' because it's located next to a primary school), followed by Mangueira later that year.	Getúlio Vargas comes into power. Inspired by European fascists, Vargas presides over an authoritarian state, playing a major role in Brazilian politics for the next two decades.

History Reads

Brazil: Five Centuries of Change (Thomas E Skidmore)

The History of Brazil (Robert Levine)

The New Brazil (Riordan Roett)

flooded the city. The British, rewarded for helping the king safely reach Brazil, gained access to Brazil's ports, and many Anglo traders and merchants set up shop in the town center. Anti-Napoleon French also arrived, as did other Europeans, creating an international air unknown until then. When the German prince and noted naturalist Alexander Philipp Maximilian arrived in Brazil in 1815, he commented on the many nationalities and mixtures of people he encountered.

Dom João VI fell in love with Rio. A great admirer of nature, he founded the botanical gardens and introduced sea bathing to the inhabitants of Rio. He had a special pier built at Caju, with a small tub at the end, in which he would immerse himself fully clothed as the waves rocked gently against it. (His wife, Carlota Joaquina, bathed in the nude.) This was long before Copacabana was opened to the rest of the city, remaining a virgin expanse of white sand framed by rainforest-covered mountains, reachable only by an arduous journey.

With the court came an influx of money and talent that helped build some of the city's lasting monuments, such as the palace at the Quinta da Boa Vista. Within a year of his arrival, Dom João VI also created the School of Medicine, the Bank of Brazil, the Law Courts, the Naval Academy and the Royal Printing Works.

Dom João VI was expected to return to Portugal after Napoleon's defeat at Waterloo in 1815, but instead stayed in Brazil. The following year his mother, Queen Dona Maria I, died, and Dom João VI became king. He refused demands to return to Portugal to rule, and declared Rio the capital of the United Kingdom of Portugal, Brazil and the Algarves. Brazil became the only New World colony to ever have a European monarch ruling on its soil.

Five years later Dom João VI finally relented to political pressure and returned to Portugal, leaving his 23-year-old son Pedro in Brazil as prince regent. In Portugal the king was confronted with the newly formed Côrtes, a legislative assembly attempting to reign in the powers of the monarchy. The Côrtes had many directives, one of which was restoring Brazil to its previous status as subservient colony. Word was sent to Dom Pedro that his authority was greatly diminished. According to legend, when Pedro received the directive in 1822, he pulled out his sword and yelled *'Independência ou morte!'* ('Independence or death!'), putting himself at the country's head as Emperor Dom Pedro I.

Portugal was too weak to fight its favorite son, not to mention the British, who had the most to gain from Brazilian independence and would have come to the aid of the Brazilians. Without spilling blood, Brazil had attained its independence and Dom Pedro I became the head of

Rio's nearest *quilombo* in the 19th century was in Leblon – then quite distant from the city. Unlike other *quilombos*, it was headed by a white, progressive businessman, Jose de Seixas Magalhães, who hid and protected slaves in his Leblon mansion and his surrounding farmlands.

1932	1937	1942	1950
Rio holds its first Carnaval parade. Mangueira wins, and quickly cements its status as the city's favorite samba school (a sentiment held by many today).	President Vargas announces a new constitution; he passes minimum wage laws in 1938, expands the military and centralizes power.	Initially maintaining neutrality, Brazil enters WWII on the Allies' side, providing raw materials, plus 25,000 troops (the only Latin American nation to do so).	Newly constructed Maracanã stadium plays center stage in the FIFA World Cup. Brazil dominates until the final, when it suffers a stunning loss to Uruguay before 200,000 fans.

the Brazilian 'empire' (despite Pedro's claims to the contrary, Brazil was a regular monarchy, not an empire since it had no overseas colonies).

Dom Pedro I ruled for only nine years. From all accounts, he was a bumbling incompetent who scandalized even the permissive Brazilians by siring numerous illegitimate children. He also strongly resisted any attempts to weaken his power by constitutional means. Following street demonstrations in Rio in 1831, he surprised everyone by abdicating, leaving the power in the hands of his five-year-old, Brazilian-born son.

Until Dom Pedro II reached adolescence, Brazil suffered through a turbulent period of unrest, which finally ended in 1840 when Dom Pedro II, at the age of 14, took the throne. Despite his youth he proved to be a stabilizing element for the country, and ushered in a long period of peace and relative prosperity. The period of industrialization began with the introduction of the steamship and the telegraph, and the king encouraged mass immigration from Europe.

Dom Pedro II's shortcomings during his half-century of rule were a bloody war with Paraguay (1864–70) and his slowness at abolishing slavery. He was well liked by his subjects, but they finally had enough of the monarchy and he was pushed from power in 1889.

The Belle Époque

Rio experienced boom days in the latter half of the 19th century. The spreading wealth of coffee plantations in Rio state (and in São Paulo) revitalized Brazil's economy, just as the city was going through substantial growth and modernization. Regular passenger ships began sailing to London (1845) and Paris (1851), and the local ferry service to Niterói began in 1862. A telegraph system and gas streetlights were installed in 1854. By 1860 Rio had more than 250,000 inhabitants, making it the largest city in South America.

For the wealthy, the goal of creating a modern European capital grew ever closer, as the city embraced all things European – with particular influence from the customs, fashion and even cuisine of Paris. The poor, however, had a miserable lot. In the 1870s and 1880s, as the rich moved to new urban areas by the bay or in the hills, Rio's marginalized lived in tenement houses in the old center of town. There, conditions were grim: streets were poorly lit and poorly ventilated, with a stench filling the narrow alleyways.

Rio's flood of immigrants added diversity to the city. On the streets, you could hear a symphony of languages – African, Portuguese, English, French – mixing with the sounds of the *bonde* (tram), of carts drawn by mules, and the cadence of various dances (maxixes, lundus, polkas and waltzes) interpreted by anonymous performers.

A true Renaissance man, Dom Pedro II had interests in many subjects – chemistry, philosophy, geology, poetry, anthropology – and he could speak over a dozen languages (including Arabic and Sanskrit). He corresponded with many great 19th-century figures, including Richard Wagner, Alexander Graham Bell and Louis Pasteur.

1954	1960	1963	1964
Following a political scandal, the military calls for the resignation of President Getúlio Vargas. He pens a melodramatic letter then shoots himself at his Rio palace.	President Juscelino Kubitschek moves the capital of Brazil from Rio to the newly constructed Brasília; Rio's political and sociocultural prominence declines.	Brazilian filmmakers create a new movement with Cinema Novo, which tackles Brazil's social problems. Director Glaubo Rocha leads the way with *Black God, White Devil*.	President Goulart is overthrown by a military coup. Troops arrive in Rio and seize power. So begins the era of dictatorship, with generals running the show for the next 20 years.

The city went through dramatic changes in the first decade of 1900, owing in large part to the work of mayor Pereira Passos. He continued the work of 'Europeanization' by widening Rio's streets and creating grand boulevards such as Av Central and Mem de Sá. The biggest of these boulevards required the destruction of 600 buildings to make way for Av Central (later renamed Rio Branco), which became the Champs Elysées of Rio, an elegant boulevard full of sidewalk cafes and promenading *cariocas*.

Passos also connected Botafogo to Copacabana by building a tunnel, paving the way for the development of the southern beaches. Despite his grand vision for Rio, his vision for the poor was one of wide-scale

THE ORIGINS OF THE FAVELA

In the Northeast, terrible droughts in the 1870s and '80s, coupled with the decline of the sugar industry, brought economic devastation. Offering a vision of hope, messianic popular movements gained support among Brazil's poor. The most famous was led by Antônio Conselheiro (Antônio the Counselor), an itinerant preacher who had wandered for years through the backlands prophesying the end of the world, defending the poor and antagonizing the authorities. He railed against the new republican government and in 1893 eventually settled with his followers at Canudos, in the interior of northern Bahia. Within 1½ years Canudos had grown to a city of 35,000.

The republican government sensed plots in Canudos to return Brazil to the monarchy. After the first attempts to subdue Canudos failed, the government sent in a federal force of 8000 soldiers – many of whom hailed from Rio – in a war of extermination that nearly wiped out every man, woman and child from Canudos. The settlement was then burned to the ground to erase it from the nation's memory.

The soldiers and their wives – some of whom were survivors taken from the Canudos massacre – returned to Rio, where they were promised land in exchange for their victory. The government, however, reneged on the promise. The soldiers, who had camped out in front of the Ministry of War, then occupied the nearby hillside of Morro da Providência.

Oddly enough, as the first tenants put up makeshift shelters and settled in, they came across the same hardy shrub they found in the arid lands surrounding Canudos. Called 'favela,' this plant caused skin irritations in all who came in contact with it – according to some accounts, the protective shrub even helped repel the army's initial invasions. Over time, hillside residents began calling their new home the Morro da Favela (perhaps in hopes that the plant would have protective benefits), and the name caught on. Within a generation, the word favela was used to describe the ever-increasing number of informal communities appearing around Rio – which quickly gathered a mix of former slaves and poverty-stricken inhabitants from the interior, who came to the city seeking a better life.

1968	1968	1968	1972
Caetano Veloso, Gilberto Gil and other musicians release 'Tropicália: ou Panis et Circencis.' Tropicália is born, a movement in music and art that takes aim at the military dictatorship.	The government passes the repressive Institutional Act 5, which purges opposition legislators, judges and mayors from public office; most political parties are banned.	The Brazilian economy booms, averaging an incredible 10% growth for the next six years. Rapid income growth continues into the 1970s.	The era of megaprojects and skyrocketing deficits begins, with the 5300km Trans-Amazonian highway. It cost nearly US$1 billion, but was never completed.

removal from the city center – a short-sighted policy that would dog the Rio (and Brazilian) government for the next 80 years. In truth, the *cortiços* (poor, collective lodgings) were breeding grounds for deadly outbreaks of smallpox, yellow fever and typhus. Sighting the widespread health and sanitation problems, the city destroyed thousands of shacks. With no homes, the poor fled to the hills, later creating some of the earliest favelas (slums, informal communities). The city also exterminated rats and mosquitoes and created a modern sewage system.

By the time Passos' term ended in 1906, Rio was the belle époque capital par excellence of Latin America. Its only possible rival in beauty was Buenos Aires.

Boom Days, Reform & Repression Under Vargas

At the end of the 19th century, the city's population exploded because of European immigration and internal migration (mostly ex-slaves from the declining coffee and sugar regions). By 1900 Rio boasted more than 800,000 inhabitants, a quarter of them foreign born (by contrast, São Paulo's population was only 300,000).

Following Passos' radical changes, the early 1920s to the late 1950s were one of Rio's golden ages. With the inauguration of some grand luxury resort hotels (the Glória in 1922 and the Copacabana Palace in 1923), Rio became a romantic, exotic destination for Hollywood celebrities and international high society, with Copacabana its headquarters. In some ways Rio's quasi-mythic status as a tropical arcadia spans its entire history, but in the 1940s and '50s its reputation as the urban Eden of Latin America was vouchsafed as the world was introduced to Carmen Miranda, a Rio icon.

This was also when radical changes were happening in the world of music and when Rio was beginning to celebrate its 'Brazilianness,' namely its mixed heritage and race. Sociologist Gilberto Freyre's influential book *Masters and Slaves* (1933) turned things upside down as Brazilians, conditioned to think of their mixed-race past with shame, began to think differently about their heritage – as an asset that set them apart from other nations of the world.

The 1930s was the era of President Vargas, who formed the Estado Novo (New State) in November 1937, making him the first Brazilian president to wield absolute power. Inspired by the fascist governments of Salazar in Portugal and Mussolini in Italy, Vargas banned political parties, imprisoned political opponents, and censored artists and the press.

Favela visits by well-known figures are increasingly common. President Rousseff, US President Obama, Prince Harry and Lady Gaga have all visited Rio favelas in recent years.

1979–80	1985	1985	1994
The decline of workers' wages leads to nationwide strikes. Unions call for justice and young workers join with intellectuals and activists to form Brazil's Workers' Party.	After a cautious period of *abertura* (opening), Brazil holds an indirect presidential election. Tancredo Neves wins and millions of Brazilians celebrate the end of military rule.	Neves dies of heart failure before taking office. His vice-presidential candidate, José Sarney, takes power but can't handle the rampant inflation and huge debt left by his predecessors.	President Collor is impeached; Vice-President Itamar Franco takes power. He introduces a new currency, the *real*, which stabilizes the economy and ushers in an economic boom.

Despite all this, many liked Vargas. The 'father' of Brazil's workers, he created Brazil's minimum wage in 1938. Each year he introduced new labor laws to coincide with Workers' Day on May 1, to sweeten the teeth of Brazil's factory workers. His vision for Brazil was not to increase the country's output, but to improve the level of education among all Brazilians.

The Military Dictatorship

Set in Rio during the military dictatorship, Bruno Barreto's film *Four Days in September* (1997) is based on the 1969 kidnapping of the US ambassador to Brazil by leftist guerrillas.

The world's fascination with Rio was severely curtailed during the rise of the military dictatorship of the 1960s. The era of repression began with press censorship, silencing of political opponents (sometimes by torture and violence) and an exodus of political defectors abroad (including musicians, writers and artists). There were numerous protests during that period (notably in 1968 when some 100,000 marched upon the Palácio Tiradentes). Even Rio's politicians opposed the military regime, which responded by withholding vital federal funding for certain social programs.

Despite the repression, the '60s and '70s witnessed profound changes in the city, with the opening of tunnels and the building of viaducts, parks and landfills. In the realm of public transportation, modernization was on the way. In the 1970s builders connected Rio with Niterói with the construction of the bay-spanning bridge, while beneath the city, the first metro cars began to run.

Meanwhile, the Zona Sul saw skyscrapers rising over the beaches of Copacabana and Leblon, with a shift of the wealthy to places further away from neglected downtown Rio. The moving of Brazil's capital to Brasília in 1960 seemed to spell the end for Centro, which became a ghost town after hours and retained none of the energy of its past. By the 1970s, its plazas and parks were dangerous places, surrounded by aging office towers.

The center of old Rio remained a bleak place until around 1985, when Brazil held its first direct presidential election in 20 years. With the slow return to civilian rule, *cariocas* turned their attention to sadly abandoned parts of the city, such as downtown. Over the next decade citizens, particularly local shop owners, launched a downtown revitalization campaign, sometimes collecting money by going door-to-door.

By 1995 it was clear that the drive was a success. Whole blocks in downtown received much-needed facelifts. Handsomely restored buildings attracted new investment, with new shops and cultural centers opening their doors alongside book publishers and art galleries. And nightlife returned to Lapa.

1994	2002	2003	2006
The Favela-Bairro project means that, over the next decade, neglected communities have access to decent sanitation, health clinics and transportation.	Lula is elected president. The former union leader serves a moderate first term, despite upper-class fears of radical agendas. Meanwhile, Brazil wins its fifth World Cup.	President Lula launches the Bolsa Família program of cash payments to 11 million of Brazil's poorest families. The program helps reduce poverty by 27% during Lula's first term.	Despite a corruption scandal in his party, Lula is reelected president. He presides over continued economic growth and receives record approval ratings.

A City Divided

Unfortunately, the latter half of the 20th century was also an era of explosive growth in the favelas, as immigrants poured in from poverty-stricken areas of the Northeast and the interior, swelling the number of urban poor in the city. The Cidade Maravilhosa (Marvelous City) began to lose its gloss as crime and violence increased, and in the 1990s it became known as the Cidade Partida (divided city), a term that reflected the widening chasm between the affluent neighborhoods of the Zona Sul and the favelas spreading across the region's hillsides.

As Rio entered the new millennium, crime remained one of the most pervasive problems afflicting the city. Violence continued to take thousands of lives, particularly in the favelas: in 2008, over 800 people were killed by police during gun battles between law enforcement and drug traffickers (12 police officers were also killed that year). Rio's middle and upper classes seemed mostly resigned to life inside gated and guarded condos, while poverty and violence surged in the slums nearby.

The government solution often failed to solve the problem. Crack troops would be sent in to take out a drug lord yet, whether or not their mission was successful, the heavy caliber raids often claimed innocent lives. This left many residents with a deep-rooted disdain for the police. Declaring war on the favelas was clearly not working; once the police left, drug lord in hand (or more likely dead), there was always someone else to take his place.

Although the first favela appeared on Rio's landscape in 1897, it wasn't until 1994 that the communities were included on maps.

A New Dawn

As a result of a worsening situation, Brazilian officials began to take a new approach. President Lula (full name Luiz Inácio Lula da Silva), who astutely saw the link between poverty and crime, announced in 2007 that Rio's favelas would receive US$1.7 billion to invest in running water, sanitation, roads and housing. He even paid a visit to the Cantagalo favela, a first for a Brazilian president. He later told a reporter that such investment – providing adequate services for the people – was the only way to combat drug lords.

On the local level, police began implementing a new approach to dealing with the drug traffickers in the favelas. Led by a new wing called the Pacifier Police Division, they would drive the drug lords out as they had done before, after which the police would stay behind in the community. In 2008 the favela Dona Marta became one of the first to be 'pacified,' and millions of reais were invested in the community, repairing or sometimes replacing houses, improving sanitation and adding a new football (soccer) pitch – though the most dramatic improvement

From 1987 to 1997, Brazilians suffered devastating hyperinflation, averaging 2000% annually. This meant rent doubled every 10 weeks, credit cards charged 25% a month in interest and food and clothing prices went up 40% a month.

2009	2010	2011	2012
Rio unveils Porto Maravilha, an R$8 billion project that will bring museums, parks, bike paths and infrastructure improvements to Rio's waterfront before the 2016 Olympics.	Rio launches Morar Carioca, an ambitious R$8 billion scheme to improve infrastructure and living conditions in all 1000 favelas by 2020.	Dilma Rousseff becomes Brazil's first female president. She enjoys widespread popularity for a largely populist agenda in her first term, though barely wins reelection in 2014.	Rio's Carnaval continues to break records, with over one million visitors drawn to the fest (29% more than expected), and revenues of nearly R$1.5 billion.

For insight into the often brutal tactics employed by police to combat drug traffickers, see the semi-fictional film *Tropa Elite* (Elite Squad, 2007), researched by former police officers and drug traffickers.

was adding a new funicular railroad that saved residents the 788-step slog to the top of the favela.

The strategy proved remarkably successful, and it's been implemented in about 20 other favelas around Rio, benefiting an estimated 400,000 residents. President Dilma Rousseff, who succeeded Lula following the 2010 election, continues to implement the policies of her predecessor in hopes of bringing substantive changes to Brazil's poorest communities.

The success of the pacification program stems in large part from the cooperation (and funding) by all three levels of government – municipal, state and federal. Working with Rousseff was Eduardo Paes, Rio's popular mayor (elected to his second term in 2012), and Sergio Cabral, the state governor. Both were instrumental in carrying out Rio's favela improvements, as well as in developments affecting other facets of the city (notably in infrastructure and civic projects surrounding the 2016 Summer Olympics).

Despite Cabral's notable successes (the homicide rate also declined substantially while he was governor), his second term ended in disgrace. Street protests erupted in 2013 over rising bus prices and the extravagant funds being lavished on stadiums, while many residents felt that poor services had become the norm. There were also allegations of corruption, when it was revealed that he allegedly used a state-funded helicopter on family trips (as well as on his commute from Leblon to Larenjeiras for work) at a cost of R$3.8 million to the taxpayers.

Local residents, for the most part, have had mixed feelings about Rio's state of progress. While there has been some improvement to social services, trash collection and the opening of over 150 new schools, violent crime remains a problem. There's also the issue of police brutality: each year in Rio more than 360 people on average are killed by police.

Meanwhile, not everyone has benefited from the Olympic preparations. Those on the losing end are, not surprisingly, favela residents. According to the book *SMH 2016: Removals in Olympic,* a staggering 67,000 people were evicted from their homes between 2009 and 2013. Amnesty International and other rights organizations have protested the tactics employed: the forcible removal of families, while police use pepper spray to disperse the crowds, followed by bulldozers that quickly demolish the buildings.

2014	2015	2015	2015
Rio, along with 11 other Brazilian cities, hosts the 2014 FIFA World Cup. The opener takes place in Maracanã stadium, which will also host the opening ceremony of the 2016 Olympics.	Rio celebrates 450 years since its founding with concerts, exhibitions and events. A 450m-long cake is displayed downtown and quickly devoured by hungry onlookers.	Angered over Brazil's economic woes and corruption scandals, protesters in Rio and dozens of other Brazilian cities call for the impeachment of President Dilma Rousseff.	In the run-up to the Summer Olympics, Rio spends R$37 billion on stadiums, infrastructure and civic beautification, adding a new metro line, a downtown light rail and new museums.

The Sounds of Rio

Rio boasts a rich musical heritage, with live music as deeply connected to Rio culture as its beaches and mountains. Foremost of all is the city's signature sound of samba, which is heard all across town, particularly in the days and weeks leading up to Carnaval. Other styles contributing to Rio's lush soundtrack include rock, pop, jazz, Música Popular Brasileira (MPB), hip-hop and *forró* – all opportunities to showcase the city's outstanding pool of musical talent.

Samba

The birth of Brazilian music essentially began with the birth of samba, first heard in the early 20th century in a Rio neighborhood near present-day Praça Onze. Here immigrants from Northeastern Brazil (mostly from Bahia) formed a tightly knit community in which traditional African customs thrived – music, dance and the Candomblé religion. Local homes provided the setting for impromptu performances and the exchange of ideas among Rio's first great instrumentalists. Such an atmosphere nurtured the likes of Pixinguinha, one of samba's founding fathers, as well as Donga, one of the composers of 'Pelo Telefone,' the first recorded samba song (in 1917) and an enormous success at the then-fledgling Carnaval.

Journalist, author and former dancer Alma Guillermoprieto vividly captures life in the favela, Mangueira, and preparations for the big Carnaval parade in her book *Samba*.

Samba continued to evolve in the homes and *botequims* (bars with table service) around Rio. The 1930s are known as the golden age of samba. By this point, samba's popularity had spread beyond the working-class neighborhoods of central Rio, and the music evolved at the same time into diverse, less percussive styles of samba. Sophisticated lyricists such as Dorival Caymmi, Ary Barroso and Noel Rosa popularized *samba canção* (melody-driven samba). (For insight into Noel Rosa's poetically charged and tragically brief life, check out the 2006 film *Noel: Poeta da Vila*.) Songs in this style featured sentimental lyrics and an emphasis on melody (rather than rhythm), foreshadowing the later advent of cool bossa nova. Carmen Miranda, one of the big radio stars of the 1930s, would become one of the first ambassadors of Brazilian music.

The 1930s were also the golden age of samba songwriting for the Carnaval. *Escolas de samba* (samba schools), which first emerged in 1928, soon became a vehicle for samba songwriting, and by the 1930s samba and Carnaval would be forever linked. Today's theme songs still borrow from that golden epoch.

Great *sambistas* (samba singers) continued to emerge in Brazil over the next few decades, although other emerging musical styles diluted their popularity. Artists such as Cartola, Nelson Cavaquinho and Clementina de Jesus made substantial contributions to both samba and styles of music that followed from it.

Traditional samba went through a rebirth over a decade ago with the opening of old-style *gafieiras* (dance halls) in Lapa. Today, Rio is once again awash with great *sambistas*. Classic *sambistas* such as Alcione and Beth Carvalho still perform, while singers such as Teresa Christina and Grupo Semente are intimately linked to Lapa's rebirth. One singer carrying on the tradition of her father is Mart'nália, daughter of samba legend Martinho da Vila. Meanwhile, the talented singer and songwriter Maria Rita, whose voice is remarkably similar to that of her late mother, Elis Regina, continues to create lush, innovative samba-influenced albums.

Bossa Nova: The Story of the Brazilian Music that Seduced the World, by Ruy Castro, captures the vibrant music and its backdrop of 1950s Rio.

Bossa Nova

In the 1950s came bossa nova (literally, new wave), sparking a new era of Brazilian music. Bossa nova's founders – songwriter and composer Antônio Carlos (Tom) Jobim and guitarist João Gilberto, in association with the lyricist-poet Vinícius de Moraes – slowed down and altered the basic samba rhythm to create a more intimate, harmonic style. This new wave initiated a new style of playing instruments and of singing.

Bossa nova's seductive melodies were very much linked to Rio's Zona Sul, where most bossa musicians lived. Songs such as Jobim's 'Corcovado' and Roberto Meneschal's 'Rio' evoked an almost nostalgic portrait of the city with their quiet lyricism.

By the 1960s, bossa nova had become a huge international success. The genre's initial development was greatly influenced by American jazz and blues, and over time the bossa nova style came to influence those music styles as well. Bossa nova classics were adopted, adapted and recorded by such musical luminaries as Frank Sinatra, Ella Fitzgerald and Stan Getz, among others.

In addition to the founding members, other great Brazilian bossa nova musicians include Marcos Valle, Luiz Bonfá and Baden Powell. Bands from the 1960s such as Sergio Mendes & Brasil '66 were also influenced by bossa nova, as were other artists who fled the repressive years of military dictatorship to live and play abroad. More recent interpreters of the seductive bossa sound include the Bahian-born Rosa Passos and the *carioca* (resident of Rio) Paula Morelenbaum. One band that brilliantly blends bossa nova with electro beats is BossaCucaNova. Their latest album, *Our Kind of Bossa* (2014), features veteran singers such as Elza Soares and Maria Rita.

Essential Listening

....

Gilberto Gil (Frevo Rasgado, 1968) – Gilberto Gil

....

Acoustic (1994) – Gilberto Gil

....

Quanta (1997) – Gilberto Gil

....

Refazenda (1996) – Gilberto Gil

....

Tropicália 2 (1994) – Gilberto Gil and Caetano Veloso

....

Tropicália, ou Panis et Circencis (1968) – Gilberto Gil, Caetano Veloso, Gal Costa and Os Mutantes

Tropicália

One of Brazil's great artistic movements, emerging in the late 1960s, was *tropicália,* a direct response to the repressive military dictatorship that seized power in 1964 (and remained in power until 1984). Bahian singers Caetano Veloso and Gilberto Gil led the movement, making waves with songs of protest against the national regime.

In addition to penning defiant lyrics, *tropicalistas* introduced the public to electric instruments, fragmentary melodies and wildly divergent musical styles. In fact, the hero of the *tropicalistas* was poet Oswald de Andrade, whose 1928 *Manifesto Antropofágico* (Cannibalistic Manifesto) supported the idea that anything under the sun could be devoured and recreated in one's music. Hence, the movement fused elements of US rock and roll, blues, jazz and British psychedelic styles into bossa nova and samba rhythms. Important figures linked to *tropicália* include Gal Costa, Jorge Ben Jor, Maria Bethânia, Os Mutantes and Tom Zé.

Although *tropicália* wasn't initially embraced by the public, who objected to the electric and rock elements (in fact, Veloso was booed off the stage on several occasions), by the 1970s its radical ideas had been absorbed and accepted, and lyrics of protest were ubiquitous in songwriting of the time.

Música Popular Brasileira (MPB)

Música Popular Brasileira (MPB) is a catchphrase to describe all popular Brazilian music after bossa nova. It includes *tropicália, pagode* (a relaxed and rhythmic form of samba) and Brazilian pop and rock. All Brazilian music has roots in samba; even in Brazilian rock, heavy metal, disco or pop, the samba sound is often present.

MPB first emerged in the 1970s along with talented musicians such as Edu Lobo, Milton Nascimento, Elis Regina, Djavan and dozens of others, many of whom wrote protest songs not unlike the *tropicalistas.* Chico Buarque is one of the first big names from this epoch, and is easily one of Brazil's greatest songwriters. His music career began in 1968 and spanned a time during which many of his songs were banned by the military dictatorship – in fact his music became a symbol of protest during that era. Today the enormously successful *carioca* artist continues to write new albums, though lately he has turned his hand to novel writing.

Jorge Ben Jor is another singer whose career, which began in the 1960s, has survived up to the present day. Highly addictive rhythms are omnipresent in Ben Jor's songs, as he incorporates African beats and elements of funk, samba and blues in his eclectic repertoire. The celebratory album *África Brasil,* alongside his debut album *Samba Esquema Novo* (with recognizable hits such as 'Mas, Que Nada!'), are among his best.

Carlinhos Brown continues to make substantial contributions to Brazilian music, particularly in the realm of Afro-Brazilian rhythms. Born in Bahia, Brown has influences that range from *merengue* (fast-paced, dance-hall music originating in the Dominican Republic) to Candomblé music to straight-up James Brown–style funk (the US artist from whom Carlinhos took his stage name). In addition to creating

The Brazilian Sound, by Chris McGowan and Ricardo Pessanha, is a well-illustrated, readable introduction to Brazilian music, with insight into regional styles and musicians (big-name and obscure). The useful discography lists essential albums to add to your collection.

BRAZIL'S FAVORITE VOICE

One of Brazil's best-loved musicians still active on the scene today is Gilberto Gil, a Grammy Award–winning singer and former minister of culture (from 2003 to 2008), who wasn't averse to singing a few songs following a meeting at, say, the World Economic Forum in Davos. The pop star made an unlikely government bureaucrat, considering his musical beginnings as an *engajado* (activist). During the 1960s he spent two years exiled in London after offending the dictatorship with his provocative lyrics.

A household name for decades, Gil hails from the Northeastern state of Bahia. Born in 1942, he was raised in a middle-class family near Salvador. His career as a troubadour began in 1965, when he moved south to São Paulo with another Bahian musician, Caetano Veloso. Between them they were responsible for *tropicália,* an influential though short-lived cultural movement that blended traditional Brazilian music with the electric guitars and psychedelia of the Beatles. Years later Veloso even recorded a Tupiniquim (an indigenous group in the Northeast) tribute to the Liverpudlian rockers – called 'Sugar Cane Fields Forever.'

Over the decades Gil has notched up hit after hit, morphing from quick-footed *sambista* to poetic balladeer to dreadlocked reggae icon.

Since the release of *Louvação* in 1967, Gil has recorded dozens of albums, including *Kaya N'Gan Daya,* a tribute to his idol Bob Marley. He's shared the stage with many performers over the years, even playing with the former UN General Secretary Kofi Annan (on bongos) in New York.

Though he's slowed down in recent years, the slender 70-something-year-old still performs, as he did at a 2012 concert on Copacabana Beach, which he headlined alongside Stevie Wonder, attracting over 500,000 fans.

by Tom Phillips

RIO PLAYLIST

One of the world's great music cultures, Brazil has an astounding array of talented musicians. A list of our favorite songs could easily fill this section, but we've limited our highly subjective pick to 25 songs from 25 different artists.

➡ 'Canto de Ossanha' – Baden Powell
➡ 'Soy Loco Por Ti, America' – Caetano Veloso
➡ 'Alvorado' – Cartola
➡ 'Samba de Orly' – Chico Buarque and Toquinho
➡ 'Flor de Lis' – Djavan
➡ 'Aguas de Março' – Elis Regina (written by Tom Jobim)
➡ 'Hoje É Dia da Festa' – Elza Soares
➡ 'Sou Brasileiro' – Fernando Abreu and Mart'nália
➡ 'Namorinho de Portão' – Gal Costa
➡ 'Quilombo, O El Dorado Negro' – Gilberto Gil
➡ 'Desafinado' – João Gilberto
➡ 'Filho Maravilha' – Jorge Ben Jor
➡ 'A Procura da Batida Perfeita' – Marcelo D2
➡ 'Novo Amor' – Maria Rita
➡ 'Carinhoso' – Marisa Monte (written by Pixinguinha)
➡ 'Travessia' – Milton Nascimento
➡ 'Ultimo Desejo' – Noel Rosa
➡ 'Besta é Tu' – Novos Baianos
➡ 'Panis et Circenses' – Os Mutantes
➡ 'Acenda O Farol' – Tim Maia
➡ 'Garota de Ipanema' (Girl from Ipanema) – Tom Jobim
➡ 'Aquarela do Brasil' – Toquinho (written by Ary Barroso)
➡ 'Velha Infância' – Tribalistas
➡ 'Não me deixe só' – Vanessa da Mata
➡ 'Felicidade' – Vinicíus de Moraes

the popular percussion ensemble Timbalada, he has a number of excellent albums of his own (notably *Alfagamabetizado*). Involved in many diverse projects, Brown was even nominated for an Oscar in 2012 for best original song ('Real in Rio' for the film *Rio*), which he and Sergio Mendes composed.

The group Da Cruz, headed by the talented Mariana da Cruz, creates lyrically rich songs with infectious disco-charged beats. The album *Disco E Progresso* (2014) features songs about a country divided between the haves and have-nots.

Rock, Pop & Hip-Hop

MPB tends to bleed into other genres, particularly into rock and pop. One artist who moves comfortably between genres is Bebel Gilberto (the daughter of João Gilberto), who blends bossa nova with modern beats on jazz-inflected bilingual albums such as *All in One* (2009). Another heiress of Brazilian traditions is the Rio-born Marisa Monte, popular at home and abroad for her fine singing and songwriting. Mixing samba, *forró* (traditional, fast-paced music from the Northeast), pop and rock, Marisa has been part of a number of successful collaborations in the music world. Her brief collaboration with Arnaldo Antunes and Carlinhos Brown resulted in the fine album *Tribalistas* (2003).

Other notable young singers who hail from a bossa line include Roberta Sá, whose last album, *Segunda Pele* (2012), features elements of bossa, jazz and even reggae; Fernanda Porto, whose music is often described as drum 'n' bossa, a blend of electronica and bossa grooves (check out her 2009 album *Auto-Retrato*); and the expat singer-songwriter and performance artist Cibelle, who incorporates a mix of pop, folk, and Brazilian sounds in her lush (mainly English-language) recordings, such as those on *The Shine of Dried Electric Leaves* (2006). Cibelle came to prominence as the main vocalist on Suba's noteworthy album *São Paulo Confessions* (1999).

With a host of Grammy nominations to her name, Céu has many fans both at home and abroad. She has recorded three albums over the last seven years, creating dreamlike melodies with elements of *tropicália*, samba, reggae and jazz. Her latest, *Caravana Sereia Bloom* (2012), is a colorful work with songs inspired by a road trip across Brazil. Her first album, the self-titled *Céu* (2007), is still considered her best.

Brazilian hip-hop emerged from the favelas of Rio sometime in the 1980s, and has been steadily attracting followers ever since. Big names such as Racionais MCs first emerged out of São Paulo, but Rio has its share of more recent success stories. One of the best on the scene is Marcelo D2 (formerly of Planet Hemp), impressing audiences with albums such as *A Procura da Batida Perfeita* (2003) and *A Arte do Barulho* (2008). Better known to international audiences is Seu Jorge, who starred in the film *Cidade de Deus* and performed brilliant Portuguese versions of Bowie songs in Wes Anderson's film *The Life Aquatic with Steve Zissou* (2004). His best solo work is *Cru* (2005), an inventive hybrid of hip-hop and ballads, with politically charged beats.

Many top hip-hop artists hail from São Paulo. A few names to look out for include Emicida, a youthful rapper admired for his cutting improvisational rhymes. Check out his funk-laden single 'Triunfo,' one of his early breakthrough songs, or his collaboration with MC Guime on the antipoverty hit 'País do Futebol.' Yet another Paulista, Rael de Rima is a fast-rapping lyricist with a strong sense of musicality, often performing with guitar and a full back-up band. MC Criolo tackles themes such as urban violence, police brutality and racism, which has made him a hit in the favelas. Following the release of his debut 2011 album, *Nó na Orelha*, he's earned a growing number of admirers. The *carioca* rapper MV Bill is a man with a message. His songs focus on youth facing the ever-present threats of drugs and violence. He's even written a book *(Falcão – Meninos do Tráfico)* and created a network of youth centers in Rio that offer kids who might otherwise be on the street classes in dancing, music and art. One emerging new artist from Rio is Fabbio Brazza, who blends rap with samba (an unlikely combo) with surprising success in songs such as 'Samba de Rap' on his 2014 album *Filho da Pátria*.

Rock has its promoters, though it enjoys far less airtime than samba. Rio gets its share of mega-rockers on world tours. It also has a few homegrown talents. The group Legião Urbana from Brasília remains one of the all-time greats among rock lovers. The band (which folded shortly after the death of lead singer Renato Russo in 1996) enjoyed enormous success in the 1980s and early 1990s, and has sold over 15 million records. Raul Seixas, Skank, O Rappa, Os Paralamas do Sucesso and the Rio-based Barão Vermelho are other essential names.

In other genres, indie-rock favorites Los Hermanos were a top band before breaking up in 2007. Check out *Ventura* (2003) or *Bloco do Eu Souzinho* (2001), a seminal pop-rock albums of its time. Vanguart, fitting somewhere in the folk-rock genre, are also a group to watch. Their self-titled debut album (2007) channeled samba, blues and classic rock.

Tropical Truth: A Story of Music and Revolution in Brazil, by Caetano Veloso, describes the great artistic experiment of *tropicália* in 1960s Brazil. Although digressive at times, Veloso captures the era's music and politics.

Raul Seixas (1945–89) is often called the father of Brazilian rock. Many of his wild rock anthems are well known, and it's not uncommon to hear shouts of 'Toca Raul!' (Play Raul!) at concerts. Curiously, best-selling author Paulo Coelho co-wrote many of his songs.

Football

Cariocas (residents of Rio), like most Brazilians, are football (soccer) mad. No one goes to work on big international game days, with everyone packing into the neighborhood *botecos* (small, open-air bars) or on the sidewalks out front to watch the game. After a big win, the whole city celebrates with rowdy nights of partying. And should the team lose, the sadness in the air is palpable. Every *carioca* has a favorite team, and will never pass up the chance to see them play live amid the roaring crowds in Maracanã.

The Game, the Fans

Futebol, by Alex Bellos (2002), is a fascinating and humorous look at the culture behind Brazil's nationwide obsession, with stories of the legendary players and the way that football has shaped Brazilian society.

Most of the world generally acknowledges that Brazilians play the world's most creative, artistic and thrilling style of football. They are also generally known as lousy defenders, but no one seems to mind since they make the attack so exciting. The fans, too, are no less fun to watch. Skillful moves and adroit dribbling past an opponent receives a Spanish-bullfight-style *'olé!'* while fans do their best to rev up the action by pounding huge drums (or the backs of the stadium seats), waving huge flags, and launching fireworks and smoke bombs (or sometimes suspicious fluids onto the seats below). Crowds are rambunctious, but no more prone to violence than in England, Spain or Italy, for instance.

The Clubs

Rio is home to four major club teams – Flamengo, Fluminense, Vasco da Gama and Botafogo – each with a die-hard local following. Apart from a couple of short breaks for the Christmas and New Year holiday and Carnaval, professional club competitions go on all year. The major event in Rio's sporting calendar is the *classico,* when the four hometown teams play each other. Expect intense and bitter rivalry, matched in excitement only by encounters between Rio and São Paulo clubs.

Flamengo

The most successful of Rio's big four, Flamengo has an enormous fan base both in Rio and around the world – an estimated 36 million followers, which makes it the most popular football club in Brazil. Flamengo has been voted one of the most successful football clubs of the 20th century by FIFA, and it certainly doesn't lack cash flow, with annual revenue of over R$200 million. Famous players who have donned the iconic red-and-black jerseys include Zico, often hailed as the best player never to win a World Cup; Leonidas, leading scorer at the 1938 World Cup; Bebeto; Mario Zagallo and Romario. More recently, Ronaldinho Gaucho, two-time FIFA player of the year, played for Flamengo (2011–12) before making a surprise move to Atlético Mineiro in 2012. He later returned to Rio after signing with Fluminense in 2015.

Flamengo plays its home games at Maracanã; the cheering section is the *setor norte* (north sector, behind the goal). A fan is called a Flamenguista.

Fluminense

Founded by sons of the elite in Laranjeiras back in 1902, Fluminense is a highly successful club that has contributed a number of top players to the national team. It has also been hailed as the champion of the century, for winning the largest number of Campeonato Carioca titles in the 20th century (28 in all), though its successes have diminished in the current century. Famous players include Didi (1949–56), a superstar midfielder who helped Brazil win the World Cup in both 1958 and 1962, and Roberto Rivellino, who led Fluminense to the state championship in 1975 and 1976 (and was instrumental in Brazil's World Cup victory in 1970). Current stars include Fred (aka Frederico Chaves Guedes), who scored the fastest goal in Brazilian history (finding net 3.17 seconds after the game's start).

Fluminense plays its home games at Maracanã. The cheering section is the *setor sul* (south sector), behind the goal. A fan is known as a Tricolor (a reference to the maroon, green and white uniforms).

Vasco da Gama

Founded by Portuguese immigrants near the turn of the 20th century, Vasco remains the favorite club for *cariocas* of Portuguese descent. One of Vasco's all-time greats was Romario (who also played for Flamengo and Fluminense), a powerful striker who scored over 900 goals during his career. Another Vasco legend is Carlos Roberto de Oliveira, nicknamed Roberto Dinamite, who holds the most appearances for the club and is its all-time highest scorer. His passion for Vasco runs deep, and he became president of the club in 2008.

Vasco generally plays its home games at the 25,000-seat Estadio São Januário in the Zona Norte. However, bigger matches (such as the city derbies) are played at Maracanã. At such times, the cheering section is the *setor sul*, unless playing Fluminense, in which case the cheering section is the *setor norte*. The uniforms are black with a white diagonal sash. A fan is called a Vascaíno.

Botafogo

Like other clubs in Rio, Botafogo started out as a rowing club in the late 19th century and quickly embraced football after its popularization in the early 1900s. One of Brazil's oldest teams, Botafogo is the only club in Brazilian history to win titles in three different centuries. During the 1950s and '60s, some of Brazil's greatest footballers played for Botafogo, such as Garrincha, who overcame physical disabilities (including legs of uneven length) and became one of the best dribblers of all time. Another legendary player was Nilton Santos – a defender so revered that the club decided to rename their home stadium after him in 2015. Unfortunately, Botafogo's star power diminished significantly in the years after, and in 2002 it was even relegated to the second division after coming in last in the Brazilian League (though it quickly returned to the first division the following year).

Botafago plays its home games at the Estádio Nilton Santos (also known as Engenhão). The stadium was built for the 2007 Pan-Am games, and will also host the track and field events in the 2016 Summer Olympics, when it will be dubbed the Estádio Olímpico. Like Vasco, during big tournaments, Botafogo plays in Maracanã. The cheering section is the *setor sul*, unless playing Fluminense, in which case the cheering section is the *setor norte*. Botafogo players wear black-and-white striped jerseys; a fan is called a Botafoguense.

The intense interclub rivalry dubbed Fla-Flu (short for Flamengo-Fluminense) began back in 1911, when a group of disgruntled players from Fluminense left the club and went to Flamengo, creating a brand new team. Games attract huge crowds – over 175,000 in 1963, a world record for a club match.

Competitions

Apart from the World Cup, which takes place every four years, there are many other tournaments happening throughout the year. In addition to the key competitions – Campeonato Brasileiro, Copa Libertadores and Campeonato Carioca – other major championships include the Copa do Brasil, the Copa dos Campeões and the Copa América.

The Estádio das Laranjeiras, built for Fluminense in 1905, was the first football stadium constructed in Brazil. It holds 8000 people and still stands today in Laranjeiras, next to the current governor's palace.

Campeonato Brasileiro

The premier competition inside Brazil is the Campeonato Brasileiro (Brazilian Championship). Between about late July and mid-November, 20-odd top clubs play each other once each, then the eight top teams advance to a knockout phase, which culminates in a two-leg final in mid-December to decide the national championship. Since the competition's inception in 1959, São Paulo's top four teams have dominated, followed by Flamengo (five titles), Vasco (four) and Fluminense (four). Underachieving Botafogo has won the championship only twice.

Copa Libertadores

The annual Copa Libertadores is South America's most important football tournament. It's contested by the best-performed clubs from South America and Mexico, and is watched by millions around the world – the event is broadcast in over 130 countries. It kicks off in February, with the final tournament staged between June and August. Since it was first held in 1960, Argentinean teams have won the most titles (24), followed by Brazil (17). Rio's Flamengo and Vasco da Gama have each won the tournament once.

PELÉ

One of the world's most famous players – still widely considered to be the greatest who ever played the game – is Pelé. He's not just a legendary footballer who has been named the greatest footballer of all time. He was also Brazil's first black government minister (for sport from 1995 to 1998) and has even been knighted by Queen Elizabeth II.

Pelé has come a long way since he was born Edson Arantes do Nascimento in a humble Minas Gerais town on October 23, 1940. Yet despite his stardom, his public image remains impeccable. He's never smoked, has never been photographed with a drink in hand, and has never been involved with drugs.

In a 22-year career, the teams on which Pelé played gained 53 titles, including three World Cups (the first, in Sweden in 1958, when he was just 17 years old) and back-to-back world club championships (with Santos in 1962 and 1963) among many others. Despite lucrative offers to play in Europe, Pelé never did so – in fact, President Janio Quadros had Pelé declared a national treasure in 1971 so that he could not be transferred to a European club.

Pelé retired from the Brazilian team in 1971 and from Santos in 1974. In 1975 the New York Cosmos coaxed him north to the US, where he played until 1977, when the team won the American championship. He finally retired for good at the end of that year, after a game between the Cosmos and Santos in which he played the first half for the Cosmos and the second half with Santos.

In 1366 games (112 for the Brazilian national team), he scored 1282 goals, making him Brazil's all-time highest goal scorer. When he scored his 1000th goal in 1969 in Maracanã stadium, he dedicated it to the children of Brazil.

Pelé, who maintains an oceanfront home in Rio, continues to be a goodwill ambassador for sport, and still commands enormous respect – as evidenced by the roar of the crowd when he made a surprise appearance at the end of the Summer Olympics in London in 2012. In Brazil, Pelé is known simply as 'O Rei' (The King).

Campeonato Carioca

Each of Brazil's 26 states holds its own championship. Running from January through March, the Campeonato Carioca is the Rio state championship, and one of the oldest held in Brazil – contested since 1906. Although other teams around the state compete, the winner, not surprisingly, is usually one of the big four. Flamengo (33 titles) and Fluminense (31) have dominated, followed by Vasco (23 titles) and Botafogo (20).

Racial Barriers

In 1902, when Oscar Cox, an Anglo-Brazilian, and some of his friends created Rio's first club, Fluminense, it was initially an aristocratic and all-white affair. Black players would not break down the racial barriers until the 1920s, when Vasco da Gama began championing black and multiracial players. By the 1930s, Brazil was already gaining fame for its talented players, some of whom were black or mulatto and came from poor families, thus inverting the elite-only sport into a sport for the poor and disenfranchised.

European Vacation

Until recently, most of the best players left Brazil for more lucrative contracts with European clubs. Over the last decade, however, many Brazilian stars have returned home to play for more adoring fans and not insubstantial contracts. The strengthening of the real against the euro, along with Brazil's economic boom, has allowed top Brazilian clubs to offer salaries near to the wages Brazilian players earn in Europe. TV rights and corporate sponsorship have also helped deepen the pockets of Brazilian clubs. The return of more players to Brazil, coupled with the ongoing growth of new talent into the big clubs, could help transform Brazil into one of the world's footballing giants – on the club level as well as the international level.

The Afro-Brazilian player and *carioca* Leonidas da Silva is one of Brazil's early football legends. He played for Vasco, Fluminense and Flamengo, leading each team to the state championship and helping to break down racial barriers. In 1938 he also scored the only bicycle kick goal in World Cup history.

The World Cup

Bringing the World Cup back to Brazil had long been a dream of the football-crazed nation. In 2007, when the nation learned that it had won the right to host the 2014 tournament, spontaneous celebrations erupted across town, and tens of thousands took to Copacabana Beach to rejoice in the good news. The South American giant last staged the big sporting event in 1950, when Brazil lost in the dramatic final against Uruguay before some 200,000 fans in Rio's Maracanã stadium. This infamous day was later called *'maracanaço'* and the term is still in common parlance.

Brazil, the most successful football nation in the history of the game (with five World Cup victories), became the fifth country to host the event twice. Aside from Rio, where the opener and final took place, 11 other cities across the country staged games; this, too, was historic, as it was the only time the World Cup was held in more than 10 cities. Brazil spent a staggering R$26 billion in preparation for the event, including stadium construction, upgrades to airports, roads and other infrastructure. Unfortunately, the tournament did not end well for Brazil, who suffered a crushing 7–1 defeat at the hands of Germany in the semi-finals (Brazil subsequently lost the third-place play-off, 0–3 against the Netherlands). Germany went on to win the World Cup 1–0 over Argentina.

Architecture

The capital of Brazil for many years, Rio de Janeiro has been the architectural setting for the beautiful, the functional and the avant-garde. Today you can see a sweeping range of styles that span the 17th to the 20th centuries in buildings that often vie for attention alongside one another.

Colonial & Imperial Rio

Colonial-Era Buildings

....

Real Gabinete Português de Leitura

....

Mosteiro de São Bento

....

Igreja de NS do Carmo da Antiga Sé

....

Convento de Santo Antônio

Vestiges of the colonial era live on in downtown Rio. Some of the most impressive works are the 17th-century churches built by the Jesuits. The best examples from this, the baroque period, are the Convento de Santo Antônio and the Mosteiro de São Bento. The incredibly ornate interiors, which appear almost to drip with liquid gold, show little of the restraint that would later typify Brazilian architecture.

The artist mission (a group of artists and architects chosen to bring new life to the city) that arrived from France in the early 19th century introduced a whole new design aesthetic to the budding Brazilian empire. Neoclassicism became the official style and was formally taught in the newly founded Imperial Academy. The works built during this period were grandiose and monumental, dominated by classical features such as elongated columns and wide domes. Among the many fine examples of this period are the Museu Nacional de Belas Artes, the Theatro Municipal and the Casa França-Brasil – considered the most important from this period. There are a few curious features of the Casa: its alignment to the cardinal points, the large cross-shaped space inside and its monumental dome.

The end of the 19th century saw the continuation of this trend of returning to earlier forms and featured works such as the Real Gabinete Português de Leitura. Completed in 1887, the Royal Reading Room shows inspiration from the much earlier Manueline period (early 1500s), with a Gothic facade and the highlighting of its metallic structure.

The 20th Century

During the 20th century, Rio became the setting for a wide array of architectural styles, including neoclassical, eclectic, art deco and modernist works. During the same period, Rio also restored some of its colonial-era gems (others fell to the wrecking ball), becoming one of Latin America's most beautiful cities.

This, of course, did not happen by chance. In the early 20th century, as capital of Brazil, Rio de Janeiro was viewed as a symbol of the glory of the modern republic and the president lavished beautiful neoclassical buildings upon the urban streetscape.

The early 1900s was also the period when one of Rio's most ambitious mayors, Pereira Passos, was in office. These twin factors had an enormous influence in shaping the face of Brazil's best-known city.

Mayor Passos (in office from 1902 to 1906) envisioned Rio as the Paris of South America, and ordered his engineers to lay down grand boulevards and create manicured parks, as some of Rio's most elegant buildings rose overhead. One of the most beautiful buildings constructed during this period was the Palaçio Monroe (Monroe Palace; 1906), a re-creation of a work built for the 1904 St Louis World's Fair. The elegant neoclassical Palaçio Monroe sat on the Praça Floriano and housed the Câmara dos Deputados (House of Representatives). Unfortunately, like many other of Rio's beautiful buildings, it was destroyed in 1976 in the gross 'reurbanization' craze that swept through the city.

The fruits of this early period were displayed at the International Exposition held in Rio in 1922. This was not only the showcase for neocolonial architecture and urban design; it also introduced Brazil's most modern city to the rest of the world. Another big event of the 1920s was the completion of the Copacabana Palace, the first luxury hotel in South America. Its construction would lead to the rapid development of the beach regions.

Rio's 1930s buildings show the currents of modern European architecture, which greatly impacted upon the city's design. Rio's modernism was born along with the rise of President Vargas, who wanted to leave his mark on federal Rio through the construction of public ministries, official chambers and the residences of government power. The Ministry of Education & Health, the apotheosis of the modernist movement in Brazil, is one of the city's most significant public buildings, as it's one of the few works designed by French architect Le Corbusier, in conjunction with several young Brazilian architects. (Another Le Corbusier–influenced design is the Aeroporto Santos Dumont, completed in 1937.)

The 1930s was also the era of the art deco movement, which was characterized by highly worked artistic details and an abundance of ornamentation. Good specimens include the central train station and the statue of Cristo Redentor (Christ the Redeemer) on Corcovado.

Architecture in Print
....

The Curves of Time: the Memoirs of Oscar Niemeyer
....
When Brazil Was Modern: A Guide to Architecture, 1928–1960 (Lauro Cavalcanti)
....
Roberto Burle Marx: The Lyrical Landscape (Marta Iris Montero)

ARCHITECTURE OSCAR NIEMEYER

Oscar Niemeyer

Oscar Niemeyer is one of the giants of 20th-century architecture. Working in the firm of Lúcio Costa, Niemeyer and Costa championed the European avant-garde style in Brazil, making a permanent impact on the next 50 years of Brazilian design. Costa and Niemeyer collaborated on many works, designing some of the most important buildings in Brazil. One of their early successes was their Ministry of Education & Health (built between 1939 and 1943). It was one of Brazil's finest 1930s modernist designs, and a unique collaboration with famed Swiss-French architect Le Corbusier.

In Rio, Niemeyer and Costa broke with the neoclassical style and developed the functional style, with its extensive use of steel and glass,

....

ARCHITECTURAL ICONS

Copacabana Palace (p171)	The neoclassical gem that came to represent a glitzy new era.
Arcos da Lapa (p140)	The 18th-century aqueduct is a widely recognized landmark that also lies at the epicenter of Rio's resurgent music scene in Lapa.
Maracanã Football Stadium (p150)	Brazil's temple to football and its largest stadium, fresh off a dramatic makeover for the 2014 World Cup.
Museu do Amanhã (p128)	Santiago Calatrava's striking new building on Praça Mauá, and a symbol for Rio's waterfront renaissance.
Theatro Municipal (p123)	The flower of the belle époque and the costliest opera house constructed outside of Europe.

and lack of ornamentation. The Museu de Arte Moderna (inaugurated in 1958) and the Catedral Metropolitana (begun in 1964) are good examples of this style. One of the most fascinating modern buildings close to Rio is the Niemeyer-designed Museu do Arte Contemporânea (MAC) in Niterói. Its fluid form and delicate curves are reminiscent of a flower in bloom (though many simply say it resembles a spaceship). It showcases its natural setting and offers mesmerizing views of Rio. The MAC is a pivotal part of the Caminho de Niemeyer (Niemeyer Way), a collection of seven buildings scattered along the waterfront in Niterói.

Niemeyer, whose work is known for its elegant curves – the female form was one of his inspirations – became famous for his work designing the nation's capital. He was a longtime Rio resident, and remained passionate about architecture and quite active in the field up until his death in 2012 at the age of 104.

A lifelong communist, Niemeyer spent much of the 1960s and 1970s in exile, during the height of the military dictatorship. His political affiliations also prevented him from working in the US during the Cold War.

Recent Projects

The huge amount of investment for the 2016 Olympic Games has led to many new developments around the city.

In 2013, Rio officially inaugurated the Cidade das Artes (City of the Arts) in Barra da Tijuca. The controversial project, originally slated to open in 2008, ran significantly over budget (the projected R$86-million cost eventually ran to over R$500 million). The ultra-modern 90,000-sq-meter complex houses a high-tech, 1800-seat concert hall, as well as theaters, a chamber music hall and terrace with picturesque views over Barra. The building is the new base of the Brazilian Symphony Orchestra, and designed by the Pritzker prize–winning French architect Christian de Portzamparc.

The revitalization of Rio's derelict port area is also seeing a host of new developments. The Museu de Arte do Rio on Praça Mauá cleverly joins two existing buildings – one a neoclassical early-20th-century mansion, the other a modernist building (and former train station). The unusual juxtaposition serves as an apt metaphor for the mix of classical and contemporary works inside. It opened in 2014. Nearby, the dramatic Santiago Calatrava–designed Museu do Amanhã (Museum of Tomorrow) juts out into the water, with a cantilevered roof and a sculptural facade for which Calatrava is so well known. It opened in late 2015.

In Copacabana, the cutting-edge Museu do Imagem e Som (Museum of Image and Sound) will bring a bold new look to Copacabana's boxy, skyscraper-lined waterfront when it opens in 2016. The design by New York architectural firm Diller Scofidio + Renfro (the team behind the famous High Line in Manhattan) integrates the building into its dramatic setting – between seafront and hilly backdrop. Public access, outdoor ramps and open-air space (including an open-air rooftop amphitheater) ensures a building accessible to all.

Survival Guide

TRANSPORTATION.. 204

**GETTING TO
RIO DE JANEIRO.......204**
Air.................... 204
Land................... 204

**GETTING AROUND
RIO DE JANEIRO.......205**
Bicycle................ 205
Boat.................. 205
Bus................... 205
Car................... 206
Metro................. 206
Minivan............... 206
Taxi.................. 206
Train..................207
Tram..................207

TOURS...............207
Bay Cruises............207
Bicycle Tours..........207
City Tours.............207
Favela Tours...........207
Helicopter Tours....... 208
4WD Tours............ 208
Walking Tours......... 208

DIRECTORY A–Z....209
Courses.............. 209
Electricity............210
Embassies
& Consulates...........210
Emergency............210
Gay & Lesbian
Travelers..............210
Internet Access........210
Legal Matters.......... 211
Medical Services....... 211
Money................. 211
Opening Hours..........212
Post..................212
Safe Travel.............212
Telephone.............212
Time..................213
Tourist Information.....213
Travelers
with Disabilities.........213
Visas..................213
Volunteering...........214
Women Travelers.......214

LANGUAGE........215

Transportation

GETTING TO RIO DE JANEIRO

Flying is the easiest way to get to Rio, with some flights stopping first in São Paulo (one hour away). High-season prices for a return ticket from gateways in North America and Europe typically run from US$900 to US$1400. Long-distance buses arrive in Rio from Chile and Argentina.

Flights, cars and tours can be booked online at www.lonelyplanet.com.

Air

Galeão (GIG)

Rio's Galeão international airport (Aeroporto Internacional Antônio Carlos Jobim; www.riogaleao.com) is 15km north of the city center on Ilha do Governador. It has left-luggage facilities, an internet cafe, ATMs and currency-exchange desks, pharmacies and a few shops and restaurants.

BUS
Premium Auto Ônibus (www.premiumautoonibus.com. br; one way R$15) operates safe air-con buses from the international airport along several different itineraries. For the Zona Sul, take No 2018, which heads southward through the *bairros* (districts) of Glória, Flamengo and Botafogo, and along the beaches of Copacabana,

Ipanema and Leblon to Barra da Tijuca (and vice versa) every 30 minutes from 5:30am to 11pm . The driver will stop wherever you ask.

It takes 75 minutes to two hours depending on traffic. Heading to the airport, you can catch this bus from in front of the major hotels along the main beaches, but you have to flag them down.

If you're going straight to Barra, it's faster to take bus No 2918 instead. There's also a bus that links to Santos Dumont airport (No 2101) and a line to the bus station (No 2145).

TAXI
From Galeão, a yellow-and-blue *comum* (common) taxi costs around R$65 to R$90 to Copacabana or Ipanema, depending on traffic (more on Sunday and late at night). A charge of R$2 per piece of luggage also applies.

More expensive, slightly fancier radio taxis charge a set fare of about R$130 to Copacabana or Ipanema.

Keep in mind that traffic can lead to long delays on the return journey to the airport. Allow up to two hours during peak times (4pm to 7pm).

Santos Dumont (SDU)

Aeroporto Santos Dumont, used by some domestic flights, is by the bay, in the city center, 1km east of Cinelândia metro station. It

has ATMs, a few shops and an internet cafe.

BUS
The No 2018 **Premium Auto Ônibus**, which departs from Galeão, stops at Santos Dumont before continuing south to Copacabana and Ipanema.

LIGHT RAIL
Rio's new light rail (the VLT), slated to begin operations in April 2016, runs from the Santos Dumont airport to the Rodoviária (bus station) via Praça Mauá. This isn't particularly useful for travelers, unless you're catching an onward bus or staying near Praça Mauá. Another line from the airport to Centro may be added in the future, which would provide handy access to the metro.

TAXI
From the domestic airport, *comum* taxis cost about R$32 to Copacabana and R$38 to Ipanema. A radio taxi runs R$59 to Copacabana and R$74 to Ipanema.

Land

Long-Distance Bus

Buses leave from the sleek **Rodoviária Novo Rio** (Map p261; ☑3213-1800; Av Francisco Bicalho 1), 2km northwest of Centro. There's a Riotur desk here for city info.

CLIMATE CHANGE & TRAVEL

Every form of transport that relies on carbon-based fuel generates CO_2, the main cause of human-induced climate change. Modern travel is dependent on airplanes, which might use less fuel per mile per person than most cars but travel much greater distances. The altitude at which aircraft emit gases (including CO_2) and particles also contributes to their climate change impact. Many websites offer 'carbon calculators' that allow people to estimate the carbon emissions generated by their journey and, for those who wish to do so, to offset the impact of the greenhouse gases emitted with contributions to portfolios of climate-friendly initiatives throughout the world. Lonely Planet offsets the carbon footprint of all staff and author travel.

A small booth near the exit at Novo Rio bus station organizes the yellow taxis out the front. Sample fares (with one bag) are about R$50 to the international airport, R$40 to Copacabana and Ipanema, and R$35 to Santa Teresa.

You can buy bus tickets online at www.clickbus.com or www.brasilbybus.com with a PayPal account. After purchasing, you'll receive the booking reference and ticket number. At the bus station, you'll enter these at the self-service kiosks. Type in the booking number first, press 'avançar,' enter your ticket number, then press 'imprimir' (print), and then your tickets will be printed.

A handful of travel agents also sell bus tickets. **Guanatur** (Map p244; ☑2548-3275; www.guana turismo.com.br; Rua Dias da Rocha 16A, Copacabana; ☺9am-6pm Mon-Fri, to noon Sat) and **Dantur** (☑2557-7144; www.dantur.com.br; Largo do Machado 29, loja 47, Flamengo; ☺9am-6:30pm Mon-Fri, to 1pm Sat) sell tickets for many lines. The commission charge is R$6 per ticket.

GETTING AROUND RIO DE JANEIRO

Rio is a fairly easy city to navigate, with an efficient metro system, a public bike-sharing system and hurtling buses. The neighborhoods themselves are perfect for getting around on foot.

Bicycle

Rio has many kilometers of bike paths along the beach, around Lagoa and along Parque do Flamengo. In addition to a public bike-sharing scheme, you can rent bikes from stands along the east side of Lagoa Rodrigo de Freitas for around R$15 per hour and at various bike shops along the bike path between Copacabana and Ipanema.

For an excellent guided bike tour, contact Rio by Bike (p205).

Bike Rio (☑4003-6054; www.mobilicidade.com.br/bike-rio.asp) Pedal yourself around the city on bright orange bikes found at over 250 stations throughout Rio. After registering on the website, you can buy a monthly pass (R$10) or a day pass (R$5). Instructions are in English at the stations and the bikes are released via cell phone or app. The downside: you can only register and use the service if you have a Brazilian cell number.

Velô Bike Store (Map p244; ☑3442-4315; Francisco Otaviano 20, Copacabana; per hr/day R$15/70, electric bike per hr R$30; ☺9am-7pm Mon-Fri, 9am-4pm Sat, 10am-4pm Sun) One of

several shops conveniently located on the cycle path between Ipanema and Copacabana.

Boat

Rio has several islands in the bay that you can visit by ferry, including Ilha de Paquetá and Ilha Fiscal. Another way to see the city is by taking the commuter ferry to Niterói. Niterói's main attraction is the Museu do Arte Contemporânea, but many visitors board the ferry just for the fine views of downtown and the surrounding landscape. The **ferry** (Map p254; ☑0800-721-1012; www.grupoccr.com.br/barcas; one way/return R$5/10) departs every 20 minutes from Praça XV (Quinze) de Novembro in Centro.

Bus

Rio's new BRS (Bus Rapid System) features dedicated public-transportation corridors in Copacabana, Ipanema, Leblon and Barra. Fares on most buses are around R$3.40.

Every bus has its key destination displayed on the illuminated signboard in front. If you see the bus for you, hail it by sticking your arm straight out (drivers won't stop unless flagged down).

Car

Driving & Parking

In the city itself, driving can be a frustrating experience even if you know your way around. Traffic snarls and parking problems do not make for an enjoyable holiday. Be aware that Rio has extremely strict drink-driving laws, with a fine of around R$2000 for those with a blood-alcohol content of over 0.06. Changing police checkpoints are set up nightly around the city.

Rental

Hiring a car is fairly simple as long as you have a driver's license, a credit card and a passport. Most agencies require renters to be at least 25 years old, though some will rent (with an added fee) to younger drivers.

Prices start around R$120 per day for a car without air-conditioning, but they go down a bit in the low season. If you are quoted prices on the phone, make sure they include insurance, which is compulsory.

Car-rental agencies can be found at both airports or scattered along Av Princesa Isabel in Copacabana.

At the international airport, **Hertz** (☎0800-701-7300; www.hertz.com), **Localiza** (☎0800-979-2000; www.localiza.com) and **Unidas** (☎2295-3628; www.unidas.com.br) provide rentals. In Copacabana, among the many are **Hertz** (☎2275-7440; Av Princesa Isabel 500) and **Localiza** (☎2275-3340; Av Princesa Isabel 150).

Metro

Rio's **metro system** (www.metrorio.com.br; ⊙5am-midnight Mon-Sat, 7am-11pm Sun) is an excellent way to get around. During Carnaval the metro operates nonstop from 5am Saturday morning until at least 11pm on Tuesday. Both lines are air-conditioned, clean, fast and safe. The main line goes from Ipanema–General Osório to Saens Peña, connecting with the secondary line to Estácio (which provides service to São Cristóvão, Maracanã and beyond). The main stops in Centro are Cinelândia and Carioca.

An ambitious R$2.5 billion expansion should be complete by June 2016. A new line (linha 4) connects Ipanema to Barra da Tijuca. It runs from General Osório to Jardim Oceânico with stops in Ipanema, Leblon and São Conrado. A spur to Gávea will eventually link it to the rest of the line.

You can purchase a cartão pré-pago (prepaid card) from a kiosk in any metro station using cash (no change given) with a minimum of R$5 or more. You can then recharge it at any kiosk. Free subway maps are available from most ticket booths.

Minivan

Minivans (called vans in Rio) are an alternative form of transportation in Rio and usually much faster than buses. They run along Av Rio Branco to the Zona Sul as far as Barra da Tijuca. On the return trip, they run along the coast almost all the way into the city center. They run frequently, and cost between R$2.50 and R$5. They do get crowded, and are not a good idea if you have luggage. Call out your stop (para!) when you want to disembark.

Taxi

Rio's yellow taxis are prevalent throughout the city. They are generally a speedy way to zip around and are usually safe. The flat rate is around R$5.20, plus around R$2.05 per km (and R$2.50 per km at night and on Sunday). Radio taxis are 30% more expensive than regular taxis. No one tips taxi drivers, but it's common to round up the fare.

In Rocinha and some other favelas, moto-taxis (basically a lift on the back of a motorcycle) are a handy

---

METRO-BUS TICKETS

The **Metrô Na Superfície** (Surface Metro; www.metrorio.com.br) subway bus consists of modern, silver buses that make limited stops as they shuttle passengers to and from metro stations. For most destinations, a one-way ticket costs the same as a single metro ride (R$3.70) but includes both the bus and the metro ride.

The most useful one for travelers is the line to Jardim Botânico, which departs from Botafogo station. It stops at Cobal do Humaitá, Rua Maria Angélica, the Hospital da Lagoa, the edge of Jardim Botânico, Praça Santos Dumont, Gávea Trade Center and PUC.

You can also go to Barra by metro bus (the No 525 Expresso Barra). This operates much like the metrô na superfície, with limited stops, but covers a much larger distance. The integrated metro-bus ticket costs around R$5 and departs from Praça General Osório station, with stops at Posto 9 (Ipanema beach), Posto 12 (Leblon beach), São Conrado Fashion Mall, Praia do Pepino (São Conrado), Shopping Downtown, Barra Shopping and Casa Shopping, among others.

way to get around, with short rides (usually from the bottom of the favela to the top or vice versa) costing R$2 (though they may ask R$5 of foreigners).

If you have a smartphone, you can use a free app such as 99Taxis or Easy Taxi to hail a cab. Uber may also survive in Rio. Or you can call one of the radio-taxi companies.

Coopertramo (☎2209-9292)
Cootramo (☎3976-9944)
Transcoopass (☎2209-1555)
Transcootour (☎2590-2220)

Train

The suburban train station, **Estação Dom Pedro II** (Central do Brasil; ☎2111-9494; Av Presidente Vargas, Praça Cristiano Ottoni, Centro), is one of Brazil's busiest commuter stations, but it's not the safest area to walk around. To get there, take the metro to Central station and head upstairs. This is the train station that was featured in the Academy Award–nominated film *Central do Brasil* (Central Station).

Tram

Rio was once serviced by a multitude of *bondes* (trams), with routes throughout the city. The only remaining line is the *bonde* to Santa Teresa, which partially reopened (1.7km of its 10km of tracks) in 2015. Currently, it begins at the **bonde station** (Lélio Gama 65) in Centro and travels over the scenic Arcos da Lapa and along Rua Joaquim Murtinho only as far as Largo do Guimarães, on Rua Almirante Alexandrino in the heart of boho Santa Teresa, before turning around.

Work on the line continues. From Largo do Guimarães, the tracks will eventually split, with one line (Paula Matos) to continue along a northwestern route,

terminating at Largo das Neves. The longer route (Dois Irmãos) will continue from Largo do Guimarães uphill and southwest before terminating near the water reservoir at Dois Irmãos.

TOURS

There are many ways to experience Rio, whether by boat, helicopter, 4WD or good old-fashioned walking.

Bay Cruises

With its magnificent coastline, Rio makes a fine backdrop for a cruise.

Saveiros Tours (Map p249; ☎2225-6064; www.saveiros. com.br; Marina de Glória, Glória; cruises from R$55) Saveiros leads daily two-hour cruises out over Baía de Guanabara in large schooners. The route follows the coastline of Rio and Niterói with excellent views of Pão de Açúcar (Sugarloaf Mountain), the MAC, Ilha Fiscal and the old fort of Urca. You'll sail under the Niterói bridge. Departs from Marina de Glória.

Bicycle Tours

Rio by Bike (☎96871-8933; www.riobybike.com; tours R$100-125) Two Dutch journalists operate this cycling outfit, and their excellent pedaling tours combine a mix of scenery and cultural insight. It's a great way to get an overview of the city, with guides pointing out key landmarks and describing key events that have shaped Rio. Tours last three to four hours and travel mostly along bike lanes separated from traffic.

Bike in Rio (☎98474-7740; www.bikeinriotours.com; tours R$85-170) Offers fun three- to five-hour bicycle tours around Rio. One itinerary takes in Parque do Flamengo and Copacabana, another goes around

Ipanema and Lagoa, a third explores Lapa and downtown Rio, and another takes you to Santa Marta favela (via bicycle and cable-car).

City Tours

A number of private guides lead customized tours around the city, taking in the major sights, leading nightlife and organizing just about anything Rio has to offer.

Brazil Expedition (☎99998-2907; www.brazilexpedition. com; city tours R$120) The friendly English-speaking guides run a variety of traditional tours around Rio, including trips to Cristo Redentor, nightlife outings to samba schools, game-day trips to Maracanã Football Stadium, street-art tours and favela tours.

Marcelo Esteves (☎99984-7654; marcelo.esteves@ hotmail.com; 5-/8hr tours US$200/300) A highly experienced multilingual Rio expert offering private tours around the city.

Madson Araújo (☎99395-3537; www.tourguiderio. com; 5hr tours from US$350) Professional English- and French-speaking guide offering custom-made day or night tours around Rio.

Favela Tours

Favela Tour (☎3322-2727; www.favelatour.com.br; tours R$90) Marcelo Armstrong's insightful tour pioneered favela tourism. A three-hour excursion takes in Rocinha and Vila Canoas.

Paulo Amendoim (☎99747-6860; www.favela tourrio.com; tours R$75) Recommended guide Paulo Amendoim is the former president of Rocinha's residents association. He seems to know everyone in the favela, and leads a warm and personalized tour that helps visitors see beyond the stereotypes.

Be A Local (☑9643-0366; www.bealocal.com; tours R$80) Offers daily trips into Rocinha (you'll ride up by moto-taxi, and walk back down), with stops along the way. It also organizes a night out at a *baile* (dance) funk party in Castelo das Pedras on Sunday.

Helicopter Tours

Helisight (☑2511-2141; www.helisight.com.br; per person 6-/15-/30min flights R$260/650/900) Offering helicopter tours since 1991, Helisight has seven different itineraries, all giving gorgeous views over the city. There's a three-person minimum. Helipad locations are in Floresta da Tijuca facing Corcovado; on

Morro da Urca, the first cable-car stop up Pão de Açúcar; and on the edge of Lagoa.

4WD Tours

Jeep Tour (☑2108-5800; www.jeeptour.com.br; 4hr tours R$142) Tours go to the Floresta da Tijuca in a large, open-topped 4WD. It includes a stop at the Vista Chinesa, then on to the forest for an easy hike and a stop for a swim beneath a waterfall, before making the return journey.

Walking Tours

Free Walker Tours (☑97101-3352; www.free walkertours.com) This well-organized outfit runs a free walking tour that takes in a bit of history and culture in downtown Rio. You'll visit the Travessa do Comércio, Praça

XV, Cinelândia, the Arcos da Lapa and the Selarón steps, among other places. Although it's free, the guide asks for tips at the end: by our reckoning, R$50 seems fair for the insightful three-hour walk. The tour departs at 10:30am Monday through Saturday from Largo da Carioca (exit C out of Carioca metro station). Just show up (reservations aren't necessary). The same outfit also leads pub crawls in Ipanema and Lapa (each R$55), as well as a free Copacabana walking tour.

Lisa Rio Tours (☑99894-6867; www.lisariotours. com; tours from US$41) Lisa Schnittger, a German expat who has lived in Rio for many years, leads a wide range of recommended tours. Some of her most popular excursions explore the colonial history of downtown, the bohemian side of Santa Teresa and Afro-Brazilian culture in Rio.

Directory A–Z

Courses

Cooking

Cook in Rio (Map p244; ☑8761-3653; www.cookinrio. com; 2nd fl, Belfort Roxo 161; per person US$75) There aren't many cooking classes available in English in Rio, other than this notable exception, which offers one-day courses where you'll learn how to make a rich *moqueca* (seafood stew cooked in coconut milk) or a decadent pot of *feijoada* (black beans and pork stew).

Language

Most language institutes charge high prices for group Portuguese courses. You can often find a private tutor for less. Hostels are a good place to troll for instructors, with ads on bulletin boards posted by native-speaking language teachers available for hire.

Casa do Caminho Language Centre (Map p236; ☑2267-6552; www.casado caminho-languagecentre. org; Farme de Amoedo 135, Ipanema; private classes per hr R$70, 4-week, 80hr courses R$1400; ☎) Offers competitively priced classes, with intensive group classes – four hours a day for five days for R$450. Profits go toward the Casa do Caminho (www. casadocaminhobrasil.org) orphanages in Brazil.

Instituto Brasil-Estados Unidos (IBEU; Map p244; ☑2548-8430; http://portu guese.ibeu.org.br; 5th fl, NS de Copacabana 690, Copacabana; 36hr courses R$1900) One of the oldest, more respected language institutions in the city.

Carioca Languages (Map p244; ☑2146-8414; www. carioca-languages.com; room 201, NS de Copacabana 807, Copacabana; 4-week, 60hr courses R$1500) Located in Co-pacabana, with a wide range of courses and private instruction.

Music

Maracatu Brasil (Map p250; ☑2557-4754; www.maracatu brasil.com.br; 2nd fl, Ipiranga 49, Laranjeiras; ⊘10am-6pm Mon-Sat) is the best place in Rio to study percussion, and students have the opportunity to perform in music events throughout the city.

Instructors here offer courses in a number of different drumming styles: Amazonian rhythms, samba, conga drums, *candomblé* and much more, plus private lessons in guitar and other instruments.

If you plan to stick around a while, you can sign up for group classes (from R$165 a month) or hire an instructor for private classes. On the 1st floor of the building, Maracatu sells instruments.

PRACTICALITIES

Currency

The monetary unit of Brazil is the *real* (R$; pronounced hay-*ow*); the plural is *reais* (pronounced hay-*ice*).

Newspapers & Magazines

Rio Times (www.riotimesonline.com) is an English-language newspaper that publishes a monthly free print version, and maintains a website updated weekly. *Veja* is the country's best-selling weekly magazine. In Rio, it comes with the *Veja Rio* insert, which details the weekly entertainment options; available on Sunday. *Jornal do Brasil* and *O Globo* are Brazil's leading dailies.

Smoking

Banned in restaurants and bars; some hotels have rooms for smokers.

Weights & Measures

Brazil uses the metric system.

Electricity

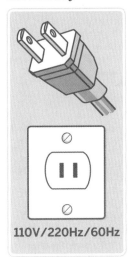

110V/220Hz/60Hz

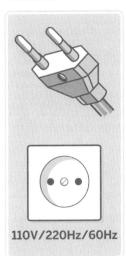

110V/220Hz/60Hz

Embassies & Consulates

Many foreign countries have consulates or embassies in Rio. You'll find consulates listed in the back of Riotur's monthly *Guia do Rio*.

Argentinian Consulate (☑2553-1646; http://crioj. cancilleria.gov.ar; Praia de Botafogo 228, Sobreloja/1st fl, Botafogo)

Australian Consulate (☑3824-4624; http://brazil. embassy.gov.au; 23rd fl, Av Presidente Wilson 231, Centro)

Canadian Consulate (☑2543-3004; www.brasil. gc.ca; 13th fl, Av Atlântica 1130, Copacabana)

French Consulate (☑3974-6699; http:// riodejaneiro.ambafrance-br. org; Av Presidente Antônio Carlos 58, Centro)

UK Consulate (☑2555-9600; www.reinounido.org.br; 2nd fl, Praia do Flamengo 284, Flamengo)

US Consulate (☑3823-2000; http://brazil.usembassy. gov; Av Presidente Wilson 147, Centro)

Emergency

To call emergency telephone numbers in Rio you don't need a phone card.

Ambulance (☑192)

Fire Department (☑193)

Police (☑190)

Tourist Police (☑2332-2924; cnr Afrânio de Melo Franco & Humberto de Campos, Leblon; ☺24hr) Report robberies to the tourist police; no major investigation is going to occur, but you will get a police form to give to your insurance company.

Gay & Lesbian Travelers

Rio is the gay capital of Latin America. There's no law against homosexuality in Brazil. During Carnaval, thousands of gay expatriate Brazilians and foreign tourists fly in for the festivities. Transvestites steal the show at all Carnaval balls, especially the gay ones. Outside Carnaval, the gay scene is fairly subdued. The most gay-friendly street in town is Farme de Amoedo in Ipanema, with cafes, restaurants and drinking spots.

You may hear or read the abbreviation GLS, particularly in the entertainment section of newspapers and magazines. It stands for Gays, Lesbians and Sympathizers, and when used in connection with venues or events basically indicates that anyone with an open mind is welcome. In general, the scene is much more integrated than elsewhere, and the majority of parties involve a pretty mixed crowd.

The **Rio Gay Guide** (www.riogayguide.com) is an excellent website full of information for gay and lesbian tourists in Rio, including sections on Carnaval, nightlife and bathhouses.

Internet Access

Most accommodations – including hostels and mid-range hotels – provide wi-fi access. It's usually free, though some luxury hotels still charge exorbitant rates for it. You'll also find free wi-fi in most cafes and in many restaurants, as well as in some shopping malls.

Given the widespread availability of wi-fi and the popularity of smartphones, internet cafes are a vanishing breed, though there are still a few scattered around Copacabana and other areas of the Zona Sul. Most places charge between R$6 and R$12 an hour.

@Onze (Marquês de Abrantes 11, Flamengo; ☺9am-11:30pm) There's no Skype, but this peaceful spot serves up tasty sandwiches, salads, desserts and microbrews you can enjoy while browsing the web.

Blame It on Rio 4 Travel (☑3813-5510; www.blame itonrio4travel.com; Xavier da Silveira 15B, Copacabana) Excellent travel agency run by a friendly and knowledge-able US expat. Internet access available.

Legal Matters

You are required by law to carry some form of identi-fication. For travelers, this generally means a passport, but a certified copy of the relevant ID page will usually be acceptable.

In the last few years, Rio has gotten serious about drunk driving, and the penalties for driving under the influence are severe. Marijuana and cocaine are plentiful in Rio, and both are very illegal. An allegation of drug trafficking or posses-sion provides the police with the perfect excuse to extract a not-insignificant amount of money from you – and Brazilian prisons are brutal places. If you are arrested, know that you have the right to remain silent, and that you are innocent until proven guilty. You also have a right to visitation by your lawyer or a family member.

Medical Services

Some private medical facili-ties in Rio de Janeiro are on par with US hospitals. The UK and US consulates have lists of English-speaking physicians.

Hospitals

Clínica Galdino Campos (☎2548-9966; www.galdino campos.com.br; NS de Copa-cabana 492, Copacabana; ☺24hr) The best hospital for foreigners, with high-quality care and multilingual doctors (who even make outpatient calls). The clinic works with most international health plans and travel-insurance policies.

Pharmacies

Pharmacies stock all kinds of drugs and sell them much

more cheaply than in many other countries. However, when buying drugs anywhere in South America, be sure to check the expiration dates and specific storage condi-tions. Some drugs that are available in Brazil may no longer be recommended, or may even be banned, in other countries. Common names of prescription medicines in South America are likely to be different from the ones you're used to; ask a pharmacist before taking anything you're not sure about.

There are scores of phar-macies in town, a number of which stay open 24 hours.

Drogaria Pacheco (NS de Copacabana 115, Copacabana; ☺7am-11pm)

Drogaria Pacheco (☎2511-7871; Visconde de Pirajá 455, Ipanema; ☺7am-11pm)

Money

The *real* is made up of 100 *centavos*. Most prices are quoted in *reais*, though some tour operators and hoteliers prefer to list their rates in US dollars or euros.

ATMs

ATMs are the handiest way to access money in Rio. Unfortunately, there has been an alarming rise in card cloning, with travelers returning home to find un-authorized withdrawals on their cards. When possible, use high-traffic ATMs in bank buildings during bank-ing hours. Always cover your hands when inputting your PIN, and check your account frequently to make sure you haven't been hacked.

ATMs for most card net-works are widely available. Citibank, Bradesco, Banco do Brasil and the Banco-24Horas all accept foreign cards (Itaú does not).

You can find ATMs in the following locations:

Banco do Brasil With branches in Centro (Senador Dantas 105,

Centro); Copacabana (NS de Copacabana 1292, Copa-cabana) and Galeão inter-national airport (1st fl, Terminal 1, Galeão international airport).

Citibank Branches at Centro (Rua da Assembléia 100, Centro); Ipanema (Visconde de Pirajá 260, Ipanema) and Leblon (Visconde de Pirajá 1260A, Leblon).

Changing Money

For exchanging cash, *casas de cambio* (exchange offices) cluster behind the Copacabana Palace hotel in Copacabana and along Visconde de Pirajá near Praça General Osório in Ipanema.

Credit Cards

Visa is the most widely accepted credit card in Rio; MasterCard, American Express and Diners Club are also accepted by many hotels, restaurants and shops.

Credit-card fraud is rife in Rio so be very careful. When making purchases keep your credit card in sight at all times. Have staff bring the machine to your table or fol-low them up to the cashier – don't give them your card.

Tipping

In restaurants the *serviço* (service charge) is usually included in the bill and is mandatory; when it is not included in the bill, it's cus-tomary to leave a 10% tip. If a waiter is friendly and help-ful, you can give more.

There are many other places where tipping is not customary but is a welcome gesture. The workers at local juice stands, bars and coffee corners, and street-and beach-vendors, are all tipped on occasion. Parking assistants receive no wages and are dependent on tips, usually about R$4. Taxi driv-ers are not usually tipped, but it is common to round up the fare.

Opening Hours

Standard opening hours in Rio:

Restaurants noon–3pm and 6–11pm

Bars 6pm–2am Monday to Friday and from noon Saturday; some open Sunday as well

Nightclubs 11pm–5am Thursday to Saturday

Shops 9am–6pm Monday to Friday, 9am–1pm Saturday

Malls 10am–10pm Monday to Saturday, 3–10pm Sunday

Banks 9am–3pm Monday to Friday

Post

Postal services are decent in Brazil, and most mail gets through. Airmail letters to the US and Europe usually arrive in a week or two. For Australia and Asia, allow three weeks.

There are yellow mailboxes on the street, but it's safer to go to a post office (correios). Most post offices are open 8am to 6pm Monday to Friday, and until noon on Saturday.

Branches include **Botafogo** (Map p252; Praia do Botafogo 324, Botafogo), **Copacabana** (Map p244; NS de Copacabana 540, Copacabana) and **Ipanema** (Map p236; Prudente de Morais 147, Ipanema).

Safe Travel

Rio gets a lot of bad international press about violence, though security has generally improved in the last few years. Regardless, to minimize your risk of becoming a victim, you should take some basic precautions. First off: dress down and leave expensive (or even expensive-looking) jewelry, watches and sunglasses at home.

Copacabana and Ipanema beaches have a police presence, but robberies still occur on the sands, even in broad daylight. Don't take anything of value with you to the beach. Late at night, don't walk on any of the beaches.

Buses are sometimes targets for thieves. Avoid taking them after dark, and keep an eye out while you're on them. Take taxis at night to avoid walking along empty streets and beaches. Don't walk around deserted areas – Centro is barren and can be unsafe on Sunday.

Get in the habit of carrying only the money you'll need for the day, so you don't have to flash a wad of reais when you pay for things. Cameras and backpacks attract a lot of attention. Plastic shopping bags nicely disguise whatever you're carrying. If headed to Maracanã Football Stadium, take only your spending money for the day and avoid the crowded sections. Safety in the favelas has improved, but it's still best to go with someone who knows the area.

If you have the misfortune of being robbed, slowly hand over the goods. Thieves in the city are only too willing to use their weapons if given provocation.

Telephone

Public phones are nicknamed orelhões (floppy ears). They take a cartão telefônico (phone card), which are available from newsstands and street vendors in denominations of R$5 to R$20.

To phone Rio from outside Brazil, dial your international access code, then ✆55 (Brazil's country code), ✆21 (Rio's area code) and the number.

To make a local collect call, dial ✆9090, then the number. For calls to other cities, dial ✆0, then the code of your selected long-distance carrier, then the two-digit area code, followed by the local number. You need to choose a long-distance carrier that covers both the place you are calling from and the place you're calling to. Carriers advertise their codes in areas where they're prominent, but you can usually use Embratel (code ✆21) or Telemar (code ✆31) nationwide.

To make an intercity collect call, dial ✆9 before the ✆0xx (the 'xx' representing the two-digit carrier as explained above, ie '21,' '31' or a host of other Brazilian carriers). A recorded message in Portuguese will ask you to say your name and where you're calling from, after the tone.

Cell Phones

The celular (cell phone) is ubiquitous in Rio. Cell phones have nine-digit numbers beginning with 9.

Brazil uses the GSM 850/900/1800/1900 network, which is compatible with North America, Europe and Australia, but the country's 4G LTE network runs on 2500/2690 (for now), which is not compatible with many North American and European smartphones.

Good news for some Americans: if you have an LTE/GSM-capable device (like certain models of the iPhone6) on Sprint or T-Mobile, you can get unlimited texting and data in Brazil on certain plans – though on the 2G network (meaning data is quite slow/nonexistent). You can, however, purchase additional data for better use. Check to see if your iPhone is compatible at www.apple.com/iphone/LTE.

Calls to cell phones are more expensive than calls to landlines. Cell phones have city codes like landlines, and if you're calling from another city, you have to use them. TIM (www.tim.com.br), Claro (www.claro.com.br), Oi (www.oi.com.br) and Vivo (www.vivo.com.br) are the major operators.

Foreigners can purchase a local SIM with a passport instead of needing a Brazilian CPF (tax ID number), though this ability is often ignored by cellular providers – prepare for a battle.

If you have an unlocked GSM phone, you can simply buy a SIM card (called a *chip*) for around R$10 to R$20. Among the major carriers, TIM generally has the most hassle-free service. You can then add minutes by purchasing additional airtime from any newspaper stand. Incoming calls are free.

Time

Brazil has four official time zones. Rio, in the southeastern region, is three hours behind Greenwich Mean Time (GMT) and four hours behind during the northern-hemisphere summer. Rio also observes daylight-saving time, pushing the clocks one hour forward from mid-October to mid-February.

Tourist Information

Riotur's multilingual website (www.rioguiaoficial.com.br) is a good source of information.

All of the Riotur offices distribute maps and the bimonthly *Rio Guide,* which is packed with information and major seasonal events. As well as branches at Galeão international airport's **Terminal 1** (☑3398-4077; Domestic Arrival Hall; ☺6am-11pm) and **Terminal 2** (☑3367-6213; International Arrival Hall; ☺6am-11pm), you'll find information kiosks at the following locations:

Riotur Centro (Map p254; Candelária 6; ☺9am-6pm Mon-Fri, to 3pm Sat) Handy tourist info kiosk on a pedestrian lane in a historic part of Centro.

Riotur Copacabana (Map p244; ☑2541-7522; Princesa Isabel 183; ☺9am-6pm Mon-Fri, to 3pm Sat) Good for information on events during Carnaval.

Riotur Ipanema (Map p236; Visconde de Pirajá & Joana Angélica; ☺8am-9pm) Useful info kiosk in the heart of Ipanema.

Riotur Kiosk Copacabana Beach (Map p244; ☑2547-4421; Av Atlântica, near Hilário de Gouveia; ☺8am-9pm) Tourist info at a kiosk overlooking the beach.

Riotur Lapa (Map p258; Mém de Sá btwn Arcos da Lapa & Lavradio; ☺9am-6pm) Tourist info in Lapa.

Riotur Leblon (Map p240; Ataulfo de Paiva & Dias Ferreira; ☺8am-6pm) Tourist info at the entrance to Leblon's best eat street.

Travelers with Disabilities

Rio is probably the most accessible city in Brazil for travelers with disabilities to get around, but that doesn't mean it's always easy. It's convenient to hire cars with driver-guides, but for only one person the expense is quite high compared to the cost of the average bus tour. If there are several people to share the cost, it's definitely worth it. For transport around the city, contact **Coop Taxi** (☑3295-9606).

The metro system has electronic wheelchair lifts, but it's difficult to know whether they're actually functional. Major sites are only partially accessible – there are about 10 steps to the gondola base of Pão de Açúcar, for instance; and although there is access to the base of Cristo Redentor, there are about two dozen steps to reach the statue itself. **Jeep Tour** (☑2108-5800; www.jeeptour.com.

br; 4hr tours R$142) offers excursions for mobility-impaired travelers.

The streets and sidewalks along the main beaches have curb cuts and are wheelchair accessible, but most other areas do not have cuts. Most of the newer hotels have wheelchair-accessible rooms, but many restaurants have entrance steps.

Visas

Brazil has a reciprocal visa system, so if your home country requires Brazilian nationals to secure a visa, then you'll need one to enter Brazil. US, Canadian and Australian citizens need visas, but UK, New Zealand, French and German citizens do not. You can check your status with the Brazilian embassy or consulate in your home country.

If you do need a visa, arrange it beforehand. Visas are not issued on arrival and you won't be permitted into the country without one. Tourist visas are issued by Brazilian diplomatic offices. They are valid upon arrival in Brazil for a 90-day stay and are renewable in Brazil for an additional 90 days. In most Brazilian embassies and consulates, visas are processed in five to 10 days. You will need to present one passport photograph, a round-trip or onward ticket (or a photocopy of it) and a valid passport. If you decide to return to Brazil, your visa is valid for anywhere from one year (for Australians) to 10 years (for Americans). Each visit, however, you are allowed only a 90-day stay (or 180 days max if you renew it). Multiple visits are allowed, but you may only stay a total of 180 days each year.

The fee for visas is also reciprocal. It's usually between US$35 and US$65, though for US citizens visas cost US$160.

ZIKA VIRUS: WARNING FOR PREGNANT TRAVELERS

Brazil has experienced an outbreak of Zika virus infections since 2015. Transmitted by mosquitoes, Zika rarely causes illness (only one in five infected people will experience the flu-like symptoms). The virus, however, has been linked to microcephaly (abnormally small head size with possible brain damage) in babies born to women who were infected while pregnant. The CDC (Centers for Disease Control & Prevention) has recommended pregnant women to consider postponing travel to Brazil (and other countries where virus transmission is ongoing).

Applicants under 18 years of age wanting to travel to Brazil must also submit a notarized letter of authorization from a parent or legal guardian.

Entry/Exit Card

On entering Brazil, all tourists must fill out an entry/exit card (cartão de entrada/saida); immigration officials will keep half, you keep the other. Don't lose this card! When you leave Brazil, the second half of the entry/exit card will be taken by immigration officials. They will also stamp your passport, and if for some reason they are not granting you the usual 90-day stay in Brazil, the number of days will be written beneath the word *Prazo* (Period) on the stamp in your passport.

Volunteering

Río Voluntário (☑2262-1110; www.riovoluntario.org.br; Room 508, Av Marecal Floriano 38, Centro) The Rio-based organization supports several hundred local volunteer organizations, from those involved in social work and the environment to health care. It's an excellent resource for finding volunteer work.

Iko Poran (☑3217-1475; www.ikoporan.org; Rua do Oriente 280, Santa Teresa) Links the diverse talents of volunteers with those required by needy organizations from its base in Rio. Previous volunteers have worked as dance, music, art and language instructors, among other things. Iko Poran also provides housing options for volunteers.

Task Brasil (www.taskbrasil.org.uk) UK-based Task Brasil is a laudable organization that places volunteers in Rio. Here, you'll have to make arrangements in advance and pay a fee that will go toward Task Brasil projects and your expenses as a volunteer.

Women Travelers

In Rio, foreign women traveling alone will scarcely be given a sideways glance. Although machismo is an undeniable element in the Brazilian social structure, it is less overt here than in many other parts of Latin America. Flirtation (often exaggerated) is a prominent element in Brazilian male-female relations. It goes both ways and is nearly always regarded as amusingly innocent banter. You should be able to stop unwelcome attention by merely expressing displeasure.

Language

Portuguese is spoken by around 190 million people worldwide, 90% of whom live in Brazil. Brazilian Portuguese today differs from European Portuguese in approximately the same way that British English differs from American English. European and Brazilian Portuguese have different spelling, pronunciation and, to some extent, vocabulary. For example, in Portugal, the word for 'train' is *comboio* and in Brazil you'd say *trem*.

Most sounds in Portuguese are also found in English. The exceptions are the nasal vowels (represented in our colored pronunciation guides by ng after the vowel), which are pronounced as if you're trying to make the sound through your nose, and the strongly rolled r (represented by rr in our pronunciation guides). Also note that the zh sounds like the 's' in 'pleasure'. The stressed syllables (generally the second-last syllable of a word) are indicated with italics. If you keep these few points in mind and read our pronunciation guides as if they were English, you'll have no problems being understood. The abbreviations (m) and (f) indicate masculine and feminine gender, whereas (sg) and (pl) stand for 'singular' and 'plural' respectively.

BASICS

Hello.	*Olá.*	o·*laa*
Goodbye.	*Tchau.*	tee·*show*
How are you?	*Como vai?*	ko·mo vai
Fine, and you?	*Bem, e você?*	beng e vo·*se*
Excuse me.	*Com licença.*	kong lee·*seng*·saa

WANT MORE?

For in-depth language information and handy phrases, check out Lonely Planet's *Brazilian Portuguese Phrasebook*. You'll find it at **shop.lonelyplanet.com**, or you can buy Lonely Planet's iPhone phrasebooks at the Apple App Store.

Sorry.	*Desculpa.*	des·*kool*·paa
Yes./No.	*Sim./Não.*	seeng/nowng
Please.	*Por favor.*	por faa·*vorr*
Thank you.	*Obrigado.* *Obrigada.*	o·bree·*gaa*·do (m) o·bree·*gaa*·daa (f)
You're welcome.	*De nada.*	de naa·daa

What's your name?
Qual é o seu nome?　kwow e o se·oo no·me

My name is ...
Meu nome é ...　me·oo no·me e ...

Do you speak English?
Você fala inglês?　vo·se faa·laa eeng·gles

I don't understand.
Não entendo.　nowng eng·teng·do

ACCOMMODATIONS

Do you have a single/double room?
Tem um quarto de solteiro/casal?　teng oom kwaarr·to de sol·tay·ro/kaa·zow

How much is it per night/person?
Quanto custa por noite/pessoa?　kwang·to koos·taa porr noy·te/pe·so·aa

Can I see it?
Posso ver?　po·so verr

campsite	*local para acampamento*	lo·kow paa·raa aa·kang·paa·*meng*·to
guesthouse	*hospedaria*	os·pe·daa·*ree*·a
hotel	*hotel*	o·*tel*
youth hostel	*albergue da juventude*	ow·*berr*·ge daa zhoo·veng·*too*·de
air-con	*ar condicionado*	aarr kong·dee·syo·*naa*·do
bathroom	*banheiro*	ba·*nyay*·ro
bed	*cama*	ka·maa
window	*janela*	zhaa·*ne*·laa

DIRECTIONS

Where is ...?
Onde fica ...? — ong·de fee·kaa ...

What's the address?
Qual é o endereço? — kwow e o eng·de·re·so

Could you please write it down?
Você poderia escrever — vo·se po·de·ree·aa es·kre·verr
num papel, por favor? — noom paa·pel porr faa·vorr

Can you show me (on the map)?
Você poderia me — vo·se po·de·ree·aa me
mostrar (no mapa)? — mos·traarr (no maa·paa)

at the corner	na esquina	na es·kee·naa
at the traffic lights	no sinal de trânsito	no see·now de trang·zee·to
behind ...	atrás ...	aa·traaz ...
in front of ...	na frente de ...	naa freng·te de ...
left	esquerda	es·kerr·daa
near ...	perto ...	perr·to ...
next to ...	ao lado de ...	ow laa·do de ...
opposite ...	do lado oposto ...	do laa·do o·pos·to ...
right	direita	dee·ray·taa
straight ahead	em frente	eng freng·te

EATING & DRINKING

What would you recommend?
O que você — oo ke vo·se
recomenda? — he·ko·meng·daa

What's in that dish?
O que tem neste prato? — o ke teng nes·te praa·to

I don't eat ...
Eu não como ... — e·oo nowng ko·mo ...

Cheers!
Saúde! — sa·oo·de

That was delicious.
Estava delicioso. — es·taa·vaa de·lee·see·o·zo

Bring the bill/check, please.
Por favor traga — porr faa·vorr traa·gaa
a conta. — aa kong·taa

I'd like to reserve a table for ...	Eu gostaria de reservar uma mesa para ...	e·oo gos·taa·ree·aa de he·zer·vaarr oo·maa me·zaa paa·raa ...
(eight) o'clock	(às oito) horas	(aas oy·to) aw·raas
(two) people	(duas) pessoas	(doo·aas) pe·so·aas

Key Words

| bottle | garrafa | gaa·haa·faa |
| breakfast | café da manha | ka·fe daa ma·nyang |

KEY PATTERNS

To get by in Portuguese, mix and match these simple patterns with words of your choice.

When's (the next flight)?
Quando é — kwaang·do e
(o próximo vôo)? — (o pro·see·mo vo·o)

Where's the (tourist office)?
Onde fica — ong·de fee·kaa
(a secretaria — (aa se·kre·taa·ree·aa
de turismo)? — de too·rees·mo)

I'm looking for (a hotel).
Estou procurando — es·to pro·koorr·ang·do
(um hotel). — (oom o·tel)

Do you have (a map)?
Você tem — vo·se teng
(um mapa)? — (oom maa·paa)

Is there (a bathroom)?
Tem (banheiro)? — teng (ba·nyay·ro)

I'd like (a coffee).
Eu gostaria de — e·oo gos·taa·ree·aa de
(um café). — (oom kaa·fe)

I'd like to (hire a car).
Eu gostaria de — e·oo gos·taa·ree·aa de
(alugar um carro). — (aa·loo·gaarr oom kaa·ho)

Can I (enter)?
Posso (entrar)? — po·so (eng·traarr)

Could you please (help me)?
Você poderia — vo·se po·de·ree·aa
me (ajudar), — me (aa·zhoo·daarr)
por favor? — por faa·vorr

Do I have to (get a visa)?
Necessito — ne·se·see·to
(obter visto)? — (o·bee·terr vees·to)

cold	frio	free·o
cup	xícara	shee·kaa·raa
dessert	sobremesa	so·bre·me·zaa
dinner	jantar	zhang·taarr
drink	bebida	be·bee·daa
entree	entrada	eng·traa·daa
fork	garfo	gaarr·fo
glass	copo	ko·po
hot (warm)	quente	keng·te
knife	faca	faa·kaa
lunch	almoço	ow·mo·so
market	mercado	merr·kaa·do
menu	cardápio	kaar·da·pyo
plate	prato	praa·to
restaurant	restaurante	hes·tow·rang·te
spicy	apimentado	aa·pee·meng·taa·do
spoon	colher	ko·lyerr

| vegetarian food | comida vegetariana | ko·mee·daa ve·zhe·taa·ree·a·naa |
| with/without | com/sem | kong/seng |

Meat & Fish

beef	carne de vaca	kaar·ne de vaa·kaa
chicken	frango	frang·go
crab	siri	see·ree
fish	peixe	pay·she
fruit	frutas	froo·tas
lamb	carneiro	karr·nay·ro
meat	carne	kaar·ne
oyster	ostra	os·traa
pork	porco	porr·ko
seafood	frutos do mar	froo·tos do maarr
shrimp	camarão	ka·ma·rowng
tuna	atum	aa·toong
veal	bezerro	be·ze·ho
vegetable	legumes	le·goo·mes

Fruit & Vegetables

apple	maçã	maa·sang
apricot	damasco	daa·maas·ko
asparagus	aspargo	aas·paarr·go
avocado	abacate	aa·baa·kaa·te
beetroot	beterraba	be·te·haa·baa
cabbage	repolho	he·po·lyo
capsicum	pimentão	pee·meng·towng
carrot	cenoura	se·no·raa
cherry	cereja	se·re·zhaa
corn	milho	mee·lyo
cucumber	pepino	pe·pee·no
garlic	alho	aa·lyo
grapes	uvas	oo·vaas
lemon	limão	lee·mowng
lettuce	alface	ow·faa·se
mushroom	cogumelo	ko·goo·me·lo
nut	noz	noz
onion	cebola	se·bo·laa
orange	laranja	laa·rang·zhaa
pea	ervilha	err·vee·lyaa
peach	pêssego	pe·se·go
pineapple	abacaxí	aa·baa·kaa·shee
plum	ameixa	aa·may·shaa
potato	batata	baa·taa·taa
pumpkin	abóbora	aa·bo·bo·raa

spinach	espinafre	es·pee·naa·fre
strawberry	morango	mo·rang·go
tomato	tomate	to·maa·te
vegetables	legumes	le·goo·mes
watermelon	melancia	me·lang·see·aa

Other

bread	pão	powng
cake	bolo	bo·lo
cheese	queijo	kay·zho
chilli	pimenta	pee·meng·taa
eggs	ovos	o·vos
honey	mel	mel
ice cream	sorvete	sorr·ve·te
jam	geléia	zhe·le·yaa
lentil	lentilha	leng·tee·lyaa
olive oil	azeite	a·zay·te
pepper	pimenta	pee·meng·taa

LANGUAGE EATING & DRINKING

CARIOCA SLANG

Making an effort with the language is something Brazilians will greatly appreciate. *Díria* (slang) is a big part of the *carioca* dialect spoken by the residents of Rio. Here are a few words and phrases :

babaca ba·ba·ka – jerk

bunda boon·da – bottom/bum

Eu gosto de você. e·oo gosh·too zhi vo·se – I like you.

Falou! fa·low – Absolutely!/You said it!

Fique à vontade. feek a van·tazh – Make yourself at home.

fio dental fee·oo den·tow – dental floss, aka bikini

gata/gato ga·ta/ga·too – good-looking woman/man

Nossa! no·sa – Gosh!/You don't say! (lit: 'Our Lady')

sunga soong·ga – tiny swim shorts favored by *carioca* men

Ta ótimo!/Ta legal! ta a·che·moo/ta lee·gow – Great!/Cool!/OK!

Tudo bem? too·doo beng – Everything OK?

Tudo bem. too·doo beng – Everything's OK.

Valeu! va·le·o – Thanks.

Vamu nessa! va·moo·ne·sa – Let's go!

Signs

Banheiro	Bathroom
Entrada	Entrance
Não Tem Vaga	No Vacancy
Pronto Socorro	Emergency Department
Saída	Exit
Tem Vaga	Vacancy

rice	arroz	a·hoz
salt	sal	sow
sauce	molho	mo·lyo
sugar	açúcar	aa·soo·kaarr

Drinks

beer	cerveja	serr·ve·zhaa
coffee	café	kaa·fe
fruit juice	suco de frutas	soo·ko de froo·taas
milk	leite	lay·te
red wine	vinho tinto	vee·nyo teeng·to
soft drink	refrigerante	he·free·zhe·rang·te
tea	chá	shaa
(mineral) water	água (mineral)	aa·gwaa (mee·ne·row)
white wine	vinho branco	vee·nyo brang·ko

EMERGENCIES

| Help! | Socorro! | so·ko·ho |
| Leave me alone! | Me deixe em paz! | me day·she eng paas |

Call ...!	Chame ...!	sha·me ...
a doctor	um médico	oom me·dee·ko
the police	a polícia	aa po·lee·syaa

It's an emergency.
É uma emergência. — e oo·maa e·merr·zheng·see·aa

I'm lost.
Estou perdido. — es·to perr·dee·do (m)
Estou perdida. — es·to perr·dee·daa (f)

I'm ill.
Estou doente. — es·to do·eng·te

It hurts here.
Aqui dói. — a·kee doy

I'm allergic to (antibiotics).
Tenho alergia à (antibióticos). — te·nyo aa·lerr·zhee·aa aa (ang·tee·bee·o·tee·kos)

Where are the bathrooms?
Onde tem um banheiro? — on·de teng oom ba·nyay·ro

SHOPPING & SERVICES

I'd like to buy ...
Gostaria de comprar ... — gos·taa·ree·aa de kong·praarr ...

I'm just looking.
Estou só olhando. — es·to so o·lyang·do

Can I look at it?
Posso ver? — po·so verr

How much is it?
Quanto custa? — kwang·to koos·taa

It's too expensive.
Está muito caro. — es·taa mweeng·to kaa·ro

Can you lower the price?
Pode baixar o preço? — po·de bai·shaarr o pre·so

There's a mistake in the bill.
Houve um erro na conta. — o·ve oom e·ho naa kong·taa

ATM	caixa automático	kai·shaa ow·too·maa·tee·ko
credit card	cartão de crédito	kaarr·towng de kre·dee·to
post office	correio	ko·hay·o
tourist office	escritório de turismo	es·kree·to·ryo de too·rees·mo

TIME & DATES

What time is it?
Que horas são? — kee aw·raas sowng

It's (10) o'clock.
São (dez) horas. — sowng (des) aw·raas

Half past (10).
(Dez) e meia. — (des) e may·aa

morning	manhã	ma·nyang
afternoon	tarde	taar·de
evening	noite	noy·te
yesterday	ontem	ong·teng
today	hoje	o·zhe
tomorrow	amanhã	aa·ma·nyang

Question Words

How?	Como é que?	ko·mo e ke
What?	Que?	ke
When?	Quando?	kwang·do
Where?	Onde?	ong·de
Which?	Qual?/Quais? (sg/pl)	kwow/kais
Who?	Quem?	keng
Why?	Por que?	porr ke

Monday	segunda-feira	se·goong·daa·fay·ra
Tuesday	terça-feira	terr·saa·fay·raa
Wednesday	quarta-feira	kwaarr·taa·fay·raa
Thursday	quinta-feira	keeng·taa·fay·raa
Friday	sexta-feira	ses·taa·fay·raa
Saturday	sábado	saa·baa·do
Sunday	domingo	do·meeng·go

January	janeiro	zha·nay·ro
February	fevereiro	fe·ve·ray·ro
March	março	marr·so
April	abril	aa·bree·oo
May	maio	maa·yo
June	junho	zhoo·nyo
July	julho	zhoo·lyo
August	agosto	aa·gos·to
September	setembro	se·teng·bro
October	outubro	o·too·bro
November	novembro	no·veng·bro
December	dezembro	de·zeng·bro

TRANSPORTATION

boat	barco	baarr·ko
bus	ônibus	o·nee·boos
plane	avião	aa·vee·owng
train	trem	treng

a ... ticket	uma passagem de ...	oo·maa paa·sa·zheng de ...
1st-class	primeira classe	pree·may·raa klaa·se
2nd-class	segunda classe	se·goom·daa klaa·se
one-way	ida	ee·daa
return	ida e volta	ee·daa e vol·taa

What time does it leave/arrive?
A que horas sai/chega? aa ke aw·raas sai/she·gaa

Does it stop at ...?
Ele para em ...? e·le paa·raa eng ...

Please stop here.
Por favor pare aqui. poor faa·vorr paa·re aa·kee

bus stop	ponto de ônibus	pong·to de o·nee·boos
ticket office	bilheteria	bee·lye·te·ree·aa
timetable	horário	o·raa·ryo
train station	estação de trem	es·taa·sowng de treng

Numbers

1	um	oom
2	dois	doys
3	três	tres
4	quatro	kwaa·tro
5	cinco	seeng·ko
6	seis	says
7	sete	se·te
8	oito	oy·to
9	nove	naw·ve
10	dez	dez
20	vinte	veeng·te
30	trinta	treeng·taa
40	quarenta	kwaa·reng·taa
50	cinquenta	seen·kweng·taa
60	sessenta	se·seng·taa
70	setenta	se·teng·taa
80	oitenta	oy·teng·taa
90	noventa	no·veng·taa
100	cem	seng
1000	mil	mee·oo

I'd like to hire a ...	Gostaria de alugar ...	gos·taa·ree·aa de aa·loo·gaarr ...
bicycle	uma bicicleta	oo·maa bee·see·kle·taa
car	um carro	oom kaa·ho
motorcycle	uma motocicleta	oo·maa mo·to·see·kle·ta

bicycle pump	bomba de bicicleta	bong·baa de bee·see·kle·taa
helmet	capacete	kaa·paa·se·te
mechanic	mecânico	me·ka·nee·ko
petrol/gas	gasolina	gaa·zo·lee·naa
service station	posto de gasolina	pos·to de gaa·zo·lee·naa

Is this the road to ...?
Esta é a estrada para ...? es·taa e aa es·traa·daa paa·raa ...

(How long) Can I park here?
(Quanto tempo) Posso estacionar aqui? (kwang·to teng·po) po·so es·taa·syo·naarr aa·kee

I have a flat tyre.
Meu pneu furou. me·oo pee·ne·oo foo·ro

I've run out of petrol.
Estou sem gasolina. es·to seng ga·zoo·lee·naa

I've had an accident.
Sofri um acidente. so·free oom aa·see·deng·te

GLOSSARY

See p32 for more Carnaval terms.

açaí – juice made from an Amazonian berry

baía – bay

baile – dance party in the favelas

baile funk – dance, ball

bairro – neighborhood

baixo – popular area with lots of restaurants and bars

banda – street party

barraca – food stall

berimbau – stringed instrument used to accompany capoeira

bloco – see *banda*

bonde – tram

boteco – small neighborhood bar

botequim – bar with table service

cachaça – potent cane spirit

caipirinha – *cachaça* cocktail

Candomblé – religion of African origin

capoeira – Afro-Brazilian martial art

capela – chapel

carioca – resident of Rio

celular – cellular (mobile) phone

chope – draft beer

chorinho or **choro** – romantic, intimate samba

churrascaria – traditional barbecue restaurant

Cidade Maravilhosa – nickname for Rio de Janeiro (literally 'Marvelous City')

convento – convent

correios – post office

escola de samba – samba school

estrada – road

favela – shanty town

feijoada – black beans and pork stew

feira – open-air market

festa – party

forró – traditional fast-paced music from Northeast Brazil

frescobol – game played on the beach with two wooden racquets and a rubber ball

futebol – football (soccer)

futevôlei – volleyball played without the hands.

gafieira – dance club/dance hall

igreja – church

ilha – island

jardim – garden

lagoa – lake

largo – plaza

limão – lemon

livraria – bookshop

manioc – cassava

mar – sea

maracujá – passion fruit

maté – sweet iced tea

mirante – lookout

moqueca – seafood stew cooked in coconut milk

morro – mountain

mulatto – person of mixed black and white ancestry

museu – museum

onibus – bus

pagode – relaxed and rhythmic form of samba; first popularized in Rio in the 1970s

parque – park

posto – lifeguard station

pousada – guesthouse

praça – square

praia – beach

reais – plural of real

real – Brazil's unit of currency

rio – river

rodoviária – bus terminal

rua – street

salgados – bar snacks

sobreloja – above the store; first floor up

supermercado – supermarket

tacacá – a fragrant soup consisting of manioc paste, jambu leaves and fresh and dried shrimp

tambores – drums

Zona Norte – Northern Zone

Zona Sul – Southern Zone; specifically, the beach- and bay-side neighborhoods of Leblon, Ipanema, Copacabana, Botafogo, Flamengo and Glória.

Behind the Scenes

SEND US YOUR FEEDBACK

We love to hear from travelers – your comments keep us on our toes and help make our books better. Our well-traveled team reads every word on what you loved or loathed about this book. Although we cannot reply individually to your submissions, we always guarantee that your feedback goes straight to the appropriate authors, in time for the next edition. Each person who sends us information is thanked in the next edition – the most useful submissions are rewarded with a selection of digital PDF chapters.

Visit **lonelyplanet.com/contact** to submit your updates and suggestions or to ask for help. Our award-winning website also features inspirational travel stories, news and discussions.

Note: We may edit, reproduce and incorporate your comments in Lonely Planet products such as guidebooks, websites and digital products, so let us know if you don't want your comments reproduced or your name acknowledged. For a copy of our privacy policy visit lonelyplanet.com/privacy.

OUR READERS

Many thanks to the travelers who used the last edition and wrote to us with helpful hints, useful advice and interesting anecdotes:

Aaron Reichlin-Melnick, Charlie Kao, Hilton Silva do Nascimento, Hoffman Wolff, Ivy Krull, John Cantin, Stella Muller.

AUTHOR THANKS

Regis St Louis

Many thanks to new and old friends who helped with tips and advice. In particular I'd like to thank Cristiano Nogueira, Jakki Saysell, Alberto Armendáriz, Marcelo Esteves, Marcio Zaidan, Vitor Souza, Philip de Wit, Bindu Mathur, Thiago Mourão, Ian Papareskos, Eduardo Cruxen, and Kevin Raub. *Beijos* to Cassandra, Magdalena and Genevieve for joining me on the road.

ACKNOWLEDGEMENTS

Climate map data adapted from Peel MC, Finlayson BL & McMahon TA (2007) 'Updated World Map of the Köppen-Geiger Climate Classifcation', *Hydrology and Earth System Sciences*, 11, 163344.

Cover photograph: Copacabana Beach, Stuart Dee/Getty Images©

THIS BOOK

....

This 9th edition of Lonely Planet's *Rio de Janeiro* guidebook was researched and written by Regis St Louis. Regis also wrote the previous two editions. This guidebook was produced by the following:

Destination Editor
MaSovaida Morgan
Product Editor
Catherine Naghten
Senior Cartographer
Mark Griffiths
Book Designer
Wibowo Rusli
Assisting Editors
Carolyn Boicos, Gabrielle Innes, Susan Paterson

Cover Researcher
Naomi Parker
Thanks to Brendan Dempsey, Grace Dobell, Ryan Evans, Larissa Frost, Andi Jones, Kate Mathews, Wayne Murphy, Karyn Noble, Martine Power, Kirsten Rawlings, Luna Soo, Tony Wheeler

Index

See also separate subindexes for:

✗ **EATING P226**

♀ **DRINKING & NIGHTLIFE P227**

☆ **ENTERTAINMENT P228**

🔒 **SHOPPING P228**

🏃 **SPORTS & ACTIVITIES P228**

🛌 **SLEEPING P229**

A

accommodations 15, 163-76, see also Sleeping subindex
  Barra da Tijuca 176
  Botafogo 171-2
  Centro 173
  Copacabana 169-71
  favelas 174
  Flamengo 172-3
  Ipanema 166-9
  Jardim Botânico area 169
  language 215
  Lapa 175
  Leblon 169
  Leme 169-71
  love motels 166
  Praça Mauá 173
  Santa Teresa 173-5
  Urca 171-2
  western Rio 176
activities 18-19, 21, 49-51, see also individual activities, Sports & Activities subindex
air travel 204
Alto da Boa Vista 161
ambulance 210
AquaRio 128
architecture 19, 200-2
Arcos da Lapa 140
area codes 212
art galleries 19
ATMs 211

B

Babilônia 89
Bairro Peixoto 88
Barra da Tijuca 55, 155-62, **155**, **262**
  accommodations 176
  drinking & nightlife 160

Sights 000
Map Pages **000**
Photo Pages 000

entertainment 160-1
food 156, 157-60
highlights 12, 155
shopping 156, 161-2
sights 156, 157
sports & activities 162
transport 156
beaches 18, 74-5, 153, 160, **74-5**, see also individual beaches
Biblioteca Nacional 123
bicycle tours 207
bicycle travel 13, 205
boat tours 119, 162, 207
boat travel 205
bonde 139
books 178
  architecture 201
  football 196
  history 184
  music 191, 192, 193, 195
Bosque da Barra 157
bossa nova 192
Botafogo 13, 55, 99-107, **99**, **252**
  accommodations 171-2
  drinking & nightlife 100, 105-6
  entertainment 100, 106-7
  food 100, 103, 105
  highlights 9, 99
  shopping 107
  sights 102
  sports & activities 107
  transport 100
Botafogo football club 197
botecos 95
budget 14, 34
bus travel 204-5
business hours 34, 38, 44, 212

C

cable cars 101, 135, **135**
CADEG 153
Camboinhas 153
Campeonato Brasileiro 198

Campo de Santana 125
capoeira 50-1
car travel 206
Carnaval 7, 20, 26-32
  dates 27
  history 26-7
  tickets 30
Casa de Benjamin Constant 139
Casa do Pontal 157
Casa França-Brasil 126
Catedral Metropolitana 140
Catete 114-15, 116-18, 172, 174, **249**
caves 161
cell phones 14, 212-13
Centro 55, 120-33, **120**, **254**, **95**
  accommodations 173
  drinking & nightlife 121, 130, 132
  entertainment 132-3
  food 121, 128-30
  highlights 120, 122
  shopping 133
  sights 121, 122, 123-8
  transport 121, 126
  walks 131, **131**
Centro Carioca de Design 124
Centro Cultural Banco do Brasil 126
Centro Cultural Correios 126
Centro Cultural Justiça Federal 123
Centro Cultural Laurinda Santos Lobo 139
Centro Cultural Oi Futuro 114
Centro de Arte Hélio Oiticica 124
Chapéu Mangueira 89
chemists 211
children, travel with 24-5
Christ the Redeemer, see Cristo Redentor
churches, see individual churches

Cidade do Samba 153
Cinelândia 123-4, 128-9, 131, 132, 133, **254**
cinema, see films
cinemas 42
classical music 40-1
climate 15, 20-3
clubs 37-9, see also Drinking & Nightlife subindex
Coelho, Gonçalo 180
Colônia dos Pescadores 88
Complexo do Alemão 152, **135**
Conselheiro, Antônio 186
consulates 210
cooking courses 209
Copa Libertadores 198
Copacabana 9, 13, 55, 85-98, **85**, **244**
  accommodations 169-71
  drinking & nightlife 86, 93, 96
  entertainment 96-7
  food 86, 88-93
  highlights 9, 85, 87
  shopping 86, 97-8
  sights 87, 88
  sports & activities 98
  transport 86
Copacabana Beach 9, 87, **3**, **8**, **75**, **87**
Corcovado 112-13, **108**
Cosme Velho 114, 116, 172-3, **250**
costs 14
  drinking & nightlife 38, 44
  food 34
  free attractions 19
  sleeping 163, 164
courses
  cooking 209
  dance 45, 98, 107, 146-7
  language 209
  music 118-19, 209
credit cards 211
Cristo Redentor 10, 112-13, **3**, **10**, **5**, **112**

INDEX C-L

culture 178-9
currency 14, 209
cycling 109, *see also* bicycle tours, bicycle travel

D
dance 40
classes 45, 98, 107, 146-7
dance halls 145
dangers, *see* safety
day spas 73, 84
disabilities, travelers with 213
diving 73, 119
Dom João VI 181, 183
Dom Pedro I 182
Dom Pedro II 185
drinking & nightlife 37-9, *see also individual neighborhoods*, Drinking & Nightlife *subindex*
language 218
driving, *see* car travel

E
economy 178-9
electricity 210
Elevador do Morro do Cantagalo 59
embassies 210
emergencies 210
language 218
entertainment 40-2, *see also individual neighborhoods*, Entertainment *subindex*
Escadaria Selarón 138, **138**
Espaço Tom Jobim 79
etiquette 34, 75
events 20-3

F
favelas 13, 61, 89, 135, 152, 187, **134-5**
accommodations 174
history 186, 189
pacification 189-90
tours 207-8
feijoada 35
Feira Nordestina 152
ferries 205
festivals 7, 20-3, *see also individual festivals*

Sights 000
Map Pages **000**
Photo Pages **000**

films 41, 113, 178, 188
fire department 210
Flamengo 55, 110-19, **110**, **250**
accommodations 172-3
drinking & nightlife 111, 117-18
entertainment 111, 118
food 111, 115-16
highlights 10, 110, 112-13
shopping 118
sights 112-13, 114
sports & activities 118-19
transport 111
Flamengo football club 196
Floresta da Tijuca 12, 161, 159, **12**, **159**
Fluminense football club 197
food 13, 33-6, *see also individual neighborhoods*, Eating *subindex*
costs 34
language 216
tours 146
football 11, 50, 150-1, 196-9
Forte de Copacabana 88
Forte Duque de Caxias 88
free attractions 19
frescobol 75
Fundação Eva Klabin 80
Fundição Progresso 140
futevôlei 75, **75**

G
gafieiras 145
GaleRio 102
gardens 19, *see also individual gardens*
'Garota de Ipanema, the' 67
Gávea 55, 76-84, **76**, **242**
drinking & nightlife 77, 82-3, **94**
food 77, 81
highlights 12, 76
shopping 77, 83-4
sights 79
sports & activities 84
transport 77
gay travelers 38, 210
Gil, Gilberto 193
Gilberto, João 67, 192
'Girl from Ipanema' 67
Glória 115, 117, 119, 166, **249**
gold mining 182
Guanabara people 180-1

H
H Stern 59
hang gliding 50, 109, **108**
health 214
helicopter tours 208
hiking 49, 109, **108-9**
hip-hop music 194-5
historical sites 19, 183
history 180-90
19th century 183-5
20th century 187-9
Belle Époque 185-6
Carnaval 26-7
Cristo Redentor 113
favelas 186, 189-90
indigenous peoples 180-1
military dictatorship 188
Portuguese colonization 180-1, 182
slavery 181-2
hospitals 211
Humaitá 13, 55, 99-107, **99**, **252**
drinking & nightlife 100, 105-6
entertainment 100
food 100, 103, 105
highlights 9, 99
sights 102
transport 100

I
Igreja da Penha 153
Igreja de Nossa Senhora da Glória do Outeiro 115
Igreja de Nossa Senhora de Candelária 126
Igreja de Nossa Senhora do Carmo da Antiga Sé 125
Igreja de Nossa Senhora do Rosário e São Benedito 124
Igreja São Francisco da Penitência & Convento de Santo Antônio 124
Ilha de Paquetá 125
Ilha Fiscal 25, 127, **24**
indigenous peoples 180-1
Instituto Moreira Salles 79
internet access 210-11
Ipanema 7, 55, 56-73, **56**, **236**
accommodations 166-9
drinking & nightlife 57, 66-9
entertainment 70
food 57, 59-64
highlights 7, 56, 58

shopping 57, 70-2
sights 58, 59
sports & activities 72-3
transport 57
Ipanema Beach 7, 58, **7**, **53**, **58**, **74-5**
Itacoatiara 153
Itaipu 153
itineraries 16-17, *see also* walks

J
Jardim Botânico 79, 159, **18**, **158-9**
Jardim Botânico area 55, 76-84, **76**, **242**
accommodations 169
drinking & nightlife 77, 83
food 77, 81
highlights 12, 76
shopping 77, 83-4
sights 79-80
sports & activities 84
transport 77
Jardim Zoológico 152
Jobim, Antônio Carlos (Tom) 67, 192
juices 34

K
kayaking 51
kiosks 92

L
Lagoa 55, 76-84, **76**, **242**
drinking & nightlife 77, 83, 95
entertainment 83
food 77, 82
highlights 12, 76, 78
shopping 77
sights 78, 80
sports & activities 84
transport 77
Lagoa Rodrigo de Freitas 12, 78, **12**, **78**
language 14, 215-19
courses 209
Lapa 136-47, **136**, **258**, **9**, **94**
accommodations 175
drinking & nightlife 9, 95, 137, 143
entertainment 137, 144-6
food 137, 141-2
highlights 136, 138
safety 44

shopping 146
sights 138, 140
sports & activities 146-7
transport 137
Laranjeiras 116, 117, 118-19, **250**
Largo das Neves 139
Largo do Boticário 114
Largo do Guimarães 139
Leblon 55, 56-73, **56**, **240**
accommodations 169
drinking & nightlife 57, 69-70
entertainment 70
food 57, 64-6
highlights 56
shopping 57, 72
sights 59
sports & activities 72-3
transport 57
legal matters 211
Leme 55, 85-98, **85**, **248**
accommodations 169-71
drinking & nightlife 86, 93-6
entertainment 96-7
food 86, 93
highlights 9, 85
shopping 86, 97-8
sights 88
sports & activities 98
transport 86
lesbian travelers 38, 210
literature, *see* books
love motels 166

M
magazines 209
Maracanã Football Stadium 11, 50, 150-1, **11**, **150**
markets 35, 47, 70, 88, 146, 152, 153, *see also* Shopping *subindex*
measures 209
medical services 211
metro 13, 206
metrô na superfície 206
Mirante do Leblon 59
Mirante do Pasmado 102
mobile phones 14, 212-13
money 14, 209, 211
drinking & nightlife 38, 44
food 34
free attractions 19
sleeping 163, 164
Moraes, Vinícius de 67
Morro da Babilônia 89

Morro da Conceição 128
Morro da Providência 125
Mosteiro de São Bento 128
motorcycle travel 206
Mural de Babilônia 89
Museu Amsterdam Sauer 59
Museu Casa de Rui Barbosa 102
Museu Chácara do Céu 139
Museu da República 114
Museu de Arte do Rio 127
Museu de Arte Moderna 123
Museu de Folclore Edison Carneiro 115
Museu do Amanhã 128
Museu do Arte Contemporânea 127
Museu do Imagem e Som 88
Museu do Índio 102
Museu do Meio Ambiente 80
Museu do Primeiro Reinado 152
Museu Histórico Nacional 122, **122**
Museu Internacional de Arte Naïf do Brasil 114
Museu Nacional 152
Museu Nacional de Belas Artes 123
Museu Naval 126
Museu Villa-Lobos 102
music 40, 67, 191-5
courses 118-19, 209
Música Popular Brasileira 42, 193-4

N
Napoleon Bonaparte 183
newspapers 209
Niemeyer, Oscar 201
nightlife 37-9, *see also individual neighborhoods*, Drinking & Nightlife *subindex*
Niterói 127
notable buildings 19, 183, 201

O
Olympics 190
opening hours 34, 38, 44, 212
outdoor activities 18-19, *see also individual activities*, Sports & Activities *subindex*

P
Paço Imperial 125
paddleboarding 51, 98, 107
Palácio Tiradentes 127
Pão de Açúcar 9, 101, **3**, **8**, **101**, **108**
parks 19, *see also individual parks*
Parque da Catacumba 80
Parque da Cidade 79
Parque das Ruínas 139
Parque do Catete 115, 159
Parque do Flamengo 114, 159
Parque do Marapendi 157
Parque Ecológico Chico Mendes 157
Parque Garota de Ipanema 59
Parque Guinle 115
Parque Lage 80
Parque Nacional da Tijuca 161
Parque Olímpico 157
Passeio Público 123
Pelé 198
pharmacies 211
Pinheiro, Helô 67
Piratininga 153
Pista Cláudio Coutinho 102
Planetário 79
planning
budgeting 34
children, travel with 24-5
festivals & events 20-3
free attractions 19
itineraries 16-17
repeat visitors 13
Rio de Janeiro basics 14-15
Rio de Janeiro's neighborhoods 54-5
travel seasons 15, 20-3
police 210
politics 178-9
Ponta do Arpoador 59
Ponte Rio-Niterói 127
pop music 194-5
population 179
port redevelopment 124, 178
Portuguese language 215-19
Portuguese colonization 180-1, 182
postal services 212
Praça Floriano 123
Praça Mauá 13, 55, 120-33, **120**, **254**
accommodations 173
drinking & nightlife 121

food 121, 130
highlights 120, 122
sights 121, 122, 127-8
transport 121
Praça Tiradentes 124-5, 129
Praça XV (Quinze) de Novembro 125
Praça XV (Quinze) de Novembro area 125-7, 129-30
Praia da Barra da Tijuca 157, **108**
Praia da Joatinga 160
Praia da Prainha 160
Praia da Urca 103
Praia de Botafogo 102
Praia de Grumari 160
Praia de Guaratiba 160
Praia de Leblon 59
Praia do Pepino 160
Praia Vermelha 103

Q
Quinta da Boa Vista 152
quiosques 92

R
Real Gabinete Português de Leitura 124
religion 179
Restinga da Marambaia 160
Rio Folia 31
rock climbing 49-50, 109, **108**
rock music 194-5

S
safety 15, 44, 212
samba 31, 32, 43-6, 191-2, **94**
classes 98, 107, 146-7
schools 28, 31, 45
Sambódromo 30-1, 153, **26**, **29**
Santa Marta favela 135, **134-5**
Santa Teresa 10, 55, 136-47, **136**, **258**
accommodations 173-5
drinking & nightlife 137, 142-3
entertainment 137, 144-6
food 137, 140-1
highlights 10, 136, 138
shopping 146
sights 138, 139
sports & activities 146-7
transport 137

Seixas, Raul 195
Selarón, Jorge 138
shopping 47-8, *see also individual neighborhoods,* Shopping *subindex*
language 218
Sítio Burle Marx 157, 159
slavery 181-2
smoking 209
soccer, *see* football
sports 49-51, *see also* Sports & Activities *subindex*
stand-up paddleboarding 51, 98, 107
statues 112-13
streetcars 13
Sugarloaf Mountain, *see* Pão de Açúcar
surfing 50, 51, 109, **74, 109**

T
taxes 164
taxis 206-7
Teatro Popular 127
telephone services 212-13
theater 40
Theatro Municipal 123
time 14, 213
tipping 34, 211
tourist information 14, 213
tours 207-8, *see also* boat tours, food tours, walking tours
train travel 13, 126, 206
trams 207
transportation 204-8
language 219
travel to Rio de Janeiro 15, 204-5
travel within Rio de Janeiro 15, 205-7
Travessa do Comércio 126
trekking, *see* hiking
tropicália 192
Tupinambá people 180-1

U
Urca 55, 99-107, **99, 252**
accommodations 171-2
drinking & nightlife 100, 106

Sights 000
Map Pages **000**
Photo Pages **000**

entertainment 100, 106-7
food 100, 105
highlights 9, 99, 101
sights 101, 102-3
transport 100
walking tours 104, **104**

V
vans 206
Vargas, Getúlio 187-8
Vasco da Gama football club 197
vegetarian travelers 36
Vidigal 61, 70, 166, 168, 174
visas 14, 213-14
VLT 13, 126
volunteering 214

W
walking tours 49, 146, 208
walks
Centro 131, **131**
Urca 104, **104**
waterfalls 161
weather 15, 20-3
websites 14, 164
accommodations 15
weights 209
western Rio 55, 155-62, **155, 262**
accommodations 176
beaches 160
food 156, 157, 160
highlights 12, 155
shopping 156, 161-2
sights 156, 157
sports & activities 162
transport 156
wi-fi 210-11
women travelers 214
World Cup 150-1, 199

Z
Zika virus 214
Zona Norte 55, 148-54, **148, 261**
entertainment 149, 154
food 149, 153-4
highlights 11, 148, 150-1
sights 149, 150-1, 152-3
transport 149
zoos 152

✗ EATING

A
Aconchego Carioca 153
Al Farabi 129
AlbaMar 130
Alessandro E Federico 62
Alquimia 140
Amazônia Soul 62
Amir 91
Angu do Gomes 130
Antonia Casa e Cafe 89
Aprazível 141
Arab 90
Arab da Lagoa 82
Arataca 91
Armazém do Café 64
Azteka 62
Azumi 92

B
Bakers 91
Bar Brasil 142
Bar do David 89
Bar do Mineiro 141
Bar Urca 105
Barsa 153
Bazzar 64
Bibi Crepes 64
Bibi Sucos 90
Bira 160
Bistrô do Paço 129
Borogodó 81
Boua Kitchen & Bar 103
Boulangerie Guerin 88
Braseiro 90
Braseiro da Gávea 81
Brasileirinho 63
Brasserie Rosário 129
Bráz 81
Brigite's 66

C
Café Arlequim 129
Cafe Colombo 91
Cafe do Alto 141
Café do Bom Cachaça Da Boa 129
Cafecito 140
Cafeína 60
Cais do Oriente 130
Cantinho Cearense 92
Capricciosa 63, 91
Cariocando 116
Casa da Feijoada 64
Casa da Suíça 117

Casa Momus 142
Casa Paladino 129
Catete Grill 117
Cedro do Líbano 129
Cervantes 90
Churrascaria Palace 92
Confeitaria Colombo 129
Crepe Nouveau Art 129
CT Boucherie 65
CT Trattorie 82

D
Da Gema 154
Da Silva 128
Delírio Tropical 60
Devassa 91
Don Camillo 92
Don Pascual 160

E
El Born 90
Emporium Pax 103
Ernesto 142
Espaço 7zero6 64
Espaço Lapa Cafe 141
Espetto Carioca 92
Espírito Santa 141

F
Faraj 90
Felice Caffè 62
Fellini 65
Ferro e Farinha 116
Formidable 66
Forneria São Sebastião 62
Frontera 62

G
Galeria 1618 93
Galeto Sat's 89
Galitos Grill 60
Garota da Urca 105
Garota de Ipanema 63, **94**
Globo 92
Govinda 128
Gringo Cafe 63
Guimas 81
Gula Gula 63

H
Hortifruti 64

I
Imaculada 130
Intihuasi 116

J

Joaquina 93
Jojö 81
Juice Co 65
Julius Brasserie 105

K

Koni Store 60, 90
Kurt 64

L

La Bicyclette 81
La Carioca Cevicheria 62, 82
La Fiorentina 93
La Trattoria 91
La Veronese 60
Laffa 60
Lagoon 82
Laguna Restaurante 157
Largo das Letras 140
Lasai 105
L'Atelier du Cuisinier 130
Le Blé Noir 91
Le Depanneur 103
Livraria Prefácio 103
Luigi's 116

M

Mangue Seco
   Cachaçaria 142
Meza Bar 103
Miam Miam 103
Mike's Haus 141
Mil Frutas 60
Mironga 130
Mônaco 91

N

Nam Thai 66
Nanquim 116
Nega Teresa 140
New Natural 63
Nonna Ridolfi 89
Nova Capela 142

O

O Rei das Empanadas 90
Olympe 82
Oui Oui 103

P

Papa Gui 63
PLage Cafe 81
Prana Vegetariano 116
Prima Bruschetteria 65

R

Rancho Inn 130
Ráscal 65
Restaurante a Floresta 161
Restaurante Kioto 116
Restaurante Naturaleve 90
Restaurante Os Esquilos 161
Restaurante Quinta
   da Boa Vista 154
Rústico 140

S

Santa Satisfação 91
Santo Scenarium 142
Shirley 93
Simon Boccanegra 92
Sírio Libaneza 116
Stuzzi 65
Sushi Leblon 66

T

Taberna da Glória 117
Tacacá do Norte 115
Talho Capixaba 65
Temporada 63
Térèze 141
Terzetto Cafe 62
TT Burger 90

U

Uruguai 60

V

Vegetariano Social Club 65
Venga! 62
Vero 60
Vezpa 60, 64
Via Sete 61
Volta 81

Y

Yalla 65

Z

Zazá Bistrô Tropical 64
Zona Sul Supermarket 64
Zot 91
Zuka 66

🍷 **DRINKING &
NIGHTLIFE**

00 (Zero Zero) 82

A

Academia Da Cachaça 69
Adega Portugália 117

Alto Vidigal 70
Amarelinho 132
Anexo Bar 143
Antônio's 143
Armazém do Chopp 118
As Melhores Cervejas
   do Mundo 96

B

Bar Astor 67
Bar Bukowski 106
Bar do Alto 89
Bar do Gomes 143
Bar do Horto 83
Bar do Serafim 117
Bar do Zé 117
Bar dos Descasados 142
Bar Lagoa 83
Bar Urca 106
Bar Veloso 69
Baretto-Londra 68
Barthodomeu 68
Barzin 67
Belmonte 69, 117
Bibi Sucos 68
Blue Agave 68
Botequim Informal 96
Bracarense 69
Brewteco 69
Buraco da Lacraia 143

C

Cabaret Lounge 105
Calavera 106
Canastra 66
Casa da Matriz 106
Caverna 105
Champanharia Ovelha
   Negra 106
Cobal do Humaitá 106
Cobal do Leblon 69
Complex Esquina 111 66
Comuna 105
Crazy Cats 105

D

Delirium Cafe 68
Devassa 68, 117

E

Empório 67
Escondido 93
Espírito do Chopp 106
Estrelas da Babilônia 89

F

Fosfobox 96

G

Galeria Café 69
Garota da Urca 106
Garota de Ipanema 68, **94**
Goya-Beira 143

H

Herr Brauer 117
Hipódromo 82

J

Jazz In Champanheria 132
Jobi 69

L

La Paz 143
Le Boy 96
Leviano Bar 143
Lord Jim 68

M

Mais Que Nada 96
Mud Bug 96
Nuth 160

O

O Plebeu 106

P

Palaphita Gávea 82
Palaphita Kitch 83
Pavão Azul 96
Pizzaria Guanabara 69
Polis Sucos 68
Ponto da Bossa Nova 93

S

Samba Caffe 132
Sarau 143
Shenanigan's 68
Sindicato do Chopp 93

T

Tô Nem Aí 69
TV Bar 96

U

Usina 70

V

Vaca Atolada 143

W

Week 132

☆ ENTERTAINMENT

B
Beco das Garrafas 97
Beco do Rato 145
Bip Bip 96

C
Carioca da Gema 144
Casa da Cultura
    Laura Alvim 70
Centro Cultural Carioca 133
Centro Cultural
    Oi Futuro 118
Cidade das Artes 160
Cine Santa Teresa 146
Cinema Leblon 70
Circo Voador 144
Citibank Hall 161

D
Democráticus 144

E
Espaço Museu
    Da República 118
Espaço SESC 97
Estação Net Botafogo 107
Estação Net Ipanema 70
Estação Net Rio 106
Estudantina Musical 132

F
Fundição Progresso 146

G
Ginga Tropical 132

L
Lapa 40 Graus 144

M
Maze Inn 118
Miranda 83

O
Odeon Petrobras 132

P
Paiol 08 145
Pedra do Sal 132

Sights 000
Map Pages 000
Photo Pages **000**

R
Renascença Clube 154
Rio Scenarium 144, **94**

S
Sacrilégio 144
Sala Cecília Meireles 146
Sala Municipal
    Baden Powell 97
Semente 144
Severyna de
    Laranjeiras 118

T
Teatro do Leblon 70
Teatro Odisséia 145
Teatro Rival
    Petrobras 133
Terra Brasilis 106
Theatro Municipal 133
Trapiche Gamboa 132
TribOz 144

U
UCI - New York City Center
    161

V
Vinícius Show Bar 70

🍷 SHOPPING

10Aquim 71

A
Amsterdam Sauer 72
Antonio Bernardo 72
Argumento 72
Arlequim 133

B
Baratos de Ribeiro 107
Barra Shopping 162
Berinjela
Bossa Nova
    & Companhia 97
Botafogo Praia
    Shopping 107
Brecho de Salto Alto 97

C
Casa Ipanema 71
Casa Oliveira 133
Catherine Labouré 71
Comparsaria 107

D
Dona Coisa 83
Draco Store 98

E
Esch Café 72
Espaço Fashion 72

F
Fashion Mall 162
Feira do Rio Antigo 146
Forum 71

G
Gabinete 83
Galeria Monique
    Paton 133
Galeria River 97
Garota de Ipanema 71
Gilson Martins 70, 97
Granado 133

H
H Stern 72
Havaianas 72, 98
Hippie Fair 70

I
Índio e Arte 107
Isabela Capeto 84

L
La Vereda
    Handicrafts 146
Lapa Decor 146
Lidador 71
Livraria da Travessa 71,
    107, 133
Loja Fla 97

M
Maracatu Brasil 118
Maria Oiticica 72
Mundo Verde 98
Musicale 98

O
O Sol 83
Osklen 71
Osklen Surfing 97

P
Pé de Boi 118

R
Redley 71
Rio Design Center 162
Rio Sul Shopping 107

S
Scenarium Antique 146
Shopping da Gávea 84
Shopping Leblon 72
Shopping Siqueira
    Campos 98
Sobral 133

T
Toca do Vinícius 71
Tucum 146

V
Via Parque Shopping 162
Village 161

W
Wöllner Outdoor 71

Z
Zimpy 98

🏃 SPORTS & ACTIVITIES

B
Barra Water Shuttle 162
Blyss Yôga 73
Body Tech 73

C
Casa de Dança Carlinhos
    de Jesus 107
Climb in Rio 50
Crux Ecoadventure 50

D
Delta Flight in Rio 50
Dive Point 73

E
Eat Rio Food Tours 146
Escolinha de Vôlei 73

F
Fruit Brazil 72
Fundição Progresso 147

J

Joquei Clube 84
Jungle Me 49
Just Fly 50

L

Lagoa Aventuras 84

M

Maracatu Brasil 118
Mar do Rio 119

N

Nirvana 84
Núcleo de Dança Renata
    Peçanha 147

R

Rio Adventures 161
Rio Hiking 49, 161
Rio Natural 49
Rio Samba Dancer 98

S

Sail in Rio 119
Spa Maria Bonita 73
Spirit Surfboards 98
Surf Rio 98

T

Tandem Fly 50

Y

Yoga Bhumi 98

🛏 **SLEEPING**

A

Acapulco 171
Ace Hostel 172

Aparthotel Adagio 168
Arpoador Inn 167

B

Babilônia Rio Hostel 174
Blame It on Rio
    4 Travel 170
Bonita 167
Books Hostel 175
Brothers Hostel 172

C

Cabana Copa 169
Caesar Park 168
Cama e Café 173
Casa Áurea 173
Casa Beleza 173
Casa Bianca 175
Casa Caminho do
    Corcovado 172
Casa Cool Beans 175
Casa da Carmen e do
    Fernando 173
Casa da Gente 173
Casa Mosquito 167
Casalegre 174
Castelinho 38 175
Che Lagarto 170
Che Lagarto Ipanema 166
Che Lagarto - Suites
    Santa Clara 170
Copacabana Palace 171

D

Discovery Hostel 172
Don Pascual 176

E

Edificio Jucati 170

G

Golden Tulip Ipanema
    Plaza 168

H

Hostel Harmonia 166
Hotel Fasano 168
Hotel Praia Ipanema 168
Hotel Santa Clara 170
Hotel Santa Teresa 175
Hotelinho Urca 172

I

Ibis 172
Injoy Hostel 172
Ipanema Beach
    House 167
Ipanema For Rent 167
Ipanema Hotel
    Residência 167
Ipanema Inn 167

L

Leblon Spot Design
    Hostel 169
Lemon Spirit Hostel 169
Lighthouse Hostel 167
Love Time 166

M

Mama Ruisa 175
Mango Tree 167
Mar Ipanema 168
Margarida's Pousada 167
Marina All Suites 169
Marina Palace 169
Maze Inn 174
Mercure Arpoador 171
Mirante do Arvrão 174

O

O Veleiro 172
Olinda Rio 170
Orla Copacabana 171
Oztel 172

P

Pestana Rio Atlântica 171
Pop Art Hostel 173
Porto Bay Rio
    Internacional 171
Pousada Favelinha 174
Pouso Verde 169
Pura Vida 170

R

Rio Apartments 170
Rio Design Hotel 171
Rio Guesthouse 171
Rio Hostel 173
Rio Hostel - Ipanema 166
Rio Spot Homes 170
Rio Surf 'N Stay 176
Ritz Plaza Hotel 169

S

Shalimar 166
Sheraton 168
Sofitel Rio de Janeiro 171
Sol Ipanema 168
Solar do Cosme 173

U

Utrópico 176

V

Varandas do Vidigal 174
Vidigalbergue 174
Vila Carioca 171
Vila Galé 175
Villa Laurinda 175
Vips 166
Visconti 168

W

Walk on the Beach
    Hostel 170

Rio de Janeiro Maps

Sights

- Beach
- Bird Sanctuary
- Buddhist
- Castle/Palace
- Christian
- Confucian
- Hindu
- Islamic
- Jain
- Jewish
- Monument
- Museum/Gallery/Historic Building
- Ruin
- Shinto
- Sikh
- Taoist
- Winery/Vineyard
- Zoo/Wildlife Sanctuary
- Other Sight

Activities, Courses & Tours

- Bodysurfing
- Diving
- Canoeing/Kayaking
- Course/Tour
- Sento Hot Baths/Onsen
- Skiing
- Snorkeling
- Surfing
- Swimming/Pool
- Walking
- Windsurfing
- Other Activity

Sleeping

- Sleeping
- Camping

Eating

- Eating

Drinking & Nightlife

- Drinking & Nightlife
- Cafe

Entertainment

- Entertainment

Shopping

- Shopping

Information

- Bank
- Embassy/Consulate
- Hospital/Medical
- Internet
- Police
- Post Office
- Telephone
- Toilet
- Tourist Information
- Other Information

Geographic

- Beach
- Gate
- Hut/Shelter
- Lighthouse
- Lookout
- Mountain/Volcano
- Oasis
- Park
- Pass
- Picnic Area
- Waterfall

Population

- Capital (National)
- Capital (State/Province)
- City/Large Town
- Town/Village

Transport

- Airport
- Border crossing
- Bus
- Cable car/Funicular
- Cycling
- Ferry
- Metro station
- Monorail
- Parking
- Petrol station
- Subway/Subte station
- Taxi
- Train station/Railway
- Tram
- Underground station
- Other Transport

Note: Not all symbols displayed above appear on the maps in this book

Routes

- Tollway
- Freeway
- Primary
- Secondary
- Tertiary
- Lane
- Unsealed road
- Road under construction
- Plaza/Mall
- Steps
- Tunnel
- Pedestrian overpass
- Walking Tour
- Walking Tour detour
- Path/Walking Trail

Boundaries

- International
- State/Province
- Disputed
- Regional/Suburb
- Marine Park
- Cliff
- Wall

Hydrography

- River, Creek
- Intermittent River
- Canal
- Water
- Dry/Salt/Intermittent Lake
- Reef

Areas

- Airport/Runway
- Beach/Desert
- Cemetery (Christian)
- Cemetery (Other)
- Glacier
- Mudflat
- Park/Forest
- Sight (Building)
- Sportsground
- Swamp/Mangrove

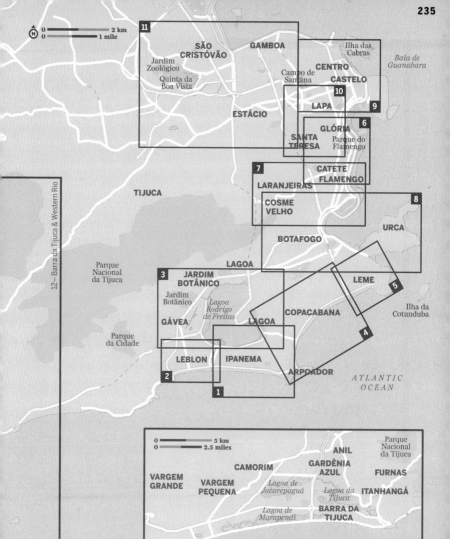

MAP INDEX

1 Ipanema (p236)

2 Leblon (p240)

3 Gávea, Jardim Botânico & Lagoa (p242)

4 Copacabana (p244)

5 Leme (p248)

6 Catete & Glória (p249)

7 Flamengo, Laranjeiras & Cosme Velho (p250)

8 Botafogo, Humaitá & Urca (p252)

9 Centro & Cinelândia (p254)

10 Santa Teresa & Lapa (p258)

11 Zona Norte (p261)

12 Barra da Tijuca & Western Rio (p262)

IPANEMA

Key on p238

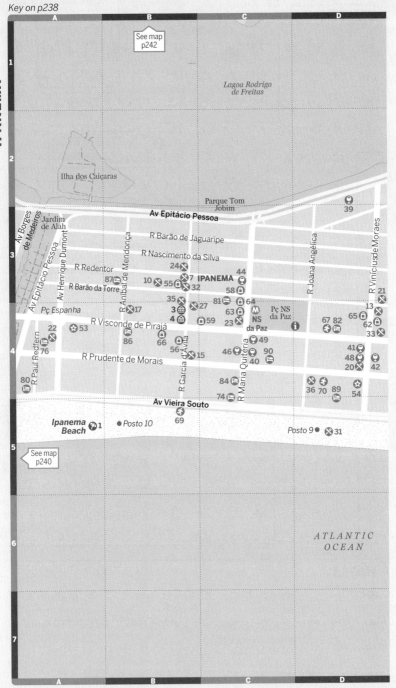

See map p242

Lagoa Rodrigo de Freitas

Ilha dos Caiçaras

Parque Tom Jobim

39

Av Epitácio Pessoa

Av Borges de Medeiros

Jardim de Alah

Av Epitácio Pessoa

Av Henrique Dumont

R Barão de Jaguaripe

R Nascimento da Silva

R Redentor

R Anibal de Mendonça

24

R Barão da Torre

87 10 55 32 7 IPANEMA 44

R Joana Angélica

R Viniciusde Moraes

58

R 21

Pç Espanha

35 81 64 13

3 27

17 4 59 23 63 M NS da Paz Pc NS da Paz 67 82 65 62

R Visconde de Pirajá

22 53 86 66 56 15 49 90 40 41 48 20 42

R Prudente de Morais

R Garcia d'Ávila

R Maria Quitéria

46

80 76

84 36 70 89 54

74

Av Vieira Souto

69

Ipanema Beach 1 Posto 10

Posto 9 31

See map p240

ATLANTIC OCEAN

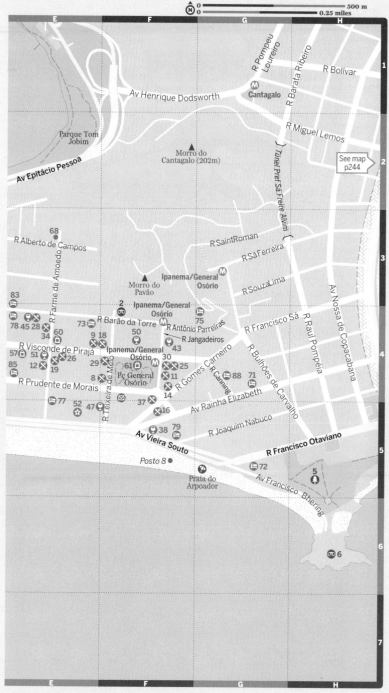

0 500 m
0 0.25 miles

R Pompeu Loureiro
R Barata Ribeiro
R Bolívar
Av Henrique Dodsworth
Cantagalo
R Miguel Lemos
Parque Tom Jobim
Av Epitácio Pessoa
Morro do Cantagalo (202m)

See map p244

R Alberte de Campos
68
R Farme de Amoedo
R SaintRoman
R Sá Ferreira
Morro do Pavão
Ipanema/General Osório
R SouzaLima
83
Av Nossa de Copacabana
Ipanema/General Osório
R Barão da Torre
75
78 45 28
73
R Antônio Parreiras
R Francisco Sá
R Raul Pompéia
34
60
9 18
50
R Jangadeiros
R Visconde de Pirajá
57
51
26
Ipanema/General Osório
43
85
12
19
30
25
R Bulhões de Carvalho
29
11
R Gomes Carneiro
88
71
8
61
R Canning
R Prudente de Morais
14
R Teixeira de Melo
77
52
47
37
16
Av Rainha Elizabeth
38
79
R Joaquim Nabuco
Av Vieira Souto
R Francisco Otaviano
Posto 8
72
5
Praia do Arpoador
Av Francisco Bhering
6

IPANEMA *Map on p236*

⊙ Top Sights — p58
1 Ipanema Beach A5

⊙ Sights — p59
2 Elevador do Morro do Cantagalo F4
3 H Stern B4
4 Museu Amsterdam Sauer B4
5 Parque Garota de Ipanema H5
6 Ponta do Arpoador H6

✖ Eating — p59
7 Alessandro E Federico B3
8 Amazônia Soul F4
9 Azteka E4
10 Bazzar B3
11 Brasileirinho F4
12 Cafeína E4
13 Capricciosa D4
14 Casa da Feijoada F4
15 Delírio Tropical B4
   Espaço 7zero6 .... (see 80)
16 Felice Caffè F5
17 Forneria São Sebastião B4
18 Frontera F4
19 Galitos Grill E4
20 Garota de Ipanema D4
21 Gringo Cafe D3
22 Gula Gula A4
23 Koni Store C4
24 La Carioca Cevicheria B3
25 La Veronese F4
26 Laffa E4
27 Mil Frutas B4
28 New Natural E4
29 Papa Gui F4
   Temporada .... (see 72)
30 Terzetto Cafe F4
31 Uruguai D5
32 Venga! B3
33 Vero D4
34 Vezpa E4
35 Via Sete B3
36 Zazá Bistrô Tropical D4
37 Zona Sul Supermarket F4

⊙ Drinking & Nightlife — p66
38 Bar Astor F5
39 Bar Lagoa D2
   Baretto-Londra .... (see 79)
40 Barthodomeu C4
41 Barzin D4
42 Blue Agave D4
43 Canastra F4
44 Complex Esquina 111 .... C3
45 Delirium Cafe E4
   Devassa .... (see 86)
46 Empório C4
47 Galeria Café F5

IPANEMA

48 Garota de Ipanema.....................................D4
   Lord Jim ....(see 76)
49 Polis Sucos C4
50 Shenanigan's..F4
51 Tô Nem Aí E4

⭐ **Entertainment** **p70**
52 Casa da Cultura Laura
   Alvim..E5
53 Estação Net Ipanema...............................A4
54 Vinícius Show Bar......................................D4

🛍 **Shopping** **p70**
55 10Aquim...B3
   Amsterdam Sauer ....(see 4)
   Antonio Bernardo ....(see 35)
56 Casa Ipanema B4
57 Catherine Labouré....................................E4
58 Forum...C3
   Garota de Ipanema.........................(see 48)
59 Gilson Martins C4
   H Stern ....(see 3)
60 Havaianas E4
61 Hippie Fair...F4
62 Lidador...D4
63 Osklen..C4
64 Redley...C4
65 Toca do Vinícius...D4
66 Wöllner Outdoor B4

🏆 **Sports & Activities** **p72**
67 Blyss Yôga...D4
68 Casa do Caminho Language
   Centre E3
69 Escolinha de Vôlei B5
70 Spa Maria Bonita.......................................D4

🛏 **Sleeping** **p166**
71 Aparthotel Adagio.....................................G4
72 Arpoador Inn...G5
73 Bonita...E4
74 Caesar Park..C4
75 Casa Mosquito...G4
76 Che Lagarto Ipanema A4
77 Golden Tulip Ipanema Plaza....................E5
78 Hostel Harmonia E4
79 Hotel Fasano..F5
80 Hotel Praia Ipanema A4
81 Ipanema Beach House C3
82 Ipanema For Rent......................................D4
83 Ipanema Hotel Residência........................E4
84 Ipanema Inn...C4
   Lighthouse Hostel ....(see 78)
85 Mango Tree..E4
86 Mar Ipanema..B4
87 Margarida's Pousada.................................B3
88 Rio Hostel – Ipanema G4
89 Sol Ipanema D5
90 Visconti..C4

LEBLON

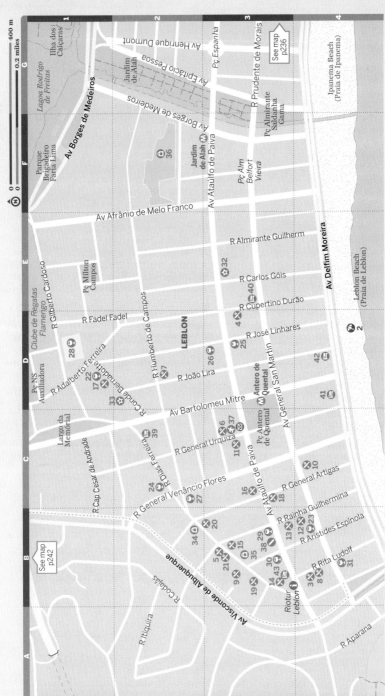

See map p236

See map p242

Lagoa Rodrigo de Freitas

Ilha dos Caiçaras

Parque Brigadeiro Faria Lima

Av Borges de Medeiros

Jardim de Aláh

Av Epitácio Pessoa

Av Henrique Dumont

Pç Espanha

R Prudente de Morais

Ipanema Beach (Praia de Ipanema)

Av Borges de Medeiros

Jardim de Alâh

Av Ataúlfo de Paiva

Pç Alm Belfort Vieira

Pç Almirante Saldanha Gama

Av Afrânio de Melo Franco

R Almirante Guilherm

Clube de Regatas Flamengo

R Gilberto Cardoso

Pç Milton Campos

R Fadel Fadel

R Humberto de Campos

LEBLON

R Carlos Góis

R Cupertino Durão

R José Linhares

Av Delfim Moreira

Leblon Beach (Praia de Leblon)

Pç NS Auxiliadora

R Adalberto Ferreira

R Conde Bernadotte

R João Lira

Av Bartolomeu Mitre

Pç Antero de Quental

Av General San Martin

Largo da Memorial

R Cap cesar de Andrade

Ruas Ferreira

R General Urquiza

R General Venâncio Flores

Av Ataúlfo de Paiva

R General Artigas

R Rainha Guilhermina

R Aristides Espínola

Av Visconde de Albuquerque

R Codajás

R Itiquira

R Rita Ludolf

Riotur Leblon

R Aparana

LEBLON

ATLANTIC OCEAN

Morro
dois Irmãos

Sheraton (300m);
Vidigal (700m)

Av Niemeyer

◎ **Sights** **p59**
1 Mirante do Leblon B5
2 Praia de Leblon D4

⊗ **Eating** **p59**
3 Armazém do Café B4
4 Bibi Crepes D3
5 Brigite's B3
   CT Boucherie .... (see 39)
6 Fellini C3
7 Formidable D2
8 Gula Gula B4
9 Hortifruti B3
10 Juice Co. C4
11 Kurt C3
12 Nam Thai B4
13 Prima Bruschetteria B3
   Ráscal .... (see 36)
14 Stuzzi B3
15 Sushi Leblon B3
16 Talho Capixaba C3
17 Vegetariano Social Club D1
18 Vezpa C3
19 Yalla B3
20 Zona Sul Supermarket C3
21 Zuka D2

◐ **Drinking & Nightlife** **p66**
22 Academia Da Cachaça C4
23 Bar Veloso C3

24 Belmonte C2
25 Bibi Sucos D3
26 Bracarense D3
27 Brewteco C2
28 Cobal do Leblon D1
29 Jobi B3
30 Pizzaria Guanabara B3
31 Usina B4

◐ **Entertainment**
32 Cinema Leblon B3
33 Teatro do Leblon B3

◐ **Shopping**
34 Argumento B4
35 Esch Café B3
   Espaço Fashion .... (see 36)
   Maria Oiticica .... (see 36)
36 Shopping Leblon F2

◐ **Sports & Activities** **p72**
37 Body Tech C3
38 Dive Point B3

◐ **Sleeping** **p169**
39 Leblon Spot Design Hostel C2
40 Lemon Spirit Hostel E3
41 Marina All Suites D4
42 Marina Palace D4
43 Ritz Plaza Hotel B3

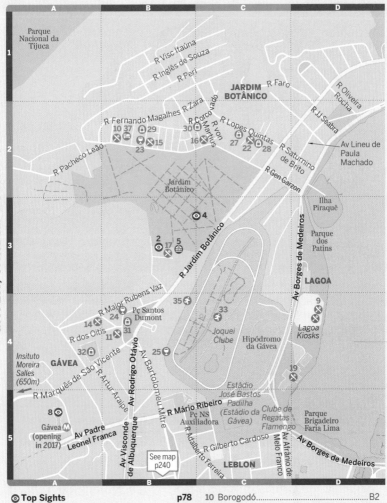

◉ Top Sights   p78
1 Lagoa Rodrigo de Freitas.........................E3

◉ Sights   p79
2 Espaço Tom Jobim...................................B3
3 Fundação Eva Klabin...............................G4
4 Jardim Botânico.......................................C3
5 Museu do Meio Ambiente.......................B3
6 Parque da Catacumba............................G4
7 Parque Lage...E1
8 Planetário...A5

◉ Eating   p80
9 Arab da Lagoa..D4

10 Borogodó...B2
11 Braseiro da Gávea..............................B4
12 Bráz...E1
13 CT Trattorie...F1
14 Guimas...A4
15 Jojô..B2
16 La Bicyclette...C2
17 La Bicyclette...B3
18 La Carioca Cevicheria........................E1
19 Lagoon..D4
20 Olympe..F1
21 PLage Cafe..E1
22 Volta..C2

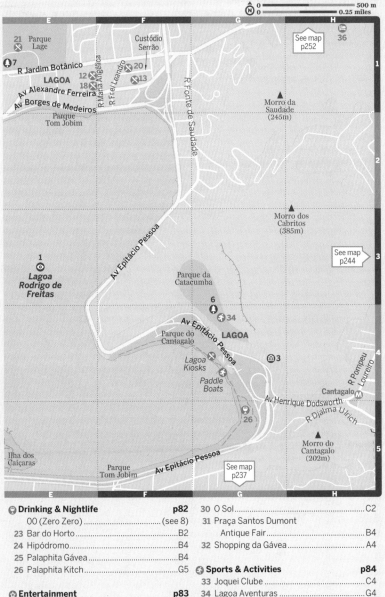

Drinking & Nightlife p82
00 (Zero Zero)....................(see 8)
23 Bar do Horto..............................B2
24 Hipódromo.................................B4
25 Palaphita Gávea.........................B4
26 Palaphita Kitch...........................G5

Entertainment p83
Miranda...............................(see 19)

Shopping p83
27 Dona Coisa................................C2
28 Gabinete....................................C2
29 Isabela Capeto...........................B2

30 O Sol...C2
31 Praça Santos Dumont
     Antique Fair.............................B4
32 Shopping da Gávea.....................A4

Sports & Activities p84
33 Joquei Clube..............................C4
34 Lagoa Aventuras........................G4
35 Nirvana.....................................B4

Sleeping p169
36 Oztel...H1
37 Pouso Verde..............................B2

COPACABANA

Key on p246

See map
p243

Parque da
Catacumba

Parque do
Cantagalo

Av Epitácio Pessoa

Av Henrique Dodsworth

70

R Décio Vilares

73

72

Pç Edmundo
Bittencourt

R Santa Clara

R Anita Garibaldi

**BAIRRO
PEIXOTO**

2

Túnel Major Vaz

R 5 de Julho

R Pompeu Loureiro

R Dias da Rocha

7

85

Guanatur
Turismo

80

11

62

Av NS de Copacabana

58

32

12

59

47

60

25

R Domingos Ferreira

16

Praia de Copacabana

Posto 4

Cantagalo

R Barata Ribeiro

R Constante Ramos

R Barão de Ipanema

R Xavier da
Silveira

R Bolívar

13

14

**BAIXO
COPA**

36

77

See map
p237

R Miguel Lemos

Rio Leopoldo Miguez

31

27

28

40

34

21

19

20

Tv Cristiano
Lacorte

R Djalma Ulrich

37

33

67

55

46

5

24

49

R Aires de
Saldanha

R Saint Roman

Túnel Pref Sá Freire Alvim

79

R Sá Ferreira

Ipanema/General
Osório

R Souza Lima

Almirante
Gonçalves

54

Posto 5

R Bulhões de Carvalho

R Francisco Sá

R Raul Pompéia

Av NS de Copacabana

43

22

66

81

82

R Júlio de Castilhos

39

Av Rainha Elizabeth

R Joaquim Nabuco

76

R Francisco Otaviano

84

44

64

65

51

74

3

4

Parque Garota
de Ipanema

ARPOADOR

Pç Coronel
Eugênio Franco

Ponta de
Copacabana

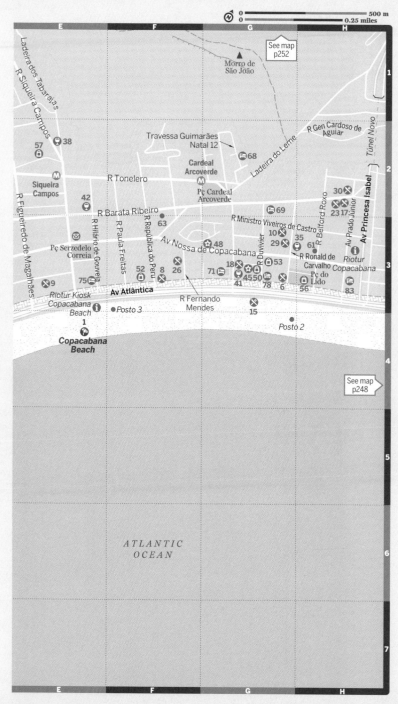

0   500 m
0   0.25 miles

See map
p252

Morro de
São João

Laderia dos Tabarajas
R Siqueira Campos

57

38

Travessa Guimarães
Natal 12

68

Cardeal
Arcoverde

R Tonelero

Siqueira
Campos

42

R Figueiredo de Magalhães

Pç Cardeal
Arcoverde

R Barata Ribeiro

69

R Gen Cardoso de
Aguiar

Ladeira do Leme

Tunel Novo

30

Av Princesa Isabel

R Belford Roxo

23 17

R Ministro Viveiros de Castro

63

R Hilário de Gouveia
R Paula Freitas
R República do Peru

Av Nossa de Copacabana

48

10
29

35

R Duvivier

61

R Prado Júnior

Pç Serzedelo
Correia

52

8

26

71

18

53

R Ronald de
Carvalho

Riotur
Copacabana

9

75

45 50

6

Pç do
Lido

83

41

78

56

Av Atlântica

Riotur Kiosk
Copacabana
Beach

Posto 3

R Fernando
Mendes

15

1

Posto 2

**Copacabana
Beach**

See map
p248

*ATLANTIC
OCEAN*

COPACABANA *Map on p244*

◉ Top Sights   **p87**
1 Copacabana Beach E4

◉ Sights   **p88**
2 Bairro Peixoto D2
3 Colônia dos Pescadores B7
4 Forte de Copacabana B7
5 Museu do Imagem e Som C5

✖ Eating   **p88**
6 Amir G3
7 Antonia Casa e Cafe D3
8 Arab F3
9 Arataca E3
10 Azumi G3
11 Bakers D3
12 Bibi Sucos D3
13 Boulangerie Guerin C4
14 Braseiro C4
Cafe Colombo .... (see 4)
15 Cantinho Cearense G3
16 Capricciosa D4
17 Cervantes H2
18 Churrascaria Palace G3
19 Devassa C4
20 Don Camillo C4
21 El Born C4
22 Faraj A5

23 Galeto Sat's H2
24 Globo C5
25 Koni Store D3
26 La Trattoria F3
27 Le Blé Noir C4
28 Mônaco C4
29 Nonna Ridolfi G3
30 O Rei das Empanadas H2
31 Restaurante Naturaleve B4
32 Santa Satisfação D3
33 Simon Boccanegra B4
TT Burger .... (see 51)
34 Zot C4

◉ Drinking & Nightlife   **p93**
35 As Melhores Cervejas do
    Mundo H3
36 Botequim Informal C4
37 Escondido C4
38 Fosfobox E2
39 Le Boy A6
40 Mais Que Nada C4
41 Mud Bug G3
42 Pavão Azul E2
Ponto da Bossa Nova .... (see 36)
43 Sindicato do Chopp B5
44 TV Bar A6

⊕ **Entertainment** **p96**
45 Beco das Garrafas G3
46 Bip Bip B5
47 Espaço SESC..D3
48 Sala Municipal Baden Powell G3

⊕ **Shopping** **p97**
49 Av Atlântica Fair.......................................B5
50 Bossa Nova & Companhia.......................G3
  Brecho de Salto Alto.........................(see 57)
  Draco Store ....(see 51)
51 Galeria River A6
52 Gilson Martins F3
  Havaianas ....(see 27)
53 Loja Fla...G3
54 Mundo Verde...B5
55 Musicale..B5
  Osklen Surfing..................................(see 51)
56 Praça do Lido Market............................. H3
57 Shopping Siqueira Campos.....................E2
58 Zimpy...D3

⊕ **Sports & Activities** **p98**
59 Body Tech (Copacabana)........................D3
60 Carioca Languages...................................D3
61 Cook in Rio... H3
62 Instituto Brasil-Estados
  Unidos D3

63 Rio Samba Dancer F3
  Spirit Surfboards............................(see 51)
64 Surf Rio B6
65 Velô Bike Store B6
66 Yoga Bhumi...B5

⊜ **Sleeping** **p169**
67 Blame It on Rio 4 Travel C4
68 Cabana Copa...G2
69 Che Lagarto...G2
70 Che Lagarto – Suites
  Santa Clara..D1
71 Copacabana Palace G3
72 Edificio Jucati..D1
73 Hotel Santa Clara D1
74 Mercure Arpoador.....................................A7
75 Olinda Rio E3
76 Orla Copacabana.......................................B6
77 Pestana Rio Atlântica................................D4
78 Porto Bay Rio
  Internacional..G3
79 Pura Vida B5
80 Rio Apartments D3
81 Rio Design Hotel B5
82 Rio Guesthouse B6
83 Rio Spot Homes...H3
84 Sofitel Rio de Janeiro...............................B6
85 Walk on the Beach Hostel C3

COPACABANA

LEME

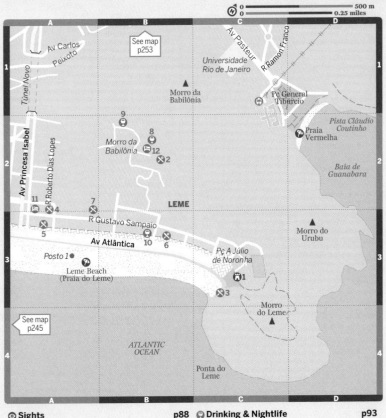

◎ Sights	p88
1 Forte Duque de Caxias	C3

⊗ Eating	p88
2 Bar do David	B2
3 Espetto Carioca	C3
4 Galeria 1618	A2
5 Joaquina	A3
6 La Fiorentina	B3
7 Shirley	A2

⊖ Drinking & Nightlife	p93
8 Bar do Alto	B2
9 Estrelas da Babilônia	B2
10 Sindicato do Chopp	B3

⊟ Sleeping	p169
11 Acapulco	A2
12 Babilônia Rio Hostel	B2

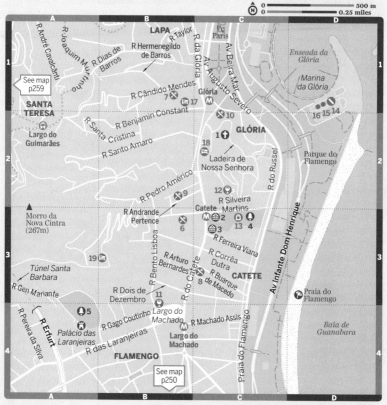

◎ Sights   p114

1 Igreja de Nossa Senhora da Glória do
   Outeiro C2
2 Museu da República C3
3 Museu de Folclore Edison Carneiro C3
4 Parque do Catete C3
5 Parque Guinle A4

⊗ Eating   p115

6 Cariocando B3
7 Casa da Suíça B1
8 Catete Grill C3
9 Ferro e Farinha B2
10 Taberna da Glória C2

○ Drinking & Nightlife   p117

11 Adega Portugália B3
12 Bar do Zé C2

✪ Entertainment   p118

Espaço Museu Da República ....(see 2)
Maze Inn ....(see 19)

○ Shopping   p118

13 Photography and Image Fair C3

✿ Sports & Activities   p119

14 Mar do Rio D1
15 Sail in Rio D1
16 Saveiros Tours D1

⊟ Sleeping

17 Discovery Hostel B1
18 Love Time C2
19 Maze Inn B3

FLAMENGO, LARANJEIRAS & COSME VELHO

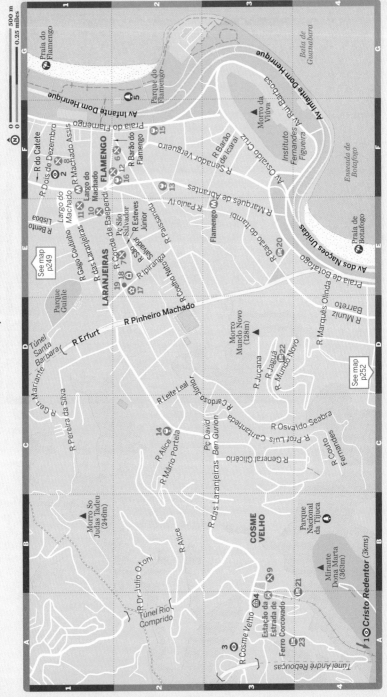

500 m
0.25 miles

Praia do Flamengo

Baía de Guanabara

Av Infante Dom Henrique

Parque do Flamengo

Morro da Viúva

Av Rui Barbosa

Instituto Fernandes Figueira

Enseada de Botafogo

R do Catete

R Dois de Dezembro

Praia do Flamengo

R Machado Assis

FLAMENGO

Largo do Machado

R Barão de Icaraí

R Barão do Flamengo

R Senador Vergueiro

See map p249

R Bento Lisboa

Largo do Machado

R Gago Coutinho

R das Laranjeiras

Pç São Salvador

R Conde de Baependi

R Esteves Júnior

R Paissandu

R Paulo IV

R Marquês de Abrantes

Flamengo

R Barão do Itambi

Praia de Botafogo

Praia de Botafogo

Av das Nações Unidas

LARANJEIRAS

R São Salvador

R Ipiranga

R Coelho Neto

R Pinheiro Machado

Parque Guinle

Túnel Santa Bárbara

R Erfurt

R Gen Mariante

R Pereira da Silva

Morro Mundo Novo (128m)

See map p252

R Jucana

R Jaguá

R Muniz Barreto

R Marquês Olinda

R Mundo Novo

R Leite Leal

R Cardoso Júnior

R Alice

R Mário Portela

R Alice

R Dr Júlio Otoni

Morro São Judas Tadeu (246m)

Pç David Ben Gurion

R das Laranjeiras

R Prof Luís Cantanheda

R Osvaldo Seabra

R General Glicério

R Couto Fernandes

COSME VELHO

Parque Nacional da Tijuca

Túnel Rio Comprido

R Cosme Velho

Estação da Estrada de Ferro Corcovado

Túnel André Rebouças

Mirante Dona Marta (363m)

Cristo Redentor (3kms)

FLAMENGO, LARANJEIRAS & COSME VELHO

◎ Top Sights   p112
1 Cristo Redentor..A4

◎ Sights   p114
2 Centro Cultural Oi Futuro.............................F1
3 Largo do Boticário.......................................A3
4 Museu Internacional de Arte Naïf do Brasil.....A3
5 Parque do Flamengo...................................G2

✖ Eating   p115
6 Intihuasi...F2
7 Luigi's..E2
8 Nanquim..F1
9 Prana Vegetariano.....................................B3

10 Restaurante Kioto.....................................E1
11 Sírio Libaneza..E1
12 Tacacá do Norte.......................................F2

◎ Drinking & Nightlife   p117
13 Armazém do Chopp...................................F2
14 Bar do Serafim..C2
15 Belmonte..F2
16 Devassa...(see 6)
    Herr Brauer.......................................(see 6)

◎ Entertainment   p118
    Centro Cultural Oi Futuro.....................(see 2)
17 Severyna de Laranjeiras..............................E2

⬛ Shopping   p118
    Maracatu Brasil................................(see 19)
18 Pé de Boi...E2

✪ Sports & Activities   p118
19 Maracatu Brasil..E2

⬛ Sleeping   p172
20 Brothers Hostel..E3
21 Casa Caminho do Corcovado....................A4
22 O Veleiro..D3
23 Solar do Cosme..A3

BOTAFOGO, HUMAITÁ & URCA

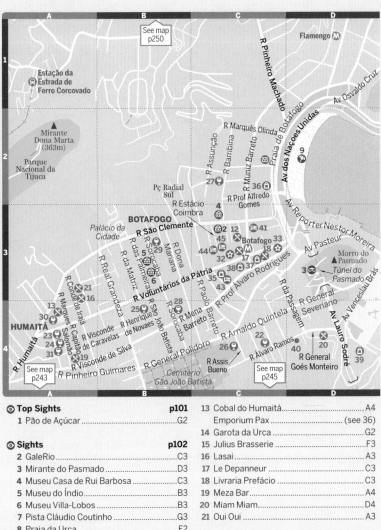

◎ **Top Sights** **p101**
1 Pão de Açúcar G2

◎ **Sights** **p102**
2 GaleRio C3
3 Mirante do Pasmado D3
4 Museu Casa de Rui Barbosa C3
5 Museu do Índio B3
6 Museu Villa-Lobos B3
7 Pista Cláudio Coutinho G3
8 Praia da Urca F2
9 Praia de Botafogo D2
10 Praia Vermelha F4

⊗ **Eating** **p103**
11 Bar Urca G2
12 Boua Kitchen & Bar C3

13 Cobal do Humaitá A4
Emporium Pax ....(see 36)
14 Garota da Urca G2
15 Julius Brasserie F3
16 Lasai A3
17 Le Depanneur C3
18 Livraria Prefácio C3
19 Meza Bar A4
20 Miam Miam D4
21 Oui Oui A3

◎ **Drinking & Nightlife** **p105**
22 Bar Bukowski C4
Bar Urca ....(see 11)
23 Cabaret Lounge A4
24 Calavera A4
25 Casa da Matriz B4

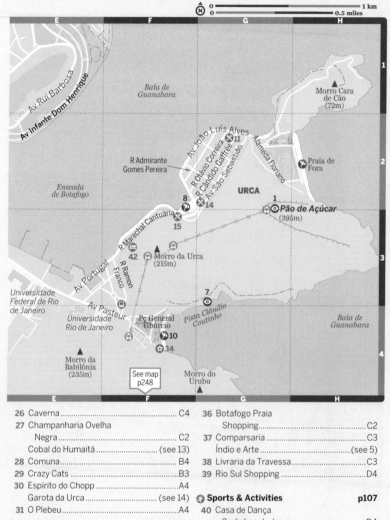

26 Caverna C4
27 Champanharia Ovelha
   Negra C2
   Cobal do Humaitá .... (see 13)
28 Comuna B4
29 Crazy Cats B3
30 Espírito do Chopp A4
   Garota da Urca .... (see 14)
31 O Plebeu A4

⊙ **Entertainment**   **p106**
32 Estação Net Botafogo C3
33 Estação Net Rio C3
34 Terra Brasilis F4

🛍 **Shopping**   **p107**
35 Baratos de Ribeiro C3

36 Botafogo Praia
   Shopping C2
37 Comparsaria C3
   Índio e Arte .... (see 5)
38 Livraria da Travessa C3
39 Rio Sul Shopping D4

⚙ **Sports & Activities**   **p107**
40 Casa de Dança
   Carlinhos de Jesus D4

🛏 **Sleeping**   **p172**
41 Ace Hostel C3
42 Hotelinho Urca F3
43 Ibis C3
44 Injoy Hostel C3
45 Vila Carioca C3

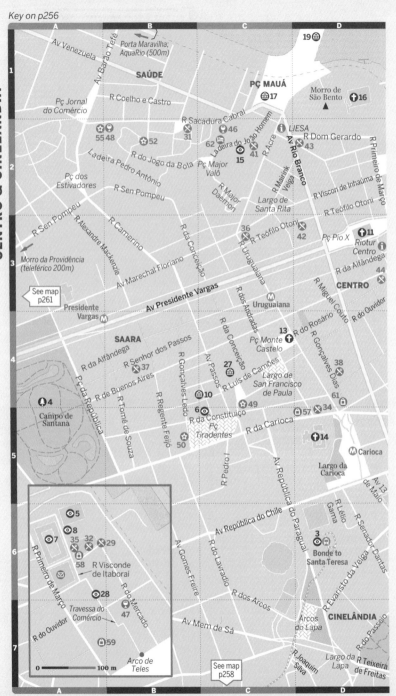

CENTRO & CINELÂNDIA

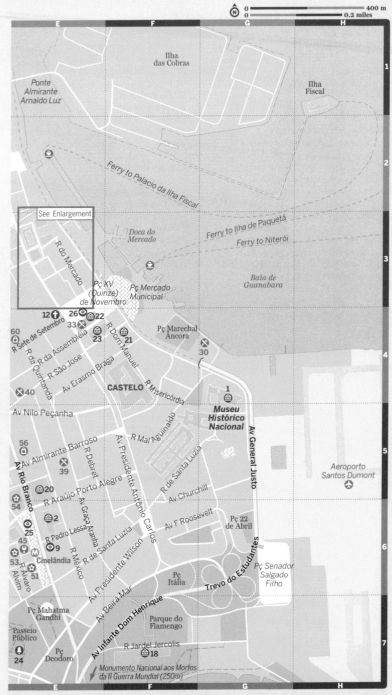

0 400 m
0 0.2 miles

Ilha
das Cobras

Ponte
Almirante
Arnaldo Luz

Ilha
Fiscal

Ferry to Palacio da Ilha Fiscal

See Enlargement

R do Mercado

Doca do
Mercado

Ferry to Ilha de Paquetá
Ferry to Niterói

Baía de
Guanabara

Pç XV
(Quinze)
de Novembro

Pç Mercado
Municipal

12   26   22
33   23
60   R Sete de Setembro   R Dom Manuel   21
R da Quintanda   R da Assembléia   R São José   Pç Marechal
Ancora
30

R Erasmo Braga

CASTELO   R Misericórdia

1
Museu
Histórico
Nacional

40

Av Nilo Peçanha

56
Av Almirante Barroso   R Mal Aguinaldo
39   R Debret   R de Santa Luzia
Av Rio Branco

Av Presidente Antônio Carlos

20
54   R Araújo Porto Alegre
2   Av Graça Aranha
25   R Pedro Lessa
45   R México
53   M   9
51   Cinelândia
R Álvaro Alvim

Av General Justo

Aeroporto
Santos Dumont

Av Churchill
Av F Roosevelt

Pç 22
de Abril

R de Santa Luzia

Av Presidente Wilson

Pç
Itália

Trevo do Estudantes

Pç Senador
Salgado
Filho

Pç Mahatma
Gandhi

Av Beira Mar

Passeio
Público

24   Pç
Deodoro

Av Infante Dom Henrique

Parque do
Flamengo

R Jardel Jercolis
18

Monumento Nacional aos Mortos
da II Guerra Mundial (250m)

CENTRO & CINELÂNDIA *Map on p254*

◎ **Top Sights** **p122**
1 Museu Histórico Nacional G4

◎ **Sights** **p123**
2 Biblioteca Nacional.....................................E6
3 Bonde Station D6
4 Campo de Santana A4
5 Casa França-Brasil A6
6 Centro Carioca de Design.........................C5
7 Centro Cultural Banco do Brasil...............A6
8 Centro Cultural Correios A6
9 Centro Cultural Justiça Federal...............E6
10 Centro de Arte Hélio Oiticica....................C4
11 Igreja de Nossa Senhora de
   Candelária...D3
12 Igreja de Nossa Senhora do Carmo da
   Antiga Sé..E4
13 Igreja de Nossa Senhora do Rosário e
   São Benedito...C4
14 Igreja São Francisco da Penitência &
   Convento de Santo Antônio..................D5
15 Morro da Conceição...................................C2
16 Mosteiro de São Bento D1

17 Museu de Arte do Rio................................C1
18 Museu de Arte Moderna...........................F7
19 Museu do Amanhã D1
20 Museu Nacional de Belas Artes............... E5
21 Museu Naval... F4
22 Paço Imperial E4
23 Palácio Tiradentes E4
24 Passeio Público..E7
25 Praça Floriano E6
26 Praça XV (Quinze) de
   Novembro.. E4
27 Real Gabinete Português de
   Leitura..C4
   Theatro Municipal .... (see 54)
28 Travessa do Comércio...............................A6

✖ **Eating** **p128**
29 Al Farabi...A6
30 AlbaMar G4
31 Angu do Gomes B2
   Bistrô do Paço .... (see 22)
32 Brasserie Rosário.......................................A6
33 Café Arlequim...E4

34 Café do Bom Cachaça Da Boa.................D5
35 Cais do Oriente...A6
36 Casa Paladino...C3
37 Cedro do Líbano...B4
38 Confeitaria Colombo D4
   Crepe Nouveau Art............................ (see 5)
   Cristóvão...(see 38)
39 Da Silva...E5
40 Govinda E4
41 Imaculada C2
42 L'Atelier du Cuisinier D3
43 Mironga D2
44 Rancho Inn..D3

◯ Drinking & Nightlife   p130
45 Amarelinho..E6
46 Jazz In Champanheria....................................C2
47 Samba Caffe...B7
48 Week..B2

◯ Entertainment   p132
49 Centro Cultural Carioca.............................C4
50 Estudantina Musical...................................B5

   Ginga Tropical....................................(see 50)
51 Odeon Petrobras...E6
52 Pedra do Sal...B2
   Teatro Do Centro Cultural Banco
      Do Brasil ....(see 7)
53 Teatro Rival Petrobras.................................E6
54 Theatro Municipal E5
55 Trapiche Gamboa...A2

◯ Shopping   p133
   Arlequim ....(see 22)
56 Berinjela..E5
57 Casa Oliveira D5
58 Galeria Monique Paton A6
59 Granado...A7
60 Livraria da Travessa.....................................E4
61 Sobral..D4

◯ Sports & Activities
   Centro Cultural Carioca..................(see 49)

◯ Sleeping   p173
62 Pop Art Hostel..C2

SANTA TERESA & LAPA

Key on p260

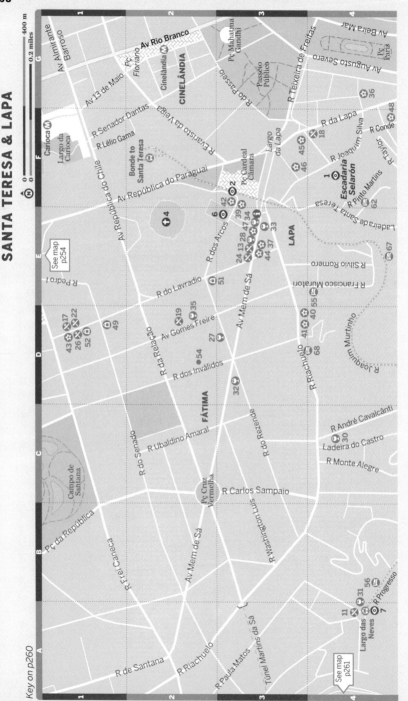

0.2 miles
400 m

Av Almirante Barroso

Av 13 de Maio

R Senador Dantas

R Lélio Gama

Carioca

Largo da Carioca

R República do Chile

R Pedro I

See map p254

Av República do Paraguai

Av República do Chile

Bonde to Santa Teresa

Pç Floriano

Av Rio Branco

Cinelândia

CINELÂNDIA

R Evaristo da Veiga

Pç Mahatma Gandhi

R do Passeio

Passeio Público

Av Teixeira de Freitas

Av Augusto Severo

Av Beira Mar

Pç Pariś

36

48

R da Lapa

R Conde

R Taylor

18

45

46

Largo da Lapa

Pç Cardeal Câmara

1

Escadaria Selarón

R Joaquim Silva

R Pinto Martins

62

Ladeira de Santa Teresa

LAPA

2

42

39

6

34

47

33

13 28

24

37

44

67

R dos Arcos

R Silvio Romero

R Francisco Muratori

51

R do Lavradio

Av Mem de Sá

40 55

41

68

R Riachuelo

R Joaquim Murtinho

17

22

43

26

52

49

19

35

Av Gomes Freire

R da Relação

27

32

54

R dos Inválidos

R André Cavalcânti

30

Ladeira do Castro

R Monte Alegre

FATIMA

R Ubaldino Amaral

R do Rezende

R do Senado

Campo de Santana

Pç Cruz Vermelha

R Carlos Sampaio

R Washington Luis

Pç da República

R Frei Caneca

R do Senado

Av Mem de Sá

56

31

11

7

Largo das Neves

R Progresso

R de Santana

R Riachuelo

R Paula Matos

Túnel Martins da Sá

See map p261

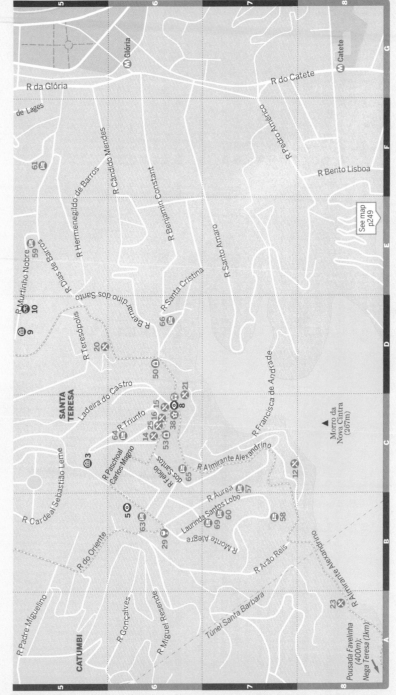

See map p249

SANTA TERESA & LAPA *Map on p258*

◎ Top Sights — p138
1 Escadaria Selarón............................F4

◎ Sights — p139
2 Arcos da Lapa..F3
3 Casa de Benjamin Constant..............C5
4 Catedral Metropolitana........................E2
5 Centro Cultural Laurinda Santos
  Lobo..B6
6 Fundição Progresso................................E3
7 Largo das Neves.......................................A4
8 Largo do Guimarães................................C6
9 Museu Chácara do Céu..........................D5
  Museu de Arte Sacra.....................(see 4)
10 Parque das Ruínas....................................D5

✕ Eating — p140
11 Alquimia...A4
12 Aprazível..C7
13 Bar Brasil...E3
14 Bar do Mineiro...C6
15 Cafe do Alto..C6
16 Cafecito...C6
17 Casa Momus..D1
18 Ernesto...F4
19 Espaço Lapa Cafe.....................................D2
20 Espírito Santa...D5
21 Largo das Letras..C6
22 Mangue Seco Cachaçaria.....................D1
23 Mike's Haus...A8
24 Nova Capela..E3
25 Rústico...C6
26 Santo Scenarium.......................................D1
  Térèze..(see 65)

◐ Drinking & Nightlife — p142
27 Anexo Bar..D3
28 Antônio's..E3
29 Bar do Gomes..B6
30 Buraco da Lacraia.....................................C4
31 Goya-Beira..B4
32 La Paz..D3
33 Leviano Bar...E3
34 Sarau..E3
35 Vaca Atolada..D2

✪ Entertainment — p144
36 Beco do Rato...G4
37 Carioca da Gema..E3
38 Cine Santa Teresa....................................C6
39 Circo Voador..F3
40 Democráticos...D3
  Fundição Progresso......................(see 6)
41 Lapa 40 Graus...D3
42 Paiol 08...F3
43 Rio Scenarium...D1
44 Sacrilégio..E3
45 Sala Cecília Meireles...............................F3
46 Semente..F3
47 Teatro Odisséia..E3
48 TribOz..F4

◉ Shopping — p146
49 Feira do Rio Antigo..................................D1
50 La Vereda Handicrafts............................D6
51 Lapa Decor..E2
52 Scenarium Antique...................................D1
53 Tucum..C6

✪ Sports & Activities — p146
  Fundição Progresso......................(see 6)
54 Núcleo de Dança Renata
  Peçanha...D2

⌂ Sleeping — p173
55 Books Hostel..E4
56 Cama e Café...B4
57 Casa Áurea..C7
58 Casa Beleza..B7
59 Casa Bianca..E5
60 Casa Cool Beans..B7
61 Casa da Carmen e do
  Fernando...F5
62 Casa da Gente...F4
63 Casalegre..B6
64 Castelinho 38...C6
65 Hotel Santa Teresa..................................C6
66 Mama Ruisa..D6
67 Rio Hostel..E4
68 Vila Galé..D4
69 Villa Laurinda..B7

ZONA NORTE

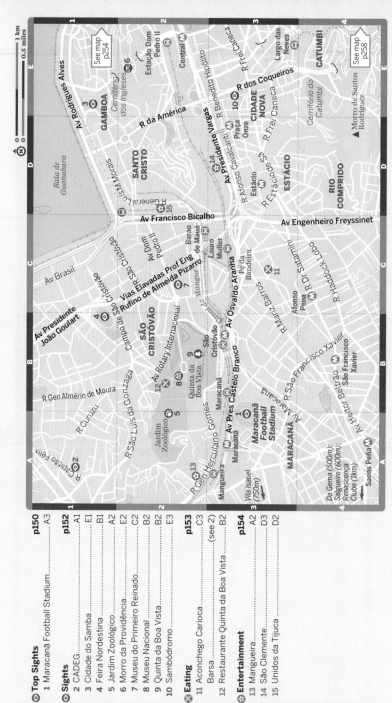

◎ **Top Sights** **p150**
1 Maracanã Football Stadium................ A3

◎ **Sights** **p152**
2 CADEG.. A1
3 Cidade do Samba.................................. E1
4 Feira Nordestina.................................... B1
5 Jardim Zoológico................................... A2
6 Morro da Providência........................... E2
7 Museu do Primeiro Reinado................ C2
8 Museu Nacional..................................... B2
9 Quinta da Boa Vista.............................. B2
10 Sambódromo.. E3

✘ **Eating** **p153**
11 Aconchego Carioca............................. C3
Barsa.. (see 2)
12 Restaurante Quinta da Boa Vista..... B2

✿ **Entertainment** **p154**
13 Mangueira... A2
14 São Clemente....................................... D3
15 Unidos da Tijuca................................. D2

BARRA DA TIJUCA & WESTERN RIO

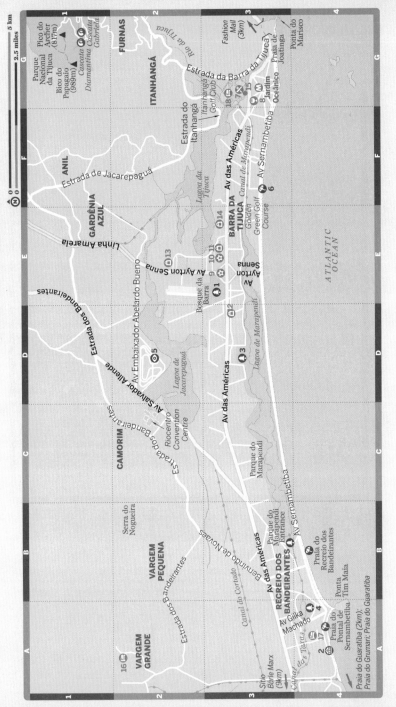

5 km
2.5 miles

Parque Nacional da Tijuca
Pico do Archer (817m)
Bico do Papagaio (989m)
Cascata Diamantina
Cascata Gabriela

FURNAS

ITANHANGÁ

Rio da Tijuca

Estrada da Barra da Tijuca

Estrada do Itanhangá

Itanhangá Golf Club

Fashion Mall (3km)

Praia de Joatinga
Ponta do Marisco

Jardim Oceânico

Estrada de Jacarepaguá

ANIL

GARDÊNIA AZUL

Linha Amarela

Estrada dos Bandeirantes

Av Embaixador Abelardo Bueno

BARRA DA TIJUCA

Av das Américas
Canal de Marapendi

Av Sernambetiba

Lagoa da Tijuca

Golden Green Golf Course

Bosque da Barra

Av Ayrton Senna

Lagoa de Marapendi

ATLANTIC OCEAN

CAMORIM

Av Salvador Allende
Estrada dos Bandeirantes

Riocentro Convention Centre

Lagoa de Jacarepaguá

Av das Américas

Serra do Nogueira

VARGEM PEQUENA

Estrada dos Bandeirantes

Benvindo de Novaes

Canal do Cortado

Av das Américas

Parque do Marapendi

Av Sernambetiba

Parque do Marapendi Entrance

Praia do Recreio dos Bandeirantes

RECREIO DOS BANDEIRANTES

Ponta do Tim Maia

Av Gilka Machado

Praia do Pontal de Sernambetiba

Burle Marx

Sítio Burle Marx (9km)

Canal das Taxas

VARGEM GRANDE

Praia do Guaratiba (2km);
Praia do Grumari; Praia do Guaratiba

BARRA DA TIJUCA & WESTERN RIO

◎ Sights   p157
1 Bosque da Barra............................E3
2 Casa do Pontal............................A4
3 Parque do Marapendi.....................D3
4 Parque Ecológico Chico Mendes........A4
5 Parque Olímpico...........................D2
6 Praia da Barra da Tijuca.................F3

✕ Eating   p157
Don Pascual.............................(see 16)
7 Laguna Restaurante.....................G3

🍸 Drinking & Nightlife   p160
8 Nuth..G3

🎭 Entertainment   p160
9 Cidade das Artes..........................E3
Citibank Hall...........................(see 13)
10 UCI – New York City Center...........E3

🛍 Shopping   p161
11 Barra Shopping...........................E3
12 Rio Design Center........................D3

13 Via Parque Shopping.....................E2
14 Village......................................E3

⚽ Sports & Activities   p162
15 Barra Water Shuttle......................G3

🛏 Sleeping   p176
16 Don Pascual...............................A2
17 Rio Surf 'N Stay...........................A4
18 Utrópico....................................G3

Our Story

A beat-up old car, a few dollars in the pocket and a sense of adventure. In 1972 that's all Tony and Maureen Wheeler needed for the trip of a lifetime – across Europe and Asia overland to Australia. It took several months, and at the end – broke but inspired – they sat at their kitchen table writing and stapling together their first travel guide, *Across Asia on the Cheap*. Within a week they'd sold 1500 copies. Lonely Planet was born.

Today, Lonely Planet has offices in Franklin, London, Melbourne, Oakland, Beijing and Delhi, with more than 600 staff and writers. We share Tony's belief that 'a great guidebook should do three things: inform, educate and amuse'.

Our Writer

Regis St Louis

Regis first visited Rio back in 2003, and he fell hard for the stunning land-scapes, the dynamic music scene, and the open and celebratory spirit of the *cariocas*. Since then he's been a frequent visitor, celebrating Carnaval (sometimes parading with a samba school), experiencing the great outdoors (climbing Pão de Açúcar, hiking remote western beaches), and charting the city's ever-changing dining scene and nightlife. Regis' articles on Rio and South America have appeared in the *Chicago Tribune*, the *Telegraph*, on BBC.com and elsewhere. He is also the coordinating author of Lonely Planet's *Brazil* and *South America on a Shoestring* guides. He splits his time between New Orleans and the tropics.

Published by Lonely Planet Publications Pty Ltd
ABN 36 005 607 983
9th edition – June 2016
ISBN 978 1 74321 767 2
© Lonely Planet 2016   Photographs © as indicated 2016
10 9 8 7 6 5 4 3 2 1
Printed in China